Mexican Immigration to the United States

A National Bureau
of Economic Research
Conference Report

Mexican Immigration to the United States

Edited by **George J. Borjas**

The University of Chicago Press

Chicago and London

GEORGE J. BORJAS is professor of economics and social policy at
the Kennedy School of Government, Harvard University, and a
research associate of the National Bureau of Economic Research.

The University of Chicago Press, Chicago 60637
The University of Chicago Press, Ltd., London
© 2007 by the National Bureau of Economic Research
All rights reserved. Published 2007
Printed in the United States of America

16 15 14 13 12 11 10 09 08 07   1 2 3 4 5
ISBN-13: 978-0-226-06632-5 (cloth)
ISBN-10: 0-226-06632-0 (cloth)

Library of Congress Cataloging-in-Publication Data

Mexican immigration to the United States / edited by George J. Borjas.
     p. cm. — (National Bureau of Economic Research conference
report)
    "Consists of papers presented at a conference held in Cambridge,
Massachusetts, in February 2005"—P. 3.
    "Contains the studies presented at the fourth NBER
conference"—P. 5.
    Includes bibliographical references and index.
    ISBN-13: 978-0-226-06632-5 (cloth : alk. paper)
    ISBN-10: 0-226-06632-0 (cloth : alk. paper)
    1. Mexican Americans—Social conditions—Congresses.
2. Mexican Americans—Cultural assimilation—Congresses.
3. Mexican Americans—Economic conditions—Congresses.
4. Mexican Americans—Employment—Congresses. 5. Alien labor,
Mexican—United States—Congresses. 6. Immigrants—United
States—Social conditions—Congresses. 7. Immigrants—United
States—Economic conditions—Congresses. 8. Mexico—
Emigration and immigration—Congresses. 9. United States—
Emigration and immigration—Congresses. I. Borjas, George J.
II. National Bureau of Economic Research.
E184.M5M522 2007
304.8'73072—dc22

                                  2006045676

Relation of the Directors to the
Work and Publications of the
National Bureau of Economic Research

1. The object of the NBER is to ascertain and present to the economics profession, and to the public more generally, important economic facts and their interpretation in a scientific manner without policy recommendations. The Board of Directors is charged with the responsibility of ensuring that the work of the NBER is carried on in strict conformity with this object.

2. The President shall establish an internal review process to ensure that book manuscripts proposed for publication DO NOT contain policy recommendations. This shall apply both to the proceedings of conferences and to manuscripts by a single author or by one or more co-authors but shall not apply to authors of comments at NBER conferences who are not NBER affiliates.

3. No book manuscript reporting research shall be published by the NBER until the President has sent to each member of the Board a notice that a manuscript is recommended for publication and that in the President's opinion it is suitable for publication in accordance with the above principles of the NBER. Such notification will include a table of contents and an abstract or summary of the manuscript's content, a list of contributors if applicable, and a response form for use by Directors who desire a copy of the manuscript for review. Each manuscript shall contain a summary drawing attention to the nature and treatment of the problem studied and the main conclusions reached.

4. No volume shall be published until forty-five days have elapsed from the above notification of intention to publish it. During this period a copy shall be sent to any Director requesting it, and if any Director objects to publication on the grounds that the manuscript contains policy recommendations, the objection will be presented to the author(s) or editor(s). In case of dispute, all members of the Board shall be notified, and the President shall appoint an ad hoc committee of the Board to decide the matter; thirty days additional shall be granted for this purpose.

5. The President shall present annually to the Board a report describing the internal manuscript review process, any objections made by Directors before publication or by anyone after publication, any disputes about such matters, and how they were handled.

6. Publications of the NBER issued for informational purposes concerning the work of the Bureau, or issued to inform the public of the activities at the Bureau, including but not limited to the NBER Digest and Reporter, shall be consistent with the object stated in paragraph 1. They shall contain a specific disclaimer noting that they have not passed through the review procedures required in this resolution. The Executive Committee of the Board is charged with the review of all such publications from time to time.

7. NBER working papers and manuscripts distributed on the Bureau's web site are not deemed to be publications for the purpose of this resolution, but they shall be consistent with the object stated in paragraph 1. Working papers shall contain a specific disclaimer noting that they have not passed through the review procedures required in this resolution. The NBER's web site shall contain a similar disclaimer. The President shall establish an internal review process to ensure that the working papers and the web site do not contain policy recommendations, and shall report annually to the Board on this process and any concerns raised in connection with it.

8. Unless otherwise determined by the Board or exempted by the terms of paragraphs 6 and 7, a copy of this resolution shall be printed in each NBER publication as described in paragraph 2 above.

Contents

Acknowledgment

This volume consists of papers presented at a conference held in Cambridge, Massachusetts, in February 2005. Funding for the project was provided by The Andrew W. Mellon Foundation. Funding for individual papers is noted in specific paper acknowledgments.

Any opinions expressed in this volume are those of the respective authors and do not necessarily reflect the views of the National Bureau of Economic Research or the sponsoring organizations.

Introduction

George J. Borjas

There has been a resurgence of international migration in many regions of the world. One of the largest flows of international migrants—regardless of whether it is measured in absolute numbers, as a percent of the population of the sending country, or as a percent of the population of the receiving country—is the flow of Mexican-born persons to the United States. By 2003, 10.2 million Mexicans, or almost 9 percent of the Mexican population, had migrated to the United States. Mexican immigrants comprised 28.3 percent of all foreign-born persons residing in the United States and accounted for 3.6 percent of the total U.S. population.

This large population flow has altered social conditions and economic opportunities in both Mexico and the United States. In fact, the rapidly increasing number of Mexicans in the U.S. population has already ignited a contentious debate over the cultural, economic, and political impact of this influx.[1] There is a great deal of concern over the possibility that the Mexican immigrant influx, which is predominantly low-skill, adversely affects working conditions for low-skill workers already residing in the United States. Similarly, there is a heated debate over the possibility that Mexican immigrants and their descendants may assimilate slowly—relative to the experience of other immigrant waves—and this slow assimilation may lead to the creation of a new underclass.

Reflecting the increased interest on issues regarding the economic impact of immigration, the National Bureau of Economic Research (NBER) has held four separate research conferences on immigration in the past two

George J. Borjas is a professor of economics and social policy at the Kennedy School of Government, Harvard University, and a research associate of the National Bureau of Economic Research.
1. See, for example, Hanson (2003) and Huntington (2004).

decades. The studies presented in the first three conferences (held in 1987, 1990, and 1998) analyzed a wide range of questions in the economics of immigration, including the decision to migrate, the determinants of assimilation, and the labor market impact of immigration on receiving countries.[2] This volume contains the studies presented at the fourth NBER conference, held in 2005. All of these studies focus specifically on issues related to Mexican immigration.

The empirical findings reported here summarize much of what is currently known about the economic impact of Mexican immigration to the United States. In addition, many of the essays address a number of new issues and report new findings. Taken together, the studies provide a historical overview of Mexican immigration, a discussion of the factors that determine the rate of assimilation of Mexican immigrants and of why the assimilation rate might differ between Mexican and non-Mexican immigrants, an evaluation of the selection mechanism that generates the non-random sample of emigrants in Mexico, an assessment of the economic impact of Mexican immigration on both the U.S. and Mexican wage structures, and a study of intergenerational mobility among Mexicans living in the United States. A common theme runs through the essays: The sheer size and uniqueness of the Mexican immigrant population in the United States ensures that the economic impact of this immigrant influx is pervasive and will likely form an important part of the discussion over many aspects of social and economic policy for decades to come.

Mexican Immigration in the United States: A Brief Overview

It is instructive to place the Mexican immigrant influx in the context of both past and current immigration to the United States. From this perspective, the historical and demographic uniqueness of recent Mexican immigration quickly becomes apparent.

The number of *legal* immigrants admitted to the United States increased substantially in the past few decades, from about 2.5 million in the 1950s to 9.1 million in the 1990s. There was also a marked increase in the size of the illegal immigrant population. In 1986, the Immigration Reform and Control Act (IRCA) granted amnesty to illegal immigrants present in the United States as of 1982. Roughly 3 million illegal immigrants qualified for this amnesty. Despite this legalization, despite higher levels of border enforcement, and despite the introduction of employer sanctions penalizing firms that knowingly hired illegal immigrants, the Immigration and Naturalization Service estimated that 5 million persons were illegally present in the United States in 1996 and that the *net* flow of illegal immigrants was on

---

2. The research essays were published in three volumes: Abowd and Freeman (1991), Borjas and Freeman (1992), and Borjas (2000).

the order of 275,000 persons per year (U.S. Immigration and Naturalization Service 1997, 197). By 2004, the size of the illegal alien population was estimated to be 10.3 million persons, and the illegal population was increasing at the rate of 700,000 persons per year (Passel 2005, 3).

The huge increase in the size of the immigrant influx in recent decades can be traced to changes in U.S. immigration policy. Prior to 1965, immigration to the United States was guided by the national-origins quota system, a visa scheme that allocated a relatively small number of legal entry visas mainly to Western European countries. The 1965 Amendments to the Immigration and Nationality Act (and subsequent revisions) repealed the national origin restrictions, increased the number of available visas, and made family ties to U.S. residents the key factor that determined whether an applicant was admitted into the country.

As a consequence of both the 1965 Amendments and of major changes in economic and political conditions in the source countries relative to the United States, the national origin mix of the immigrant flow began to change substantially in the past few decades. Over two-thirds of the legal immigrants admitted during the 1950s originated in Europe or Canada, 25 percent originated in Western Hemisphere countries other than Canada, and only 6 percent originated in Asia. By the 1990s, only 17.1 percent of the immigrants originated in Europe or Canada, 47.2 percent in Western Hemisphere countries other than Canada, and 30.7 percent originated in Asia.

A key determinant of these various trends is the influx of Mexican immigrants. The population of Mexican-born persons residing in the United States increased at an unprecedented rate in recent decades. During the 1950s, an average of 30,000 legal Mexican immigrants entered the United States each year, comprising about 12 percent of the immigrant flow. During the 1990s, an average of 225,000 Mexicans entered the United States legally each year, comprising almost 25 percent of the legal flow. Further, it is estimated that 57 percent of the illegal immigrants present in the United States in 2004 are of Mexican origin (Passel 2005, 4). If one takes into account both legal and illegal immigration, the estimated flow of Mexican immigrants to the United States during the 1990s was around 400,000 per year. The magnitude of this flow was far larger than that of any other national origin group.

The size of the large Mexican immigrant influx of the past few decades is unique not only relative to current immigration, but also even relative to the very large migration of some European national origin groups at the beginning of the twentieth century. In 1920, for example, the largest two immigrant populations were those of persons who originated in Germany or Italy, and *together* those two populations comprised about 23.7 percent of the foreign-born population at the time (U.S. Bureau of the Census 1975). As noted in the preceding, in 2004 Mexican immigrants *alone* account for 28.3 percent of the foreign-born population. Put differently, the dominant position of Mexican immigration in determining the ethnic composition of the immigrant population represents an important outlier in the history of U.S. immigration.

In fact, it is interesting to contrast recent Mexican immigration to the United States with Mexican immigration a century ago. Mexican immigration was relatively small in the early 1900s; the fraction of the U.S. population composed of Mexican immigrants was only 0.6 percent in 1920 and actually declined for several decades afterward. To ease the labor force shortage caused by World War II in the agricultural industry, the Bracero Program was launched in 1942. By 1964, when it was terminated, the guest-worker program had brought almost 5 million Mexican-born farm workers to the United States. It is very likely that the termination of the Bracero Program sparked the beginning of large-scale illegal immigration from Mexico to the United States. In 1964, for example, the Border Patrol apprehended only 41.6 thousand Mexican illegal immigrants. By 1970, the Border Patrol was apprehending 348.2 thousand Mexicans annually.[3]

As figure I.1 shows, the economic pressures for immigration from Mexico probably also helped maintain the momentum. Per capita income in Mexico relative to the United States peaked in the early 1980s at around .27. It fell dramatically during the 1980s, and has not recovered since. By 2000, Mexican per capita income was only 19 percent of that of the United States. The relative decline in the Mexican standard of living is surely an important determinant of the large increase in Mexican immigration in recent years.

It is important to note that the large increase in Mexican immigration has led to an equally large increase (with a lag) in the number of persons born in the United States of Mexican ancestry. In 1980, 3.1 percent of the native-born population was of Mexican ancestry. By 2004, 6.3 percent of the native-born population was of Mexican ancestry. If one combines the population of Mexican-born workers with that of U.S.-born workers of Mexican ancestry, these two groups accounted for 9.3 percent of the U.S. population in 2004 (as compared to only 3.9 percent in 1980). The flow of Mexican-born persons to the United States has not shown any signs of abating in recent years. As a result, the demographic and economic importance of the Mexican-origin population in the United States is bound to increase dramatically in the next few decades.

The NBER Project

The many studies that examine the economic consequences of immigration repeatedly show that one of the key determinants of the economic im-

---

3. To put these numbers into perspective, note that there were 1.7 million such apprehensions in 1986, just prior to the enactment of IRCA.

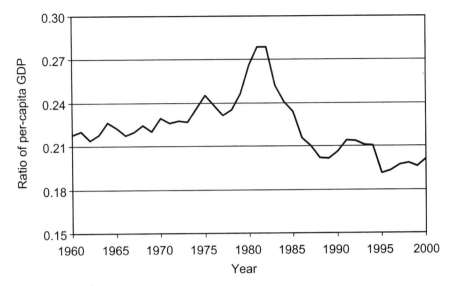

Fig. I.1   Per capita income in Mexico relative to per capita income in the United States

Source: Hanson (2006).

pact of immigration on a receiving country is the skill mix of the immigrant influx—and, particularly, how that skill mix compares to the skill mix of the native-born population.[4]

The connection between immigrant skills and the fiscal impact of immigration, for instance, is obvious. The many programs that make up the welfare state tend to redistribute resources from high-income workers to persons with less economic potential. Skilled immigrants may also assimilate quickly. They might be more adept at learning the tools and tricks of the trade that can increase the chances of economic success in the United States, such as the language and culture of the American workplace. The skill mix of immigrants also determines which native workers are most affected by immigration. Low-skill immigrants will typically harm low-skill natives, while skilled immigrants will harm skilled natives. Finally, the skills of immigrants determine the economic benefits from immigration. The United States benefits from international trade because it can import goods that are not available or are too expensive to produce in the domestic market. Similarly, the country benefits from immigration because it can import workers with scarce qualifications and abilities. In view of the importance of determining the relative skills of the immigrant population, it is not surprising that many of the studies in this volume carefully examine

4. Borjas (1994), Friedberg and Hunt (1995), and LaLonde and Topel (1996) survey the immigration literature.

the differences between the skill composition of the Mexican immigrant population and that of native workers and of other immigrants.

In their contribution to this volume, George Borjas and Lawrence Katz use the available microdata from the U.S. decennial Census to provide a sweeping account of the evolution of the Mexican-born workforce in the United States throughout the entire twentieth century. In particular, the paper describes the evolution of the relative skills and economic performance of Mexican immigrants and contrasts this evolution to that experienced by other immigrant groups arriving in the United States during the period. The paper also examines the costs and benefits of this influx. Specifically, it shows how the Mexican influx has altered economic opportunities in the most affected labor markets and discusses how the relative prices of goods and services produced by Mexican immigrants may have changed over time.

The empirical analysis of Borjas and Katz yields a number of interesting findings. It turns out, for example, that the very large differences in educational attainment between native-born workers and Mexican immigrants accounts for nearly three-quarters of the very large wage disadvantage suffered by Mexican immigrants in the U.S. workforce. Similarly, they document that the earnings of non-Mexican immigrants tend to converge to those of their native-born counterparts as the immigrants accumulate work experience in the U.S. labor market but that this type of wage convergence has been much weaker for Mexican immigrants. Finally, Borjas and Katz estimate a structural model of labor demand to document that Mexican immigration has adversely affected the earnings of less-educated native workers in recent decades. In fact, they find that practically all of the predicted reduction in the real wage of high school dropouts since 1980 can be traced to the depressing wage effects caused by the increase in the supply of low-skill workers attributable to Mexican immigration.

Francine Blau and Lawrence Kahn's essay provides a comprehensive study of the assimilation of Mexican immigrants in the U.S. labor market. The paper examines the relation between gender and assimilation in labor supply and wages, both within and across generations. Blau and Kahn document that there is a much more traditional gender division of labor in the family in Mexico than among Mexican immigrants in the United States, with women in Mexico having considerably lower labor force participation and higher fertility than their ethnic counterparts in the United States. In fact, they document a dramatic rate of assimilation in the labor supply of Mexican immigrant women. After twenty years in the United States, the very large initial differences in female labor supply between Mexican women and other women have been virtually eliminated. Further, the labor supply gap remains small in the second and third generations.

Interestingly, the pattern of rapid assimilation in labor supply behavior does not carry over to wages. Blau and Kahn's evidence on wage convergence between Mexicans and native-born workers suggests that Mexican immigrants do not exhibit rapid assimilation. Wage convergence for Mexican immigrant men tends to be relatively modest, while the evidence for women is quite mixed. The Blau-Kahn essay highlights the importance of source-country characteristics in determining the behavior of immigrants in the receiving country, at least initially. In effect, it underlines the importance of understanding the context of work decisions in the source country if one wishes to explain the source of the differences in labor market outcomes between Mexicans and non-Mexicans in the United States.

Edward Lazear's contribution continues the study of assimilation among Mexican immigrants by specifically focusing on *the* crucial question: why are assimilation rates among Mexican immigrants lower than those found in other immigrant groups? As Lazear notes, by almost any measure of socioeconomic outcomes, immigrants from Mexico have performed worse and become assimilated more slowly than immigrants from other countries. After considering a number of alternative hypotheses, Lazear argues that the lower assimilation rates of Mexican immigrants may be a consequence of U.S. immigration policy.

As noted earlier, the United States lets in far more immigrants from Mexico than from any other country. The large size of the group allows for the creation of socially vibrant and economically viable large Mexican enclaves in the United States. Lazear argues that economic theory and evidence suggests that those who live in highly concentrated communities earn lower wages, have poorer educational attainment, and do not assimilate as quickly as immigrants who live outside the enclave. Lazear's empirical analysis, however, shows that the clustering of Mexicans into highly concentrated geographic communities explains some, but not all, of the difference between their economic performance and that of other immigrants. Lazear argues that the rest of the difference may well be the result of an immigration policy that emphasizes family ties, rather than jobs or skills, in the awarding of entry visas (at least for legal immigrants). Put differently, by admitting relatively large numbers of Mexicans on a family rather than job basis, the United States selects a group of Mexican immigrants who have an economic disadvantage at the starting gate.

There are many assimilation paths for immigrant groups in the United States. Some immigrant groups, for example, have used self-employment (such as opening up small shops that cater mainly to their ethnic counterparts in the enclave) as the method of moving up the economic ladder. The study by Robert Fairlie and Christopher Woodruff notes an important puzzle. Mexico is one of the most entrepreneurial countries in the world, at least as measured by the self-employment rate of its workforce. At the same time, however, self-employment rates among Mexican immigrants in the United States are remarkably low: only about 6 percent of Mexican immigrants are self-employed, as compared to the national average of 11 percent. This differential behavior in self-employment propensities between the Mexican immigrant and the Mexican population, Fairlie and Woodruff show, appears to be an extreme outlier when examining the same relation among other immigrant groups in the United States. It seems, therefore, that Mexican immigrants are missing out on a potentially important channel of assimilation even though their source country characteristics suggest that such a path would be a relatively easy one to follow.

Fairlie and Woodruff explore several possible explanations for the relatively lower rates of self-employment among Mexican immigrants in the United States, both relative to other immigrant groups and relative to their initial conditions. One possibility is that self-employment propensities of Mexican immigrants may be lower because the socioeconomic characteristics of Mexican workers in the United States differ systematically from those of Mexican workers who remain in Mexico. They find, however, that differences in observed characteristics (such as education and age) between the two groups explain little of the gap between self-employment rates in Mexico and self-employment rates among Mexicans in the United States. Fairlie and Woodruff also show that although the industrial distribution of workers differs between the two countries, these differences cannot account for the self-employment gap. Their analysis suggests instead that barriers created by English language difficulties and legalization status may help to explain part of the relatively low rates of self-employment among Mexican immigrants.

Pablo Ibarraran and Darren Lubotsky present an in-depth analysis of the type of selection that characterizes the nonrandom flow of Mexican immigrants to the United States. Various theories of migration argue that differences in the wage structure between countries, as well as migration costs, community social capital, and access to credit markets, may be important determinants of the migration decision and that these variables generate the observed (and unobserved) differences in characteristics between the nonrandom samples of movers and stayers. Some of these theories predict that Mexican migrants may be positively selected (that is, they will be more skilled than nonmigrants), while others predict that Mexican immigrants may be negatively selected.

The primary goal of the Ibarraran-Lubotsky essay is to assess empirically if Mexican migrants are, in fact, positively or negatively selected. Using data from the 2000 Mexican and U.S. Censuses, Ibarraran and Lubotsky examine how the educational attainment of Mexican migrants to the United States compares with the educational attainment of Mexican workers who choose to remain in Mexico. Their key—and potentially controversial—finding is that low-skill Mexicans are more likely to migrate to the United States than high-skill Mexicans.[5] They argue that this evidence is consistent with the predictions of a simple Roy model of migration. As fur-

---

5. For related (and somewhat contradictory) evidence, see Chiquiar and Hanson (2005).

ther confirmation of this theoretical framework, they also show that the degree of negative selection among emigrants is larger in Mexican counties where workers typically face higher returns to education.

The study by David Card and Ethan Lewis begins by noting that although Mexican immigrants have historically clustered in only a few cities in the United States, primarily in California and Texas, this strong geographic clustering has begun to unravel in the past decade. More recent arrivals have established large immigrant communities in many new destinations. In previous decades, for example, nearly 80 percent of Mexican immigrants settled in either California or Texas. By 2000, however, fewer than half of the most recent Mexican immigrants settled in those two states. Many cities that had negligible Mexican immigrant populations in 1990—such as Atlanta and Raleigh-Durham—received many Mexican immigrants during the 1990s. The recent arrival of Mexican immigrants in many Southeastern cities raises many new interesting questions because of the potential impact of the immigrant influx on the labor market prospects of less-skilled African Americans.

Card and Lewis explore the causes and consequences of the recent geographic diffusion of Mexican immigrants. They find that a combination of demand-pull and supply-push factors explains most of the intercity variation in inflows of Mexican immigrants over the 1990s. Card and Lewis also note that Mexican immigration into a particular locality raises the relative supply of low-skill workers in a city. This supply shock, in turn, raises the question of how cities adapt to these demographic shifts. One possible adjustment mechanism is a shifting industry composition. Card and Lewis, however, find limited evidence for this mechanism: most of the increases in the relative supply of low-skill labor are absorbed by changes in skill intensity within narrowly defined industries, rather than a shifting industrial structure. They also seem to find little evidence of relative wage effects at the local level. The Card-Lewis study, therefore, suggests that the adjustment mechanism used by local markets to adjust to large and sudden supply shocks (composed mainly of low-skill workers) is still not well understood.

The essay by Brian Duncan and Stephen Trejo focuses specifically on the important question of how the latest wave of Mexican immigrants and their U.S.-born descendants will ultimately assimilate into the mainstream of American society. Although the large differences in educational attainment, occupation, and earnings that existed among early twentieth century waves of European immigrants narrowed substantially by the end of the twentieth century, there seems to be considerable skepticism that Mexican immigrants will follow the same processes of assimilation and adaptation.[6]

Duncan and Trejo argue that the existing literature ignores an important

6. See, for example, Portes and Zhou (1993) and Rumbaut (1994).

determinant of the rate of social mobility in the Mexican population: inter-marriage between Mexican immigrants and non-Mexicans. Their analysis shows that ignoring this factor can easily lead to a distorted picture of the social mobility likely to be experienced by the children of Mexican immigrants. The evidence, for example, shows that U.S.-born persons of Mexican ancestry who marry non-Mexicans are substantially more edu-cated and English proficient than are the Mexican Americans who marry co-ethnics. Moreover, the non-Mexican spouses of intermarried Mexican Americans also possess relatively high levels of schooling and English pro-ficiency, compared to the spouses of endogamously married Mexican Americans. Duncan and Trejo's empirical analysis documents that the children of intermarried Mexican Americans are much less likely to be identified as Mexican than are the children of endogamous Mexican mar-riages. These forces produce strong negative correlations between the edu-cation, English proficiency, employment, and earnings of Mexican Amer-ican parents and the chances that their children retain a Mexican ethnicity. Such findings raise the possibility that selective ethnic attrition biases ob-served measures of intergenerational progress for Mexican Americans.

Susan Richter, J. Edward Taylor, and Antonio Yúnez-Naude study the determinants of the flow of illegal immigrants from Mexico to the United States. They specifically focus on two major policy shifts: the 1986 IRCA and the North American Free Trade Agreement (NAFTA). The 1990s also witnessed increasing border enforcement against illegal immigration. The increased border enforcement should reduce the supply of illegal labor to the United States, but both NAFTA and IRCA could have potentially countervailing effects, at least in the short term.

Richter, Taylor, and Yúnez-Naude estimate an econometric model to test the effect of these policy changes on the flow of migrant labor from ru-ral Mexico to the United States. The models are estimated using retro-spective data from the 2003 National Mexico Rural Household Survey. Although it is nearly impossible to separately identify the impact of the various policy shifts from the concurrent economic trends, the empirical analysis suggests a number of interesting patterns. First, labor migration from rural Mexico followed an upward trend during the 1980s and 1990s, but its trend seems to be driven mainly by past migration flows, reflecting the central role of migration networks in generating further migration. Richter, Taylor and Yúnez-Naude find that policy variables seem to sig-nificantly influence migration, but their influence is relatively small, espe-cially when compared to the impact of macroeconomic variables and net-work effects.

Finally, Gordon Hanson's paper examines how Mexican emigration may have affected regional labor supply and regional earnings in Mexico. Emigration rates vary widely across Mexican regions, with workers from west-central states having the highest propensity to migrate abroad. Hanson exploits the regional persistence in these migration propensities to identify the impact of emigration on the regional wage structure in Mexico. In particular, Hanson finds that wages in high-migration states rose relative to wages in low-migration states.

There are, of course, several possible interpretations for this correlation between regional wages and supply movements. From the perspective of the economics of migration, the most interesting would be that emigration of low-skill workers raises wages in Mexico, with the effects being most pronounced in those states that have well-developed networks for sending migrants to the United States. As Hanson notes, however, emigration was not the only shock to the Mexican economy during the 1990s. Both NAFTA and the 1994–1995 Mexico peso crisis likely influenced wages and migration.

Conclusion

As a result of the continuing surge in international migration in many regions of the world, the literature investigating the economic impact of immigration on the United States and on other receiving (as well as sending) countries continues to grow rapidly. This explosion of research has substantially increased our understanding of the economic consequences of immigration. For example, the large number of immigrants admitted in the United States in recent decades has already had a major impact on the skill composition of the U.S. workforce and was likely responsible for some of the shifts in the wage structure observed in the 1980s and 1990s.

The essays presented in this volume add to our understanding of an important part of the immigration phenomenon in the United States: Mexican immigration. The essays clearly show that this immigrant influx has important economic consequences for both Mexico and the United States. Moreover, the economic impact of today's Mexican immigrants is not limited to the current generation, but will likely continue far into the future as the descendants of the Mexican immigrant population constitute an ever-larger part of the U.S. workforce.

References

Abowd, John M., and Richard B. Freeman, eds. 1991. *Immigration, trade, and the labor market.* Chicago: University of Chicago Press.

Borjas, George J. 1994. The economics of immigration. *Journal of Economic Literature* 32 (4): 1667–1717.

———. 2000. *Issues in the economics of immigration.* Chicago: University of Chicago Press.

Borjas, George J., and Richard B. Freeman, eds. 1992. *Immigration and the work force: Economic consequences for the United States and source areas.* Chicago: University of Chicago Press.

Chiquiar, Daniel, and Gordon Hanson. 2005. International migration, self-selection, and the distribution of wages: Evidence from Mexico and the United States. *Journal of Political Economy* 113 (2): 239–81.

Friedberg, Rachel, and Jennifer Hunt. 1995. The impact of immigration on host country wages, employment and growth. *Journal of Economic Perspectives* 9 (2): 23–44.

Hanson, Gordon. 2006. Illegal immigration from Mexico to the United States. *Journal of Economic Literature,* forthcoming.

Hanson, Victor Davis. 2003. *Mexifornia: A state of becoming.* San Francisco: Encounter Books.

Huntington, Samuel. 2004. *Who are we: The challenges to America's national identity.* New York: Simon & Schuster.

LaLonde, Robert J., and Robert H. Topel. 1996. Economic impact of international migration and the economic performance of immigrants. In *Handbook of population and family economics,* ed. Mark R. Rosenzweig and Oded Stark, 799–850. Amsterdam: North-Holland.

Passel, Jeffrey. 2005. *Unauthorized migrants: Numbers and characteristics.* Washington, DC: Pew Hispanic Center. http://www.pewhispanic.org/files/reports/46.pdf.

Portes, Alejandro, and Min Zhou. 1993. The new second generation: Segmented assimilation and its variants among post-1965 immigrant youth. *Annals of the American Academy of Political and Social Science* 530:74–96.

Rumbaut, Ruben G. 1994. The crucible within: Ethnic identity, self-esteem, and segmented assimilation among children of immigrants. *International Migration Review* 28 (4): 748–94.

U.S. Bureau of the Census. 1975. *Historical statistics of the United States: Colonial times to 1970.* Bicentennial ed. 2 vols. Washington, D.C.: U.S. Government Printing Office.

U.S. Immigration and Naturalization Service. Various Issues. *Statistical yearbook of the Immigration and Naturalization Service.* Washington, D.C.: U.S. Government Printing Office.

1

The Evolution of the Mexican-Born Workforce in the United States

George J. Borjas and Lawrence F. Katz

1.1 Introduction

The population of Mexican-born persons residing in the United States has increased at an unprecedented rate in recent decades. This increase can be attributed to both legal and illegal immigration. During the entire decade of the 1950s, only about three hundred thousand legal Mexican immigrants entered the United States, making up 12 percent of the immigrant flow. In the 1990s, 2.2 million Mexicans entered the United States legally, making up almost 25 percent of the legal flow (U.S. Immigration and Naturalization Service 2002). In addition, it is estimated that (as of January 2000) there were 7 million illegal aliens residing in the United States, with 4.8 million (68 percent of this stock) being of Mexican origin (U.S. Department of Commerce 2004). As a result of the increase in the number of legal and illegal Mexican immigrants, nearly 9.2 million Mexican-born persons resided in the United States in 2000, comprising about 29.5 percent of the foreign-born population (U.S. Bureau of the Census 2003).

It is instructive to place the Mexican immigrant influx of the late twentieth century in the context of earlier immigrant flows. In 1920, toward the end of the first great migration, the largest two national origin populations enumerated by the 1920 Census were Germans and Italians, and together these two populations comprised about 23.7 percent of the foreign-born population at the time (U.S. Bureau of the Census 1975). From this perspective, it is clear that the Mexican-born population of the late twentieth

George J. Borjas is a professor of economics and social policy at the Kennedy School of Government, Harvard University, and a research associate of the National Bureau of Economic Research. Lawrence F. Katz is a professor of economics at Harvard University, and a research associate of the National Bureau of Economic Research.

century is historically unprecedented, being both numerically and proportionately larger than any other immigrant influx in the past century.

This paper analyzes the evolution of Mexican immigration as a component of the U.S. workforce during the twentieth century. As a result of the rapidly increasing Mexican immigrant influx described earlier, the fraction of the workforce composed of Mexican-born workers increased rapidly after 1970. As the top panel of figure 1.1 shows, only 0.4 percent of the workforce aged eighteen–sixty-four in 1970 was composed of Mexican-born workers. By 2000, the Mexican immigrant share had increased to 4.0 percent. The increase is even larger in the male workforce, where 0.5 percent of working men were Mexican-born in 1970 and 5.1 percent in 2000.[1]

It is of interest to contrast the explosion of Mexican workers in the U.S. workforce in the late twentieth century with the demographic trends at the beginning of the century. Although Mexican immigration was relatively small in the early 1900s, the relative number of Mexican immigrants in the U.S. workforce increased to 0.6 percent in 1920 (and continued rising until the late 1920s). The halting of European migration to the United States with the outbreak of World War I followed by Congressional action to restrict immigration combined with strong labor demand in the booms of the late 1910s and the 1920s engendered substantial efforts by U.S. employers to recruit Mexican laborers through private labor contractors (Massey, Durand, and Malone 2002).[2] Remarkably, the Mexican immigrant share went into a long steady decline after the 1920s that lasted for several decades. It was not until the 1970s that the Mexican immigrant share of the workforce was at least as large as it was in the 1920s!

The reasons for the declining Mexican share in the workforce are not entirely clear.[3] Until 1965, there was not a numerical limitation on immigration from countries in the Western Hemisphere. In theory, at least, legal migration from Mexico was guided by a "first-come, first-served" approach. Potential immigrants applied for entry and local consular officials had a great deal of discretion in determining which applicants would be provided entry visas.

1. Tabulations from the Current Population Survey indicate that the Mexican immigrant share of the workforce has continued rising rapidly in recent years. The Mexican immigrant share of the overall workforce aged eighteen–sixty-four reached 4.7 percent in 2005 and had risen to 6.2 percent for males and 2.9 percent for females.

2. Mexican immigrants were exempted from the head tax and literacy test imposed on new arrivals in 1917 and from the national origin quotas of the immigration restriction acts of the 1920s.

3. Massey, Durand, and Malone (2002) argue that the weak U.S. labor market of the Great Depression generated more hostile attitudes of U.S. citizens toward Mexican immigrants and created political pressures leading to several highly publicized mass deportations of Mexican immigrants over the course of the 1930s. These changing economic incentives and immigration policies may have played a key role in stemming Mexican migration to the United States and even in reducing the absolute number of Mexican working in the United States during the 1930s.

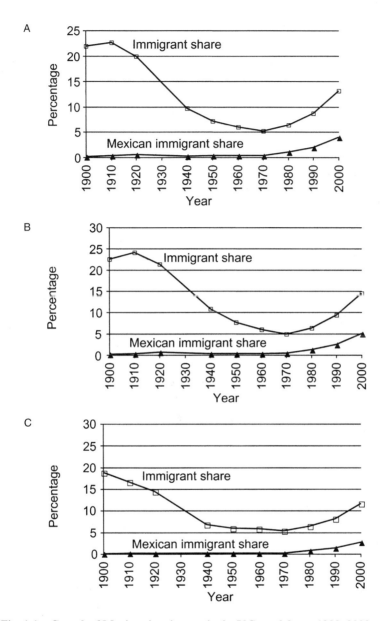

Fig. 1.1   Growth of Mexican immigrants in the U.S. workforce, 1900–2000:
A, **All workers;** *B,* **Male workers;** *C,* **Female workers**

Note: All statistics are calculated using the sample of workers aged eighteen–sixty-four.

To ease the labor force shortage caused by World War II in the agricultural industry during the early 1940s, the Bracero Program was launched on August 4, 1942. This guest-worker program brought almost 5 million Mexican-born farm workers to the United States between 1942 and 1964, when it was abruptly terminated by the United States. The main reason given for the discontinuation of the program at the time was the assertion that the Bracero Program depressed the wages of native-born Americans in the agricultural industry (Massey and Liang 1989; Marcell 1994).

The latest wave of illegal immigration from Mexico began in the late 1960s, after the discontinuation of the Bracero Program. There is, in fact, a clear link between the end of the Bracero Program and the beginning of the illegal alien flow, at least as measured by the number of Mexican nationals aliens apprehended as they attempt to enter the United States illegally. The number of Mexican illegal aliens apprehended by the Border Patrol began to increase soon after the Bracero Program ended. In 1964, for example, the Border Patrol apprehended only 41.6 thousand Mexican illegal aliens. By 1970, apprehensions were up to 348.2 thousand annually. In 1986, about 1.7 million Mexican illegal aliens were apprehended (U.S. Immigration and Naturalization Service, various issues).

Although the discontinuation of the Bracero Program may help explain why illegal immigration accelerated in the 1960s and 1970s, there are several questions that remain unanswered. The wage gap between Mexico and the United States has been large for many decades, and it is far from clear that it is larger now than it was at the beginning or middle of the twentieth century. Why then didn't we observe large flows of Mexican immigrants prior to the 1970s? It is possible, of course, that the policy changes initiated by the 1965 Amendments and subsequent legislation, which made family reunification the central goal of immigration policy, could have eased the entry of Mexicans in the United States, but, at least in theory, Mexican immigration was not greatly restricted prior to the post-1965 policy shifts. Why did so few Mexicans take advantage of it? Or were the institutional barriers placed at the consular level in Mexico so forbidding that relatively few Mexicans even bothered to apply to enter the United States?

We do not know the answers to these questions. What we do know, however, is that the Mexican immigrant population today stands out from the rest of the immigrant population in two striking ways. It is well known, of course, that there has also been a sizable increase in the number of non-Mexican immigrants admitted to the United States. Nevertheless, Mexican immigrants comprise an ever-larger fraction of the foreign-born stock of the United States (see figure 1.2). Second, as we will document, Mexican immigrants tend to have demographic and socioeconomic characteristics that differ significantly not only from that of the native-born population, but from that of other immigrants as well. In general, the economic per-

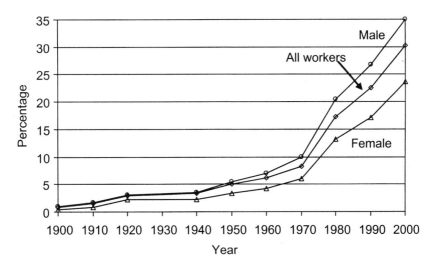

Fig. 1.2   Mexican immigrants as a share of U.S. immigrant workforce
Note: All statistics are calculated using the sample of workers aged eighteen–sixty-four.

formance of Mexican immigrants lags significantly behind that of other immigrant groups, and this lagging performance is, to an important extent, transmitted to future generations of native-born workers of Mexican ancestry.

This paper differs from earlier contributions in the immigration literature by focusing specifically on the evolution of the Mexican-born workforce in the United States.[4] We use data drawn from the Integrated Public Use Microdata Samples (IPUMS) of the U.S. Decennial Census throughout the entire twentieth century to describe the demographic and economic evolution of this population. The paper examines the evolution of the relative skills and economic performance of Mexican immigrants and contrasts this evolution to that experienced by other immigrants arriving in the United States during the period. The paper also examines the costs and benefits of this influx by examining how the Mexican influx has altered economic opportunities in the most affected labor markets and by discussing how the relative prices of goods and services produced by Mexican immigrants may have changed over time.

4. Important exceptions include Feliciano (2001), who examines the economic performance of Mexican immigrants through 1990; Camarota (2001), who attempts a cost-benefit analysis of Mexican immigration; and Trejo (2003), who studies the intergenerational mobility of Mexican-origin workers in the U.S. labor market. Broader analyses of immigrant and Hispanic labor market performance in the United States include Borjas (1985, 1995), Funkhouser and Trejo (1995), and LaLonde and Topel (1992).

1.2 Data and Key Trends

The analysis uses data drawn from all of the available IPUMS of the U.S. Decennial Census between 1900 and 2000.[5] This long-term look at the available data helps to provide a historical account of the evolution and economic performance of Mexican immigrants in the U.S. workforce.

Throughout the analysis, a person is classified as an "immigrant" if he or she was born in a foreign country; all other workers are classified as "natives."[6] Persons who are immigrants and who were born in Mexico comprise the sample of Mexican immigrants. The pre-1970 censuses comprise (roughly) a 1 percent random sample of the population. Beginning with 1980, the data comprise a 5 percent random sample of the population. The entire available sample in each census is used in the empirical analysis.

In each census, the study is restricted to persons aged eighteen–sixty-four who work in the civilian sector, are not enrolled in school, and do not reside in group quarters.[7] When appropriate, the sampling weights reported in the IPUMS data are used in the calculations.

1.2.1 The Geographic Sorting of Mexican Immigrants

Table 1.1 begins the empirical analysis by documenting how the geographic sorting of Mexican immigrants in the United States changed over the twentieth century. The top panel of the table reports the share of the stock of Mexican immigrants (both male and female) who reside in a particular state at a particular point in time, while the bottom panel reports the fraction of the state's workforce that is composed of Mexican immigrants.

---

5. General-use IPUMS samples are currently available for every decennial census in the twentieth century except for 1930. A preliminary 1930 sample became available after the empirical analysis was completed for this paper.

6. Persons born abroad of American parents and persons born in a U.S. possession are also classified as natives. It is important to note that the census data contain both legal Mexican immigrants as well as those illegal immigrants who answered the census questionnaire.

7. In the 1940–2000 samples, the study is also restricted to workers who report positive weeks worked and hours worked weekly and positive earnings in the calendar year prior to the survey. Prior to 1980, the information on hours worked refers to hours worked last week; in the 1980–2000 Censuses, the information refers to usual hours worked weekly. In the 1960–1970 Censuses, weeks worked are reported as a categorical variable. We imputed weeks worked for each worker as follows: 6.5 weeks for thirteen weeks or less, 20 for fourteen–twenty-six weeks, 33 for twenty-seven–thirty-nine weeks, 43.5 for forty–forty-seven weeks, 48.5 for forty-eight–forty-nine weeks, and 51 for fifty–fifty-two weeks. Similarly, in the 1960–1970 Censuses, hours worked last week are reported as a categorical variable. We imputed weekly hours worked for each worker as follows: 7.5 hours for one–fourteen hours, 22 for fifteen–twenty-nine hours, 32 for thirty–thirty-four hours, 37 for thirty-five–thirty-nine hours, 40 for forty hours exactly, 44.5 for forty-one–forty-eight hours, 54 for forty-nine–fifty-nine hours, and 70 for at least sixty hours. In the 1940–1980 Censuses, the top coded annual salary is multiplied by 1.5. We calculated a wage rate for each worker by taking the ratio of annual earnings to the product of weeks worked and hours worked weekly. We restrict the analysis in each census to workers whose calculated hourly wage rate lies between $1 and $250 (in 1999 dollars).

Table 1.1   **Regional concentration of the Mexican-born workforce, selected states**

	1900	1910	1920	1940	1950	1960	1970	1980	1990	2000
Percentage of Mexican immigrants residing in:										
Arizona	17.2	10.7	12.5	7.6	5.4	4.1	4.0	3.0	3.3	4.4
California	7.8	19.9	17.9	40.4	40.3	44.6	55.1	58.7	57.4	42.1
Colorado	0.0	1.3	3.1	1.9	1.0	0.9	0.4	0.8	0.8	2.0
Florida	0.0	0.2	0.1	0.0	0.0	0.2	0.4	0.5	1.4	2.2
Georgia	0.0	0.0	0.1	0.0	0.0	0.1	0.0	0.1	0.5	2.2
Illinois	1.6	0.2	1.4	3.0	2.5	6.6	8.2	8.6	7.3	7.3
Kansas	0.0	12.2	2.9	2.2	1.5	0.7	0.3	0.3	0.4	0.7
New Jersey	0.0	0.0	0.0	0.0	0.2	0.0	0.3	0.1	0.3	0.8
New Mexico	10.9	5.3	4.2	2.8	1.7	1.4	1.0	1.0	1.1	1.1
New York	0.0	0.7	0.6	1.5	0.7	1.7	0.5	0.5	1.1	1.7
North Carolina	0.0	0.0	0.0	0.0	0.0	0.1	0.0	0.1	0.2	2.0
Texas	62.5	46.2	50.6	35.3	39.1	33.2	23.4	21.2	20.0	19.9
Mexican immigrants as percentage of state's workforce										
Arizona	19.3	17.1	23.6	7.8	4.3	2.3	2.2	2.9	4.8	10.2
California	0.7	2.3	2.9	2.2	2.0	1.8	2.4	6.2	9.8	14.8
Colorado	0.0	0.5	2.0	0.9	0.4	0.4	0.2	0.6	1.1	4.8
Florida	0.0	0.1	0.1	0.0	0.0	0.0	0.1	0.1	0.5	1.6
Georgia	0.0	0.0	0.0	0.0	0.0	0.0	0.0	0.0	0.4	2.8
Illinois	0.1	0.0	0.1	0.1	0.1	0.4	0.6	1.8	3.1	6.5
Kansas	0.0	2.7	1.2	0.7	0.5	0.2	0.1	0.3	0.7	2.9
New Jersey	0.0	0.0	0.0	0.0	0.0	0.0	0.0	0.0	0.2	1.0
New Mexico	10.6	6.0	8.6	3.2	1.8	1.2	1.0	2.1	4.0	7.3
New York	0.0	0.0	0.0	0.0	0.0	0.1	0.0	0.1	0.3	1.1
North Carolina	0.0	0.0	0.0	0.0	0.0	0.0	0.0	0.0	0.2	2.6
Texas	3.4	4.3	7.7	3.1	3.0	2.4	1.9	3.7	6.0	10.9

Note: All statistics are calculated using the sample of workers aged eighteen–sixty-four.

The top panel of table 1.1 reports an important trend: a steady and substantial redistribution in Mexican immigration from Texas to California throughout much of the twentieth century. In 1900, for example, 62.5 percent of Mexican immigrants lived in Texas, and only 7.8 percent lived in California. By 1950, roughly equal numbers of Mexican immigrants lived in Texas (39.1 percent) and California (40.3 percent). By 1980, almost 60 percent of Mexican immigrants lived in California, and the fraction of those living in Texas had further declined to 21.2 percent. Between 1980 and 2000, however, California seemed to become a relatively less attractive destination for Mexican immigrants. By 2000, the fraction of Mexican immigrants living there had declined to 42.1 percent. Note, however, that this decline was not accompanied by an increase in the fraction choosing to reside in Texas; that share was relatively constant over the period.

Table 1.1 also shows that the recent decline in the relative share of Mexican immigrants who choose to live in California has been accompanied by a remarkable increase in Mexican immigration to states that had never been the recipients of large numbers of these immigrants. In 1980, for example, Mexican immigrants had, at best, a negligible presence in both North Carolina and Georgia. By 2000, however, almost 3 percent of the workforce in each of these states was composed of Mexican immigrants. Similarly, less than 1 percent of workers in Colorado were Mexican-born in 1980; by 2000, almost 5 percent of Colorado's workforce was Mexican-born. Although often noted in the popular press, this remarkable and sudden shift in the geographic sorting of Mexican immigrants in the United States has received little systematic analysis, and the reasons leading to the dramatic geographic redistribution are still not well understood.[8]

Because there were relatively few Mexican immigrants living in the United States at the beginning of the twentieth century, it is worth noting that even though nearly two-thirds of Mexican immigrants lived in Texas in 1900, only 3.4 percent of the Texas workforce was Mexican-born. By 2000, however, nearly 14.8 percent of the California workforce and 10.9 percent of the Texas workforce were Mexican-born. The relative importance of Mexican immigration as a component of the workforce of the main immigrant-receiving states, therefore, now stands at a historic high. The growth has been most dramatic in California. In 1970, only 2.4 percent of California's workforce was Mexican-born. By 2000, this statistic had increased sixfold, to 14.8 percent.

1.2.2   Trends in Educational Attainment and Occupation

The skill composition of the Mexican immigrant workforce differs strikingly from that of the native workforce as well as from that of other immigrants. We begin the description of the skill composition of the various groups by comparing the trend in the educational attainment of native working men with that of Mexican immigrant men. The census provides data on educational attainment beginning in 1940, so that this phase of the study focuses on the trends in the post-1940 period. As table 1.2 shows, 67.3 percent of male native-born working men were high-school dropouts in 1940.[9] This high native dropout rate was lower than that of Mexican immigrant men, where 94.6 percent had not completed high school. To provide a point of reference for these statistics, the table also reports that 84.4 percent of non-Mexican immigrant working men at that time were high school dropouts.[10]

8. See Card and Lewis (2005) for an initial analysis of the geographic redistribution of Mexican immigrants during the 1990s.

9. We refer to anyone with fewer than twelve years of completed schooling as a high school dropout.

10. Information on literacy in the 1900 to 1920 censuses suggests a similar educational gap for Mexican immigrant workers in the early twentieth century. For example, the literacy rate for Mexican-born male workers was 50.1 percent in 1910 as compared to 92.8 percent for native-born male workers and 87.0 percent for non-Mexican immigrant working men.

Table 1.2   **Percent distribution of educational attainment**

	1940	1950	1960	1970	1080	1990	2000
			Male workers				
Native-born							
High school dropouts	67.3	61.3	52.0	38.4	23.8	12.9	8.7
High school graduates	20.0	24.2	27.8	35.2	39.1	36.0	34.5
Some college	6.4	7.4	9.4	11.9	16.8	26.6	29.4
College graduates	6.3	7.1	10.8	14.5	20.3	24.5	27.4
Mexican immigrants							
High school dropouts	94.6	91.2	88.3	82.6	77.2	70.4	63.0
High school graduates	3.0	6.7	6.7	11.7	14.3	19.0	25.1
Some college	1.0	1.5	2.7	3.6	5.7	7.8	8.5
College graduates	1.4	0.6	2.4	2.2	2.9	2.8	3.4
Non-Mexican immigrants							
High school dropouts	84.4	76.4	64.5	45.5	30.2	21.0	17.0
High school graduates	9.2	14.5	16.8	23.9	26.7	26.0	25.8
Some college	2.8	4.0	8.3	11.7	15.2	21.3	20.9
College graduates	3.7	5.1	10.4	18.9	27.9	31.7	36.3
			Female workers				
Native-born							
High school dropouts	50.6	46.3	42.4	31.2	19.2	9.8	6.5
High school graduates	32.1	35.3	37.6	45.3	47.3	38.7	32.8
Some college	9.5	10.1	11.0	12.6	17.9	29.9	33.5
College graduates	7.8	8.3	9.0	11.0	15.6	21.6	27.3
Mexican immigrants							
High school dropouts	84.5	82.4	83.9	77.3	72.9	64.7	57.0
High school graduates	12.5	10.3	11.4	16.9	17.7	21.9	26.6
Some college	2.1	4.4	2.7	4.5	7.0	10.5	11.8
College graduates	0.9	2.9	2.0	1.4	2.4	3.0	4.5
Non-Mexican immigrants							
High school dropouts	79.2	68.5	59.3	43.9	30.1	20.0	15.5
High school graduates	15.8	22.3	25.5	33.7	35.2	31.1	27.6
Some college	2.8	5.0	9.6	12.6	16.8	24.0	24.4
College graduates	2.2	4.2	5.7	9.9	17.9	24.9	32.6

Note: All statistics are calculated using the sample of workers aged eighteen–sixty-four.

By 2000, the fraction of male native-born workers who are high school dropouts had fallen by almost 60 percentage points, to 8.7 percent. In contrast, the fraction of Mexican-born high school dropouts had fallen by only about 30 percentage points, to 63 percent. Again, as a reference point, note that the fraction of high school dropouts in the non-Mexican immigrant population had fallen by almost as much as in the native-born workforce, to 17 percent. As a result of these trends, the data indicate a remarkable fact: the population of male high school dropouts in the United States has become disproportionately Mexican-born. In 1940, 0.5 percent of all male high school dropouts were Mexican immigrants. Even as recently as 1980, only 4.1 percent of male high school dropouts were Mexican immigrants. By 2000, however, 26.2 percent of all male high school dropouts were Mexican-born.

The growing disadvantage of Mexican immigrants at the bottom of the educational attainment distribution is matched by an equally growing disadvantage at the top of the distribution, where a fast-growing number of native workers and non-Mexican immigrants are college graduates. In 1940, there was relatively little difference in college graduation rates among the three groups; by 2000, however, there is a wide gulf separating college graduation rates between Mexican immigrants and the other groups. In particular, 6.3 percent of native working men were college graduates in 1940, and this fraction had quadrupled to 27.4 percent by 2000. Similarly, 3.7 percent of non-Mexican immigrant men were college graduates in 1940, and this fraction had increased almost tenfold to 36.3 percent by 2000. In contrast, only 1.4 percent of Mexican immigrant men in 1940 were college graduates; by 2000, the college graduation remained a minuscule 3.4 percent in this group of workers.

The bottom panel of table 1.2 reports the trends in the education distribution for working women. The trends are similar to those reported for the various groups of working men, though not as dramatic. For example, the high school dropout rate of native women dropped by 44 percentage points between 1940 and 2000 (from 50.6 to 6.5 percent), as compared to the almost 60 percentage point drop experienced by native men. Similarly, the high school dropout rate for Mexican immigrant women dropped by 28 percentage points (from 84.5 to 57.0 percent), as compared to the 32 percentage point drop experienced by Mexican immigrant men. These data patterns presage a systematic finding in much of our analysis: the differences exhibited by the various groups of working women mirror those exhibited among the respective groups of working men but are less extreme. As a result of this similarity, much of the discussion that follows will focus on the trends observed in the sample of working men (even though many of the tables will report the respective statistics for working women). By focusing on the trends exhibited by working men, we can avoid the difficult conceptual and econometric issues introduced by the interpretation of skill and wage trends for working women during a period of rapidly rising female labor force participation rates.

Finally, table 1.3 illustrates the changing occupational distribution of Mexican immigrants by listing the "Top Ten" occupations employing these workers. The IPUMS data recode the very different occupation codes used by the various censuses into a single occupation categorization based on the 1950 Census definitions. We use this simplifying recoding to compare the occupation distribution of workers across censuses.

Not surprisingly, such low-skill occupations as laborers, farm laborers, gardeners and cooks, dominate the occupational distribution of Mexican

Table 1.3 Percent of Mexican immigrants employed in "Top 10" occupations

Occupation (1950 coding)	1900	1910	1920	1940	1950	1960	1970	1980	1990	2000
Male workers										
Operatives, nec (690)	0.0	1.0	1.7	7.2	10.8	10.6	18.2	20.1	16.0	15.5
Laborers, nec (970)	43.3	44.4	42.8	24.9	22.6	17.1	11.1	11.7	11.9	11.7
Farm laborers (820)	15.0	26.4	21.1	32.2	24.3	17.7	14.9	10.5	9.5	6.3
Gardeners (930)	0.0	0.0	0.0	1.2	0.6	1.5	2.9	2.6	4.8	5.8
Cooks (754)	0.0	0.0	0.2	1.3	0.9	1.4	1.7	3.3	4.9	5.4
Truck drivers (683)	0.0	2.2	0.2	1.9	3.5	4.4	2.8	2.2	3.5	4.2
Managers, proprietors nec (290)	1.7	1.4	1.5	1.6	1.2	3.1	2.2	3.4	3.9	3.9
Carpenters (510)	0.0	1.2	1.4	1.3	1.5	1.5	1.8	2.3	2.5	3.6
Janitors (770)	0.0	0.0	0.2	1.0	1.2	1.8	3.4	4.0	4.4	3.5
Foremen, nec (523)	0.0	0.0	0.4	0.7	1.5	1.4	1.6	2.4	1.9	3.2
Female workers										
Operatives, nec (690)	0.0	5.0	10.1	31.5	30.9	29.8	34.9	35.8	26.9	21.2
Private household (720)	50.0	25.0	16.0	14.7	10.3	13.6	5.4	2.8	4.2	9.0
Clerical workers (390)	0.0	0.0	0.8	1.8	2.9	3.2	2.8	5.1	5.4	7.6
Farm laborers (820)	0.0	30.0	13.9	5.6	2.9	4.7	7.4	8.7	7.7	5.0
Cooks (754)	0.0	0.0	1.3	0.9	1.5	2.7	1.8	2.4	3.7	4.9
Janitors (770)	0.0	0.0	0.0	0.7	0.0	0.5	0.9	2.7	5.0	4.5
Service, except private household, nec (790)	25.0	0.0	1.3	1.8	2.9	4.0	4.3	1.9	2.3	4.3
Cashiers (320)	0.0	0.0	0.0	0.0	1.5	0.5	2.0	2.1	3.3	3.7
Managers, officials, proprietors, nec (290)	0.0	0.0	3.8	0.0	4.4	2.0	1.2	1.7	2.7	3.3
Attendants, nec (731)	0.0	0.0	0.0	0.0	0.0	0.2	0.1	1.7	2.1	2.9

Notes: All statistics are calculated using the sample of workers aged eighteen–sixty-four. Occupations ranked according to their 2000 share of employment of Mexican immigrants.

immigrants. It is worth noting, however, that there seems to be much less occupational clustering among Mexican immigrants in the late 1900s than there was at the beginning of the century. In 1900, for example, almost two-thirds of Mexican immigrant men were employed as laborers or farm laborers. In 2000, the largest concentration of Mexican immigrant men is found in operatives (not elsewhere classified), which employs "only" 15.5 percent of the workers.

1.2.3   Trends in the Relative Wage

The growing disadvantage in the educational attainment of Mexican immigrants clearly implies a growing disadvantage in relative wages. Beginning in 1940, the IPUMS reports the worker's annual earned income in the year prior to the census. We divided the reported annual earned income by the reported number of weeks worked (in the subsample of workers who reported a positive number of weeks worked) to calculate the weekly wage for each worker.[11]

Table 1.4 documents that the relative log weekly wage of both Mexican and non-Mexican immigrants fell steeply between 1940 and 2000. Panel A of the table reports the trend in the log weekly wage of male Mexican and non-Mexican immigrants relative to the log weekly wage of native-born working men. It is instructive to begin the discussion by observing the trend in the relative log weekly wage of non-Mexican immigrants. Table 1.4 shows that there was a sizable and steady decline in the relative wage of non-Mexican immigrants between 1940 and 2000. In 1940, the typical non-Mexican immigrant man earned about .18 log points more than the typical native worker. By 2000, the typical non-Mexican immigrant man earned about .03 log points less than the typical native-born worker. This decline in the relative immigrant economic performance of immigrants has been a subject of intensive (and contentious) debate (Borjas 1985, 1995; Chiswick 1986; LaLonde and Topel 1992; Yuengert 1994).

The table also shows that, although the magnitude of the wage disadvantage of Mexican immigrant men is much larger than that of their non-Mexican counterparts, there has *not* been a steady downward trend in relative economic performance among Mexican immigrants. For example, the log weekly wage of Mexican immigrants was –.48 log points lower than that of native-born workers in 1940. This wage disadvantage, in fact, narrowed to around –.39 log points by 1970, before growing again to –.53 log points in 2000. It is worth stressing that although the relative economic performance of Mexican immigrants does not seem to have worsened substantially over the past few decades, Mexican immigrants have always

11. The sample includes self-employed workers. The worker's annual earned income is then defined as the sum of wage and salary income and self-employment income, except in 1940 when the Census does not report detailed information on self-employment income. Similar trends are revealed when the analysis is restricted only to salaried workers.

Table 1.4 **Trends in immigrant wages relative to native-born workers**

	1940	1950	1960	1970	1980	1990	2000
			Male workers				
A. Unadjusted wage gap							
Mexican immigrants	−.475	−.385	−.365	−.390	−.408	−.544	−.533
	(.022)	(.030)	(.016)	(.014)	(.004)	(.003)	(.002)
Non-Mexican immigrants	.175	.131	.104	.072	−.022	−.004	−.034
	(.005)	(.007)	(.005)	(.005)	(.002)	(.002)	(.002)
B. Adjusted wage gap, adjusts for education, age							
Mexican immigrants	−.453	−.352	−.249	−.205	−.148	−.149	−.144
	(.020)	(.028)	(.015)	(.013)	(.003)	(.003)	(.002)
Non-Mexican immigrants	.092	.093	.102	.035	−.048	−.042	−.073
	(.004)	(.007)	(.004)	(.004)	(.002)	(.002)	(.001)
C. Adjusted wage gap, adjusts for education, age, state of residence							
Mexican immigrants	−.444	−.377	−.304	−.255	−.202	−.208	−.176
	(.019)	(.027)	(.014)	(.013)	(.003)	(.003)	(.002)
Non-Mexican immigrants	−.016	.019	.016	−.027	−.062	−.104	−.106
	(.004)	(.007)	(.004)	(.004)	(.002)	(.002)	(.001)
			Female workers				
D. Unadjusted wage gap							
Mexican immigrants	−.329	−.193	−.335	−.217	−.135	−.316	−.401
	(.056)	(.068)	(.033)	(.025)	(.005)	(.004)	(.003)
Non-Mexican immigrants	.026	.065	.052	.057	.060	.081	.036
	(.009)	(.013)	(.007)	(.006)	(.002)	(.002)	(.002)
E. Adjusted wage gap, adjusts for education, age							
Mexican immigrants	−.247	−.104	−.177	−.049	.035	−.015	−.074
	(.051)	(.064)	(.031)	(.023)	(.005)	(.004)	(.003)
Non-Mexican immigrants	.080	.123	.100	.078	.045	.072	.025
	(.008)	(.013)	(.007)	(.006)	(.002)	(.002)	(.002)
F. Adjusted wage gap, adjusts for education, age, state of residence							
Mexican immigrants	−.246	−.132	−.230	−.094	−.038	−.120	−.137
	(.050)	(.062)	(.031)	(.023)	(.005)	(.004)	(.003)
Non-Mexican immigrants	−.013	.021	−.001	.010	.011	−.017	−.035
	(.008)	(.012)	(.007)	(.006)	(.002)	(.002)	(.002)

Notes: Standard errors are in parentheses. The numbers of observations in the male regressions are as follows: 208,729 in the 1940 Census; 79,824 in the 1950 Census; 362,823 in the 1960 Census; 393,653 in the 1970 Census; 2,546,859 in the 1980 Census; 2,809,917 in the 1990 Census; and 3,164,510 in the 2000 Census. The numbers of observations in the female regressions are: 74,101 in the 1940 Census; 33,777 in the 1950 Census; 163,027 in the 1960 Census; 227,736 in the 1970 Census; 1,961,549 in the 1980 Census; 2,405,910 in the 1990 Census; and 2,800,811 in the 2000 Census. The reported coefficients are log wage gaps relative to native-born workers.

suffered a substantial handicap in the labor market. A log point difference of –.53 implies an approximate 41 percent wage gap relative to natives for Mexican immigrants, as compared to only a 3 percent wage gap for the non-Mexican immigrant population in 2000.

As we showed earlier, there has been an increasing gap in educational attainment between Mexican immigrants and native-born workers. It is of interest to determine, therefore, whether differences in educational attainment and other observed measures of human capital explain the sizable wage gap between Mexican immigrants and native men. To illustrate the key importance of observable socioeconomic characteristics in determining the relatively low wage of Mexican immigrants, we estimated the following generic regression model separately in each census:

$$(1) \qquad \log w_{jt} = \mathbf{X}_{jt}\beta_t + \delta_t \mathbf{I}_{jt} + \varepsilon_{jt},$$

where w_{jt} gives the log weekly wage of worker j in year t; $\mathbf{X}$ is a vector of socioeconomic characteristics (defined below); and I_{jt} is a vector of two variables indicating if worker j is a Mexican immigrant or a non-Mexican immigrant. Depending on the specification of the regression model, the vector $\mathbf{X}$ can contain a vector of dummy variables indicating the worker's education (less than high school, high school graduate, some college, or college graduate), a third-order polynomial in the worker's age, and a vector of fixed effects indicating the state of residence.[12]

Panel B of table 1.4 reports the estimated coefficients of the parameter vector δ when the vector of standardizing variables includes only the worker's education and age. The results are striking. In 1940, the observed difference in socioeconomic characteristics, and particularly educational attainment, explain almost nothing of the sizable wage gap between Mexican immigrants and native-born men. The observed wage gap was –.475 log points, and the adjusted wage gap was –.453. By 1970, the minimal set of variables included in the vector $\mathbf{X}$ is an important determinant of the wage gap. In 1970, the observed wage gap stood at –.390 log points, and the adjusted wage gap was –.205 so that the observed human capital variables explained roughly half of the observed wage gap. Beginning in 1980, the adjusted wage gap has remained stable at around –.15 log points so that a very large fraction of the observed wage gap (over 70 percent of the –.53 wage gap in 2000) can be attributed to differences in socioeconomic characteristics, and particularly the very large difference in educational attainment.[13]

12. This regression model can be easily expanded to allow for different vectors of coefficients for the various groups. This more general specification leads to results that are similar to those reported in the paper. For simplicity, we choose to report the findings from the most basic regression specification.

13. The fact that age and educational attainment explain a large part of the wage gap in recent decades but almost none of the gap in 1940 and 1950 is explained by the fact that, although there was a large gap in educational attainment in the earlier years, Mexican immigrants were substantially older than native workers in 1940 and 1950 and roughly the same

It also turns out that by 2000 the observed differences in human capital—and again most particularly the observed difference in educational attainment—explains practically all of the wage gap between non-Mexican immigrants and Mexican immigrants. In 2000, for example, the adjusted relative wage of non-Mexican immigrants is −.07 log points, in contrast to a −.14 log point difference for Mexican immigrants. The .07 log point difference in adjusted relative wages between the two groups of immigrant workers stands in sharp contrast to the .50 log point difference in observed wages. Put differently, practically the entire wage gap between the two groups of immigrants can be explained through the fact that they differ in their levels of observed human capital—particularly educational attainment.

Panel C of table 1.4 replicates the regression analysis after adding in a vector of fixed effects indicating the worker's state of residence. These fixed effects could conceivably be very important as there is a great deal of geographic clustering among immigrants, and the states where immigrants tend to cluster may be high-wage states. The regression coefficients reported in the table, however, indicate that the quantitative changes in the size of the adjusted wage gaps are relatively small so that none of the key findings reported previously are affected by the inclusion of the state fixed effects.

Finally, the bottom panels of table 1.4 replicate the analysis using the sample of female workers. As noted earlier, the trends tend to be quite similar to those found among working men. In 2000, the relative wage of female Mexican immigrants stood at −.40 log points, as compared to an advantage of +.04 log points for female non-Mexican immigrants. Much of the wage disadvantage experienced by Mexican immigrant women, however, disappears once the regression model controls for differences in educational attainment among the groups. In particular, the −.40 log point wage gap falls to a −.07 wage gap when the regression model controls for educational attainment and age. In other words, a minimal set of skill characteristics explains about 80 percent of the wage gap between Mexican and native women.

1.2.4 Cohort Effects

The literature that documents the trends in immigrant skills stresses the importance of cohort and assimilation effects in generating the secular trends in the wage gap between immigrants and natives reported in table 1.4. After all, the wage of Mexican (or non-Mexican) immigrants may be changing over time either because—even at the time of entry—newer waves of immigrants have different skills than earlier waves or because ear-

---

age as natives after 1970. For example, the mean age of Mexican immigrants in 1940 was 45.9 years, as compared to 36.4 years for natives. In 2000, the mean age of the two groups is 40.7 and 40.5 years, respectively.

lier waves are acquiring valuable skills as they adapt to the U.S. labor market. It is of great interest to investigate the relative importance of both of these factors to examine the wage evolution experienced by the Mexican-born workforce in the United States.

Instead of developing a parametric model to summarize the various trends, we use a simple framework that attempts to characterize the underlying trends without imposing any structure on the data. Consider, in particular, the trend in the relative wage of immigrants who, as of the time of the census, have been in the United States fewer than five years.[14] The trend in the relative wage of these immigrants would identify the cohort effect that characterizes the most recent wave observed in each of the censuses.[15] Panel A of table 1.5 reports the relative wage of these newly arrived Mexican and non-Mexican immigrants in each of the censuses where the data are available.

The data clearly suggest a steady decline in the relative wage of successive waves of newly arrived Mexican immigrants from 1940 through 1990. The most recently arrived Mexican immigrant wave enumerated in the 1940 Census (i.e., the 1945–1949 arrivals) earned –.34 log points less than natives in 1940. By 1990, the latest wave of Mexican immigrants enumerated in that census earned .81 log points less than natives. This decline was reversed slightly in the 1990s. In 2000, the latest wave of Mexican immigrants earned .76 log points less than native workers. To provide some perspective, note that a –.76 log wage gap implies a 53 percent wage differential between Mexican immigrants and natives at the time of arrival.

A similar decline in the relative wage of successive immigrant cohorts—although the magnitude of the relative wage disadvantage is not as large—is clear in the sample of non-Mexican immigrants. In 1940, the most recently arrived non-Mexican immigrants earned .10 more log points than native workers; by 1970, the relative wage of the most recent cohort stood at –.16; by 1990 it stood at –29. This long-term decline in the relative wage of newly arrived immigrants was reversed in the 1990s. In 2000, the newly arrived non-Mexican immigrants earned .20 log points less than native workers.

The relative wage trends of successive immigrant cohorts of both Mexican and non-Mexican immigrants, therefore, imply a very similar trend in cohort effects in the period between 1940 and 1990—a decline in the relative earnings of newly arrived immigrants from 1940 through 1990 and then a reversal in the 1990s. This reversal was relatively modest for Mexican immigrants and quite sharp for non-Mexican immigrants.

Two points are worth emphasizing about these trends. First, although

14. The 1950 Census does not provide this information so that the relative wage of the most recently arrived five-year cohort cannot be measured.
15. This assertion, of course, assumes that the period effect is neutral between the immigrant population and the baseline reference group.

Table 1.5   **Trends in the relative wage of newly arrived immigrants**

	1940	1950	1960	1970	1980	1990	2000
		Male workers					
A. Unadjusted wage gap							
Mexican immigrants	−.342		−.526	−.593	−.647	−.812	−.764
	(.258)		(.044)	(.031)	(.007)	(.006)	(.004)
Non-Mexican immigrants	.101		−.074	−.160	−.218	−.289	−.203
	(.042)		(.014)	(.011)	(0.004)	(0.004)	(.003)
B. Adjusted wage gap, adjusts for education, age							
Mexican immigrants	−.408		−.316	−.254	−.214	−.201	−.164
	(.230)		(.039)	(.028)	(.006)	(.005)	(.004)
Non-Mexican immigrants	−.004		−.077	−.177	−.210	−.200	−.149
	(.037)		(.013)	(.010)	(.004)	(.003)	(.003)
C. Adjusted wage gap, adjusts for education, age, state of residence							
Mexican immigrants	−.459		−.396	−.325	−.272	−.277	−.187
	(.219)		(.038)	(.027)	(.006)	(.005)	(.004)
Non-Mexican immigrants	−.111		−0.166	−.238	−.230	−.272	−.180
	(.035)		(.012)	(.010)	(.004)	(.003)	(.003)
		Female workers					
D. Unadjusted wage gap							
Mexican immigrants			−.557	−.286	−.248	−.503	−.544
			(.084)	(.056)	(.011)	(.010)	(.007)
Non-Mexican immigrants	−.125		−.046	.018	−.040	−.137	−.150
	(.053)		(.019)	(.014)	(.005)	(.005)	(.004)
E. Adjusted wage gap, adjusts for education, age							
Mexican immigrants			−.334	−.072	.001	−.092	−.096
			(.079)	(.053)	(.011)	(.009)	(.006)
Non-Mexican immigrants	−.004		.018	.054	−.025	−.078	−.100
	(.048)		(.018)	(.013)	(.005)	(.004)	(.004)
F. Adjusted wage gap, adjusts for education, age, state of residence							
Mexican immigrants			−.395	−.133	−.078	−.214	−.144
			(.077)	(.052)	(.011)	(.009)	(.006)
Non-Mexican immigrants	−.119		−.086	−.022	−.066	−.181	−.155
	(.046)		(.017)	(.013)	(.005)	(.004)	(.004)

Notes: Standard errors are in parentheses. A newly arrived immigrant has been in the United States five years or less as of the time of the Census. The numbers of observations in the male regressions are as follows: 186,314 in the 1940 Census; 343,028 in the 1960 Census; 377,656 in the 1970 Census; 2,416,854 in the 1980 Census; 2,612,394 in the 1990 Census; and 2,820,033 in the 2000 Census. The numbers of observations in the female regressions are as follows: 69,147 in the 1940 Census; 154,868 in the 1960 Census; 217,844 in the 1970 Census; 1,856,973 in the 1980 Census; 2,250,119 in the 1990 Census; and 2,541,595 in the 2000 Census. The reported wage coefficients are log wage gaps relative to native-born workers.

the U-shaped trends in cohort effects are very similar between the two groups of immigrants, the magnitude of the relative wage disadvantage at the time of entry is far greater for the Mexican population. In 2000, the typical newly arrived Mexican immigrant earned 53.4 percent less than the typical native worker, as compared to an 18.4 percent wage disadvantage for non-Mexican immigrants.

Second, a recent study by Borjas and Friedberg (2004) documents that the uptick in the cohort effect for (all) immigrants who arrived in the late 1990s can be explained in terms of a simple story that has significant policy relevance. In particular, the uptick documented in the entire sample of immigrants disappears when the relatively small number of immigrants who are employed as computer scientists and engineers is excluded from the analysis.[16] In both 1980 and 1990, fewer than 5 percent of the newly arrived immigrants worked in these high-tech occupations. By 2000, however, 11.1 percent of the newly arrived immigrants worked in these occupations.

Although the census data do not provide information on the type of visa immigrants used to enter the country, it is probably not a coincidence that this increase in the relative number of high-tech immigrants occurred at the same time that the size of the H-1B visa program grew substantially. This program allows employers to sponsor the entry of temporary workers in specialty occupations. In fact, 70 percent of the workers entering the country with an H-1B visa in 2000 are employed either in computer-related occupations or in engineering (U.S. Immigration and Naturalization Service 2002). Between 1990 and 1994, about 100,000 H-1B visas were granted each year. In 1996, this number increased to 144,548; to 240,947 in 1998; and to 302,326 in 1999 (U.S. Immigration and Naturalization Service, various issues). It seems, therefore, that the insourcing of high-tech workers through the H-1B program reversed the long-standing trend of declining relative skills in successive cohorts of new immigrants.

It is extremely unlikely, however, that the H-1B program can explain the modest uptick observed in the cohort effects for Mexican immigrants during the late 1990s. After all, the number of Mexican-born workers in the newly arrived sample in the 2000 Census who are employed as computer scientists or engineers is minuscule (0.6 percent for Mexican immigrants as compared to 9.5 percent for non-Mexican immigrants). It seems, therefore, that the improvement in the relative economic status of newly arrived Mexican immigrants in the late 1990s may reflect either an increase in the overall skills of the sample or a period effect that is not yet fully understood (although it is well known that wages for low-skill workers increased

---

16. The occupation codes used to define the sample of computer scientists and engineers in each census are: 80–93 in 1960; 3, 4, and 6–23 in 1970; 44–59, 64, and 229 in 1970 and 1980; 100–111 and 132–153 in 2000.

markedly during this period as shown, for example, in Autor, Katz, and Kearney 2005).

Panel B of table 1.5 continues the analysis of the cohort effects by reporting the adjusted wage differential between the sample of newly arrived immigrants and native-born workers when the regression model includes the age and education variables, and panel C adds the state of residence fixed effects. The adjusted log wage differentials reported in the table are obtained by estimating a regression model similar to that presented in equation (1), but including only the samples of native workers and the most recently arrived immigrants in each census. The comparison of the adjusted (from panel B) and unadjusted log wage gaps reveal a number of interesting findings. First, a minimal vector of skill characteristics explains a great deal of the wage gap between newly arrived Mexican immigrants and native workers, but explains only a relatively small part of the wage gap between non-Mexican immigrants and natives. For example, in 2000 there was a −.76 unadjusted log wage gap between recent Mexican immigrants and natives. Adjusting for differences in education and age reduces the wage gap to −.16 log points so that the observed skill characteristics explain about 80 percent of the observed wage gap. In contrast, the observed wage gap for recent non-Mexican immigrants is −.20 log points, and the adjusted wage gap is −.16 log points so that differences in education and age explain only about one-fifth of the observed wage gap in this population.

A second important insight provided by table 1.5 is that the very large wage gap between non-Mexican and newly arrived Mexican immigrants is almost entirely due to differences in educational attainment and age, particularly in recent years. In 2000, for example, the regression coefficients imply that there was an unadjusted wage gap of −.56 log points between Mexican and non-Mexican immigrants but that adjusting for education and age reduced this wage gap to only about −.015 log points. In short, the regressions yield the important conclusion that the reason that recent Mexican immigrants earn far less than their non-Mexican counterparts appears to have little to do with the fact that they are Mexican but has almost everything to do with the fact that they are far less educated than their counterparts.

It is worth noting that the trend in relative wages between immigrants and native workers may also be reflecting differential period effects on the wages of the various groups, particularly toward the latter part of the period under study. After all, there were historic changes in the U.S. wage structure during the 1980s and 1990s, and these changes did not affect all skill groups equally (Autor, Katz, and Kearney 2005; Katz and Murphy 1992; Murphy and Welch 1992). There was, for instance, a sizable increase in the wage gap between highly educated and less-educated workers. Because Mexican immigrants are relatively unskilled, the changes in the wage structure imply that the relative wage of Mexican immigrants would have fallen between 1980 and 2000 even if the relative skills of Mexican immigrants had remained constant.

We use a simple approach to show that the wage trends documented in tables 1.4 and 1.5 are not greatly affected by the changes in the wage structure. In particular, we calculated the median wage of Mexican or non-Mexican immigrants in each of the census years starting in 1960 and computed the fraction of native workers whose wage lies below the immigrant median. This approach, of course, results in a statistic that marks the placement of the median Mexican or non-Mexican immigrant in the native wage distribution. As shown in table 1.6, the results of this analysis strongly resemble those provided by the trends in the mean log wage gap between immigrant and native workers. Among male workers, for example, the trend in the log wage gap between newly arrived Mexican immigrants and native workers suggested a general decline in the relative skills of the successive immigrant cohorts between 1960 and 2000. Similarly, the percentile analysis reported in table 1.6 shows that the median newly arrived Mexican immigrant in 1960 placed at the 17th percentile of the native wage distribution, while the median newly arrived Mexican immigrant in 2000 placed at the 12th percentile.

Table 1.6 also reports the percentile placement of the immigrant workers after adjusting the data for differences in educational attainment, age, and state of residence between immigrants and natives. These adjusted placements are calculated by obtaining the residuals from a log weekly wage regression estimated separately by census year and gender. The adjusted placement reported in the table gives the fraction of native workers who have a residual from this regression below that of the median residual in the samples of Mexican or non-Mexican workers. As with the trends in the adjusted mean wage gap, the trend in the adjusted percentile placement suggest a decline in the relative economic status of newly arrived non-Mexican immigrants from 1960 through 1990 and an increase in the relative status of newly arrived Mexican immigrants throughout the entire 1960–2000 period.[17]

1.2.5   Economic Assimilation

The 1960–2000 Census data can also be used to measure the extent of "economic assimilation," the improvement in the relative wage of a specific immigrant cohort over time.[18] We define an *immigrant cohort* in terms of

17. It is worth noting that the change in the wage of entry cohorts over time is distorted by changes in census coverage—particularly as more-recent censuses have attempted to count a greater fraction of the population of illegal immigrant.

18. It is believed that as many as one-third of the immigrants in the United States eventually return to their origin countries. Suppose that the return migrants are disproportionately composed of workers with lower than average wages. The intercensal tracking of a particular immigrant cohort would then indicate an improvement in relative wages even if no wage convergence is taking place. Alternatively, if the return migrants are the successes, the rate of

Table 1.6   Placement of median immigrant in native wage distribution

	Percentile placement of median Mexican immigrant					Percentile placement of median non-Mexican immigrant				
	1960	1970	1980	1990	2000	1960	1970	1980	1990	2000
Male										
All immigrant	26.2	22.0	23.6	19.7	19.0	53.6	53.4	47.7	47.8	45.5
Recent immigrants	17.0	14.7	14.1	12.4	12.3	40.5	34.2	30.3	27.7	32.8
Male[b]										
All immigrants	26.7	27.1	33.4	34.9	37.8	49.6	46.7	43.6	41.2	41.9
Recent immigrants	19.5	22.4	28.0	29.8	35.9	35.9	29.0	29.6	28.3	36.6
Female[a]										
All immigrants	27.5	33.5	38.1	30.6	25.9	50.7	52.1	52.4	52.3	49.7
Recent immigrants	19.8	31.7	32.1	22.8	20.9	43.7	47.4	44.1	37.8	36.0
Female[b]										
All immigrants	29.0	39.1	42.9	38.6	37.6	46.6	48.0	48.5	46.2	45.7
Recent immigrants	21.7	36.5	40.3	32.4	36.4	41.6	42.8	41.1	34.1	36.0

[a]Unadjusted placement: fraction of the relevant native workforce that has a wage below that of the median of the Mexican or non-Mexican immigrant.

[b]Adjusted placement: the fraction of the relevant native workforce that has a residual from a wage regression that lies below the median residual of the Mexican or non-Mexican immigrant, where the regression includes a vector of educational attainment fixed effects, a third-order polynomial in the worker's age, and a vector of fixed effects indicating the worker's state of residence.

calendar year of arrival *and* age at arrival. One can then use the decennial censuses to calculate the wage differential between newly arrived immigrants and similarly aged natives as of 1970; to recalculate the wage gap between these same two groups ten years later in the 1980 Census when the workers are ten years older; and to recalculate it again later in the 1990 and 2000 Censuses when the groups are twenty and thirty years older, respectively.

Consider initially the economic assimilation experienced by non-Mexican immigrants. Table 1.7 reports the economic assimilation trends for various cohorts of this group of immigrants. Figure 1.3 summarizes the results by illustrating the assimilation trends for workers who arrived in the United States when they were twenty-five to thirty-four years old. To simplify the presentation, much of our discussion will focus directly on the groups illustrated in figure 1.3.[19]

wage convergence would be underestimated. Because of data limitations, the selection mechanism generating the return migration flow is not well understood. An important exception is the work of Ramos (1992), who analyzes the return migration decisions of Puerto Ricans living in the United States.

19. The assimilation profile of the cohort of immigrants that entered the United States between 1955 and 1959 is incomplete because the cohort cannot be identified in the 1980 and 1990 Censuses.

Table 1.7   Evolution of relative wage of non-Mexican immigrants over time (relative to native workers)

Year of entry	Age at migration	1960	1970	1980	1990	2000
1955–1959	25–34	−0.039	0.127			
	35–44	−0.080	0.067			
	45–54	−0.122	−0.005			
1965–1969	5–14				0.087	0.110
	15–24			−0.019	0.062	0.037
	25–34		−0.107	0.014	0.101	0.124
	35–44		−0.182	−0.138	−0.017	
	45–54		−0.268	−0.231		
1975–1979	5–14					0.107
	15–24				0.054	0.055
	25–34			−0.176	−0.017	−0.018
	35–44			−0.203	−0.130	−0.065
	45–54			−0.291	−0.178	
1985–1989	15–24					−0.043
	25–34				−0.174	−0.096
	35–44				−0.262	−0.262
	45–54				−0.345	−0.354
1995–1999	25–34					0.004

Note: The "age at migration" reflects the age of the workers at the time of the Census immediately following the arrival of the immigrant cohort.

Consider the group of non-Mexican immigrants who arrived in the late 1960s at a relatively young age, when they were twenty-five to thirty-four years old. Figure 1.3 shows that these immigrants earned .11 log points less than comparably aged native workers at the time of entry. Let's now move forward in time ten years to 1980, when both the immigrants and the natives are thirty-five to forty-four years old. The wage disadvantage experienced by these immigrants has now been reversed, and the non-Mexican immigrant relative wage is .01 log points greater than that of comparably aged native workers. The economic assimilation of this group continues during the 1980s so that the 1990 Census shows that the wage of this group of non-Mexican immigrants is about .10 log points greater than that of comparably aged natives. Finally, the data reveal relatively little additional wage growth during the 1990s as both native and immigrant workers near retirement. In sum, the process of economic assimilation exhibited by this cohort reduced the initial wage disadvantage of these immigrants by just over 20 log points over a thirty-year period—with most of the wage growth occurring in the first twenty years after immigration. Because this immigrant cohort had a relatively high wage at the time of entry, the process of economic assimilation allowed the immigrants to narrow the wage disadvantage by catching up and overtaking comparable native workers.

The experience of other groups of non-Mexican immigrants who arrived

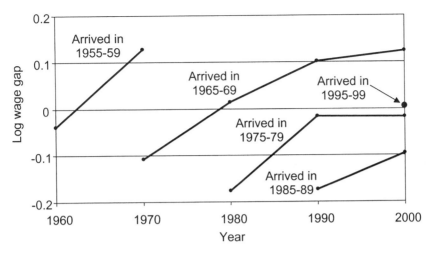

Fig. 1.3 Wage growth of non-Mexican immigrant cohorts over time, relative to natives (relative wage of immigrants who arrived when they were twenty-five–thirty-four years old)

at a relatively young age (between twenty-five and thirty-four) yields roughly the same type of wage convergence regardless of the calendar year when they arrived in the United States. Consider, for instance, the non-Mexican workers who arrived in the United States in the late 1970s. They started out with a wage disadvantage of .18 log points, and this disadvantage had disappeared within a decade. In short, the evidence suggests that non-Mexican immigrants experience reasonably rapid wage convergence, with the process of economic assimilation increasing the relative wage of the non-Mexican immigrants who arrived at around age thirty by 20 log points over the first two decades.

Contrast now these assimilation rates with those found in the population of similarly aged (i.e., twenty-five–thirty-four at the time of arrival) Mexican immigrants, as reported in table 1.8 and illustrated in figure 1.4. The figure reveals far less evidence of a consistent pattern of economic improvement for a particular cohort of immigrants over time. Although there is a great deal of variability in the data (perhaps due to sampling error or to period effects), the age-earnings profiles for the various cohorts of Mexican immigrants represented in the figure provide little evidence that these immigrants experience systematic and persistent wage growth as they accumulate experience in the U.S. labor market. To be specific, consider the evolution of relative wages for the Mexican immigrants who arrived in the late 1960s. They experienced a –.59 log point wage disadvantage at the time of entry; this disadvantage was narrowed substantially to –.45 log points by 1980, but then it began to grow again, to –.54 log points in 1990 and –.52

Table 1.8   Evolution of relative wage of Mexican immigrants over time (relative to native workers)

Year of entry	Age at migration	1960	1970	1980	1990	2000
1955–1959	25–34	−0.381	−0.352			
	35–44	−0.626	−0.381			
	45–54	−0.835	−0.660			
1965–1969	5–14				−0.173	−0.271
	15–24			−0.231	−0.360	−0.440
	25–34		−0.593	−0.445	−0.537	−0.517
	35–44		−0.628	−0.529	−0.606	
	45–54		−0.711	−0.524		
1975–1979	5–14					−0.261
	15–24				−0.352	−0.423
	25–34			−0.543	−0.603	−0.591
	35–44			−0.759	−0.783	−0.646
	45–54			−0.816	−0.753	
1985–1989	15–24					−0.361
	25–34				−0.626	−0.554
	35–44				−0.880	−0.716
	45–54				−1.029	−0.732
1995–1999	25–34					−0.574

Note: See notes to table 1.7.

log points in 2000, as the group of older workers now approached retirement age. Similarly, the sample of Mexican immigrants who arrived in the late 1970s, for example, experienced a flat assimilation path over their observable life cycle. In short, the evidence clearly indicates that the path of economic assimilation experienced by Mexican immigrants differs strikingly from that experienced by non-Mexican immigrants.

Tables 1.7 and 1.8 report more detailed evidence on the rate of economic assimilation for other cohorts of non-Mexican and Mexican immigrants who arrived at different ages. The evidence clearly suggests that immigrants (regardless of whether they are Mexican) who enter the United States at older ages enter with a greater disadvantage and experience less economic assimilation. For example, the relative wage of Mexican immigrants who arrived in the United States in the late 1970s when they were forty-five to fifty-four years old was −.82 log points at the time of entry. This group's relative wage had improved slightly to −.75 log points by 1990. Similarly, the relative wage of comparably aged non-Mexican immigrants who entered the country in the late 1970s was −.29 at the time of entry and had improved modestly to −.18 log points by 1990.

In contrast, the data indicate that immigrants who enter the United States as children have a much smaller wage disadvantage when they first enter the labor market. Consider, for instance, the wage experience of non-Mexican immigrants who entered the United States in the late 1960s when

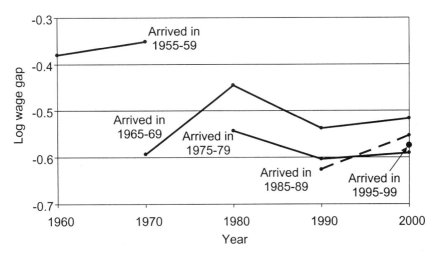

Fig. 1.4   Wage growth of Mexican immigrant cohorts over time, relative to natives (relative wage of immigrants who arrived when they were twenty-five–thirty-four years old)

they were five to fourteen years old. These persons are first observed in the labor market in 1990 when they are twenty-five to thirty-four years old. Their entry wage stands at +.09 log points. Similarly, the wage of the respective cohort of Mexican immigrants is –.17 log points in 1990. Although Mexican immigrants still suffer a disadvantage, the size of the disadvantage is far smaller than that experienced by groups of Mexican immigrants who entered the United States at older ages (and, as we shall see momentarily, is roughly similar to the wage disadvantage experienced by U.S.-born workers of Mexican ancestry).

A number of data and conceptual problems suggest that we should interpret the evolution of relative wages for specific cohorts of Mexican immigrants with some caution. For instance, it could be argued that the rates of economic assimilation convergence reported in table 1.8 are misleading because they compare the wage growth experienced by the typical Mexican immigrant with the wage growth experienced by the typical U.S.-born worker. As we have seen, however, the educational attainment of the typical Mexican immigrant is much lower than the educational attainment of the typical native worker. In 1990, for example, only 4 percent of male native workers had eight or fewer years of schooling, as compared to 57 percent of male Mexican immigrants.

This huge difference in the human capital of the two groups suggests that it may be of interest to compare the wage growth experienced by Mexican immigrants with the wage growth experienced by natives who face somewhat similar economic opportunities. Figure 1.5 replicates the economic

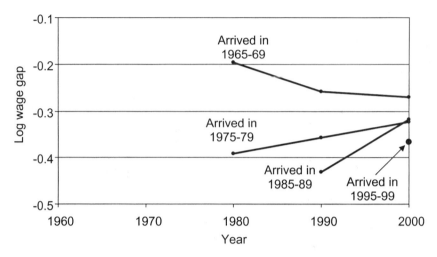

Fig. 1.5   Wage growth of Mexican immigrant cohorts over time, relative to Mexican natives (relative wage of immigrants who arrived when they were twenty-five–thirty-four years old)

assimilation analysis by using a different native group as the reference group—namely the sample of native-born workers who report they have Mexican ancestry.[20] The information on Mexican ancestry is available on a consistent basis only beginning with the 1980 Census so that this phase of the research focuses on the 1980–2000 period.

It is of interest to contrast the age-earnings profiles illustrated in figures 1.4 and 1.5. This contrast reveals two important findings. First, there is a much smaller wage gap between Mexican immigrants and Mexican natives than between Mexican immigrants and the typical native-born worker. For example, recently arrived Mexican immigrants aged twenty-five–thirty-four in 1980 earned .50 log points less than the typical young native worker at the time, but earned only –.04 log points less than the typical U.S.-born worker of Mexican ancestry. Second, although there is a great deal of variability in the age-earnings profiles, there is somewhat more evidence of a catching up effect for Mexican immigrants relative to U.S. natives of Mexican ancestry. Figure 1.5, in fact, suggests that Mexican immigrants (at least starting with those arriving in the 1970s) experience roughly a .10 log point catching up effect during their first decade in the United States.

There is even stronger evidence of wage convergence when the Mexican immigrants are compared to native workers who have the same educa-

20. The next section discusses the construction of the sample of Mexican-born workers in the post-1980 censuses in detail.

tional attainment. As shown in the preceding, the fraction of Mexican men who are high school dropouts hovered around 90 percent prior to 1960 and was still around 63 percent even by 2000. It is of interest, therefore, to contrast how the bulk of the Mexican immigrant workforce fares relative to the (shrinking) sample of native high school dropouts. Figure 1.6 shows that the wage of Mexican immigrant high school dropouts increases significantly during their first decade in the United States *relative to that of native high school dropouts.* For example, the newly arrived immigrants aged twenty-five–thirty-four in 1970 earned –.46 log points less than native high school dropouts, but this wage gap had narrowed to –.17 log points by 1980. Note, however, that this wage convergence slows down considerably (if not stops altogether) after ten years in the United States so that Mexican immigrants earn less than comparably aged native high school dropouts even after twenty years in the country.

In addition to the problems introduced by the choice of a baseline group, it is worth stressing that the interpretation of the wage evolution experienced by a particular Mexican immigrant cohort as a measure of economic assimilation ignores the fact that the sample composition of the Mexican immigrant sample is likely changing over time because of return migration. The proximity of Mexico to the United States, and the presumed large back-and-forth migration flows between the two countries, suggests that

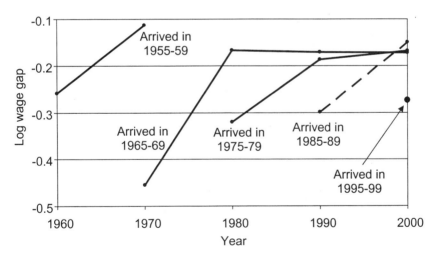

Fig. 1.6   Wage growth of Mexican immigrant cohorts over time, relative to native worker, restricted to sample of high school dropouts (relative wage of immigrants who arrived when they were twenty-five–thirty-four years old)

Note: The samples of Mexican immigrants and native workers are restricted to male workers who are high school dropouts.

Mexican immigrants may have relatively large outmigration rates.[21] It is evident that the use of synthetic cohorts created by matching particular groups of workers across census surveys may not lead to an accurate assessment of economic assimilation for a population that has a large transient component.[22]

Suppose, for instance, that the return migrants are disproportionately composed of workers who have lower than average wages. The intercensal tracking of a particular immigrant cohort (defined in terms of calendar year of entry and age at migration) would then indicate an improvement in relative wages even if no wage convergence is taking place. Alternatively, the rate of wage convergence would be underestimated if the return migrants are the successes.

The United States does not collect any information on either the size or the skill composition of the outmigrant flow. As a result, the available census data cannot conclusively determine the biases introduced by selective return migration on the observed rate of economic assimilation. Nevertheless, there are relatively simple ways of ascertaining the potential importance of this bias. For example, let $\overline{w}_0$ be the relative log weekly wage of a cohort of Mexican immigrants at the time of entry ($t = 0$), and let w_1^S be the relative log weekly wage of the sample of survivors in the following period (that is, the relative wage of those immigrants who chose to remain in the United States). Assume that there is no sample attrition in the native-born population and that a fraction r of the immigrants will return to Mexico between $t = 0$ and $t = 1$. We can then write the *observed* rate of wage convergence for this particular cohort of immigrants as

$$(2) \qquad w_1^S - \overline{w}_0 = w_1^S - [(1 - r) w_0^S + r w_0^R],$$

where w_0^S is the average relative entry wage of immigrants who remained in the United States and w_0^R is the average relative entry wage of the immigrants who returned to Mexico. It is instructive to rewrite equation (2) as

$$(3) \qquad w_1^S - \overline{w}_0 = (w_1^S - w_0^S) + r(w_0^S - w_0^R),$$

which shows the relation between the *observed* rate of wage growth and the true rate of wage growth ($w_1^S - w_0^S$) actually experienced by the sample of survivors. The observed rate of wage growth is a biased measure of the true rate of wage convergence as long as the skill composition of the sample of

---

21. Borjas and Bratsberg (1996), for example, estimate that about 25.9 percent of the *legal* Mexican immigrants who arrived between 1970 and 1974 had left the United States by 1980. This outmigration rate compares to a rate of 21.5 percent for all legal immigrants who arrived between 1970 and 1974.

22. The multiple border crossings made by many Mexican immigrants raises issues concerning the accuracy of their responses to the census question on year of arrival in the United States (Redstone and Massey 2004).

survivors differs from that of the sample of return migrants (that is, as long as $w_0^S \neq w_0^R$).

We do not have any direct empirical evidence indicating the extent to which the entry wage of Mexican immigrants who remain in the United States differs from the entry wage of Mexican immigrants who return to Mexico. Equation (3), however, suggests that the numerical importance of the bias introduced by nonrandom return migration will not be very large for reasonable parameter values. Suppose, for instance, that the rate-of-return migration among Mexican immigrants who were enumerated by the U.S. Census at some point of their U.S. sojourn is as high as 30 percent. If the wage differential between the Mexicans who remain in the United States and those who leave is on the order of .2 log points (favoring the immigrants who return to Mexico), equation (3) then indicates that the true rate of wage convergence is about 6 log points higher than the observed rate of wage convergence. The data in table 1.8, however, suggest that there would still be relatively little evidence of substantial wage convergence even if we add 6 log points to the wage growth experienced by the surviving Mexican immigrants. In short, it is very unlikely that the bulk of the Mexican immigrant influx will ever reach wage parity with the native-born workforce.

1.3 Native-Born Workers of Mexican Ancestry

As noted earlier, beginning with the 1980 Census, we can observe the socioeconomic characteristics of native-born persons who are of Hispanic origin and who in addition claim that their Hispanic ancestry is of Mexican origin. The number of native-born workers of Mexican ancestry in the U.S. workforce has grown rapidly in the past twenty years and is inevitably going to grow even faster in the future. As a result, it is of great interest to determine the skills and characteristics of these workers in the labor market. Note that this population does not necessarily consist of only second-generation workers, as many workers of higher-order generations may claim Mexican ancestry. Nevertheless, the entry of many second-generation workers of Mexican ancestry in the near future is bound to lead to a substantial increase in the demographic and economic importance of this population in the U.S. labor market.

There has been a rapid growth in the size of the population of native-born workers who are of Mexican ancestry in the past two decades. In 1980, 2.3 percent of the native-born male workforce and 2.3 percent of the native-born female workforce was of Mexican ancestry. By 2000, these statistics had increased to 3.1 and 3.0 percent. It is of interest to note that if one combines the population of Mexican-born workers with that of U.S.-born workers of Mexican ancestry, the 2000 Census indicates that these two groups combined make up 7.7 percent of the male workforce in the United States and 5.4 percent of the female workforce. These statistics stand in sharp contrast to the data in 1980, where only 3.5 percent of the male workforce and 2.9 percent of the female workforce could be classified as of Mexican origin.

Table 1.9 documents the sizable difference in the distributions of educational attainment between native-born Mexicans and other native-born workers. Like their immigrant counterparts, native-born Mexicans have disproportionately large high school dropout rates and disproportionately low rates of college graduation. In 2000, for example, 21.0 percent of

Table 1.9   **Distribution of educational attainment for Mexican native-born workers**

	1980	1990	2000
Male workers			
Native-born of Mexican ancestry			
High school dropouts	45.5	27.6	21.0
High school graduates	33.4	38.6	40.0
Some college	14.3	24.7	27.7
College graduates	6.7	9.1	11.3
All other native-born workers			
High school dropouts	23.3	12.5	8.3
High school graduates	39.3	35.9	34.3
Some college	16.8	26.7	29.5
College graduates	20.6	24.9	27.9
Mexican immigrants			
High school dropouts	77.2	70.4	63.0
High school graduates	14.3	19.0	25.1
Some college	5.7	7.8	8.5
College graduates	2.9	2.8	3.4
Female workers			
Native-born of Mexican ancestry			
High school dropouts	39.6	23.0	16.5
High school graduates	42.0	41.1	38.4
Some college	13.4	27.2	32.1
College graduates	5.0	8.7	13.0
All other native-born workers			
High school dropouts	18.8	9.4	6.2
High school graduates	47.4	38.6	32.6
Some college	18.1	30.0	33.5
College graduates	15.8	22.0	27.7
Mexican immigrants			
High school dropouts	72.9	64.7	57.0
High school graduates	17.7	21.9	26.6
Some college	7.0	10.5	11.8
College graduates	2.4	3.0	4.5

Note: All statistics are calculated using the sample of workers aged eighteen–sixty-four.

native-born Mexicans were high school dropouts, and only 11.3 percent were college graduates. This contrasts strikingly with the 8.3 percent of native-born non-Mexicans who were high school dropouts and 27.9 percent who were college graduates. It is worth stressing that although native-born Mexicans have relatively low educational attainment (relative to other native-born workers), they are far more educated than the Mexican immigrant workforce, where dropout rates are around 63 percent in 2000.

The sizable differences in the educational attainment (as well as in the occupations) of Mexican native workers and other natives inevitably lead to equally sizable differences in log weekly wages between the two groups. We use the generic regression framework given by equation (1) to estimate the adjusted wage differentials separately in each of the censuses since 1980. We expand the immigration status variable to include dummy variables indicating if the worker is native-born of Mexican ancestry, an immigrant of Mexican origin, a non-Mexican immigrant, and a native-born worker of non-Mexican ancestry (the omitted group).

Panel A of table 1.10 reports the trend in the unadjusted relative log weekly wage between the various groups and the baseline group of non-Mexican native born workers. In 1980, the unadjusted log weekly wage of Mexican immigrants was .41 log points below that of non-Mexican natives. By 2000, this gap had grown to –.54 log points. It turns out that the economic status of native-born workers of Mexican ancestry also deteriorated significantly over this period, from –.24 log points in 1980 to –.31 log points in 2000.

The table also shows, however, that as with the Mexican immigrant sample, observable variables, and particularly educational attainment, tend to explain much of the gap between native-born Mexicans and the baseline group. By adjusting simply for differences in educational attainment and age, the observed log wage gap of –.31 log points for Mexican natives falls to –.08 log points. In other words, nearly three-quarters of the wage differential between native-born workers of Mexican ancestry and other native-born workers is due to differences in a minimal set of observable measures of educational attainment and age.[23]

The empirical analysis in the previous section was unable to document that Mexican immigrants experience substantial rates of economic assimilation during the immigrants' work life. The empirical analysis summarized in table 1.10 shows that a large part of the wage disadvantage of Mexican immigrants is likely to persist into the next generation. It seems, therefore, that the very large Mexican immigrant influx that entered the United States in recent decades has experienced and will likely continue to experience a very different path of economic adaptation than other immi-

23. See also Trejo (1997).

Table 1.10   Trends in the relative wage of the Mexican-origin population

	1980	1990	2000
Male workers			
A. Relative weekly wage (relative to other natives)			
Mexican immigrant	−.414	−.553	−.543
	(.004)	(.003)	(.002)
Other immigrant	.017	−.004	−.044
	(.002)	(.002)	(.002)
Native-born of Mexican ancestry	−.238	−.298	−.310
	(.003)	(.003)	(.003)
B. Adjusted relative weekly wage (adjusts for education, age)			
Mexican immigrant	−.151	−.154	−.148
	(.003)	(.003)	(.002)
Other immigrant	−.049	−.045	−.076
	(.002)	(.002)	(.001)
Native-born of Mexican ancestry	−.075	−.098	−.075
	(.003)	(.002)	(.002)
Female workers			
C. Relative weekly wage (relative to other natives)			
Mexican immigrant	−.137	−.319	−.405
	(.005)	(.004)	(.003)
Other immigrant	.058	.077	.032
	(.002)	(.002)	(.002)
Native-born of Mexican ancestry	−.093	−.134	−.150
	(.003)	(.003)	(.003)
D. Adjusted relative weekly wage (adjusts for education, age)			
Mexican immigrant	.036	−.015	−.073
	(.005)	(.004)	(.003)
Other immigrant	.045	.072	.025
	(.002)	(.002)	(.002)
Native-born of Mexican ancestry	.015	.013	.022
	(.003)	(.003)	(.003)

Notes: Standard errors are in parentheses. The numbers of observations in the regressions are as follows: 2,546,859 in the 1980 Census; 2,809,917 in the 1990 Census; and 3,164,510 in the 2000 Census. The reported wage coefficients are log wage gaps relative to native-born workers of non-Mexican ancestry.

grant waves. The reasons for the lagging economic performance of this large and fast-growing population will likely be a central concern of social science research for decades to come.

1.4   Labor Market Impact and Economic Benefits

Economic theory implies that immigration should lower the wage of competing workers and increase the wage of complementary workers. For example, an influx of foreign-born laborers reduces the economic opportunities for laborers—all laborers now face stiffer competition in the labor market. At the same time, high-skill natives may gain substantially. They pay less for the services that laborers provide, such as painting the house and mowing the lawn, and natives who hire these laborers can now specialize in producing the goods and services that better suit their skills.

Because of the policy significance associated with determining the impact of immigration on the employment opportunities of native workers, a large literature developed in the past two decades attempting to measure this impact. The starting point for much of this literature is the fact that immigrants in the United States cluster in a small number of geographic areas. Many studies exploit this geographic clustering to define the empirical exercise that purports to measure the labor market impact of immigration.[24] The typical study defines a metropolitan area (or state) as the labor market that is penetrated by immigrants. The study then goes on to calculate a cross-city correlation measuring the relation between the native wage in a locality and the relative number of immigrants in that locality. A negative correlation, indicating that native wages are lower in markets with many immigrants, would suggest that immigrants worsen the employment opportunities of competing native workers.

There is a great deal of dispersion in the findings in this literature. Nevertheless, there is a tendency for the estimated cross-city correlations to cluster around zero, helping to create the conventional wisdom that immigrants have little impact on the labor market opportunities of native workers, perhaps because immigrants do jobs that natives do not want to do.

Recent research, however, raises two questions about the validity of interpreting near-zero cross-city correlations as evidence that immigration has no labor market impact. First, immigrants may not be randomly distributed across labor markets. If immigrants tend to cluster in cities with thriving economies (and high wages), there would be a built-in positive correlation between immigration and wages. This positive correlation would attenuate, and perhaps even reverse, whatever negative impact immigration might have had on wages in local labor markets.

Second, natives may respond to the wage impact of immigration by moving their labor or capital to other cities. For example, native-owned firms see that cities in Southern California flooded by low-skill immigrants pay lower wages to laborers. Employers who hire laborers will want to relocate to those cities. The flow of jobs to the immigrant-hit areas cushions the adverse effect of immigration on the wage of competing workers in those localities. Similarly, laborers living in Michigan were perhaps thinking about moving to California before the immigrants entered that state. These laborers learn that immigration reduced their potential wages in California, and they may instead decide to remain where they are or move elsewhere.

---

24. Representative studies include Altonji and Card (1991), Card (1990, 2001), and Grossman (1982).

Moreover, some Californians might leave the state to search for better opportunities.

The flows of capital and labor tend to equalize economic conditions across cities. As a result, intercity comparisons of native wage rates will not be very revealing: capital flows and native migration diffuse the impact of immigration across the national economy. In the end, all laborers, regardless of where they live, are worse off because there are now many more of them.

Because local labor markets adjust to immigration, a number of recent studies have emphasized that the labor market impact of immigration may be measurable only at the national level.[25] Borjas (2003) used this insight to examine the link between immigration and the evolution of wages for specific skill groups in the past few decades. His study indicates that by analyzing national trends in the labor market and by defining skill groups in terms of both educational attainment and work experience, one can make substantial progress in determining how immigration alters the employment and earnings opportunities of native workers.

The empirical analysis reported in this section estimates a labor demand model developed by Borjas (2003) to simulate the impact of the Mexican immigrant influx on the wages of competing workers. We restrict the simulation to male workers observed in the 1980 and 2000 Censuses. As in Borjas (2003), the men are classified into four distinct education groups: persons who are high school dropouts, high school graduates, persons who have some college, and college graduates. Work experience is defined as the number of years that have elapsed since the person completed school.[26] The analysis is restricted to workers with one to forty years of experience. Workers are then grouped into eight different experience groups, indicating if the worker has one–five years of experience, six–ten years, eleven–fifteen years, and so on. There are, therefore, a total of thirty-two skill groups in the labor market (four education and eight experience groups).

As in Borjas (2003), suppose the aggregate production function for the national economy at time t is

$$(4) \qquad Q_t = (\lambda_{Kt} K_t^v + \lambda_{Lt} L_t^v)^{1/v},$$

where Q is output, K is capital, L denotes the aggregate labor input; and $v = 1 - 1/\sigma_{KL}$, with σ_{KL} being the elasticity of substitution between capital

---

25. Borjas, Freeman, and Katz (1997) proposed the hypothesis that the labor market impact of immigration may only be measurable at the national level.

26. The analysis assumes that the age of entry into the labor market is seventeen for the typical high school dropout, nineteen for the typical high school graduate, twenty-one for the typical person with some college, and twenty-three for the typical college graduate. We restrict the analysis to persons who have between one and forty years of experience. By restricting the sample to male workers, we are assuming a form of production separability between men and women in the production process. The inclusion of women in the analysis does not greatly affect the results, even though the allocation of women into the various labor market experience groups likely contains a great deal of measurement error.

and labor $(-\infty < v \leq 1)$. The vector λ gives technology parameters that shift the production frontier, with $\lambda_{Kt} + \lambda_{Lt} = 1$. The aggregate L_t incorporates the contributions of workers who differ in both education and experience. Let

$$(5) \qquad L_t = \left(\sum_i \theta_{it} L_{it}^\rho \right)^{1/\rho},$$

where L_{it} gives the number of workers with education i at time t, and $\rho = 1 - 1/\sigma_E$, with σ_E being the elasticity of substitution across these education aggregates $(-\infty < \rho \leq 1)$. The θ_{it} give time-variant technology parameters that shift the relative productivity of education groups, with $\Sigma_i \theta_{it} = 1$. Finally, the supply of workers in each education group is itself given by an aggregation of the contribution of similarly educated workers with different experience. In particular,

$$(6) \qquad L_{it} = \left(\sum_j \alpha_{ij} L_{ijt}^\eta \right)^{1/\eta},$$

where L_{ijt} gives the number of workers in education group i and experience group j at time t (given by the sum of N_{ijt} native and M_{ijt} immigrant workers); and $\eta = 1 - 1/\sigma_X$, with σ_X being the elasticity of substitution across experience classes within an education group $(-\infty < \eta \leq 1)$. Equation (6) assumes that the technology coefficients α_{ij} are constant over time, with $\Sigma_j \alpha_{ij} = 1$.

Borjas (2003) shows that the key parameters σ_X and σ_E can be estimated by regressing the log wage of particular education-experience groups on the log of the size of the workforce in the various cells and instrumenting the supply variable by the immigrant share in that skill cell.[27] We reestimated the econometric framework using data from the 1960–2000 IPUMS samples.[28] Our elasticity estimates are $\sigma_X = 3.0$ and $\sigma_E = 2.4$. The empirical

27. This instrument would be valid if the immigrant influx into particular skill groups were independent of the relative wages offered to the various skill categories. It is likely, however, that the number of immigrants in a skill group responds to shifts in the wage structure. Income-maximizing immigration would generate larger flows into those skill cells that had relatively high wages. This behavioral response builds in a positive correlation between the size of the immigrant influx and wages in a skill group. The elasticity estimates reported in the following, therefore, understate the negative wage impact of a relative supply increase.

28. More precisely, the model generates two estimating equations. The first regresses the log wage of a skill group (defined by education and experience) on various fixed effects and on the log of the size of the workforce in that group. This regression identifies σ_X. The second aggregates the data to the education group level and regresses the log wage of an education group on vectors of fixed effects and on the log of the size of the workforce in the education group. This regression identifies σ_E. The estimation of the second-stage regression requires an assumption about the trends in relative demand for various skill groups. In particular, Katz and Murphy (1992) documented that the secular trend in relative demand shifts for high-skill workers in a CES framework could be approximated by linear trends specific to each education group. This approximation became an important identification restriction for the estimation of the elasticity of substitution across education groups in Card and Lemieux (2001) and Borjas (2003). More recently, Autor, Katz, and Kearney (2005) documented that the

implementation of the three-level constant elasticity of substitution (CES) technology described in the preceding does not use any data on the aggregate capital stock so that σ_K cannot be directly estimated. Hamermesh (1993, 92) concludes that the aggregate U.S. economy can be reasonably described by a Cobb-Douglas production function, suggesting that σ_{KL} equals one. We use this estimate in the simulation reported in the following.

The factor price elasticity giving the impact on the wage of factor y of an increase in the supply of factor z is defined by

(7)
$$\varepsilon_{yz} = \frac{d \log w_y}{d \log L_z}.$$

It is easy to show that the factor price elasticities depend on the income shares accruing to the various factors and on the three elasticities of substitution that lie at the core of the three-level CES framework.[29] The marginal productivity condition for the typical worker in education group s and experience group x can be written as $w_{sx} = D(K, L_{11}, \ldots, L_{18}, \ldots, L_{41}, \ldots, L_{48})$. *Assuming that the capital stock is constant,* the net impact of immigration on the log wage of group (s, x) is

(8)
$$\Delta \log w_{sx} = \varepsilon_{sx,sx} m_{sx} + \sum_{j \neq x} \varepsilon_{sx,sj} m_{sj} + \sum_{i \neq s} \sum_{j} \varepsilon_{sx,ij} m_{ij},$$

where m_{ij} gives the percentage change in labor supply due to immigration in cell (i, j). Because the size of the native labor force in each skill group is shifting over time, define m_{ij} as

(9)
$$m_{ij} = \frac{M_{ij,2000} - M_{ij,1980}}{0.5(N_{ij,1980} + N_{ij,2000}) + M_{ij,1980}}$$

so that the baseline population used to calculate the percent increase in labor supply averages out the size of the native workforce in the skill cell and treats the preexisting immigrant population as part of the native stock.

---

growth rate in the relative demand for skilled workers slowed in the 1990s. In particular, they find a 20 percent decline in the secular growth rate of demand for skilled workers during the 1990s as compared to the growth rate prior to the 1990s. To capture this break in the secular trend, we included education-specific splines in the marginal productivity equation that identifies σ_E (instead of simple linear trends). For each education group, this variable is defined by a linear trend that increases at the rate of one per year between 1960 and 1990. The trend variable then increases at a rate of 0.8 per year between 1990 and 2000. Our estimate of the inverse elasticity $1/\sigma_X$ is .332 (with a standard error of .129), while the estimate of the inverse elasticity $1/\sigma_E$ is .413 (312). The inverse elasticity of substitution across education groups is estimated imprecisely because there are only twenty observations in the second-stage regression. To improve the precision, we estimated the second-stage model using annual data from the Current Population Surveys from 1963 through 2003. The estimated inverse elasticity was .307 (.094). Despite the data differences, the estimates of the inverse elasticity of substitution across education groups are roughly similar.

29. We assume that the share of income accruing to all labor groups is 0.7. We then used data from the 1990 Census to calculate the income share accruing to each of the various education-experience cells.

Table 1.11	Comparing the actual impact of the 1980–2000 immigrant influx with a counterfactual of no Mexican immigration during period (predicted percent change in the weekly wage; %)	
Specification/Group	Actual impact	Counterfactual: No Mexican immigration
Short-run: Capital is fixed		
All workers	−3.4	−2.7
High school dropouts	−8.2	−0.5
High school graduates	−2.2	−1.4
Some college	−2.7	−2.4
College graduates	−3.9	−3.9
Long-run: Capital is perfectly elastic		
All workers	0.0	0.0
High school dropouts	−4.8	2.2
High school graduates	1.2	1.4
Some college	0.7	0.3
College graduates	−0.5	−1.2

Notes: The simulation models in equations (8) and (11) generate wage effects for specific education-experience cells. We used the share of income accruing to each of the skill groups in 2000 to calculate the weighted aggregates reported in this table. The predicted percent changes refer to the product of the predicted log wage change times 100.

The top panel of table 1.11 summarizes the results of the simulation. Before proceeding to discuss the results, note that the equation (8) gives the predicted change in the log wage for *each* skill (i.e., education-experience) group. We use the share of income accruing to each of the skill groups in 2000 to calculate the weighted aggregates reported in the table. The immigrant influx of the 1980s and 1990s lowered the wage of most native workers, particularly of those workers at the bottom and top of the education distribution. The wage fell by 8.2 percent for high school dropouts and by 3.9 percent for college graduates. In contrast, the wage of high school graduates fell by just over 2 percent. Overall, the immigrant influx from 1980 to 2000 is estimated to have reduced the wage of the typical native worker by 3.4 percent.

This framework provides a simple mechanism for establishing the labor market impact of Mexican immigration. In particular, we simulated the model to predict a new set of labor market impacts under the counterfactual assumption that there had been *no* Mexican immigration (either legal or illegal) between 1980 and 2000. This assumption redefines the labor supply shocks defined in equation (1). In particular, consider

$$(10) \qquad m_{ij}^* = \frac{M_{ij,2000}^* - M_{ij,1980}}{0.5(N_{ij,1980} + N_{ij,2000}) + M_{ij,1980}},$$

where $M^*_{ij,2000}$ gives the size of the immigrant workforce in skill group (i, j) in 2000 under the assumption that *no* Mexican immigrants entered the United States between 1980 and 2000.[30]

The second column of table 1.11 shows the predicted labor market effects when the supply shocks are given by equation (1). Mexican immigration, which is predominantly low skill, accounts for all of the adverse impact of immigration on low-skill native workers. It is also worth noting that the earnings of college graduates would still have been reduced by 3.9 percent from immigration even if there had been no Mexican immigration. Under the constant capital stock scenario, our estimates imply the influx of low-skill Mexican immigrants did not work to improve the wage of high-skill workers.

As emphasized in the preceding, these simulations assume the capital stock is constant so that the results summarized in the top panel of table 1.11 represent the short-run impact of immigration. An alternative simulation would measure the impacts under the assumption that the capital stock adjusts completely to the increased labor supply. In effect, this alternative simulation would assume that the rental price of capital (rather than the capital stock) is constant. In other words, the adjustment of the capital stock to immigration would reduce the rental rate of capital back to its preexisting equilibrium level.

The maintained assumption that σ_{KL} equals one implies that the predicted long-run wage impact on the log wage of group (s, x) is

$$(11) \qquad \Delta \log w_{sx} = s_K \tilde{K} + \varepsilon_{sx,sx} m_{sx} + \sum_{j \neq x} \varepsilon_{sx,sj} m_{sj} + \sum_{i \neq s} \sum_j \varepsilon_{sx,ij} m_{ij},$$

where s_K is capital's share of income (assumed to be 0.3), and $\tilde{K}$ is the percent change in the capital stock induced by immigration. The assumption that σ_{KL} is unity implies that the change in the capital stock is a weighted average of the immigrant supply shocks in the various education-experience groups, where the weights are the shares of income accruing to the various groups.[31] It is worth noting that equation (11) differs from equation (8) only by adding the constant $s_K \tilde{K}$ to each group. Put differently, full capital adjustment alters the absolute wage impact of immigration but leaves the relative wage effects unchanged. In addition, it *must* be the case that the aggregate wage change must be identically equal to zero (when the skill-specific effects are aggregated using the group's income share as weights) because the production function in (4) has constant returns to

---

30. More precisely, the variable $M^*_{ij,2000}$ is defined as the immigrant stock reported in the 2000 Census after omitting from the count all Mexican-born persons who reported arriving between 1980 and 2000.

31. To simplify notation, let n be the subscript indicating the education-experience skill group $(n = 1, \ldots, 32)$. The implied change in the capital stock $\tilde{K} = \Sigma_n s_n m_n / s_L$, where s_L is labor's share of income.

scale.[32] As a result, the relative wage effects of immigration are much better measured by this approach than the absolute wage effects of immigration—because the relative wage effects are directly estimated using variation across groups and time in the size of immigrant supply shocks, but the absolute wage effect depends crucially on (difficult-to-assess) assumptions about the response of the capital stock to the immigrant supply shift.

The bottom panel of table 1.11 uses equation (11) to predict the long-run impact of the 1980–2000 immigrant influx. As expected, the wage impact of immigration is muted in the long run as capital adjusts to the increased workforce. Although the average wage in the economy is unaffected by immigration, the unbalanced nature of the immigrant supply shock in terms of the skill distribution implies that there are still distributional effects. The first column of the table reveals that high school dropouts still experience a sizable wage reduction, even in the long run, of about 4.8 percentage points. The long-run increase in the capital stock, however, removes almost the entire wage loss from immigration suffered by college graduates and leads to wage improvements for high school graduates and those with some college.

The second column of the panel shows the predicted long-run impact under the counterfactual that no Mexicans migrated to the United States between 1980 and 2000. It is evident that in the absence of Mexican immigration, U.S. low-skill workers would have benefited (through a 2.2 percent wage increase for dropouts) from the complementarities that arise when the immigrant influx is composed mainly of high-skill workers.

Immigration may also affect the economic welfare of natives through its impact on the relative prices of goods and services.[33] The skill distribution of Mexican immigrants and their concentration in low-skill occupations suggest that Mexican immigration may serve to expand the supply and lower the U.S. prices of nontraded goods and services that are low-skill labor intensive. In fact, a much larger share of Mexican immigrants than of U.S. natives is employed in low-skill service jobs such as private household occupations, food preparation occupations, and gardening. In 2000, for example, 20.9 percent of Mexican immigrants and only 6.5 percent of native-born workers were employed in the subset of occupations classified as "food preparation and serving" or "buildings and grounds cleaning and maintenance." American consumers who spend more on low-skill inten-

---

32. The choice of the weights is not a trivial decision. For example, Ottaviano and Peri (2005) carry out a similar simulation where they use employment shares as weights and conclude that immigration raises the average wage in the labor market, even though the first-degree homogeneous production function would imply that the average wage must remain constant under the assumption of full capital adjustments.

33. Rivera-Batiz (1983) provides a useful summary of the implications of alternative multisector trade models for the distributional impacts on rich countries of low-skill immigration from poor to rich countries.

sive nontraded goods and services will tend to disproportionately benefit from the recent wave of Mexican immigration.

Some recent exploratory work has exploited cross-area variation in changes in low-skill immigrants as a share of the workforce to estimate the impacts of increased low-skill immigration on the supply and prices of low-skill intensive services. This approach will tend to understate the price impacts on nontraded services intensively employing new low-skill immigrants to the extent the expansion in the overall national supply of less-educated workers also affects low-immigrant receiving areas by altering native labor and capital flows. Khananusapkul (2004) finds using U.S. Census data from 1970 to 2000 that a 1 percentage point increase in the share of low-skill female immigrants in a metropolitan area increases the proportion of private household workers by 6 percentage points and lowers the wages in the private household sector by 3 percent. This evidence indicates a direct supply expansion in the low-skill female intensive sector when more low-skill female immigrants are available in a labor market.

Cortes (2005) examines the impacts on prices and consumer expenditures for nontraded goods and services of changes in the workforce share of low-skilled immigrants (mainly Mexican immigrants) across U.S. metropolitan areas from 1990 to 2000. Her estimates imply that an increase in the share of low-skill immigrants in an area significantly reduces the prices of goods and services in low-skilled immigrant-intensive industries such as housekeeping and gardening. Cortes finds that low-skilled immigration in the 1990s improved the purchasing power of high-skilled U.S. natives, but it worked to reduce the purchasing power of native high school dropouts as the negative wage impacts of immigration for less-skilled workers greatly outweighed the price reductions for a limited set of nontraded goods and services.

The large growth and predominantly low-skilled nature of Mexican immigration to the United States over the past two decades appears to have played a modest role in the widening of the U.S. wage structure by adversely affecting the earnings of less-educated native workers and improving the earnings of college graduates. The estimates in table 1.11 imply that Mexican immigration from 1980 to 2000 reduced the wages of U.S. high school dropouts relative to college graduates by 7.7 percent. U.S. natives (especially high-skill natives) appear to have benefited from greater availability and reduced prices of nontraded goods and services that are intensive in low-skill labor.

1.5   Summary

This paper uses the IPUMS data from 1900 through 2000 to document the evolution of the Mexican-born workforce in the U.S. labor market. It is well known, of course, that there has been a rapid rise in Mexican immigration to the United States in recent years. Interestingly, the share of Mexican immigrants in the U.S. workforce *declined* steadily beginning in the 1920s before beginning to rise in the 1960s. It was not until 1980 that the relative number of Mexican immigrants in the U.S. workforce was at the 1920s level.

The analysis of the economic performance of these immigrants throughout the twentieth century yields a number of interesting and potentially important findings:

1. Mexican immigrants have much less educational attainment than either native-born workers or non-Mexican immigrants. These differences in human capital account for nearly three-quarters of the very large wage disadvantage suffered by Mexican immigrants in recent decades.

2. Although the earnings of non-Mexican immigrants converge to those of their native-born counterparts as the immigrants accumulate work experience in the U.S. labor market, this type of wage convergence has been much weaker on average for Mexican immigrants than for other immigrant groups.

3. Although native-born workers of Mexican ancestry have levels of human capital and earnings that far exceed those of Mexican immigrants, the economic performance of these native-born workers lags behind that of native workers who are not of Mexican ancestry. Much of the wage gap between the two groups of native-born workers can be explained by the large difference in educational attainment between the two groups.

4. The large Mexican influx in recent decades widened the U.S. wage structure by adversely affecting the earnings of less-educated native workers and improving the earnings of college graduates. These wage effects have, in turn, lowered the prices of nontraded goods and services that are low-skill labor intensive.

There is little evidence that the influx of Mexican-born workers into the United States is slowing down as we enter a new century, and there is also little evidence that the skill composition of the Mexican influx is changing from what it has been in the past. The continued migration of Mexican workers into the United States and the inevitable rapid growth of the group of native-born workers of Mexican ancestry suggest that the economic consequences of this low-skill migration influx are only beginning to be felt.

References

Altonji, Joseph G., and David Card. 1991. The effects of immigration on the labor market outcomes of less-skilled natives. In *Immigration, trade, and the labor market,* ed. J. M. Abowd and R. B. Freeman, 201–34. Chicago: University of Chicago Press.

Autor, David H., Lawrence F. Katz, and Melissa S. Kearney. 2005. Trends in U.S. wage inequality: Re-Assessing the revisionists. NBER Working Paper no. 11627. Cambridge, MA: National Bureau of Economic Research, September.

Borjas, George J. 1985. Assimilation, changes in cohort quality, and the earnings of immigrants. *Journal of Labor Economics* 3:463–89.

———. 1995. Assimilation and changes in cohort quality revisited: What happened to immigrant earnings in the 1980s? *Journal of Labor Economics* 13:201–45.

———. 2003. The labor demand curve *is* downward sloping: Reexamining the impact of immigration on the labor market. *Quarterly Journal of Economics* 118: 1335–74.

Borjas, George J., and Bernt Bratsberg. 1996. Who leaves? The outmigration of the foreign-born. *Review of Economics and Statistics* 78:165–76.

Borjas, George J., Richard B. Freeman, and Lawrence F. Katz. 1997. How much do immigration and trade affect labor market outcomes? *Brookings Papers on Economic Activity,* Issue no. 1:1–67. Washington, DC: Brookings Institution.

Borjas, George J., and Rachel Friedberg. 2004. The trend in immigrant earnings and skills over the 1990s. Harvard University. Working Paper.

Camarota, Stephen A. 2001. *Immigration from Mexico: Assessing the impact on the United States.* Washington, DC: Center for Immigration Studies.

Card, David. 1990. The impact of the Mariel boatlift on the Miami labor market. *Industrial and Labor Relations Review* 43:245–57.

———. 2001. Immigrant inflows, native outflows, and the local labor market impacts of higher immigration. *Journal of Labor Economics* 19:22–64.

Card, David, and Thomas Lemieux. 2001. Can falling supply explain the rising return to college for younger men? A cohort-based analysis. *Quarterly Journal of Economics* 116:705–46.

Card, David, and Ethan Lewis. 2005. The diffusion of Mexican immigrants during the 1990s: Explanations and impacts. Chapter 6, this volume.

Chiswick, Barry R. 1986. Is the new immigration less skilled than the old? *Journal of Labor Economics* 4:168–92.

Cortes, Patricia. 2005. The effect of low-skilled immigration on U.S. prices: Evidence from CPI data. Massachusetts Institute of Technology. Manuscript, November.

Feliciano, Zadia. 2001. The skill and economic performance of Mexican immigrants from 1910 to 1990. *Explorations in Economic History* 38:386–409.

Funkhouser, Edward, and Stephen J. Trejo. 1995. The labor market skills of recent male immigrants: Evidence from the current population surveys. *Industrial and Labor Relations Review* 48:792–811.

Grossman, Jean Baldwin. 1982. The substitutability of natives and immigrants in production. *Review of Economics and Statistics* 54:596–603.

Hamermesh, Daniel S. 1993. *Labor demand.* Princeton, NJ: Princeton University Press.

Katz, Lawrence F., and Kevin M. Murphy. 1992. Changes in the wage structure, 1963–87: Supply and demand factors. *Quarterly Journal of Economics* 107:35–78.

Khananusapkul, Phanwadee. 2004. Do low-skilled female immigrants increase the labor supply of skilled women? Harvard University. Manuscript, February.

LaLonde, Robert J., and Robert H. Topel. 1992. The assimilation of immigrants in the U.S. labor market. In *Immigration and the work force: Economic consequences for the United States and source areas,* ed. G. J. Borjas and R. B. Freeman, 67–92. Chicago: University of Chicago Press.

Marcell, Ronald O. 1994. Bracero Program hurt domestic farm workers. *Borderlands* 12:13–14.

Massey, Douglas S., Jorge Durand, and Nolan J. Malone. 2002. *Beyond smoke and mirrors.* New York: Russell Sage Foundation.

Massey, Douglas S., and Zai Liang. 1989. The long-term consequences of a temporary worker program: The U.S. Bracero experience. *Population Research and Policy Review* 8:199–226.

Murphy, Kevin M., and Finis Welch. 1992. The structure of wages. *Quarterly Journal of Economics* 107:285–326.

Ottaviano, Gianmarco I. P., and Giovanni Peri. 2005. Rethinking the gains from immigration: Theory and evidence from the U.S. NBER Working Paper no. 11672. Cambridge, MA: National Bureau of Economic Research, October.

Ramos, Fernando. 1992. Out-Migration and return migration of Puerto Ricans. In *Immigration and the work force: Economic consequences for the United States and source areas,* ed. G. J. Borjas and R. B. Freeman, 49–66. Chicago: University of Chicago Press.

Redstone, Ilana, and Douglas S. Massey. 2004. Coming to stay: An analysis of the U.S. Census question on immigrants' year of arrival. *Demography* 41:721–38.

Rivera-Batiz, Francisco L. 1983. Trade theory, distribution of income, and immigration. *American Economic Review* 73:183–87.

Trejo, Stephen J. 1997. Why do Mexican-Americans earn low wages? *Journal of Political Economy* 105:1235–68.

———. 2003. Intergenerational progress of Mexican-origin workers in the U.S. labor market. *Journal of Human Resources* 38:467–89.

U.S. Bureau of the Census. 1975. *Historical statistics of the United States: Colonial times to 1970.* Bicentennial ed. Part 1. Washington, DC: GPO.

———. 2003. *The foreign born population: 2000.* Census 2000 Brief. http://www.census.gov/prod/2003pubs/c2kbr-34.pdf.

U.S. Department of Commerce, U.S. Census Bureau. 2004. *Statistical abstract of the United States: 2004–2005.* Washington, DC: GPO.

U.S. Immigration and Naturalization Service. Various Issues. *Statistical yearbook of the Immigration and Naturalization Service.* Washington, DC: GPO.

Yuengert, Andrew. 1994. Immigrant earnings, relative to what? The importance of earnings function specification and comparison points. *Journal of Applied Econometrics* 9:71–90.

2

Gender and Assimilation among Mexican Americans

Francine D. Blau and Lawrence M. Kahn

2.1 Introduction

A steady flow of new immigration has led the foreign-born share of the U.S. population to rise from 4.8 percent in 1970 to 11.1 percent in 2000. Perhaps more dramatically, the percentage of the accumulated foreign-born population that came from Europe or Northern America fell from 70.4 to 18.5 percent between 1970 and 2000, with a corresponding increase in the Asian and Latin American share from 28.3 percent in 1970 to 78.2 percent in 2000 (see the U.S. Bureau of the Census Web site at http://www.census.gov). By far, the largest source of immigration in recent years has been Mexico. For instance, from 1991 to 2000, 24.7 percent (2.25 million) of the 9.095 million immigrants to the United States came from Mexico, with the next largest source, the Philippines, sending only 5.5 percent (504,000) of the total. And Mexican immigration has been growing in both absolute and relative terms as immigration from Mexico was 454,000 (13.7 percent of the total) in 1961–1970.[1] By 2003, people of Mexican heritage

Francine D. Blau is the Frances Perkins Professor of Industrial and Labor Relations and Labor Economics at Cornell University, and a research associate of the National Bureau of Economic Research. Lawrence M. Kahn is professor of labor economics and collective bargaining at Cornell University.

The authors thank the Russell Sage Foundation for research support. We are grateful to Joseph Altonji; George Borjas; Darren Lubotsky; an anonymous referee and participants at the NBER Mexican Immigration Conference (February 2005) and Preconference (August 2004) in Cambridge, Massachusetts for helpful comments and suggestions; Chris Woodruff for providing us with tabulations of Mexican Census data; and Fidan Kurtulus for collecting labor force participation data. Portions of this paper were written while the authors were visiting fellows in the economics department of Princeton University, supported by the Industrial Relations Section. We are very grateful for this support.

1. These figures are taken from U.S. Department of Homeland Security, Office of Immigration Statistics (2003), table 2.

comprised fully 8.2 percent of the U.S. adult population, a figure that is about 70 percent as large as the incidence of the black non-Hispanic population (11.7 percent).[2]

In addition to making up a large and growing portion of the U.S. population, Mexican Americans are, on average, poorer and less educated than U.S. residents of European heritage (Browne 1999; Cobb-Clark and Hildebrand 2004). Since it is well known that poverty in the United States falls disproportionately on women and children (Blank 1997), a study of gender and labor market outcomes of Mexican Americans could yield important insights into this issue. And, of particular relevance to the issues considered in this paper, Mexican Americans come from an origin country with a much more traditional division of labor in the family and lower relative and absolute female human capital levels than the United States. For example, female labor force participation rates remain considerably lower in Mexico than in the United States, although the difference has declined in recent years: the Mexican female participation rate was 15.6 percent in 1970 and 39.4 percent in 2000, compared to rates of 41.5 and 58.8 percent in the United States (see the International Labour Organization [ILO] Web site at http://www.laborsta.ilo.org).[3] Fertility was higher in Mexico than in the United States, although, in this case, the difference has declined considerably in recent years, reflecting a sharp drop in fertility in Mexico: the total fertility rate in Mexico was 6.5 total births per woman as of 1970 and 2.8 as of 1998, compared to U.S. rates of 2.5 and 2.1. Adult illiteracy rates for women in Mexico were 22 percent in 1980 and 11 percent in 1998, compared to male rates of 14 percent and 7 percent, respectively; for the United States, illiteracy was below 5 percent in all cases (Blau, Ferber and Winkler 2002, 384–85). Moreover, according to Mexican Census data for 1990, among those age sixteen–sixty-five, men averaged 7.0 years of schooling, compared to only 6.4 for women.[4] Educational attainment rose for both men and women in Mexico between 1990 and 2000: in 2000, men averaged 8.1 years and women 7.6 years. These are of course much lower than average U.S. schooling levels of thirteen–fourteen years for men and women according to Current Population Survey (CPS) data. And, while women's schooling in Mexico grew very slightly faster than men's between 1990 and

2. This is based on data from the March 2003 Current Population Survey.

3. Especially in developing countries, participation rates may be an incomplete measure of economic activity because they often do not count subsistence and family-based activities, although it might be argued that an indicator focusing on market-based work is not altogether inappropriate in that it is this type of involvement that is most important in the United States. A measure that implicitly adjusts for these problems (at least to the extent that they affect men and women similarly) is the ratio of female to male participation rates. It tells a similar story to the female participation rates: these ratios were .227 (Mexico) and .531 (United States) in 1970, and .472 (Mexico) and .781 (United States) in 2000.

4. We are grateful to Chris Woodruff for supplying this information from the Mexican census.

2000, a noticeable gender gap in educational attainment among Mexicans remained. In light of these large differences between the labor market status and preparedness of women in Mexico and those in the United States, Mexico represents a potentially interesting case in which to examine the assimilation of women into the U.S. labor market. Do Mexican immigrant families exhibit a more traditional division of labor than U.S. families as Mexican residents do? To what extent do gender patterns in labor market attachment and success among Mexican Americans converge to U.S.-native patterns within and across generations?

In this paper, we use the March CPS Annual Demographic Files for 1994–2003 to study the assimilation of Mexican American women and men, including both Mexican immigrants and the native born of Mexican heritage. While many analyses of immigration use the decennial censuses, we employ the CPS files because, since 1994, the Current Population Surveys contain information not only on immigration status but also on the birthplace of respondents' parents, thus allowing for intergenerational comparisons. Data on parents' birthplace have not been available in the census since 1970. The outcomes we consider include marriage and fertility, labor supply, unemployment, wages, and occupation and industry distribution. The repeated cross-sections in the CPS allow us to examine issues of assimilation among immigrants from a variety of arrival cohorts using the synthetic cohort approach proposed in Borjas (1985). Moreover, we also study assimilation across generations by analyzing these outcomes for second- and third-generation Mexican Americans. Examining progress across generations provides a more comprehensive study of assimilation than the traditional immigration literature that has, for the most part, focused on success at arrival and over time in the United States for those born in other countries. The children of immigrants may do considerably better in the United States than the immigrants themselves, and their fortunes need to be taken into account in evaluating the experience of immigrants (Card, DiNardo, and Estes 2000; Card 2004).

We begin by examining outcomes for all Mexican American adults and then consider married individuals separately. This enables us to confirm our aggregate findings for this group—one that is most likely to manifest traditional labor market patterns. Moreover, while, for the most part, research on immigrants has studied the behavior of individuals, analyzing immigrant behavior in a family context makes sense in general and may be particularly relevant to understanding women's assimilation. Baker and Benjamin (1997) propose a family investment model in which, upon arrival, husbands invest in their human capital, while wives work to provide the family with liquidity during this investment period. With increased time in the destination country, husbands' labor supply increases rapidly due to their growing skills, while wives' labor supply falls off in part because they originally took dead-end jobs upon arrival in order to finance their husbands' investments in human capital. Baker and Benjamin provide some evidence consistent with this model using data on Canada over the 1986–1991 period. However, using data for the United States from the 1980 and 1990 U.S. Censuses, Blau et al. (2003) did not find evidence consistent with the family migration model.[5] Specifically, they find that immigrant husbands and wives both worked less than comparable natives upon arrival and that both had positive assimilation profiles in labor supply, eventually overtaking the labor supply of comparable natives.

In the family migration model, married women are clearly secondary earners in the immigrant family. The Blau et al. (2003) results for the United States suggest more similar economic behavior of men and women within the immigrant family.[6] Blau et al. report that labor supply assimilation patterns for men and women in the United States were very similar for each major sending region, including the Central American region defined to include Mexico. However, as a group coming from a source country with highly traditional gender roles, it is possible that patterns for Mexican immigrants would more closely approximate the family investment model than immigrants from Central America generally or other regions. Thus, we reexamine this question here. In addition, we include more recent data and study more dependent variables in the current paper, such as marriage, education, unemployment, occupational and industrial segregation, and fertility, than in this earlier work.

2.2   Recent Research on Labor Market Outcomes for Mexican Americans

Several authors have recently examined the assimilation of Mexican Americans into the U.S. labor market both within and between generations, although none has specifically studied gender differences in the assimilation process or assessed the relevance of the family migration model for Mexican Americans. Trejo (1997, 2003), for example, studied human capital and wages for men of Mexican origin versus white non-Hispanic native men for 1979 and 1989. He found that although men of Mexican origin earned considerably less than whites, most of these differences were

5. Studies by Long (1980), Duleep and Sanders (1993), and Macpherson and Stewart (1989) for the United States are all at least partially consistent with the idea that married immigrant women are more likely to work while their husbands are investing in human capital. However, unlike Blau et al. (2003), each of these studies is based on a single cross section of data.

6. In a recent paper, Duleep and Dowhan (2002) use matched Social Security earnings and 1994 CPS data to track the longitudinal earnings growth of immigrant versus native women. They find that more recent immigrant cohorts' earnings start low relative to natives' but rise quickly with time in the United States and eventually catch up to natives'. In contrast, earlier cohorts' initial earnings were at least as high as natives' but then either increased only a little or actually dropped. The results for the more recent cohorts are similar to the changes in hourly earnings reported by Baker and Benjamin (1997) for Canada and Blau et al. (2003) for the United States.

explained by the former's relatively low human capital levels. Moreover, while both the relative human capital levels and the return to investment in human capital rose between the first and second generations, this progress stalled between the second and third generations (Trejo 1997, 2003). A cross-sectional study of the wages of men and women for a sample of individuals of Mexican origin by Livingston and Kahn (2002) also found some progress of immigrants between the first and second generations that apparently stalled in the third generation.

Corcoran, Heflin, and Reyes (1999) summarize trends in labor market outcomes for Mexican American women using census data to compare outcomes for Mexican American women and white non-Hispanic women over the 1970–1990 period. They find that the relative wages and employment attachment of Mexican Americans fell over the 1980s, probably reflecting, in part, the growing immigrant share among Mexican American women. They also find that, in the cross section, long-term immigrants (i.e., those with over ten years of U.S. residence) had better wage outcomes and higher employment levels than short-term immigrants, while Mexican American women born in the United States had higher wages and employment incidence than long-term immigrants, although they still lagged considerably behind white non-Hispanic women in this regard. These findings suggest assimilation across generations and either assimilation among immigrants with more time in the United States or declining labor market success among more recent cohorts of immigrants.

Baker (1999) provides some additional descriptive information on demographic patterns using the 1970, 1980, and 1990 Censuses. Specifically, while immigrant Mexican American women were in each year roughly equally likely as white non-Hispanic women to be married, U.S.-born Mexican American women were less likely to be married than white non-Hispanic women. Moreover, Mexican immigrants had more children than white non-Hispanics and so did U.S.-born Mexican American women. However, these Mexican-white differentials in fertility were smaller for U.S.-born Mexican Americans and also fell progressively from 1970 to 1990 for each nativity group. Relative fertility levels were thus falling for Mexican American women over time and across generations.

Unlike the earlier work that studied only men or only women, we explicitly analyze gender differences in demographic and labor market outcomes for Mexican Americans. And, in contrast to the descriptive studies, we explicitly analyze assimilation in a regression context and may thus estimate how much assimilation occurs in the first generation with exposure to the U.S. economy and labor market as well as identify the impact of measured covariates versus behavioral changes in the assimilation of Mexican Americans, both within and across generations. Moreover, unlike the Livingston and Kahn (2002) study of Mexican-origin workers, we make explicit comparisons with a native base group and also examine a much wider array of outcomes than their focus on hourly earnings. And, in contrast to all of these studies, we also examine the family context in which these outcomes occur. This means, for example, controlling for family related variables in analyzing individual outcomes. Thus, in addition, by making explicit gender comparisons, we are able to arrive at conclusions about assimilation with respect to gender roles.

2.3   Data and Descriptive Patterns

We use the 1994–2003 March CPS Annual Demographic Supplement files to study gender and Mexican American assimilation. These files contain information on the respondent's country of birth, the country(ies) of birth of his or her mother and father, and whether the individual is of Mexican origin. We can thus construct samples of Mexican immigrants, second-generation Mexican Americans (defined as individuals who were born in the United States who had at least one parent born in Mexico), and U.S.-born individuals of Mexican origin whose parents were both born in the United States (the third generation). Our comparison group comprises third-generation, U.S.-born non-Hispanic whites (non-Hispanic whites). Using ten years of pooled cross-sectional data provides us with fairly large samples of Mexican Americans in each generation (see table 2A.1) and allows us to distinguish the impact of immigrant cohort from that of time in the United States (Borjas 1985).[7]

Our analyses of intergenerational mobility compare outcomes for immigrants with those of second- and third-generation Mexican Americans. Immigrants observed as of 1994–2003, the time window of our data, may not be representative of the parents of second-generation Mexican Americans also observed at that time, although there is likely to be some overlap. By using the same data to observe all three generations, we are in effect assuming that contemporary Mexican immigrants are in some sense similar to those of the 1950s, 1960s, and 1970s, when the parents of many of the second-generation Mexican Americans in our sample would have been in the prime working ages. An alternative would be to use data for an earlier period to observe outcomes for the first generation. Each approach has strengths and weaknesses, and recent research suggests they may not pro-

7. As in all analyses based on pooled cross-section data, we cannot observe return migration. Results may be biased if those who remain in the United States are a self-selected group of more or less successful immigrants. In addition, there may be recall errors and ambiguities of interpretation among respondents to the CPS question on when they arrived in the United States, as immigrants may enter and leave the United States several times. In a paper analyzing such issues using a recently developed data base that allows one to correct for such factors (the New Immigrant Survey Pilot [NISP]), Redstone and Massey (2004) find that traditional analyses of wages and years of U.S. experience yield similar results under the census and NISP definition of years in the United States.

duce the same estimates of intergenerational assimilation. For example, Smith (2003) finds more apparent progress in wages and schooling across generations among Hispanic Americans when he pools census and CPS data for the 1940–1997 period than when he bases his estimate on a single cross-section (the 1970 Census).

Looking at one cross-section (or, in our case, a single ten-year period) may yield a biased estimate of intergenerational assimilation if unmeasured immigrant cohort characteristics have changed. On the other hand, as Trejo (1997) points out, the time series approach may also be problematic. Between the 1950s–1970s and 1994–2003, there were many legal and economic changes that themselves could have influenced the economic success of Mexican American immigrants. Trejo specifically mentions the passage of the Civil Rights Act of 1964, which outlawed discrimination based on national origin (as well as race and sex). Thus, part of any apparent progress of Mexican Americans in general or Mexican American women in particular across generations between earlier years and the current period may have been due to changes in the legal and social environment that impacted all generations rather than to assimilation of the second generation. Working in the opposite direction, we may note that rising returns to education and unmeasured skills probably had an independent effect lowering the relative fortunes of most Mexican Americans in the 1990s relative to the earlier period. This development would cause us to underestimate true intergenerational assimilation.[8] Finally, the prohibition of sex discrimination by the Civil Rights Act is also relevant to our study as we are interested in gender differences in outcomes, as are the considerable changes in social norms and attitudes about gender roles that have occurred since the earlier period. These developments could have had a differential impact on Mexican American women's labor force behavior and outcomes relative to a native reference group, although the direction of this bias is unclear. Taking into account these considerations, our approach to measuring the intergenerational assimilation of Mexican Americans is to compare all three generations under the same legal, economic, and social environment: the 1994–2003 period. However, by looking at estimated immigrant cohort effects, we will be able to simulate outcomes for the immigrants from an earlier cohort and also to assess the extent to which results are sensitive to which immigrant cohort is used in the simulation.

In interpreting our findings for assimilation across generations, special caution is warranted regarding the third generation. While first- and second-generation individuals may be objectively identified in terms of their own or their parents' place of birth, third-generation Mexican Americans

---

8. For analyses of the returns to education and unmeasured skills in the context of immigrant assimilation, see LaLonde and Topel (1992) and Borjas (1995).

must identify themselves as of Mexican origin. If there is self-selection in reporting, results may be biased.[9] For example, if among third-generation Mexican Americans, those who self-identify as of Mexican origin are less well assimilated than those who do not, assimilation of third-generation Mexican Americans relative to the native-born, non-Hispanic reference group will be understated.[10]

Table 2.1 contains some descriptive information on demographic and labor market outcomes for Mexican Americans and non-Hispanic white–third-generation Americans. The entries in table 2.1 are predicted levels of these outcomes from regressions controlling for ethnicity or generation, a quartic in age and year. We control for age even at this descriptive stage because there are age differences across samples due to past immigration patterns, and we wish to describe Mexican American–non-Hispanic white contrasts net of this compositional factor.[11] The following regression was estimated separately by gender:

$$(1) \quad y_{it} = b_0 + b_1 age_{it} + b_2 age_{it}^2 + b_3 age_{it}^3 + b_4 age_{it}^4 + c_1 Meximm_{it}$$
$$+ c_2 Mexsecgen_{it} + c_3 Mexthirdgen_{it} + d_t + u_{it},$$

where i indexes individuals, and t indexes survey years, and y is a demographic or labor market outcome, age is the person's age in years, Meximm, Mexsecgen, and Mexthird are, respectively, dummy variables for Mexican immigrants, and second- and third-generation Mexican Americans, d is a year effect, and u is a disturbance term. We define a second-generation Mexican American as someone born in the United States who had at least one parent who was born in Mexico. Two versions of equation (1) were estimated: (a) one which included all immigrants and (b) one which included only those who migrated to the United States at age eighteen or older (adult immigrants).[12] We show results for adult immigrants, in addition to those for all immigrants, because those who migrated as children are likely to be more assimilated to U.S. labor markets than those who migrated as

9. Of course, as noted previously, even for immigrants biases may arise due to self-selection in return migration, recall bias, and ambiguities in defining length of residence in the United States.

10. For a fuller consideration of these issues, see, for example, Duncan and Trejo (chap. 7 in this volume), who find some indirect evidence consistent with the idea that more assimilated Mexican Americans are less likely to self-identify as having a Mexican heritage.

11. Within each of the ethnicity or generation subsamples (i.e., third-generation non-Hispanic whites, Mexican immigrants, and second- and third-generation Mexican Americans), the average age of men and women was similar, but average age varied across subsamples. Non-Hispanic whites averaged thirty-nine years of age, Mexican immigrants thirty-four–thirty-five years (thirty-eight–thirty-nine years for adult immigrants), second-generation Mexican Americans thirty-two years, and third-generation Mexican Americans thirty-four–thirty-five years.

12. Results for second- and third-generation Mexican Americans are based on regressions that include all immigrants, although the findings were similar in regressions with the immigrant sample restricted to adult migrants.

Table 2.1   Age- and year-corrected levels of demographic, human capital and wage outcomes for Mexican Americans and native non-Hispanic whites (third generation), 1994–2003

	Education		Married, spouse present		No. of children <18 yrs	
	Level	SE	Level	SE	Level	SE
Men						
Native, non-Hispanic whites	13.723	0.015	0.687	0.003		
Mexican Americans						
All immigrants	9.094	0.024	0.704	0.004		
Adult immigrants	8.254	0.028	0.663	0.005		
Second generation	12.651	0.035	0.650	0.006		
Third generation	12.533	0.030	0.657	0.005		
Women						
Native, non-Hispanic whites	13.856	0.014	0.705	0.003	1.458	0.007
Mexican Americans						
All immigrants	9.162	0.023	0.776	0.004	2.159	0.012
Adult immigrants	8.280	0.027	0.758	0.005	2.138	0.014
Second generation	12.670	0.031	0.670	0.006	1.845	0.016
Third generation	12.498	0.026	0.657	0.005	1.724	0.013

	Currently employed		Annual work hours		Currently in labor force	
	Level	SE	Level	SE	Level	SE
Men						
Native, non-Hispanic whites	0.869	0.002	2096.81	5.17	0.909	0.002
Mexican Americans						
All immigrants	0.872	0.004	1963.80	8.03	0.933	0.003
Adult immigrants	0.863	0.004	1886.38	9.78	0.930	0.004
Second generation	0.818	0.005	1947.97	11.77	0.878	0.005
Third generation	0.818	0.004	1919.15	10.10	0.877	0.004
Women						
Native, non-Hispanic whites	0.764	0.003	1463.48	5.50	0.792	0.003
Mexican Americans						
All immigrants	0.480	0.004	935.22	9.08	0.536	0.004
Adult immigrants	0.444	0.005	838.42	10.91	0.503	0.005
Second generation	0.672	0.006	1353.53	12.38	0.725	0.006
Third generation	0.687	0.005	1342.21	10.51	0.730	0.005

	Unemployed | In labor force		Log wages (FT)	
	Level	SE	Level	SE
Men				
Native, non-Hispanic whites	0.047	0.001	2.985	0.005
Mexican Americans				
All immigrants	0.070	0.002	2.468	0.007
Adult immigrants	0.077	0.003	2.354	0.008
Second generation	0.079	0.003	2.810	0.011
Third generation	0.074	0.003	2.771	0.009

(*continued*)

Table 2.1   (continued)

	Unemployed ǀ In labor force		Log wages (FT)	
	Level	SE	Level	SE
Women				
Native, non-Hispanic whites	0.039	0.001	2.717	0.005
Mexican Americans				
All immigrants	0.114	0.003	2.213	0.010
Adult immigrants	0.125	0.003	2.079	0.012
Second generation	0.085	0.003	2.582	0.012
Third generation	0.065	0.003	2.533	0.010

Notes: Based on pooled equations with a quartic in age, year dummies, and dummies for each Mexican American generation. Results for adult immigrants are based on regression with native non-Hispanic whites, and the three Mexican American generations pooled, where the immigrant generation includes only those who migrated at age eighteen or older. Sample for number of children under age eighteen is restricted to respondents who are age fifty or less; sample for log wages is full-time wage and salary workers. Predictions assume the mean age: thirty-nine years and year = 2003. Native, non-Hispanic whites are limited to third generation.

adults (Friedberg 1993). The sample for equation (1) includes only Mexican Americans and third-generation non-Hispanic whites who were age sixteen–sixty-five, and the entries in table 2.1 assume the sample mean for age (thirty-nine years) and the 2003 year effect. In all regressions and descriptive statistics, we use CPS sampling weights adjusted so that each year receives the same weight. We consider immigrants (or adult immigrants) as a group now for comparison purposes, although later we will discuss the role of immigrant cohort and time in the United States.

The results in table 2.1 indicate that, as is well known, Mexican immigrants have much lower levels of schooling than the non-Hispanic white reference group: 4.6 to 4.7 years less for all immigrants and 5.5 to 5.6 years for adult immigrants.[13] Assuming a 10 percent rate of return to education (approximately the rate obtained in our wage regressions reported in the following), this difference in years of schooling is responsible for a wage differential of .46 to .56 log points (i.e., 58–75 percent), a sizable effect. While less well educated than non-Hispanic white natives, Mexican immigrants appear to be somewhat positively selected relative to the Mexican population. Table 2.1 shows that among Mexican adult immigrants (who presumably had largely finished their schooling when they arrived in the United States), men and women have 8.3 years of education.[14] This is

13. We mapped the CPS education categories into years of schooling using Jaeger's (1997) algorithm.
14. We confirmed the claim that adult immigrants had largely finished their schooling: controlling for age, year, immigrant cohort, and years since migration and its square, we found that years living in the United States had insignificant and small effects on current education levels for adult immigrant men and women.

higher than the reported years of schooling for men and women in Mexico obtained from Mexican census data for 1990 and 2000: 7.0–8.1 years for males and 6.4–7.6 for females. Moreover, in contrast to the situation in Mexico, Mexican men and women immigrants in the United States have the same educational attainment.[15]

While Mexican Americans lag behind native non-Hispanic whites, there is considerable convergence in education across generations; second-generation Mexican Americans have only 1.07 (males) to 1.19 (females) years less education than the non-Hispanic white reference group, while the differentials for the third generation are 1.19 (males) to 1.36 (females) years. The apparent cessation of convergence toward non-Hispanic whites' education levels after the second generation is consistent with earlier analyses of labor market outcomes for Mexican Americans discussed in the preceding. In both the second and third generations, the Mexican American educational shortfall relative to non-Hispanic whites is statistically significantly smaller for men than women, and this gender difference increases from the second to the third generations (from 0.07 to 0.17). However, the magnitude of the gender difference in convergence is small— only 0.1 years, and educational attainment of Mexican American men and women within each generation is virtually identical, in contrast to the 0.5– 0.6 year male advantage in Mexico.

Table 2.1 shows that, overall, both immigrant men and immigrant women are significantly more likely to be married, spouse present (married) than are non-Hispanic white natives; however, among adult immigrants, men are less likely to be married than the non-Hispanic white reference group, while women are still more likely to be married. This suggests that immigration may be disruptive of marriage for Mexican men—either by delaying marriage or causing spouses to live apart—but not for women. Mexican immigrant women are 5 to 7 percentage points more likely to be married than native non-Hispanic whites. The higher marriage rates of Mexican immigrant women are consistent with a greater adherence to traditional gender roles in this population but may also be related to a tendency to migrate jointly with their husbands or to reunite families, perhaps as tied movers. By the second and third generations, however, Mexican Americans of both sexes are significantly less likely to be married than non-Hispanic whites, with differentials of 3–5 percentage points. As discussed by Angrist (2002), reductions across generations in the likelihood of marriage may be due to marital search problems and the desire to marry

15. The conclusion that Mexican immigrants are positively selected with respect to education has been challenged by Ibarraran and Lubotsky (chap. 5 in this volume), who suggest negative selection. On the other hand, Chiquiar and Hanson (2005) find that Mexican immigrants come from the middle- and upper-middle portions of the educational distribution, suggesting mildly positive selection. For our purposes, the most interesting finding is that educational attainment of male and female Mexican immigrants is the same, while in Mexico, men have somewhat more education than women. Thus, Mexican female immigrants are *relatively* positively selected.

within one's own ethnic group.[16] On the other hand, the discrepancy may be explained by measured characteristics, for example, the lower levels of education of U.S.-born Mexican Americans. The following regression analysis will shed light on this.

Table 2.1 also presents results for number of own (biological or adopted) children under age eighteen living in the family. While it would be more accurate to have information on number of children ever born, by restricting the age sample for this variable to women no older than fifty and evaluating the variable at age thirty-nine, we are likely to obtain a fairly good indicator of cross-group differences in fertility.[17] Because children who live with only one parent are much more likely to live with their mothers than their fathers, we restrict our examination of fertility differences to women. Perhaps reflecting higher fertility rates in the source country, Mexican immigrant women have more children than non-Hispanic whites, and, although this differential declines across generations, it remains positive even in the third generation. As noted earlier, as of 1998, the total fertility rate for women in Mexico averaged 2.8, while in the United States, the fertility rate was 2.1, a difference of 0.7. While our measure is constructed quite differently, we obtain a very similar differential between Mexican immigrants and non-Hispanic whites: Mexican immigrant women average 2.14 to 2.16 children, roughly 0.7 more than the corresponding figure for white non-Hispanic women of 1.46. (The gap between the number of own children for Mexican immigrant women and all women residing in the United States was also 0.7.) The gap had fallen to 0.39 by the second and 0.27 by the third generation, suggesting an intergenerational assimilation of roughly 60 percent.

When we stratified the analysis of the number of children by marital status, we found similar patterns across the generations. For all generations, among either single or married individuals, Mexican Americans have more children, with a declining differential across generations; moreover, the magnitude of the Mexican American–non-Hispanic white differential was similar for married and single women. In addition, Mexican American women were more likely than non-Hispanic whites to be single parents, with significant differentials for immigrant (5.3 percentage points), adult immigrant (4.5 percentage points), second-generation (9.6 percentage points), and third-generation Mexican Americans (9.0 percentage points). We expect having larger numbers of children to be associated with less labor market attachment and lower wage offers for Mexican American versus non-Hispanic white women (Blau, Ferber, and Winkler 2002; Waldfogel 1998).

16. The disproportionately high marriage incidence among immigrant women shown in tables 2.1 and 2.2 for Mexican immigrants is similar to what Angrist (2002) finds for immigrants in general.
17. Results were similar when the age range was unrestricted.

Table 2.1 contains several measures of labor force attachment, including whether one is currently employed, total hours of work in the previous year (including those who didn't work), and whether one is in the labor force. The generational patterns with respect to these three indicators are similar. Among males, immigrants and adult immigrants are roughly equally likely to be currently in the labor force as white non-Hispanics; in contrast, among females, both groups of immigrants have much lower participation rates than white non-Hispanics. The labor force participation rate was 79.2 percent for white non-Hispanic women compared to only 53.6 percent for all female immigrants and 50.3 percent for adult female immigrants. However, Mexican American men's participation decreased by about 5 percentage points between the first and second generations, while that for women rose dramatically, to 72.5 percent. There is little further change for either group between the second and third generations. Thus, by the second generation, Mexican American women have nearly caught up to non-Hispanic white women, and the Mexican American–non-Hispanic white difference in the gender gap in participation has been almost eliminated. In the next section we will consider how much of this assimilation to U.S. gender roles occurs among immigrants with time in the United States versus across generations as well as its relationship to measured characteristics.

The relative labor market attachment of female compared to male Mexican immigrants may be compared to that in Mexico. As previously noted, in 2000 the female labor force participation rate was 39.4 percent in Mexico—this was 47.2 percent of the male rate. Mexican female labor force participation rates were 30.2 percent (35.6 percent of the male rate) in 1980 and 34.0 percent (40.7 percent of the male rate) in 1990 (see the ILO Web site at http://www.laborsta.ilo.org). These earlier rates may be relevant for comparing immigrants who arrived during the 1980s and 1990s. The ILO figures refer to individuals fifteen years of age and older, so, for purposes of comparison, we computed raw labor force participation rates for individuals sixteen years and older in the CPS with no age cutoff at the top. For all Mexican immigrants, the participation rates were 85.7 percent for men and 46.6 percent for women, for a female-to-male ratio of 54.4 percent; and, for adult Mexican immigrants, the rates were 85.8 percent for men and 43.3 percent for women, for a ratio of 50.5 percent. These figures show that Mexican immigrant women had higher absolute and relative labor force participation than women in Mexico as of 2000, but the differences were not large. The gap between labor supply of Mexican immigrant women and women in Mexico is somewhat larger if we compare current Mexican immigrants to women in Mexico as of 1980 or 1990. As noted earlier, labor force attachment of women in the United States in general is much higher than that of women in Mexico or Mexican immigrants to the United States. In particular, as of 2000, ILO data show that women's labor force participation in the United States was 58.8 percent (81.2 percent of the male rate). This is suggestive of a strong effect of source country patterns on Mexican immigrants in the United States. The observed differences between Mexican immigrants and source-country patterns could be a selection effect if migration is selective of relatively more market-oriented women from Mexico; alternatively, exposure to the U.S. labor market may bring Mexican immigrant women into the labor force. In the following, we pursue the latter issue in more detail.

Although all the labor supply measures show similar generational patterns, Mexican American employment-population rates are consistently lower relative to non-Hispanic white rates than are their labor force participation rates. This difference reflects the considerably higher unemployment rates of Mexican Americans, especially Mexican American women, compared to non-Hispanic whites, though here, too, there is dramatic intergenerational convergence for women. Mexican American male unemployment rates were 2.3–3.2 percentage points higher than those of non-Hispanic whites (a large differential, considering non-Hispanic white males' predicted rate of 4.7 percent), and there is no intergenerational convergence to native whites' levels. In contrast, the Mexican immigrant women's unemployment rate is 7.5 percentage points higher than non-Hispanic whites' (11.4 versus 3.9 percent), and the female adult immigrant unemployment rate is 8.6 percentage points higher; however, the Mexican American non-Hispanic white gap falls steadily across generations, reaching 4.6 percent by the second generation and 2.6 percent by the third generation. It is possible that Mexican immigrant women have relatively low levels of job seeking skills that prevent their locating a wage offer or that minimum wage floors are especially binding for them.[18]

The final outcome shown in table 2.1 is the log of real hourly earnings for full-time wage and salary workers.[19] The immigrant wage shortfalls are very large and roughly the same size for men and women: .505 to .517 log points for all immigrants and .634 to .641 log points for adult immigrants. These fall dramatically by the second generation, to .135–.175, and then rise several log points, to .184–.213, by the third generation. Here, we again note the lack of further convergence between the second and third generations noted in previous studies. The male shortfall is 3–4 percent larger than the female shortfall for the second and third generations, implying that the gender wage differential between Mexican Americans born in the United

18. For example, the 25th percentile of hourly wages among all wage and salary workers (both full and part time) with valid wages was only $5.27 in 2000 dollars for Mexican American immigrant women ($5.11 for adult immigrant women) at a time when the minimum wage ranged from $4.66 to $5.42 in 2000 dollars; in contrast, the 25th percentile for second- and third-generation women was $5.92 and $6.14, respectively. Corresponding figures for Mexican American men were $6.15 (immigrants), $6.04 (adult immigrants), $6.97 (second generation) and $7.47 (third generation). Thus, the minimum wage cuts into the Mexican immigrant women's wage distribution to a much larger degree than for the other Mexican American groups.

19. See the appendix for the construction of the earnings variable.

States is somewhat smaller than among non-Hispanic whites; this is a fairly general pattern among minorities (Blau, Ferber, and Winkler 2002).

2.4   Assimilation within and across Generations: Basic Regression Results

One of our key objectives is to compare the degree to which Mexican American men and women assimilate to U.S. labor market and family patterns, both within and between generations. While table 2.1 provides some important descriptive information on demographic and labor market outcomes for immigrants and later generations, in this section we present the results of regression analyses for selected dependent variables that allow us to more explicitly examine assimilation by controlling for the effect of years since migration on immigrants' outcomes and by including additional covariates which control for the human capital and locational characteristics of Mexican Americans. This specification enables us to estimate how much assimilation occurs in the first generation with exposure to the U.S. economy and labor market as well as to identify the impact of measured covariates versus behavioral changes in the assimilation of Mexican Americans, both within and across generations.

Specifically, to capture the assimilation of immigrants, we augment equation (1) by replacing the immigrant dummy variable with a full set of immigrant arrival cohort dummies and an indicator of years since migration and its square. The cohort variables refer to arrival before 1961; 1961–1970; 1971–1980; 1981–1990; 1991–1996; and 1997–2002. As previously noted, because we are pooling ten years of data, we can in principle distinguish the effects of different arrival cohorts from that of time in the United States as in Borjas (1985). In our basic models, we also control for human capital (years of schooling)[20] and location (eight Census region dummies, a metropolitan statistical area [MSA] dummy, and dummies for California and Texas, the two states with the largest incidence of Mexican Americans in the population),[21] in addition to a quartic in age and year dummies (as in the preceding). For comparison, we also estimate models with only the age and year controls, in effect allowing human capital and region to be endogenous.

With respect to immigrants, the two specifications allow us to compare immigrants both to third-generation non-Hispanic whites in general and also to those with similar measured characteristics, with the former comparison including both compositional and behavioral differences and the

20. Ibarraran and Lubotsky (chap. 5 in this volume) suggest that the U.S. Census overstates educational attainment for Mexican immigrants. If this is true, then the results we show in figures 2.1–2.9 with full controls may be biased. However, we note that all of our estimated immigrant assimilation profiles have similar slopes whether or not we control for education. Thus, our basic conclusions about the direction and magnitude of immigrant assimilation are likely to be robust with respect to possible measurement error in immigrant education.

21. California and Texas dummies were used by Trejo (1997, 2003) in his analyses of Mexican American men.

latter attempting to isolate the effect of behavioral differences. Similarly, looking across generations, comparison of the two specifications allows us to make inferences about the degree to which assimilation in labor market and family outcomes occurs through changes in the education and location variables versus behavioral changes. Table 2.2 shows regression results controlling for education and location as well as year, while table 2A.2 shows corresponding results for models that control only for age and year. Means of the explanatory variables are shown in table 2A.3. To assist in the interpretation of the regression results, figures 2.1–2.6 show implied assimilation profiles for Mexican Americans. Immigrant outcomes are usually evaluated for the 1971–1980 arrival cohort. We chose this cohort because it likely contains a large number of the parents of second-generation Mexican Americans in our 1994–2003 sample period. However, where relevant, we also discuss other arrival cohorts, particularly the 1980s cohort, as this was a period of rapidly rising returns to education, a factor that worked against the labor market success of Mexican Americans.

Turning first to the incidence of marriage shown in table 2.2 and figure 2.1, we see that, upon arrival, Mexican immigrant men are less likely and Mexican immigrant women more likely than otherwise similar non-Hispanic white natives to be married, spouse present. There is some assimilation for both sexes, with substantial male assimilation into marriage among immigrants with time in the United States and some reduction over time in females' likelihood of being married. This pattern suggests that, for males, immigration may be disruptive of marriage (either by delaying marriage or causing a temporary separation from their wives), whereas marriage may play a positive role in immigration decision of women, with some perhaps arriving as tied movers. Despite assimilation toward the lower marriage incidence of natives with similar characteristics, female immigrants continue to be more likely to be married, spouse present, than the native reference group for all cohorts. For example, the 1971–1980 arrival cohort of immigrant women has an 18.2 percentage point higher incidence of marriage upon arrival in the United States than the native reference group and continued to have an 8.4 percentage point advantage after twenty years of residence. Given their positive assimilation, male immigrants in this cohort were projected to overtake their native counterparts after eight years and to have an 11.0 percentage point higher incidence of marriage after twenty years. Thus, both male and female immigrants are characterized by more traditional marriage patterns than natives. The regression results suggest, however, that full assimilation to the marriage patterns of otherwise similar third-generation non-Hispanic whites has occurred by the second generation in which Mexican Americans of both sexes are roughly equally likely to be married as comparable natives; by the third generation, Mexican-American women are actually slightly (3 percentage points) less likely to be married than the reference group.

Assimilation rates are similar when we do not control for education and

Table 2.2   Selected regression results for demographic and labor market outcomes

| | Marriage | | | | No. of children <18 yrs | | | |
| | Men | | Women | | Women | | Women | |
	Coef.	SE	Coef.	SE	Coef.	SE	Coef.	SE
immig: pre-1961 arrival	−0.083	0.051	0.238	0.056	1.178	0.190	0.954	0.183
immig: 1961–70 arrival	−0.090	0.032	0.216	0.036	0.473	0.100	0.329	0.097
immig: 1971–80 arrival	−0.106	0.024	0.182	0.027	0.260	0.069	0.120	0.067
immig: 1981–90 arrival	−0.024	0.017	0.169	0.020	0.331	0.052	0.201	0.050
immig: 1991–96 arrival	−0.014	0.011	0.232	0.013	0.250	0.035	0.086	0.034
immig: 1997–2002 arrival	−0.079	0.010	0.154	0.012	0.045	0.030	−0.065	0.029
years since mig. (ysm)	0.017	0.002	−0.004	0.002	0.058	0.006	0.062	0.005
ysm squared (/100)	−0.028	0.004	−0.005	0.005	−0.184	0.017	−0.184	0.016
second-gen. Mexican American	−0.002	0.006	−0.007	0.006	0.373	0.015	0.371	0.014
third-gen. Mexican American	−0.006	0.005	−0.030	0.005	0.239	0.012	0.258	0.012
Control for marital status?					No		Yes	

| | Annual work hours | | | | Unemployment \| In labor force | | | |
| | Men | | Women | | Men | | Women | |
	Coef.	SE	Coef.	SE	Coef.	SE	Coef.	SE
immig: pre-1961 arrival	−187.57	99.45	−642.74	112.38	0.015	0.029	0.155	0.035
immig: 1961–70 arrival	−73.37	63.03	−653.59	73.35	0.041	0.018	0.143	0.023
immig: 1971–80 arrival	44.15	47.43	−454.92	55.59	0.006	0.013	0.103	0.018
immig: 1981–90 arrival	105.85	33.70	−463.57	39.68	−0.005	0.009	0.099	0.014
immig: 1991–96 arrival	172.72	22.20	−479.20	25.83	−0.019	0.006	0.090	0.009
immig: 1997–2002 arrival	217.77	19.32	−417.03	23.89	−0.023	0.005	0.060	0.008
years since mig. (ysm)	4.85	3.26	26.02	3.80	−0.001	0.001	−0.004	0.001
ysm squared (/100)	3.55	7.93	−23.87	9.13	−0.001	0.002	0.002	0.003
second-gen. Mexican American	−57.09	10.90	−13.66	11.46	0.019	0.003	0.034	0.003
third-gen. Mexican American	−105.02	9.24	−20.50	9.63	0.017	0.003	0.015	0.003

| | Log wages (FT) | | | |
| | Men | | Women | |
	Coef.	SE	Coef.	SE
immig: pre-1961 arrival	−0.150	0.080	−0.075	0.111
immig: 1961–70 arrival	−0.162	0.048	−0.113	0.073
immig: 1971–80 arrival	−0.166	0.036	−0.069	0.059
immig: 1981–90 arrival	−0.282	0.026	−0.157	0.045
immig: 1991–96 arrival	−0.246	0.018	−0.191	0.032
immig: 1997–2002 arrival	−0.209	0.015	−0.182	0.028
years since mig. (ysm)	0.004	0.003	−0.003	0.004
ysm squared (/100)	−0.009	0.007	0.011	0.011
second-gen. Mexican American	−0.130	0.010	−0.083	0.010
third-gen. Mexican American	−0.141	0.008	−0.094	0.008

Note: Other controls include: a quartic in age, years of schooling, eight Census region dummies, an MSA dummy, dummies for California and Texas, and year dummies.

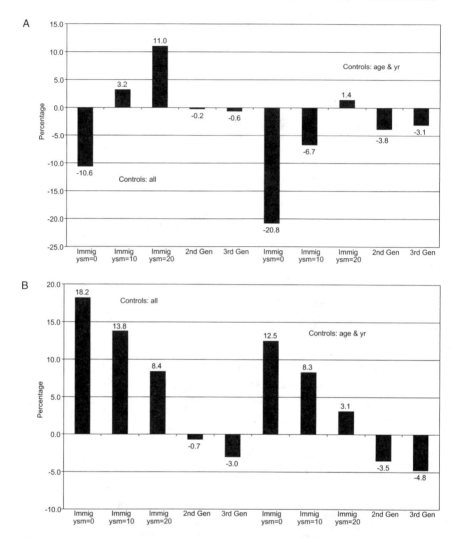

Fig. 2.1   Assimilation of Mexican Americans: *A,* **Marriage for men (1971–1980 arrival cohort for immigrants);** *B,* **Marriage for women (1971–1980 arrival cohort for immigrants)**

Note: "All" controls include age, year, education, region, MSA, California, and Texas.

location. However, as may be seen in figure 2.1 (see also tables 2.2 and 2A.2), the characteristics of Mexican Americans lower their marriage propensity. Specifically, we find that education raises the incidence of marriage, while residence in an MSA or in California or Texas lowers it, and Mexican Americans have lower levels of schooling and are more likely to live in California or Texas and in MSAs (table 2A.3). Nonetheless, as may be seen in panel B of figure 2.1, female immigrants in the 1971–1980 arrival cohort remain more likely to be married than natives, even when these controls are omitted. (This is the case for other arrival cohorts as well.) Considering subsequent generations, it appears that education and location factors, rather than a dearth of prospective partners, are sufficient to account for the lower raw marriage rates of second- and third-generation Mexican Americans compared to third-generation non-Hispanic whites observed in table 2.1 and figure 2.1, since, as we have seen, the Mexican American–non-Hispanic white differences are virtually eliminated when we control for these factors.

Consistent with higher fertility rates in Mexico than in the United States, table 2.2 indicates that Mexican immigrant women in all cohorts are estimated to have higher fertility than otherwise comparable natives upon arrival in the United States when marital status is not controlled for. However, the immigrant-native differential upon arrival has been declining with successive arrival cohorts. This trend tracks the sharp declines in fertility that have occurred in Mexico. Some of the immigrant-native differential is due to the greater propensity of immigrant women to be married. Controlling for marital status reduces the estimated immigrant-native differential substantially. Nonetheless, with the exception of the most recent arrival cohort, immigrants continue to have higher fertility than the reference group, even controlling for marital status. Immigrant women's fertility is found to *increase* relative to natives with time in the United States: table 2.2 shows significantly positive assimilation profiles for immigrant women in both specifications (see also figure 2.2). Thus, like Blau (1992), we find evidence consistent with the notion that the immigration process disrupts or delays fertility and, thus, that immigrant women's fertility increases over time in the United States relative to comparable native women—in this case further widening the immigrant-native fertility differential over time. For the 1971–1980 arrival cohort, controlling for education and location, immigrants are estimated to arrive with .26 more children than natives, and this gap rises to .70 children after twenty years of residence. The immigrant-native differences in fertility are larger—rising from .42 to .83 after twenty years—for the model that does not control for education and location, a result consistent with a negative relationship between fertility and education. Note that, as Blau (1992) points out, if the immigration process disrupts fertility, the positive effect on fertility of years since migration does not necessarily mean that no assimilation toward native fertility levels is taking place. That is, the desired number of children could potentially have been reduced by exposure to U.S. norms and labor market opportunities, but fertility nonetheless rises over time compared to natives as desired fertility is approached. The problem is that we do not observe desired fertility.

While, consistent with more traditional gender roles, Mexican immigrant women are a high fertility group relative to the native reference group

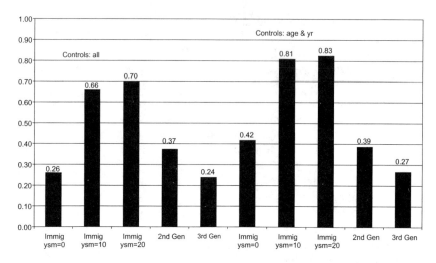

Fig. 2.2   Assimilation of Mexican Americans: Number of children < eighteen for women (1971–1980 arrival cohort for immigrants)

Note: "All" controls include age, year, education, region, MSA, California, and Texas.

with no direct evidence of assimilation towards native levels, there is clear evidence of intergenerational assimilation of Mexican American fertility toward non-Hispanic white levels. Mexican American fertility does remain higher, however: .37 higher for the second generation and .24 higher for the third generation, even controlling for measured covariates. These differences relative to non-Hispanic whites are only slightly affected by whether we control for education (and location), presumably reflecting the smaller education differentials relative to non-Hispanic whites for Mexican Americans born in the United States compared to Mexican immigrants.

As may be seen in table 2.2 and figure 2.3, upon arrival, the labor supply patterns of Mexican immigrants are much more traditional than those of otherwise similar natives in the reference group. We focus here on annual work hours, including those who worked zero hours as this variable summarizes both labor force participation and work intensity. Upon arrival, immigrant women's annual hours are considerably lower than those of the reference group, while, for cohorts arriving after 1970, men's annual hours are somewhat higher. More recent cohorts of immigrant men increased the hours differential compared to the native reference group, ceteris paribus, while, consistent with rising female labor force participation in Mexico, the gap for women decreased a bit, though the pattern is much less pronounced than we found for fertility, and the shortfall compared to the native reference group remains sizable. Unlike our results for marriage and fertility, however, we find substantial assimilation of immigrant women to the native reference group's labor supply patterns. Despite their initially higher levels, male hours show some positive assimilation as well.

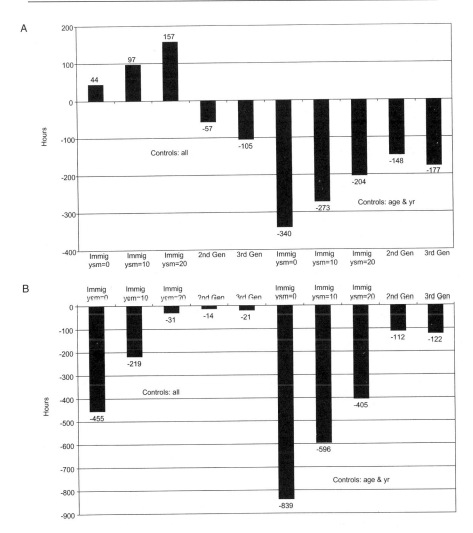

Fig. 2.3   Assimilation of Mexican Americans: *A,* **Annual hours for men (1971–1980 arrival cohort for immigrants);** *B,* **Annual hours for women (1971–1980 arrival cohort for immigrants)**

Note: "All" controls include age, year, education, region, MSA, California, and Texas.

Focusing on the dramatic results for women, we see that, upon arrival in the United States, the 1971–1980 cohort of immigrant women worked a highly significant 455 fewer hours than comparable white non-Hispanics, a large gap compared to the white non-Hispanic average of 1,281 hours per year. However, there is rapid assimilation: over half of this shortfall is eliminated after ten years as the gap falls to 219 hours, and nearly all of the rest after twenty years in the United States when immigrants are estimated to work only 31 hours less. In results not controlling for schooling or location, the labor supply effects for immigrants become much more negative, but the assimilation profiles have similar slopes to those in the models with full controls (see also table 2A.2). For example, immigrant women in the 1971–1980 arrival cohort initially work 839 hours less; after twenty years, this deficit is reduced to 405 hours. Immigrants' low levels of education thus cause them to work much less than white non-Hispanic natives of the same age.

Across generations, Mexican American men appear to be progressively less work-oriented than comparable non-Hispanic whites (table 2.2 and panel A of figure 2.3), with a 105 hour shortfall by the third generation. In contrast, second- and third-generation Mexican American women work about the same number of hours as comparable white non-Hispanics: the effects range from a fourteen-hour shortfall for the second generation that is insignificant to a twenty-one-hour shortfall for the third generation that is significant although still small compared to the average white non-Hispanic female labor supply of 1,281 hours (table 2.2 and panel B of figure 2.3). As we have seen, our estimates suggest that assimilation to the labor supply patterns of otherwise similar women in the white non-Hispanic reference group essentially occurs in the first generation. As was the case for immigrants, when we do not control for education or location (see also table 2A.2), the Mexican American hours effects become more negative for the second and third generation compared to models with full controls, although the changes in these effects are smaller than for immigrants (due to later generations' higher education levels). The hours shortfalls for U.S.-born Mexican Americans range from 148 to 177 hours for men and from 112 to 122 hours for women.

The most striking findings in these results is the dramatic assimilation of Mexican immigrant women into the U.S. labor market and the relatively rapid erosion of the highly traditional labor supply pattern exhibited by Mexican immigrants upon arrival in the United States. Female immigrants begin with a large ceteris paribus shortfall in work hours. However, within twenty years of residence, their work hours are nearly equal to those of women with the same characteristics in the third-generation–non-Hispanic white reference group, and this remains the case in the second and third generations. While male immigrants tend to work more than the reference group, ceteris paribus, this is no longer the case in subsequent generations. Thus, by the second generation, the labor supply patterns of Mexican Americans exhibit no more gender specialization than do those of third-generation non-Hispanic whites, all else equal. Even without controlling for education, there is still rapid assimilation of Mexican immigrant women into market work with time in the United States, although a sizable labor supply gap remains. The assimilation process continues across generations as U.S.-born Mexican origin women raise their education levels relative to the reference group. However, shortfalls remain for both men and women that are roughly constant between the second and third generations, suggesting a lack of further convergence in annual hours beyond the second generation, a pattern noted in previous work and for other dependent variables.

Although the annual hours measure indirectly reflects Mexican American–non-Hispanic white differences in unemployment, we also examine unemployment rates explicitly because they may provide evidence on particular labor market problems facing Mexican Americans. Like the labor supply measure, the unemployment experience of Mexican immigrants differs greatly by sex (see table 2.2 and figure 2.4). For males, the immigrant-native difference, controlling for characteristics, tends to be small, and men in recent cohorts actually have a lower unemployment rate at arrival than comparable white non-Hispanics. There is no significant effect of years since migration on the unemployment rates of immigrant men, and second- and third-generation, Mexican American men actually have 1.7–1.9 percentage points' higher unemployment than comparable white non-Hispanics.

In contrast, immigrant women have a substantially higher unemployment rate than comparable natives at arrival, but this gap decreases somewhat across cohorts. The somewhat smaller unemployment gap for more recent arrival cohorts corresponds to the cross-cohort decline we found for the labor supply gap (in turn likely reflecting rising female participation rates in Mexico) and suggests that a portion of the unemployment gap reflects job seeking skills. The stronger results are for the years since migration variable, which indicate that the unemployment gap falls substantially with time in the United States. For example, in the 1971–1980 cohort, Mexican immigrant women have a 10.3 percentage point higher unemployment rate at arrival than comparable white non-Hispanic natives. After ten years in the United States, however, the gap has fallen to 6.4 percentage points and after twenty years to 3.0 percentage points. Little further assimilation occurs generations, controlling for measured characteristics: the gap is 3.4 percentage points for the second generation and 1.5 percentage points by the third generation. When we control only for age and year, the immigrant-native difference in unemployment rates for women is much larger and remains considerable even after long residence, although substantial assimilation does take place. For example, the unemployment rate of immigrants in the 1971–1980 cohort is 14.3 percentage points higher upon arrival in the United States and is still 6.5 percentage points higher after twenty years of residence. The differential decreases to 4.7 percentage points in the second generation and 2.6 percentage points in the third generation.

We now turn to the results for wage assimilation in table 2.2, which, it may be recalled, show results for the log of real hourly earnings for full-time wage and salary workers. Given the deteriorating wage position of immigrants, we have evaluated the regression results for both the 1971–1980

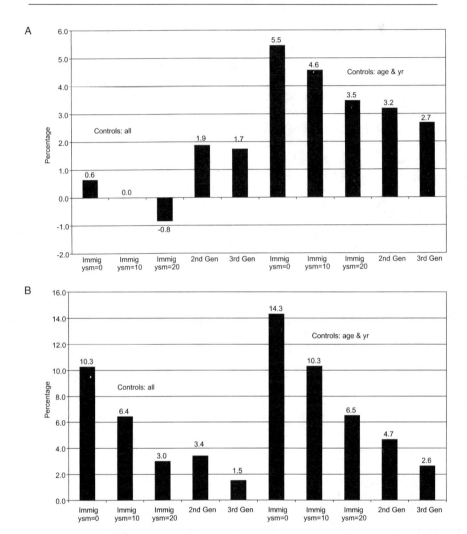

Fig. 2.4   Assimilation of Mexican Americans: *A,* **Unemployment rate for men (1971–1980 arrival cohort for immigrants);** *B,* **Unemployment rate for women (1971–1980 arrival cohort for immigrants)**

Note: "All" controls include age, year, education, region, MSA, California, and Texas.

(figure 2.5) and 1981–1990 (figure 2.6) arrival cohorts. The results for immigrant men conform to what would be expected based on the literature. There is a considerable wage gap with otherwise similar natives at arrival that tends to increase across cohorts as well as some weak evidence of positive wage assimilation with time in the United States. The wage gap for men in the 1971–1980 (1981–1990) cohort is estimated to be .17 (.28) log points on arrival and to fall to .12 (.23) log points after twenty years of res-

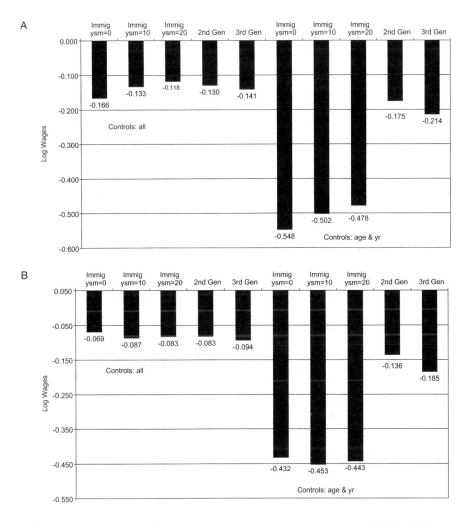

Fig. 2.5   Assimilation of Mexican Americans: *A,* Log wages for men (1971–1980 arrival cohort for immigrants); *B,* Log wages for women (1971–1980 arrival cohort for immigrants)

Note: "All" controls include age, year, education, region, MSA, California, and Texas.

idence. The wage shortfall, controlling for the full set of explanatory variables, for immigrants in the 1971–1980 cohort after twenty years in the United States was comparable to the estimated wage gaps for the second and third generations of .13–.14 log points, although that estimated for the 1981–1990 cohort was about .10 log points higher.

Our assimilation results for men can be compared with the findings in Borjas and Katz's (chap. 1 in this volume) detailed examination of Mexican

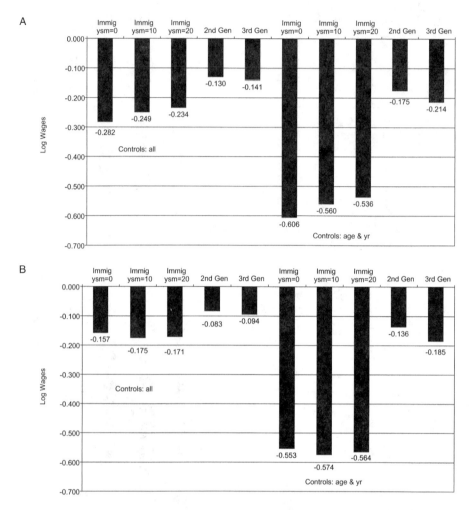

Fig. 2.6   Assimilation of Mexican Americans: *A,* **Log wages for men (1981–1990 arrival cohort for immigrants);** *B,* **Log wages for women (1981–1990 arrival cohort for immigrants)**

Note: "All" controls include age, year, education, region, MSA, California, and Texas.

immigrant men's wage assimilation (the authors did not study women's wages). Specifically, Borjas and Katz find that during the 1990–2000 period, which overlaps with our 1994–2003 period, some arrival cohorts and age groups experienced positive wage assimilation, while the relative wages of others fell. Our finding of a slightly positive overall rate of wage assimilation for men is within the authors' range of estimates for individual cohorts and age groups. And the estimated shortfalls (versus natives) we find for immigrant men in our models that do not control for education of .48–.61 log points (panel A of figures 2.5 and 2.6) are similar to those found by

Borjas and Katz for 2000 in models not controlling for education, which were mostly in the .44–.73 log point range.

The arrival log wage shortfalls for women also tend to increase over time and were .07 log points for the 1971–1980 cohort and .16 log points for the 1981–1990 cohort. In general, the log wage arrival shortfalls of immigrant women tend to be smaller than for men, a pattern we noted in the preceding for later generations as well. However, in contrast to the male pattern, there is no evidence of positive wage assimilation for women immigrants. Moreover, for women, as for men, we find little further wage assimilation across generations compared to the 1971–1980 arrival cohort of immigrants, controlling for education and location, with a wage gap of .08–.09 for the second and third generations. And, similar to men, some intergenerational wage assimilation is suggested for the 1981–1990 cohort.

The absence of wage assimilation for immigrant women may reflect the lack of data on women's actual labor market experience in the CPS. Given strong positive assimilation for labor supply, the women in the wage sample in successive years-since-migration groups will include more new entrants with relatively little labor market experience and, hence, low wages. They may be a less positively selected group in other ways as well. This may be the reason for the seeming lack of wage assimilation for women, although it is also worth noting that both we and Borjas and Katz (chap. 1 in this volume) do not find strong evidence of positive wage assimilation for men either. We investigated the selection issue for women by implementing a Heckman-style (1979) selectivity bias correction for women's wages. For this analysis, we considered all those with valid wage observations (i.e., full-time and part-time workers) as the wage sample. We identified the selection equation (a probit on a variable equaling 1 if the respondent was in the wage sample) by excluding marital status, number of children less than six years old, and number of children between seven and seventeen years old from the wage equation. We interpret the selectivity-corrected results cautiously because of these strong identification assumptions.

Ordinary least squares (OLS) wage equations for women (now including both part-time and full-time workers) showed immigrant arrival effects that were negative for all cohorts except 1971–1980 and ranged from 0.035 to –0.093, with some of the negative values significant. Moreover, there was marginally significant negative female immigrant wage assimilation of a small magnitude, where wages fell 0.068 log points over twenty years, all else equal.[22] When we implemented the selectivity bias correction, immigrant arrival effects ranged from –0.085 to –0.207 and were significant in almost every case, and there was some weak evidence of positive wage assimilation for women: after twenty years, wages rose a modest 0.054 log

22. The arrival effects are less negative, and the assimilation slope is more negative for the pooled full-time and part-time sample than for the full-time sample shown in table 2.2 and figure 2.5. In both cases, however, there is no evidence of positive wage assimilation among Mexican immigrant women in OLS regressions.

points, ceteris paribus, an effect that was similar in magnitude to the OLS estimate for men of .048; however, the women's result was not significant. Thus, the point estimate of the assimilation effect becomes more positive with the selection correction versus OLS, a difference predicted by our reasoning about the increased labor market entry of inexperienced women with time in the United States. However, the difference between the two estimates is modest and is based on strong identification assumptions. The conclusion we draw from these estimates is that neither the OLS nor the selectivity-bias corrected equations show strong evidence of positive wage assimilation for Mexican immigrant women. The quantitative similarity of the selectivity bias-corrected wage assimilation results for women and the OLS male wage assimilation results, for which selectivity bias is much less an issue, suggests that Mexican immigrants' wage offers do not improve much with assimilation beyond, of course, the normal increase in wages that all workers obtain with potential work experience.

Figures 2.5 and 2.6 as well as table 2A.2 show that the wage shortfalls of each Mexican American group are much larger when the controls for education and location are omitted; this, of course, reflects the lower educational attainment of Mexican Americans relative to the reference group of third-generation non-Hispanic whites. Viewing the data in this way, however, does give a more substantial role for intergenerational wage assimilation due to the increasing educational attainment of Mexican Americans across generations. So, for example, in the 1971–1980 cohort, controlling only for age and year, even after twenty years in the United States, the pay shortfalls for immigrants are much larger than for later generations: .48 log points for immigrant men and .44 log points for immigrant women versus .18–.21 log points for men and .14–.19 log points for women for later generations. Thus, the increase in education achieved by subsequent generations of Mexican Americans relative to immigrants leads to a substantial closing of the raw pay gap relative to third-generation white non-Hispanics. However, we again note a lack of further convergence, in this case for log wages, beyond the second generation.

The results considered previously may be biased by changes in the age composition of a specific immigration cohort across successive cross sections (Friedberg 1993). Specifically, more recent cross sections will include more immigrants in the particular cohort who immigrated as children. The assimilation process is likely to be quite different for those who immigrated as children compared to adult immigrants. For this reason, we repeated the analyses in table 2.2 with the immigrant sample restricted to adult immigrants (see table 2A.4). The results were very similar. One exception was that there was somewhat more positive assimilation with time in the United States for men's annual work hours; however, even here, the relationship was much steeper for immigrant women than immigrant men.

In addition to analyzing wages and employment, we also show some evidence on the industrial and occupational progression of Mexican Americans within and across generations. Sectoral representation can be an important indicator of the degree of integration into American society. Table 2A.5 shows the distributions of workers across occupations and industries.[23] We distinguish immigrants according to whether they migrated as adults, and we also show separate statistics for immigrants who were in the United States at least ten years. Comparing these long-term immigrants to the overall immigrant sample shows the combined effects of time in the United States as well as selective return migration and changing cohort characteristics.

Looking first at industry distribution, one of the most dramatic differences between Mexican immigrants and the white non-Hispanic reference group is that Mexican immigrants, especially men, are much more likely to work in agriculture. However, by the second generation, the Mexican American female incidence of farm work is virtually the same as for non-Hispanic whites, while that for Mexican American men is only slightly higher than that of non-Hispanic white men. And by the third generation, male agricultural employment is virtually indistinguishable from that of non-Hispanic whites. There is also a dramatic cross-generation movement of Mexican American women out of nondurable manufacturing into health and education services. A similar but less dramatic development also characterizes the movement of Mexican-American men across generations out of construction.

Regarding occupations, there is a notable movement across generations of Mexican American men out of personal service, farmworker, and operative jobs into managerial and professional jobs. For women, there is a dramatic move out of operative and personal service jobs into managerial, professional, and, especially, clerical occupations. While most of this occupational movement occurs across generations, there appears also to be some upgrading of immigrants with time in the United States, as suggested by the results for long-term versus all immigrants. Of course, these latter differences may also be due to cohort effects or selective return migration.

Tables 2.3 and 2.4 summarize the impact of these occupational and industrial shifts on segregation indexes by gender (table 2.3) and by ethnicity (table 2.4).[24] Looking first at table 2.3, we see that differences in industry segregation by gender between Mexican Americans and the non-Hispanic

---

23. In 2003, there was a major change in CPS occupation and industry codes based on the changes in these codes adopted in the 2000 Census. Crosswalk information available at the Census Web site (http://www.census.gov/hhes/www/ioindex/crosswalks.html) was used to assign incumbents in the 2003 CPS to the 1990 Census categories employed in earlier CPSs on the basis of the category into which the largest number of individuals in their detailed occupation or industry would have been allocated.

24. The segregation index is defined, for example for gender, as the fraction of the male or female work force that would have to change jobs in order to achieve parity. It is equal to $.5 \cdot \Sigma_i |m_i - f_i|$, where i represents sector (occupation or industry), and m_i and f_i are, respectively, the proportions of the total male and female work force employed in sector i. As elsewhere, the reference group for the analysis by ethnicity is white non-Hispanic natives.

Table 2.3   Occupational and industrial segregation indexes, by gender

	Industry	Occupation
White non-Hispanic natives with native parents	0.337	0.360
Mexican immigrants	0.336	0.394
In U.S. at least 10 yrs	0.345	0.393
Migrated age 18 or higher	0.335	0.391
Migrated age 18 or higher, in U.S. at least 10 yrs	0.346	0.397
Second-generation Mexican Americans	0.356	0.416
Third-generation Mexican Americans	0.347	0.446

Table 2.4   Occupational and industrial segregation indexes relative to white non-Hispanic natives with native parents

	Industry		Occupation	
	Men	Women	Men	Women
Mexican immigrants	0.264	0.320	0.411	0.478
In U.S. at least 10 yrs	0.218	0.270	0.378	0.435
Migrated age 18 or higher	0.280	0.373	0.447	0.580
Migrated age 18 or higher, in U.S. at least 10 yrs	0.233	0.349	0.420	0.571
Second-generation Mexican Americans	0.100	0.070	0.178	0.149
Third-generation Mexican Americans	0.079	0.062	0.185	0.122

white native reference group are not very large. The level of industry segregation by gender of immigrants is very similar to that of non-Hispanic whites, and there is actually a slight increase in gender segregation by industry across generations. The differences between Mexican Americans and the reference group in occupational segregation by gender are larger and exhibit an interesting cross-generational pattern. Among immigrants, there is only slightly more occupational segregation by gender than non-Hispanic white natives. However, the occupational segregation index *rises* steadily across generations of Mexican Americans.

The results in table 2.4, which show segregation indexes by ethnicity, shed some light on the rising gender segregation across generations for Mexican Americans. For industry and, especially, occupation, there is a more dramatic reduction across generations in segregation versus non-Hispanic whites for Mexican American women than men. Specifically, the industrial segregation index (Mexican Americans versus non-Hispanic whites) falls 25.8 percentage points for immigrants as a whole to the third generation for women but only 18.5 percentage points for men, while the occupational segregation index falls 35.6 percentage points for women but only 22.6 percentage points for men. The result is a slight increase in gender segregation by industry and a more substantial one by occupation. Focusing on the latter increase, table 2A.5 shows that Mexican American men have moved into white-collar jobs to a lesser extent than Mexican American women. For example, table 2A.5 shows that 11.8 percent of Mexican immigrant men and 28.0 percent of Mexican immigrant women worked in managerial, professional, clerical, or sales jobs; by the third generation, these figures were 34.7 percent for men and fully 68.8 percent for women.[25]

2.5   The Family Migration Model: Regression Results

Our data can be used to study the relevance of the family migration model for Mexican American immigrants. This exercise is additionally of interest because it enables us to ascertain whether we obtain similar findings to those in the preceding when we focus on married individuals and explicitly take into account spouses' characteristics. To address these questions, we constructed a file using the CPS data that consisted of married individuals for whom we could identify the ethnicity and nativity of both husband and wife. We restricted the sample to women (men) who were of Mexican origin and to a reference group of women (men) who were themselves third-generation white non-Hispanics and were married to third-generation white non-Hispanics. (The latter constitute the reference category in the female and male regressions.) Recall that the family migration model asserts that immigrant women upon arrival work to support their husbands' human capital investments but later reduce their labor supply. This model thus implies positive cohort arrival effects and negative assimilation profiles for women's work hours; in addition, the model suggests that women do not invest in their own human capital, implying perhaps less positively sloped wage assimilation profiles for women than men.

As may be seen in table 2.5, Mexican Americans of both sexes have a very high probability—82 to 83 percent—of having a Mexican American spouse. This incidence is particularly high for immigrants, with 92 percent of both men and women having a spouse who is of Mexican origin. Fully 84 percent of female immigrants and 79 percent of male immigrants have spouses who are themselves Mexican immigrants. Although we do not know when these marriages took place, the higher percentage of female than male Mexican immigrants whose spouse is a Mexican immigrant is consistent with our preceding finding that immigration tends to be a family decision for women and that the incidence of being married (spouse present) is high upon arrival in the United States. Of course, marriages to

---

25. Tables 2.4 and 2A.5 also show that the occupation and industry distribution of adult immigrants is more dissimilar to non-Hispanic whites than is the case for immigrants in general and that, among immigrants, there is more integration (relative to non-Hispanic whites) among long-term immigrants than for the immigrant group as a whole. (This latter pattern is especially pronounced for the "all immigrants" group.) These patterns for adult immigrants are consistent with their larger educational shortfalls, while those for long-term immigrants may be due to assimilation, cohort effects, or selective return migration.

Table 2.5   Ethnicity and nativity of marriage patterns, married Mexican American women and men

	Fraction of husbands who were:			
	Mexican immigrants	Second-generation Mexican Americans	Third-generation Mexican Americans	Mexican-American: All generations
A. Married Mexican American women (wife's generation)				
Mexican American immigrants	0.835	0.057	0.028	0.920
Second-generation Mexican Americans	0.321	0.247	0.172	0.740
Third-generation Mexican Americans	0.098	0.122	0.479	0.699
All Mexican American wives	0.540	0.106	0.181	0.827

	Fraction of wives who were:			
	Mexican immigrants	Second-generation Mexican Americans	Third-generation Mexican Americans	Mexican-American: All generations
B. Married Mexican American men (husband's generation)				
Mexican American immigrants	0.792	0.079	0.045	0.916
Second-generation Mexican Americans	0.219	0.256	0.226	0.701
Third-generation Mexican Americans	0.060	0.099	0.505	0.664
All Mexican American husbands	0.512	0.109	0.196	0.817

fellow immigrants may also occur in the United States or involve bringing a spouse to the United States from Mexico. The probability of having a spouse who is of Mexican origin declines across generations for both women and men: decreasing from 92 percent for immigrants to 74 (70) percent for second-generation women (men) and 70 (66) percent for third-generation women (men). Nonetheless, marriage outside the Mexican-origin group still characterizes only 30–34 percent of third-generation married Mexican Americans.[26]

Table 2.6 contains selected regression results for three dependent variables that are of central importance in forming a picture of married women's assimilation and evaluating the family investment hypotheses: the number of children for married women and annual work hours and log hourly earnings for married women and married men. The explanatory variables include both own and spouse characteristics for education, age, migration cohort, and years since migration. In addition, there is a full set of shift terms for each combination of own and spouse Mexican American generation as well as dummies for spouse white non-Hispanic and spouse other non-Mexican origin. Based on these regressions, figures 2.7–2.9 show assimilation profiles for Mexican immigrant women and men with an immigrant spouse who came to the United States at the same time (relative to the reference group of third-generation white non-Hispanics who were married to third-generation white non-Hispanics).

We begin by considering the results for annual hours, which are the key variable for the family investment hypothesis, and also the variable for which we obtained the most striking evidence of assimilation for the full sample of Mexican American women. As may be seen in the table and figure 2.7, the results for married women are quite similar to those for the full female population and thus do not support the family migration model. Married immigrant women tend to have large ceteris paribus labor supply shortfalls upon arrival in the United States and steep positive assimilation with time in the United States. So, for example, married women in the 1971–1980 arrival cohort who have a Mexican immigrant spouse who arrived in the same period are estimated to supply 556 hours less per year when they first come to the United States; however, after ten years in the United States, the shortfall has been reduced by more than half to 265 hours, and after twenty years, to only 36 hours. Immigrant men also have an hours shortfall at arrival and positive assimilation profiles; however, these are both less dramatic than for women: for married men who migrated with a Mexican spouse, the arrival hours shortfall for the 1971–1980 cohort is 272 hours, a differential that falls to 109 hours after ten years and

26. We again note, however, that third-generation Mexican Americans must self-identify. Marriage outside the Mexican American community may reduce their propensity to self-identify as Mexican American or at least be correlated with a reduced propensity to so identify. Again, see Duncan and Trejo (chap. 7 in this volume).

Table 2.6 Selected results for demographic and employment outcomes, married couple sample

	No. of children <18 yrs		Annual work hours		Log wages (FT)	
	Coef.	SE	Coef.	SE	Coef.	SE
A. Married women						
education	−0.026	0.001	68.49	1.00	0.097	0.001
spouse education	0.0062	0.0006	−8.98	0.43	0.0031	0.0003
immig: pre-1961 arrival	0.476	0.250	−835.70	172.85	0.025	0.160
immig: 1961–70 arrival	−0.079	0.155	−926.21	124.09	−0.061	0.122
immig: 1971–80 arrival	−0.084	0.120	−777.13	101.22	−0.114	0.106
immig: 1981–90 arrival	0.026	0.095	−733.33	77.97	−0.187	0.085
immig: 1991–96 arrival	−0.041	0.073	−729.16	59.08	−0.217	0.065
immig: 1997–2002 arrival	−0.165	0.070	−725.28	57.72	−0.202	0.061
spouse immig: pre-1961 arrival	0.604	0.208	−38.58	155.68	0.045	0.146
spouse immig: 1961–70 arrival	0.298	0.147	89.50	123.06	0.058	0.117
spouse immig: 1971–80 arrival	0.270	0.124	220.94	103.63	0.116	0.101
spouse immig: 1981–90 arrival	0.139	0.098	135.84	79.77	0.020	0.079
spouse immig: 1991–96 arrival	0.106	0.077	161.19	63.00	0.055	0.061
spouse immig: 1997–2002 arrival	0.090	0.077	149.58	63.68	0.077	0.062
years since migration (ysm)	0.050	0.008	43.41	6.27	0.007	0.008
ysm squared (/100)	−0.141	0.023	−54.75	14.07	−0.018	0.017
spouse years since migration (sysm)	0.019	0.008	−11.17	6.01	−0.008	0.006
sysm squared (/100)	−0.064	0.017	23.68	11.15	0.019	0.012
Mex imm, spouse second-gen. Mexican	0.157	0.072	−53.79	56.94	0.016	0.052
Mex imm, spouse third-gen. Mexican	−0.012	0.089	−40.70	70.65	−0.030	0.060
second-gen. Mexican, spouse Mex immig	0.219	0.063	−70.35	51.43	−0.124	0.041
Both second-gen. Mexican	0.322	0.050	−8.49	36.69	−0.067	0.029
second-gen. Mexican, spouse third-gen. Mexican	0.340	0.055	87.72	43.75	−0.083	0.032
third-gen. Mexican, spouse Mex imm	0.304	0.072	−127.66	58.73	−0.111	0.046
third-gen. Mexican, spouse second-gen. Mexican	0.252	0.052	99.78	38.80	−0.095	0.028
Both third-gen. Mexican	0.336	0.026	−3.48	20.26	−0.124	0.016
B. Married men						
education			49.97	0.77	0.076	0.001
spouse education			2.37	0.34	0.0024	0.0003
immig: pre-1961 arrival			−448.36	133.57	−0.222	0.103
immig: 1961–70 arrival			−294.15	103.05	−0.282	0.075
immig: 1971–80 arrival			−141.68	86.72	−0.263	0.063
immig: 1981–90 arrival			−74.30	66.73	−0.326	0.049
immig: 1991–96 arrival			−40.52	51.68	−0.327	0.038
immig: 1997–2002 arrival			−103.89	53.14	−0.241	0.039
spouse immig: pre-1961 arrival			124.85	147.37	−0.004	0.117
spouse immig: 1961–70 arrival			−33.47	105.57	−0.008	0.078
spouse immig: 1971–80 arrival			−129.98	86.06	−0.027	0.062
spouse immig: 1981–90 arrival			−127.36	65.58	−0.099	0.048

Table 2.6   (continued)

	No. of children <18 yrs		Annual work hours		Log wages (FT)	
	Coef.	SE	Coef.	SE	Coef.	SE
spouse immig: 1991–96 arrival			−49.92	49.06	−0.060	0.036
spouse immig: 1997–2002 arrival			−61.23	48.47	−0.115	0.035
years since migration (ysm)			11.65	5.24	0.018	0.004
ysm squared (/100)			1.08	10.38	−0.033	0.009
spouse years since migration (sysm)			7.04	5.21	−0.005	0.004
sysm squared (/100)			−25.66	11.28	0.006	0.009
Mex imm, spouse second-gen Mexican			−59.82	42.86	−0.003	0.031
Mex imm, spouse third-gen Mexican			−140.93	50.28	−0.053	0.037
second-gen. Mexican, spouse Mex immig			27.05	47.90	−0.107	0.035
Both second-gen. Mexican			−94.26	31.69	−0.146	0.024
second-gen. Mexican, spouse third gen. Mexican			−72.14	33.45	−0.189	0.024
third-gen. Mexican, spouse Mex imm			−67.38	57.66	−0.158	0.042
third-gen. Mexican, spouse second gen. Mexican			−171.15	36.93	−0.208	0.027
Both third-gen. Mexican			−145.14	17.22	−0.185	0.013

Notes: Controls include age, spouse age, region, msa, calif, texas, and dummies for spouse white non-Hispanic, and spouse other non-Mexican origin. Female sample includes white non-Hispanic third-generation women married to white non-Hispanic third-generation men and married women of Mexican origin; male sample includes white non-Hispanic third-generation men married to white non-Hispanic third-generation women and married men of Mexican origin.

actually becomes a 4-hour excess after twenty years. In earlier work using 1980 and 1990 Census data (Blau et al. 2003), we showed that, among immigrants to the United States in general, married men and women had similarly steep assimilation profiles relative to average hours worked by natives. Moreover, in supplementary unpublished results for Blau et al. (2003), we found that for the Central American sending region, married immigrant women's work hours increased by about 106 with twenty years in the United States, compared to a very similar figure of 116 for married men. Mexican immigrants in the 1990s and early 2000s stand out from both the overall pattern for immigrants in general and for immigrants from the Central American region in that the profile for Mexican immigrants is much steeper for women than men. This conclusion holds both absolutely and relative to average labor supply.[27]

27. Of course, in our earlier work, we used 1980 and 1990 Census data, and in the current paper, we use data from the more recent 1994–2003 period. But it does appear that Mexican immigrant women's work hours assimilate especially rapidly.

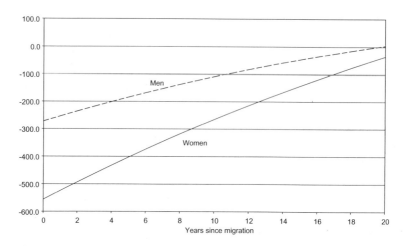

Fig. 2.7 **Assimilation profiles for married Mexican immigrant men and women who immigrated with Mexican spouse, annual work hours, 1971–1980 arrival cohort**

Second- and third-generation–Mexican American women married to second- or third-generation Mexican-American men have smaller deficits (or in some cases, slightly higher work hours) relative to comparable white natives than immigrants from the 1971–1980 cohort at arrival or after ten years in the United States—table 2.6 shows hours effects of –8 to +100 work hours relative to the white non-Hispanic reference group. However, as in the case of the full sample, most of the convergence in labor supply patterns to otherwise similar individuals in the white non-Hispanic reference group occurs in the first generation.

Turning to assimilation in log wages we again find similar patterns to those observed for the full sample (see table 2.6). Figure 2.8 shows results for immigrant men and women who migrated from Mexico with their spouse in the 1971–1980 or 1981–1990 period. Except for women in the 1971–1980 arrival cohort, we see large wage deficits with otherwise similar native non-Hispanic whites in the reference group, and wage profiles for the 1981–1990 cohort are considerably lower than those for the 1971–1980 cohort. As in the full sample, while men's wages rise with time in the United States (wage assimilation is actually steeper for married men than for the full sample), there is no evidence of positive wage assimilation for women. This pattern is consistent with the family migration model in that men appear to be investing in their own human capital, while women's wages are seemingly not affected by time in the United States. However, the same reasoning we used earlier about the potential effects of selectivity on immigrant women's wage assimilation applies here. Specifically, it is possible that the women with longer U.S. residence in the wage sample include more recent labor force entrants with less experience and thus may be less posi-

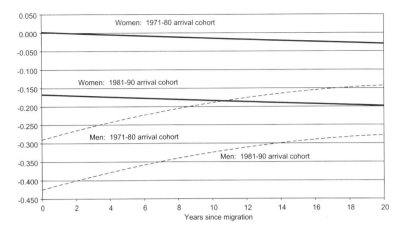

Fig. 2.8   Assimilation profiles for married Mexican men and women who immigrated with Mexican spouse, log hourly earnings, full-time wage and salary workers, 1971–1980 and 1981–1990 arrival cohorts

tively selected than the female sample of full-time workers among more recent arrivals. However, when we implemented Heckman (1979) selectivity bias correction techniques for married women (identified this time by the exclusion of number of children under six and number of children between six and seventeen years old), we still did not find any evidence of positive wage assimilation for immigrant women.[28]

As in the preceding, we do not find much evidence of wage convergence across generations, controlling for measured characteristics. For example, for immigrant men from the 1971–1980 (1981–1990) arrival cohort, the wage deficit relative to the white non-Hispanic reference group falls from .29 (.43) log points at arrival to .14 (.28) after 20 years. For second- and third-generation men married to U.S.-born Mexican origin women, the pay shortfall for men ranges from .15 to .21 log points, suggesting some evidence of moderate intergenerational wage assimilation only for the 1981–1990 cohort. For women in the 1971–1980 cohort, there is hardly any wage gap relative to comparable white non-Hispanics. But for women in the 1981–1990 cohort, the gaps are .17 log points at arrival and .20 log points after twenty years. Mexican American women of later generations married to U.S.-born Mexican origin men have ceteris paribus log wage deficits of .06 to .12 relative to white non-Hispanics. Again, little intergenerational assimilation is implied for the 1971–1980 cohort and some modest improvement across generations is suggested for the 1981–1990 cohort.

Finally, we may consider evidence of assimilation in fertility. As was the

28. In both table 2.6 and in the selectivity-bias corrected results, there was a modestly negative, insignificant wage profile for immigrant women who migrated with their husbands.

case for the full sample, married Mexican immigrant women (who migrated with a Mexican spouse) tend to have more children than their counterparts upon arrival in the United States, though this difference has been declining with successive cohorts and has recently become negative. Fertility compared to otherwise similar individuals in the white non-Hispanic reference group then increases further with time in the United States. (Note the own and spouse cohort and years-since-migration (YSM) effects must be summed to make this comparison.) For example, in the 1971–1980 cohort, women have somewhat more (.19) children than comparable white non-Hispanic women upon arrival, a gap that rises to .76 after 20 years in the United States. The 1997–2002 cohort that begins with .075 *fewer* children than comparable white non-Hispanics is estimated to have .50 more children after twenty years. The fertility difference falls across generations, but the fertility of second- and third-generation–Mexican-American women in Mexican American families is still a bit higher than the native reference group: .22 to .34 (second generation) and .25 to .34 (third generation). However, based on the declining relative fertility of newer cohorts of immigrants, we might expect excess fertility of future second- and third-generation–Mexican American women to be even smaller than this.

The positive relationship between fertility and time in the United States that we obtain for immigrants is illustrated in figure 2.9 for the 1971–1980 arrival cohort. This relationship could be consistent with the family investment model: fertility may be deferred while wives' focus on the labor market in order to support their husband's human capital investments.

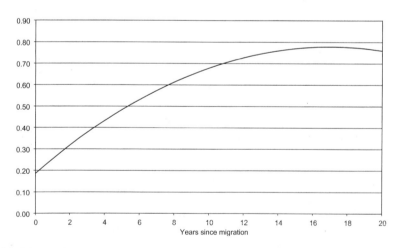

Fig. 2.9   Assimilation profile for married Mexican immigrant women who immigrated with Mexican spouse, number of children under eighteen, 1971–1980 arrival cohort

However, this is unlikely given the strong *positive* assimilation that we have found for wives' labor supply. In light of this, we believe that the pattern of fertility most likely represents a disruption of fertility due to immigration. One factor leading the family to defer fertility may be a desire to postpone at least some childbearing to a time when the family is on a firmer financial footing. But, again, given the labor supply patterns we observe, this is likely to be a time when both spouses are faring better in terms of labor market incomes.

2.6   Conclusions

This paper has examined gender and the labor market and demographic assimilation of Mexican Americans, both within and across generations. Published data show a much more traditional gender division of labor in the family in Mexico than in the United States, with women in Mexico having considerably lower labor force participation and higher fertility than those in the United States as well as lower education both absolutely and relative to Mexican men. Our data suggest that these source country patterns strongly influence the outcomes and behavior of Mexican immigrants on arrival in the United States. Both male and female immigrants have much lower levels of education than the native reference group (third-generation non-Hispanic whites), although immigrants of both sexes have somewhat higher levels of education than the average for Mexico and gender differences in educational attainment among immigrants are minimal. Educational attainment of Mexican American men and women increases substantially between the first and second generations, but not beyond. Controlling for education and other characteristics including location on arrival in the United States, immigrant women are more likely to be married with spouse present and have higher fertility and much lower labor supply than the native reference group. The key question then is how these patterns change with time in the United States of immigrants and over the second and third generations.

Our most striking finding is the dramatic assimilation in labor supply for female immigrants with time in the United States. For example, upon arrival in the United States, the 1971–1980 cohort of Mexican women had a ceteris paribus shortfall of 455 hours relative to non-Hispanic whites; this fell to 219 hours after ten years of residence and 31 hours after twenty years. The gap remained small in the second and third generations. Consistent with a more traditional division of labor in the first generation, immigrant men's annual hours tended to be somewhat higher than those of non-Hispanic whites upon arrival, all else equal, and showed moderate positive assimilation with time in the United States. In contrast, Mexican American men in later generations actually have somewhat lower labor supply than natives. Taking the male and female results together, Mexican American–non-Hispanic white differences in gender specialization in labor supply are very small for long-term immigrants and are entirely eliminated by the second generation.

When we do not control for education and other characteristics, however, immigrants, as a low education group, have hours shortfalls relative to non-Hispanic whites for both men and women; the gaps are quite sizable for women and remain large, even with positive assimilation in hours. In the case of women, particularly, there is assimilation between the first and second generation, due to rising educational attainment, but no further progress between the second and third generation.

Wage differences between female immigrants and non-Hispanic whites, controlling for other factors, are far less marked than labor supply differences and tend to be smaller than the immigrant–non-Hispanic white wage gap for men, though both show a deteriorating wage position of immigrants beginning in the 1980s. While male wage gaps decline modestly with exposure to the U.S. labor market, in contrast to the labor supply results, we find no evidence of positive wage assimilation for women. This may reflect the limitations of the synthetic cohort approach. Positive assimilation in employment means that, as years since migration increase, the wage sample likely includes more new labor market entrants and may be less positively selected in other ways as well. We present some evidence based on a correction for selectivity bias that is consistent with this reasoning, although wage assimilation, even based on these analyses, is quite moderate. For both men and women, rising educational attainment in subsequent generations contributes to a considerable narrowing of the raw wage gap with non-Hispanic whites, but we again find no evidence of convergence beyond the second generation. The lack of further assimilation between the second and third generation thus characterizes our findings for education, labor supply, and wages and mirrors results from some earlier studies of Mexican Americans.

Results for assimilation on the demographic outcomes are also mixed. Over time in the United States, female immigrants assimilate toward the native reference group but remain more likely to be married, ceteris paribus. While male immigrants are actually less likely to be married with spouse present than otherwise similar non-Hispanic whites upon arrival, their marriage incidence increases with time in the United States and, after long residence, they are predicted to be more likely to be married than natives. Across generations, both male and female immigrants assimilate to the patterns in the native non-Hispanic white reference group, controlling for characteristics including education, and are no more likely to be married. When controls for education and other characteristics are omitted, second- and third-generation–Mexican-American men and women are both less likely to be married than non-Hispanic whites.

While immigrant women have higher fertility than non-Hispanic whites, all else equal, the immigrant-native differential upon arrival has been declining with successive arrival cohorts, reflecting sharp declines in fertility in the source country. In contrast to the findings for marriage, however, we find no evidence that the higher fertility of Mexican immigrant women on arrival assimilates toward native levels. Rather, the gap tends to increase still further with time in the United States; this is consistent with the hypothesis that that immigration disrupts or delays immigrant women's fertility, causing their relative fertility to rise with residence in the United States and counterbalancing or obscuring whatever assimilation might have otherwise taken place. These disruptions may be due to men arriving in the United States before their wives, delayed courtship, or delayed marriage. Unfortunately we don't have data on the time of marriage that might allow us to distinguish among these explanations. While the size of the Mexican American–non-Hispanic white fertility differential declines across generations, it is not eliminated.

Finally, we separately examined results for married men and women and confirmed our findings based on the full sample, including the dramatic assimilation in labor supply of immigrant women, for this group. This means further that we did not support the family investment model, which has recently been proposed as a model of the immigrant assimilation process in a family context (e.g., Baker and Benjamin 1997). This view holds that, upon arrival, immigrant husbands invest in their human capital, while wives work to provide the family with liquidity during the investment period. The model predicts rapid positive assimilation in labor supply for husbands and decreases in wives' labor supply over time relative to the native reference group. On the contrary, we found positive assimilation in labor supply for both immigrant husbands and wives, with dramatically faster assimilation for wives.

Appendix

Creation of Hourly Earnings Variable

To analyze hourly earnings, we restrict our sample to wage and salary workers who were employed full time (defined as those with at least thirty-five usual weekly work hours). Wage and salary workers were defined as those with zero self-employment and zero farm self-employment income in the prior year who were wage and salary workers for their longest job during that year. The CPS reports two wage and salary income variables: one for the main job and one for all other jobs. The main job values were top-coded at $99,000 for 1994 and 1995; $150,000 for 1996–2002; and $200,000

for 2003. The values for all other jobs were topcoded at $99,999 for 1994
and 1995; $25,000 for 1996–2002; and $35,000 for 2003. For the main job
earnings variables, we used the following conventions for topcoding: for
1994–2002, we multiplied the topcoded value by 1.45, and for 2003, we
forced all topcoded values to equal $150,000 × 1.45. For the other jobs
variable, we forced all values above $25,000 to equal $25,000 and then multiplied this by 1.45. We then added the adjusted variables to form annual
wage and salary earnings. These were converted to hourly earnings by di-
viding by weeks worked times usual hours per week. We then defined
hourly earnings in 2000 dollars using the personal consumption expenditures gross domestic product (GDP) deflator. We kept only those values between $2 and $200 in 2000 dollars. Results were not sensitive to alternative
assumptions about topcoding.

Table 2A.1   Sample sizes for basic regression analyses

Group	Men	Women
Third-generation white, non-Hispanics	286,531	300,008
Mexican Americans		
Immigrants	20,733	18,858
Second generation	7,456	8,214
Third generation	11,348	12,664

Table 2A.2   Selected regression results for demographic and labor market outcomes, controlling only for age and year

| | Marriage | | | | No. of children <18 yrs | |
| | Men | | Women | | Women | |
Dependent variable	Coef.	SE	Coef.	SE	Coef.	SE
immig: pre-1961 arrival	−0.171	0.051	0.189	0.056	1.319	0.190
immig: 1961–70 arrival	−0.191	0.033	0.158	0.036	0.598	0.100
immig: 1971–80 arrival	−0.208	0.024	0.125	0.027	0.417	0.069
immig: 1981–90 arrival	−0.117	0.017	0.116	0.020	0.477	0.052
immig: 1991–96 arrival	−0.095	0.011	0.186	0.013	0.396	0.034
immig: 1997–2002 arrival	−0.157	0.010	0.115	0.012	0.184	0.030
years since mig. (ysm)	0.017	0.002	−0.004	0.002	0.058	0.006
ysm squared (/100)	−0.028	0.004	−0.005	0.005	−0.188	0.017
second-gen. Mexican American	−0.038	0.005	−0.035	0.005	0.386	0.014
third-gen. Mexican American	−0.031	0.005	−0.048	0.005	0.266	0.012

| | Annual work hours | | | | Unemployment | | In labor force | |
| | Men | | Women | | Men | | Women | |
	Coef.	SE	Coef.	SE	Coef.	SE	Coef.	SE
immig: pre-1961 arrival	−482.3	101.2	−949.3	114.4	0.052	0.029	0.191	0.036
immig: 1961–70 arrival	−438.0	64.1	−1000.9	74.6	0.086	0.018	0.179	0.023
immig: 1971–80 arrival	−340.3	48.1	−839.0	56.4	0.055	0.013	0.143	0.018
immig: 1981–90 arrival	−234.4	34.1	−835.0	40.2	0.038	0.009	0.139	0.014
immig: 1991–96 arrival	−130.8	22.4	−839.2	26.0	0.019	0.006	0.127	0.009
immig: 1997–2002 arrival	−82.8	19.4	−751.5	24.0	0.012	0.005	0.092	0.008
years since mig. (ysm)	6.6	3.3	26.9	3.9	−0.001	0.001	−0.004	0.001
ysm squared (/100)	1.2	8.1	−25.9	9.3	−0.001	0.002	0.001	0.003
second-gen. Mexican American	−148.2	10.7	−111.8	11.3	0.032	0.003	0.047	0.003
third-gen. Mexican American	−177.2	9.0	−122.2	9.3	0.027	0.003	0.026	0.002

| | Log wages (FT) | | | |
| | Men | | Women | |
	Coef.	SE	Coef.	SE
immig: pre-1961 arrival	−0.402	0.087	−0.335	0.126
immig: 1961–70 arrival	−0.459	0.052	−0.394	0.084
immig: 1971–80 arrival	−0.548	0.039	−0.432	0.068
immig: 1981–90 arrival	−0.606	0.028	−0.553	0.051
immig: 1991–96 arrival	−0.573	0.019	−0.560	0.036
immig: 1997–2002 arrival	−0.541	0.016	−0.563	0.032
years since mig. (ysm)	0.006	0.003	−0.004	0.005
ysm squared (/100)	−0.011	0.007	0.015	0.012
second-gen. Mexican American	−0.175	0.010	−0.136	0.011
third-gen. Mexican American	−0.214	0.008	−0.185	0.009

Table 2A.3   Means of explanatory variables, by group

Explanatory variable	Non-Hispanic whites		Immigrants		Mexican Americans			
	Third generation				Second generation		Third generation	
	Men	Women	Men	Women	Men	Women	Men	Women
age	38.90	39.18	34.20	35.21	31.58	31.82	34.14	34.85
age squared	1,687.5	1,710.7	1,298.6	1,379.9	1,190.9	1,207.0	1,324.7	1,372.4
age^3	79,370.5	80,928.9	54,159.1	59,350.8	52,102.3	52,987.5	56,966.0	59,629.1
age^4	3,959,187	4,058,389	2,444,970	2,755,546	2,535,968	2,581,753	2,647,491	2,792,618
education	13.240	13.220	8.670	8.667	11.718	11.683	11.913	11.847
immig: pre-1961 arrival	0	0	0.020	0.023	0	0	0	0
immig: 1961–70 arrival	0	0	0.060	0.068	0	0	0	0
immig: 1971–80 arrival	0	0	0.215	0.218	0	0	0	0
immig: 1981–90 arrival	0	0	0.351	0.323	0	0	0	0
immig: 1991–96 arrival	0	0	0.218	0.248	0	0	0	0
immig: 1997–2002 arrival	0	0	0.135	0.120	0	0	0	0
years since mig. (ysm)	0	0	14.34	14.69	0	0	0	0
ysm squared (/100)	0	0	3.1	3.2	0	0	0	0
year = 1994	0.102	0.102	0.085	0.086	0.093	0.087	0.089	0.085
year = 1995	0.102	0.102	0.094	0.090	0.093	0.094	0.084	0.085
year = 1996	0.102	0.101	0.092	0.093	0.097	0.093	0.089	0.089
year = 1997	0.100	0.100	0.099	0.093	0.099	0.095	0.092	0.089
year = 1998	0.100	0.100	0.099	0.097	0.105	0.096	0.099	0.096
year = 1999	0.100	0.101	0.095	0.097	0.093	0.099	0.110	0.109

year = 2000	0.100	0.100	0.100	0.103	0.090	0.102	0.108	0.109
year = 2001	0.099	0.099	0.102	0.106	0.097	0.107	0.102	0.112
year = 2002	0.098	0.098	0.117	0.116	0.115	0.111	0.112	0.109
year = 2003 (omitted category)	0.097	0.097	0.118	0.120	0.118	0.115	0.117	0.116
lives in metropolitan area	0.762	0.762	0.905	0.912	0.900	0.901	0.856	0.861
lives in California	0.079	0.078	0.460	0.493	0.456	0.450	0.286	0.294
lives in Texas	0.057	0.057	0.200	0.213	0.284	0.302	0.421	0.431
New England Census Division	0.055	0.055	0.002	0.001	0.001	0.001	0.002	0.002
Middle Atlantic Census Division	0.133	0.134	0.032	0.023	0.007	0.007	0.006	0.005
East North Central Census Division	0.190	0.190	0.081	0.071	0.073	0.069	0.053	0.050
West North Central Census Division	0.092	0.090	0.018	0.015	0.015	0.015	0.022	0.018
South Atlantic Census Division	0.173	0.173	0.058	0.038	0.022	0.023	0.025	0.023
East South Central Census Division	0.071	0.073	0.006	0.004	0.002	0.002	0.006	0.005
West South Central Census Division	0.099	0.099	0.207	0.218	0.290	0.309	0.431	0.441
Mountain Census Division	0.065	0.064	0.108	0.112	0.116	0.109	0.156	0.145
Pacific Census Division (omitted category)	0.122	0.121	0.488	0.516	0.474	0.465	0.300	0.311
Sample size	286,531	300,008	20,733	8,858	7,456	8,214	11,348	12,664

Table 2A.4   **Selected regression results for demographic and labor market outcomes (adult immigrants only)**

Dependent variable	Marriage				No. of children <18 yrs			
	Men		Women		Women		Women	
	Coef.	SE	Coef.	SE	Coef.	SE	Coef.	SE
immig: pre-1961 arrival	0.036	0.085	0.146	0.088				
immig: 1961–70 arrival	−0.054	0.046	0.184	0.051	0.706	0.199	0.583	0.192
immig: 1971–80 arrival	−0.100	0.032	0.138	0.035	0.314	0.090	0.197	0.087
immig: 1981–90 arrival	−0.077	0.023	0.100	0.025	0.172	0.066	0.082	0.063
immig: 1991–96 arrival	−0.052	0.015	0.191	0.016	0.150	0.044	0.011	0.043
immig: 1997–2002 arrival	−0.116	0.012	0.132	0.014	−0.005	0.036	−0.103	0.034
years since mig. (ysm)	0.022	0.003	−0.002	0.003	0.088	0.008	0.091	0.008
ysm squared (/100)	−0.046	0.008	−0.006	0.008	−0.344	0.031	−0.346	0.030
second-gen. Mexican American	−0.0002	0.006	−0.006	0.006	0.377	0.015	0.373	0.014
third-gen. Mexican American	−0.005	0.005	−0.030	0.005	0.241	0.012	0.260	0.012
Control for marital status					No		Yes	

	Annual work hours				Unemployment		In labor force	
	Men		Women		Men		Women	
	Coef.	SE	Coef.	SE	Coef.	SE	Coef.	SE
immig: pre-1961 arrival	−79.6	165.0	−378.5	178.4	0.014	0.055	0.151	0.060
immig: 1961–70 arrival	−135.2	90.4	−692.9	102.8	0.085	0.025	0.054	0.032
immig: 1971–80 arrival	−29.1	62.4	−453.2	70.9	0.033	0.017	0.084	0.023
immig: 1981–90 arrival	−20.7	45.2	−471.9	51.4	0.018	0.012	0.087	0.018
immig: 1991–96 arrival	27.1	29.2	−551.5	33.1	−0.009	0.008	0.091	0.012
immig: 1997–2002 arrival	96.4	22.8	−486.1	27.7	−0.019	0.006	0.055	0.009
years since mig. (ysm)	17.7	5.0	29.8	5.6	−0.002	0.001	−0.004	0.002
ysm squared (/100)	−22.2	15.2	−27.7	16.9	0.001	0.004	0.004	0.006
second-gen. Mexican American	−54.2	10.9	−12.4	11.5	0.019	0.003	0.034	0.003
third-gen. Mexican American	−103.5	9.3	−20.6	9.7	0.017	0.003	0.015	0.003

	Log wages (FT)			
	Men		Women	
	Coef.	SE	Coef.	SE
immig: pre-1961 arrival	−0.079	0.178	−0.185	0.223
immig: 1961–70 arrival	−0.191	0.071	−0.051	0.102
immig: 1971–80 arrival	−0.172	0.046	−0.007	0.076
immig: 1981–90 arrival	−0.341	0.034	−0.170	0.059
immig: 1991–96 arrival	−0.303	0.023	−0.220	0.042
immig: 1997–2002 arrival	−0.247	0.018	−0.243	0.032
years since mig. (ysm)	0.002	0.004	−0.004	0.007
ysm squared (/100)	0.002	0.012	0.013	0.019
second-gen. Mexican American	−0.127	0.010	−0.082	0.010
third-gen. Mexican American	−0.138	0.008	−0.093	0.008

Note: Other controls include: a quartic in age, years of schooling, eight Census region dummies, an MSA dummy, dummies for California and Texas, and year dummies.

Table 2A.5   Industrial and occupational distribution, by gender

	White, non-Hispanic natives with native parents		Mexican immigrants		Mexican immigrants, in U.S. at least 10 years		Mexican immigrants (mig. age ≥18)		Mexican immigrants (mig. age ≥18, in U.S. at least 10 years)		Second-generation Mexican Americans		Third-generation Mexican Americans	
	Men	Women	Men	Women	Men	Women	Men	Women	Men	Women	Men	Women	Men	Women
Industry														
Agriculture	0.034	0.015	0.149	0.066	0.138	0.053	0.163	0.080	0.160	0.071	0.047	0.016	0.035	0.011
Mining	0.009	0.002	0.006	0.001	0.007	0.001	0.004	0.001	0.005	0.000	0.009	0.001	0.014	0.002
Construction	0.117	0.016	0.179	0.008	0.170	0.007	0.181	0.007	0.164	0.005	0.117	0.011	0.126	0.011
Mfg. nondurable	0.068	0.048	0.105	0.151	0.102	0.145	0.109	0.179	0.110	0.186	0.074	0.042	0.072	0.038
Mfg. durable	0.132	0.052	0.116	0.086	0.128	0.095	0.115	0.087	0.131	0.100	0.090	0.043	0.099	0.044
Transportation	0.057	0.024	0.036	0.012	0.046	0.014	0.031	0.010	0.041	0.012	0.068	0.022	0.062	0.022
Communication utilities	0.035	0.017	0.007	0.005	0.009	0.005	0.006	0.003	0.006	0.003	0.029	0.016	0.033	0.025
Wholesale trade	0.051	0.025	0.043	0.036	0.048	0.038	0.043	0.037	0.048	0.041	0.051	0.028	0.052	0.023
Retail trade	0.160	0.210	0.208	0.247	0.185	0.219	0.202	0.235	0.176	0.197	0.216	0.268	0.200	0.245
Finance, real estate and insurance	0.051	0.083	0.015	0.031	0.019	0.039	0.014	0.022	0.020	0.026	0.030	0.073	0.033	0.071
Business and repair services	0.073	0.050	0.070	0.062	0.068	0.058	0.070	0.063	0.067	0.055	0.080	0.046	0.072	0.053
Private household services	0.001	0.009	0.004	0.065	0.003	0.056	0.004	0.079	0.004	0.072	0.002	0.016	0.002	0.012
Other personal services	0.006	0.021	0.006	0.038	0.006	0.037	0.007	0.043	0.006	0.045	0.007	0.022	0.008	0.021
Entertainment and rec. services	0.022	0.021	0.016	0.009	0.016	0.010	0.016	0.008	0.017	0.009	0.024	0.019	0.020	0.020
Health services	0.032	0.141	0.011	0.061	0.013	0.077	0.008	0.052	0.010	0.070	0.032	0.122	0.030	0.138
Education services	0.049	0.130	0.014	0.058	0.020	0.073	0.013	0.042	0.019	0.053	0.044	0.128	0.047	0.130

(*continued*)

Table 2A.5 (continued)

	White, non-Hispanic natives with native parents		Mexican immigrants		Mexican immigrants, in U.S. at least 10 years		Mexican immigrants (mig. age ≥18)		Mexican immigrants (mig. age ≥18, in U.S. at least 10 years)		Second-generation Mexican Americans		Third-generation Mexican Americans	
	Men	Women	Men	Women	Men	Women	Men	Women	Men	Women	Men	Women	Men	Women
Other professional services	0.038	0.040	0.005	0.008	0.006	0.009	0.004	0.004	0.004	0.003	0.014	0.031	0.019	0.024
Social services	0.016	0.057	0.006	0.044	0.008	0.048	0.006	0.042	0.008	0.044	0.016	0.055	0.017	0.062
Public administration	0.047	0.040	0.005	0.012	0.007	0.016	0.003	0.006	0.004	0.008	0.050	0.041	0.058	0.047
Occupation														
Manager	0.159	0.144	0.031	0.037	0.040	0.045	0.025	0.026	0.031	0.030	0.084	0.093	0.085	0.108
Professional & technical	0.163	0.223	0.024	0.045	0.032	0.052	0.017	0.031	0.020	0.028	0.087	0.130	0.094	0.142
Clerical	0.052	0.245	0.025	0.108	0.032	0.133	0.017	0.060	0.021	0.067	0.080	0.303	0.077	0.292
Sales	0.122	0.136	0.038	0.090	0.044	0.092	0.032	0.064	0.037	0.066	0.108	0.168	0.091	0.146
Personal service	0.058	0.125	0.166	0.304	0.138	0.273	0.170	0.351	0.145	0.320	0.102	0.151	0.092	0.160
Protective service	0.026	0.006	0.005	0.003	0.007	0.003	0.002	0.002	0.003	0.002	0.031	0.008	0.038	0.007
Health service	0.003	0.029	0.002	0.032	0.002	0.041	0.001	0.030	0.001	0.043	0.005	0.038	0.005	0.045
Farm manager	0.014	0.005	0.005	0.001	0.005	0.001	0.005	0.002	0.006	0.002	0.003	0.001	0.002	0.001
Farmworker	0.023	0.006	0.151	0.075	0.136	0.063	0.168	0.092	0.160	0.087	0.049	0.014	0.038	0.008
Craft	0.194	0.019	0.231	0.049	0.243	0.050	0.235	0.052	0.247	0.055	0.192	0.021	0.216	0.022
Operative, exc. transportation equip.	0.063	0.036	0.136	0.200	0.137	0.195	0.141	0.233	0.150	0.248	0.076	0.042	0.076	0.040
Transportation equipment operative	0.067	0.009	0.066	0.006	0.080	0.007	0.060	0.005	0.074	0.004	0.075	0.010	0.088	0.009
Laborer	0.056	0.016	0.121	0.051	0.104	0.045	0.127	0.053	0.104	0.049	0.108	0.023	0.098	0.022

Note: Sample includes all workers with a reported occupation and industry for the previous year.

References

Angrist, Joshua. 2002. How do sex ratios affect marriage and labor markets? Evidence from America's second generation. *Quarterly Journal of Economics* 117 (3): 997–1038.

Baker, Michael, and Dwayne Benjamin. 1997. The role of the family in immigrants' labor-market activity: An evaluation of alternative explanations. *American Economic Review* 87 (4): 705–27.

Baker, Susan Gonzalez. 1999. Mexican-origin women in southwestern labor markets. In *Latinas and African American women at work,* ed. Irene Browne, 244–69. New York: Russell Sage Foundation.

Blank, Rebecca M. 1997. *It takes a nation: A new agenda for fighting poverty.* New York: Russell Sage Foundation.

Blau, Francine D. 1992. The fertility of immigrant women: Evidence from high-fertility source countries. In *Immigration and the work force: Economic consequences for the United States and source areas,* ed. George J. Borjas and Richard B. Freeman, 93–133. Chicago: University of Chicago Press.

Blau, Francine D., Marianne A. Ferber, and Anne E. Winkler. 2002. *The economics of women, men, and work.* 4th ed. Upper Saddle River, NJ: Prentice Hall.

Blau, Francine D., Lawrence M. Kahn, Joan Moriarty, and Andre Souza. 2003. The role of the family in immigrants' labor-market activity: An evaluation of alternative explanations: Comment. *American Economic Review* 93 (1): 429–47.

Borjas, George J. 1985. Assimilation, changes in cohort quality, and the earnings of immigrants. *Journal of Labor Economics* 3 (4): 463–89.

———. 1995. Assimilation and changes in cohort quality revisited: What happened to immigrant earnings in the 1980s? *Journal of Labor Economics* 13 (2): 201–45.

Browne, Irene, ed. 1999. *Latinas and African American Women at work.* New York: Russell Sage Foundation.

Card, David. 2004. Is the new immigration really so bad? IZA Discussion Paper no. 1119. Bonn, Germany: Institute for the Study of Labor, April.

Card, David, John DiNardo, and Eugena Estes. 2000. The more things change: Immigrants and the children of immigrants in the 1940s, the 1970s, and the 1990s. In *Issues in the economics of immigration,* ed. George J. Borjas, 227–69. Chicago: University of Chicago Press.

Chiquiar, Daniel, and Gordon Hanson. 2005. International migration, self-selection, and the distribution of wages: Evidence from Mexico and the United States. *Journal of Political Economy* 113 (2): 239–81.

Cobb-Clark, Deborah A., and Vincent Hildebrand. 2004. The wealth of Mexican Americans. IZA Discussion Paper no. 1150. Bonn, Germany: Institute for the Study of Labor, May.

Corcoran, Mary, Colleen M. Heflin, and Belinda C. Reyes. 1999. The economic progress of Mexican and Puerto Rican women. In *Latinas and African American women at work,* ed. Irene Browne, 105–38. New York: Russell Sage Foundation.

Duleep, Harriet Orcutt, and Daniel J. Dowhan. 2002. Revisiting the family investment model with longitudinal data: The earnings growth of immigrant and U.S.-born women. IZA Discussion Paper no. 568. Bonn, Germany: Institute for the Study of Labor, September.

Duleep, Harriet Orcutt, and Seth Sanders. 1993. The decision to work by married immigrant women. *Industrial and Labor Relations Review* 46 (4): 677–90.

Friedberg, Rachel M. 1993. Immigration and the labor market. PhD diss. Massachusetts Institute of Technology.

Heckman, James J. 1979. Sample selection bias as a specification error. *Econometrica* 47:153–62.

International Labour Organization. International Labour Organization Web site. http://www.laborsta.ilo.org.

Jaeger, David A. 1997. Reconciling the old and new Census Bureau education questions: Recommendations for researchers. *Journal of Business & Economic Statistics* 15 (3): 300–309.

LaLonde, Robert J., and Robert H. Topel. 1992. The assimilation of immigrants in the U.S. labor market. In *Immigration and the work force: Economic consequences for the United States and source areas,* ed. George J. Borjas and Richard B. Freeman, 67–92. Chicago: University of Chicago Press.

Livingston, Gretchen, and Joan R. Kahn. 2002. An American dream unfulfilled: The limited mobility of Mexican Americans. *Social Science Quarterly* 83 (4): 1003–1012.

Long, James E. 1980. The effect of Americanization on earnings: Some evidence for women. *Journal of Political Economy* 88 (3): 620–29.

Macpherson, David A., and James B. Stewart. 1989. The labor force participation and earnings profiles of married immigrant females. *Quarterly Review of Economics and Business* 29 (3): 57–72.

Redstone, Ilana, and Douglas S. Massey. 2004. Coming to stay: An analysis of the U.S. Census question on immigrants' year of arrival. *Demography* 41 (4): 721–38.

Smith, James P. 2003. Assimilation across the Latino generations. *American Economic Review* 93 (2): 315–19.

Trejo, Stephen J. 1997. Why do Mexican Americans earn low wages? *Journal of Political Economy* 105 (6): 1235–68.

———. 2003. Intergenerational progress of Mexican-origin workers in the U.S. labor market. *Journal of Human Resources* 38 (3): 467–89.

U.S. Bureau of the Census. 2000. Industry and occupation 2000: Crosswalks Web site. http://www.census.gov/hhes/www/ioindex/crosswalks.html.

U.S. Department of Homeland Security, Office of Immigration Statistics. 2003. *Yearbook of immigration statistics 2002.* Washington, DC: Office of Immigration Statistics.

Waldfogel, Jane. 1998. Understanding the "family gap" in pay for women with children. *Journal of Economic Perspectives* 12 (1): 137–56.

3

Mexican Assimilation
in the United States

Edward P. Lazear

Immigrants to the United States from Mexico become assimilated into American society much less rapidly than do other groups. A few facts from the 2000 U.S. Census make the slowness of Mexican integration apparent.

1. About 80 percent of non-Mexican immigrants are fluent in English. Among Mexicans, the number is 49 percent.

Figure 3.1 shows the differences across groups in graphic detail. The groups depicted in the graph are the largest subgroups in the 2000 Census. Mexicans clearly have the lowest average levels of fluency.

English fluency depends on the amount of time that an individual has been in the country. Figure 3.2 makes clear that Mexicans start below other groups in levels of English fluency when they arrive in the United States and never catch up. The curves never converge. Other Hispanics start above and stay above Mexicans. Non-Hispanics are significantly more fluent in English than Hispanics at all times after arrival in the United States.

2. Non-Mexican (working) immigrants have average wage income of on average $21,000 per year. Mexican immigrants have average wage income of on average $12,000 per year.

3. The typical non-Mexican immigrant has a high school diploma. The typical Mexican immigrant has less than an eighth grade education. Part of this may reflect differences in educational systems of the native country.

Edward P. Lazear is currently chairman of the Council of Economic Advisers. He is also the Jack Steele Parker Professor of Human Resources Management and Economics in the Graduate School of Business, and the Morris Arnold Cox Senior Fellow at the Hoover Institution, both at Stanford University.

This research was supported by CRESST and NBER. I am grateful to participants at the NBER conference on Mexican immigration and, especially, to Charlie Brown for many useful suggestions. I also thank Ben Ho for comments and assistance.

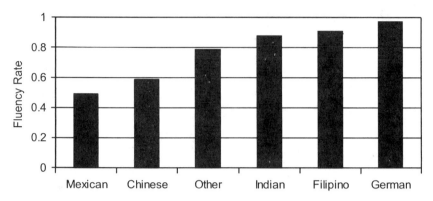

Fig. 3.1   English fluency among immigrant groups

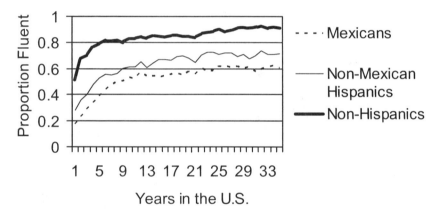

Fig. 3.2   Fluency

This is not the whole story. Even among immigrants who came to the United States before they were five years old and whose entire schooling was in the United States, those Mexican born have average education levels of 11.7 years, whereas those from other countries have average levels of education of 14.1 years.[1]

4. Even when compared to other Hispanics, Mexican immigrants fare badly, with 62 percent of non-Mexican Hispanics being fluent in English as compared to only 49 percent for Mexican immigrants. Mexican average incomes are about 75 percent that of other Hispanic immigrants, and Mexican immigrants have about 2.5 fewer years of schooling.

1. The sample is restricted to those who are now at least twenty-three years old so that schooling is completed for most in the sample.

The numbers leave little doubt that Mexican immigrants do not move into mainstream American society as rapidly as do other immigrants.

Three other facts are worth noting. First, Mexican immigrants live in communities[2] where about 15 percent of the residents are also born in Mexico. Non-Mexican immigrants live in counties where fewer than 3 percent of the residents are from their specific native land. As I have argued elsewhere, the incentive to become assimilated depends in large part on the proportion of individuals in one's community who do not speak his native language or share his culture. Correcting for the difference in living patterns eliminates just about half of the fluency difference between Mexicans and other immigrants.

Second, Mexican immigrants account for a much higher proportion of the immigrant population than any other single group. Mexicans are 29 percent of immigrants in the 2000 Census. Other large groups are from the Philippines, Germany, China, and India and have shares roughly an order of magnitude smaller. Mexico is about 20 percent larger in population than the Philippines, but has about one-tenth the population of either India or China. This suggests that it is easier to obtain entry to the United States from Mexico than it is from most other countries.

Third, Mexicans come to the United States disproportionately on the basis of family connections. Other groups, most notable, Indians, come in at high levels based on job performance.

3.1 Model

The model used here comes from Lazear (1999). Only a sketch of the theory is provided here.

Culture facilitates trade. This is most clear in the case of language. If two agents speak the same language, they can negotiate a contract without the use of a translator. While language may be the most important manifestation of a shared culture, a common culture allows the traders to have common expectations and customs, which enhances trust.

The focus is on incentives to become assimilated, and the model presented here defines *trade* to include nonmarket interaction as well.[3] In the simplest structure, assume that an individual randomly encounters one and only one other individual in each period. Let the expected value to one

2. Strictly speaking, the census 5 percent sample uses Public Use Microdata Area (PUMA), which is a geographic unit that is akin to county, but not the same thing in most cases.

3. The empirical literature on the economic returns to assimilation began with Chiswick (1978). More to the point of this analysis is the work by McManus, Gould, and Welch (1983), which shows that English speaking Hispanic Americans do better in the labor market than non-English speaking ones. Also, Chiswick (1991) finds that both speaking and reading fluency affect earnings, with reading fluency playing the more important role. Chiswick (1993) studies the acquisition of Hebrew language skills in Israel. As in the United States, Chiswick finds that the ability to speak the majority language increases earnings in Israel.

party of meeting another individual with whom one can trade be normalized to be 1. For simplicity, let there be only two cultures in a country, labeled A and B. Define p_a as the proportion of individuals who belong to culture A in equilibrium and p_b as the proportion of individuals who belong to culture B in equilibrium. The majority culture is A, which means that $p_a > p_b$. It is possible that $p_a + p_b > 1$ as one individual can belong to two cultures as, for example, in the case of bilingual persons. In order for trade to occur, an individual must encounter another individual with his own culture. If the per-trader value of a trade is 1, then the expected gains from trade that accrues to As and Bs are

(1) $$R_a = p_a$$

and

$$R_b = p_b.$$

Since $p_a > p_b$, $R_a > R_b$, individuals from the majority are richer than those from the minority.

Either type of individual can acquire the culture of the other group. The interest here is in minorities who acquire or choose not to acquire the language or culture of the majority. By becoming assimilated, they have the ability to trade with the majority group as well as members of their own minority. In the case of language, this can be thought of as becoming fluent in the majority language, while retaining the ability to speak the native tongue.

It is costly to acquire the new culture or to learn the new language. Define t_j as an individual specific cost parameter that measures (inversely) the efficiency with which individual j acquires the new culture with $t_j \sim g(t_j)$ having distribution $G(t_j)$.

A monocultural B receives income p_b. If the minority member becomes bicultural, every encounter results in a trade, but t_j is spent learning the ways of the majority. Thus, the B acquires the A culture if and only if

$$(1 - t_j) > p_b$$

or if and only if

(2) $$t_j < 1 - p_b.$$

It follows that

(3)   Proportion of Bs who learn A = $\text{prob}(t_j < 1 - p_b)$

$$= G(1 - p_b).$$

Proportion $G(1 - p_b)$ of the Bs are sufficiently efficient at acquiring the new culture to make it worthwhile.

Because $G(1 - p_b)$ is decreasing in p_b, the proportion of a minority group that becomes assimilated into the majority culture is decreasing in the proportion of the population comprising the minority group. Also, $p_a > p_b$ guarantees that the proportion of majority members who learn the minority language is smaller than the proportion of minority members who learn the majority language.

As p_b decreases, the minority group becomes smaller relative to the majority, which means that random contact with another is less likely to result in a trade. When p_b is very small, minority members must be assimilated in order to survive in the society.

The key insight from this model is that high proportions of similar-cultured individuals in a community retard the rate of assimilation. This effect goes part of the way to explaining the slow assimilation of Mexicans into American society. Because Mexicans live in communities with other Mexicans to a larger degree (by far) than other ethnic groups, Mexicans incentives to assimilate are reduced relative to other immigrants. But this is not the entire story. As will be shown in the following, were Mexicans in communities that resembled those of other immigrants, about half of the gap between their fluency rates and that of other immigrant groups would be closed.

3.2   Empirical Analysis

3.2.1   Data

The data come from the 2000 U.S. Census, 5 percent sample. The 5 percent sample provides far more observations than are needed, but only the 5 percent sample contains the detailed information on residential location that is necessary to perform the analysis. As a result, the 5 percent Census Public Use sample was the starting point, but from it, only one in five individuals were selected (randomly) to be included in the sample used for analysis.

The variables, their definitions, and means are given in table 3.1.

The basic argument is that slow assimilation is a characteristic of those who live in concentrated communities where a large proportion of individuals are born in their native land. The fundamental result is shown in table 3.2. Linear probability models are presented for ease of interpretation. Logit result, also provided, are virtually identical.

The basic result is clear in column (1). Those who live in concentrated areas are far less likely to be fluent in English. The coefficient on cntyprop (the proportion of individuals who are born in the respondents native country) is around –1. This implies that going from a PUMA where everyone was born in the respondent's native land to one in which no others were born in the respondent's native land would change fluency rates from zero to 1.

It is useful to do the same analysis for Mexicans and non-Mexican im-

Table 3.1   **Immigrant sample: Includes all in sample not born in the United States**

Variable	Definition	Mean	Standard deviation
fluent	Dummy: 1 if respondent claims fluency in English	.71	.45
cntyprop	Proportion of other residents in PUMA who are born in respondent's native country	.06	.10
yrus	Years in United States	17.3	14.9
cnty2	$(cntyprop)^2$	.014	.037
cntyyr	$(cntyprop)(yrus)$	.98	2.22
edyrs	Highest grade of schooling completed in years	10.8	5.1
Mexican	Dummy: 1 if born in Mexico	.29	.45
Latin	Dummy: 1 if hispanic origin	.44	.5
cntyed	$(cntyprop)(edyrs)$	.55	1.0

migrants separately. This is done in columns (3) and (4). The coefficients are smaller for Mexicans than for non-Mexicans, perhaps reflecting non-linearities in part that will be discussed in the following.

For now, it is most instructive to use these results in order to find out how much of the difference between Mexican and non-Mexican immigrant fluency can be explained by living patterns. The mean level of cntyprop is .151 for Mexicans and .027 for non-Mexicans. The mean level of yrus is 13.8 for Mexicans and 18.8 for non-Mexicans. Using the coefficients from column (1), were Mexicans to have the same mean levels of cntyprop and yrus as other the non-Mexican immigrants, the predicted fluency rate would be 65 percent instead of the actual 49 percent, which closes about half of the gap between Mexican and non-Mexican immigrants. This is sizeable and important but does not eliminate the fluency gap between Mexican and non-Mexican immigrants.

As noted, there are large differences between the coefficients in columns (3) and (4). In particular, the cntyprop coefficient is much smaller for Mexicans than for non-Mexicans. Thus, if the experiment is that of raising other immigrants' level of cntyprop to that of Mexicans, column (4) is relevant. The interpretation is that if non-Mexicans had levels of cntyprop as high (and yrus as low) as Mexicans, they would be about 15 percent less fluent than they are now, reducing their fluency rate to about 65 percent or again accounting for half of the difference. But if the experiment is that of taking Mexicans in their current communities and giving them the measured attributes of the non-Mexican immigrants, then column (3) is relevant and fluency would rise by only 7 percent or about one-fourth of the gap.

3.2.2 Return Migration

The preceding model is an investment model, and the return to investing in language and cultural assimilation depends on the length of time during

Table 3.2   **Fluency results**

			Regression					
			No			Logit		
	Regression	Logit	Mexicans	Mexicans				
Variable	(1)	(2)	(3)	(4)	(5)	(6)	(7)	(8)
cntyprop	−1.062	−5.108	−.988	−.241	−4.212	−10.778	−4.874	−4.315
	(.007)	(.040)	(.012)	(.014)	(.066)	(.114)	(.140)	(.146)
yrus	.00650	.04585	.00497	.00868	.04998	.08112	.07914	.06220
	(.00005)	(.00038)	(.00005)	(.00014)	(.00046)	(.00087)	(.00089)	(.00094)
cntyyr					−.055	−.087	−.076	−.047
					(.003)	(.003)	(.003)	(.003)
cnty2						19.95	10.06	8.11
						(.29)	(.32)	(.34)
yrus2						−.00067	−.00070	−.00048
						(.00002)	(.00002)	(.00002)
Mexican							−.13	.12
							(.01)	(.01)
Latin							−1.09	−.95
							(.01)	(.01)
edyrs								.1348
								(.0009)
constant	.662	.552	.729	.408	.492	.478	.859	−.518
	(.001)	(.007)	(.001)	(.003)	(.008)	(.009)	(.010)	(.014)
r-square	0.1083		.0675	.0426				
Log likelihood		−168,137			−167.989	−164,919	−158,468	−147,397
N	308,345	308,345	218,330	90,015	308,345	308,345	308,345	308,345

which an individual expects to remain in the country. There are two reasons why this might be shorter for Mexicans than for non-Mexican immigrants. First, Mexico shares a border with the United States, and travel between the two is likely to be lower cost and more frequent. Second, and related, there may be a high proportion of illegal immigrants from Mexico who show up in the census data. If illegals have a shorter expected duration of stay in the United States or find it more difficult to avail themselves of the resources necessary to become assimilated and learn English, then Mexican immigrants may be adversely affected.

Evidence supports the basic ingredient behind this argument, namely that duration of time over which the language will be used affects the probability of assimilation as measured by English fluency. Including an age variable in the regression reported in table 3.2, column (1) yields a coefficient of −.00678 with a standard error of .00005. If one thinks of each additional year of age as shorting the horizon over which English will be used by about one year, then the preceding logic that relates to return migration finds support. The effect is large. A forty-year-old immigrant is about 14 percent less likely to be fluent in English than a twenty-year-old immigrant.[4]

3.2.3   Two Mechanisms

There are two interpretations of the results of table 3.2, both of which are consistent with the theory. One is that English is learned more rapidly by immigrants who are in integrated communities, viewing locational choice as exogenous.

The second interpretation is one of endogenous location choice. Immigrants who do not speak English may be more likely to locate in areas where there are many others who speak their language. This second view reflects the same mechanism described in this paper. Individuals who are not fluent in English move to high cntyprop areas precisely because they cannot interact with others unless they do. If it were unnecessary to be with individuals who share language to interact, the locational pattern of immigrants would be uncorrelated with English fluency. Immigrants might still cluster just because different areas settle at different times, and immigrant waves are time dependent, but there would be no reason to expect that those who did not live in highly immigrant concentrated neighborhoods would be more likely to attain English fluency.

The two interpretations are more a question of timing than of substance. Immigrants who know English had to make a decision to learn it at some point in the past. That decision was likely influenced by their desire to trade with other English speakers. Those who learn English after coming to the United States perform the same calculation but do so at a later stage. Thus, the sorting story differs from the learning story primarily on the timing at which English was learned, not on the motives for learning English.[5]

The coefficients in column (5) of table 3.2 allow these effects to be disentangled. If learning while in United States is the primary mechanism, then one would expect the effect of clustering to operate through the interaction with the yrus variable. Each year in the United States should be less valuable to English fluency for individuals who are in high cntyprop areas. In fact, that is what is found. Both mechanisms seem operative. Even when yrus = 0, the effect of cntyprop on fluency is large and strong. Those who move to concentrated areas start out with a fluency deficit relative to other immigrants. It is also true, however, that those who live in concentrated areas are less likely to become fluent with each additional year in the United

---

4. Additionally, the sample contains young children who may not be fluent in any language. As a result, the regression run in column (1) of table 3.2 was repeated excluding children under five, eight, and ten years of age. The coefficients on both the cntyprop and yrus variables were virtually unaffected (although statistically different) by the different exclusion restrictions.

5. It is likely that those who come to the United States are not a random sample of the language-learning skill distribution. Those who find it easiest to learn English will receive higher wages when they come to the United States and are therefore more likely to emigrate from their native land.

States than those who live in less-concentrated areas. Comparing the typical Mexican residence where cntyprop equals .151 to the typical non-Mexican immigrant's residence where cntyprop equals .027 implies a reduction in the effect of years in the United States by (.151 − .027) (−.055)/.05 = −.136 or by 13.6 percent of the effect of years in the United States. Both mechanisms are large and important.

Two caveats are in order. Because the data are from a single cross section and not a panel, years in the United States is not simply a duration variable but also reflects different cohorts. Those who have been in the United States longer are from an earlier cohort. To the extent that cohorts vary over time in their learning skills as argued by Borjas (1985), part of the positive effect of time in the United States reflects cohort effects. Not only would this show up as a shifter in the constant term (yrus), but it also could be related to the interaction (yrus)(cntyprop). But the effect seems to go in the wrong direction. Because the sign is negative, being in a highly concentrated area hurts learning more for early cohorts than for later cohorts. One might expect that better learners would be more immune to being in a highly concentrated area than slower learners. It is possible, however, that an argument could be made in the other direction.

Second, it is possible that those who are high-cost learners also go to highly concentrated areas. If true, then it is not only concentration per se that reduces the incentive to learn but also the fact that concentrated areas have poorer language learners.

Incidentally, there is evidence that country of origin, not merely language, is relevant, at least in terms of residential pattern. Natives of Mexico do not live in the same neighborhoods as natives of Cuba or Puerto Rico. The correlation between the proportion of a community that is Mexican and the proportion that is non-Mexican Hispanic is actually negative (−.27). If language were the only relevant factor, one would expect the correlation to be positive.[6]

Column (6) of table 3.2 allows nonlinear terms to enter the logit. Not surprisingly, effects are highly nonlinear. Initial years in the United States matter more than subsequent years for fluency, and going from .01 to .02 cntyprop has a larger negative effect on fluency than going from .30 to .31 cntyprop. The nonlinearity is not sufficient, however, to account for the very large differences between the linear coefficients on cntyprop in columns (2) and (3). Running linear probability regressions for Mexicans and non-Mexicans separately, while including quadratic terms, still yields very different coefficients between the two groups. Effects of cntyprop are much more damped for the Mexican group.

The logit reported in column (7) of table 3.2 shows that Hispanics are

6. See Kalnins and Chung (2004) for a study that shows that large hotels that are run by Indians do better when there are other Indians in the community, the interpretation being that individuals learn from others who share culture. Language is not the issue because virtually all are English speakers.

less fluent in English than other groups and that Mexicans are less fluent than Hispanics. The cntyprop variable is not the whole story as already discussed previously. Both Latin and Mexican variables are important even when cntyprop is included in the logit. The difference between Mexicans and other Hispanics in fluency is more pronounced than the coefficient on the Mexican dummy in column (7) would suggest. The average level of fluency among non-Mexican Hispanics is 62 percent, whereas the average level of fluency among Mexican Hispanics is 49 percent. Recall that the logit holds cntyprop constant, but Mexicans live in more concentrated communities than other Hispanics. Non-Mexican Hispanics live in communities where the average value of cntyprop is .06. Mexicans live in communities where the average value of cntyprop is .15. But note that the non-Mexican Hispanic value of .06 is well above the .02 value for non-Hispanics. The average level of fluency among non-Hispanic immigrants is 84 percent.

3.2.4   Other Potential Measures

The key variable, cntyprop, is a measure of the proportion of individuals in the census unit, PUMA, who were born in the respondent's native country. But the PUMA can be quite a large area and may not be the variable that best measures living patterns or typical encounters among individuals of various ethnic categories. For one thing, there may be a small proportion of individuals in a PUMA, but enough of them may be concentrated in a sufficient small area to provide the kind of social network that mitigates the adverse consequences lack of English skills.

There is no way using the Public Use Microdata Samples (PUMS) Census data to get more refined measures than PUMA. It might be possible to do more with the exact communities and cities using other qualitative data. The effect of using an imperfect proxy of the variable that is desired has the effect of reducing the estimated coefficient. This is a standard errors-in-variables problem that biases the coefficient toward zero. (There is no obvious reason why the measurement error would be correlated with the observed variable, making it something other than white noise.) As such, the estimated effect probably understates the true effect of concentration to the extent that cntyprop measures badly the interaction or residence group in question.

3.2.5   The Role of Income and Education

Not surprisingly, education is closely associated with English fluency. Those who acquire more education become fluent in English, and those who plan to attain high levels of education tend to be more fluent in English. Column (8) of table 3.2 is identical to column (7), except that column (8) holds constant years of education attained. The shape of the relation of fluency to cntyprop changes slightly but remains almost the same. But it is clear that education is importantly related to fluency. Every additional year of education increases fluency by 2.7 percent, so going from an eighth grade education to high school graduation increases expected fluency by 11 percent.

Education is not independent of cntyprop. Those who live in high cntyprop areas get fewer years of education. Table 3.3 reports the results. In the regression in column (1), only individuals who grew up in the United States and who have likely completed their education are included. Specifically, only individuals who were older than twenty-three and who were younger than six when they came to the United States are included.

Just as in the logit on fluency, the relation of education to cntyprop is negative and convex. There are two additional points worth noting. First, even holding cntyprop constant, Mexicans and other Hispanics obtain fewer years of education than other immigrants. Second, cntyprop is a measure of current residence, not necessarily the residence where the individual was raised. So again, the exact mechanism is in question. Is living in a highly concentrated area detrimental to educational attainment, or do those who fail to get educated choose to live in concentrated areas?

The effect of concentration on fluency is more pronounced for the highly educated. Although having high levels of education implies more fluency, this is less true when the education is obtained in concentrated areas. Again, to make this claim, it is necessary that current cntyprop is a good proxy for the cntyprop relevant when the individual was growing up.

Table 3.3   **Education and income results**

Variable	Education regression (1)	Fluency logit (2)	Log income regression	
			(3)	(4)
cntyprop	−4.48	−3.51	−1.41	−.37
	(.99)	(.16)	(.02)	(.02)
yrus		.0618	.0089	.0087
		(.0009)	(.0002)	(.0002)
cnty2	6.22	8.07		
	(2.43)	(.34)		
Mexican	−1.78	.11		
	(.10)	(.01)		
Latin	−.29	−.94		
	(.07)	(.01)		
edyrs				.0715
				(.0005)
constant	14.19	−.58	9.614	8.712
	(.02)	(.02)	(.004)	(.008)
r-square	.0967		.0305	.1078
Log likelihood		−147,343		
N	19,711	308,345	226,664	226,664

3.2.6   Income and Concentration

Income is lower for individuals who live in highly concentrated areas, given education, and years in the United States. As before, the direction of causation is unclear. Those who have low incomes might choose to live in concentrated areas because rents are lower. Alternatively, those who live in concentrated areas never acquire the skills that are relevant to communities outside the concentrated ones in which they reside.

There is some suggestion of causation from cntyprop to income, however, which comes from comparing columns (3) and (4) of table 3.3. If the causation went the other way, there would be little reason to expect that holding education constant will kill off so much of the effect, as it does when it is included in the income regression. The most natural interpretation of the results is that those who live in concentrated areas obtain less education, and this has very detrimental effects on earnings. The rest of the effect in column (4) may reflect additional reductions in earnings that come from living in a concentrated area, or it may simply reflect an income effect.

The failure to identify causation in the results makes clear that it is very difficult to draw policy conclusions from the results. For example, it might be tempting to suggest that individuals might be subsidized to move out of concentrated areas.[7] However, the choice of living in a concentrated area may simply be one of allocating income optimally. Even if the causation runs from concentration to income, there are costs of transition when individuals move to other areas, and those costs need to be taken into account. However, the estimates in table 3.3 can provide an upper bound to the benefits from moving from concentrated to less concentrated areas.

There may also be effects on subsequent generations. Having parents who live in concentrated areas implies that children grow up in concentrated areas. The spillover effects across generations may be quite large, suggesting additional gains to subsidizing moves outside of concentrated areas.[8] (The effect must be a general equilibrium one, however. If one individual in a concentrated area is simply replaced by another similar immigrant as rent prices adjust, nothing is gained.) Unfortunately, these effects cannot be identified in the data because we only know current residence and not residence during childhood for those who are already in the labor market.

3.3   Welfare

Can welfare explain some of the difference between Mexican and non-Mexican assimilation? Theory suggests that it might. When an individual

---

7. See Kling, Ludwig, and Katz (2004) on moving to opportunity.
8. See Lazear (1986) for analysis of the effects of parental education and residential location choice on income.

can obtain government support, the value of assimilation is reduced. Welfare places a floor on the amount that an individual can earn. In the absence of government transfers, the condition for acquiring the majority culture, from equation (2), is

$$1 - t_j > p_b.$$

A government transfer program can be thought of as guaranteeing some average level of surplus, S. If

$$S > 1 - t_j > p_b,$$

then an individual who would have become assimilated in the absence of the government transfer will remain monocultural and will merely accept the transfer. Reducing the size of government transfers would increase the rate of assimilation in the society.

Is this what is going on, and does it affect Mexican immigrants differently from non-Mexican immigrants? The evidence suggests that it is not the explanation. Mexicans are somewhat more likely (13.1 percent versus 9.5 percent) to be on welfare than other immigrants and have almost the same amount received given that they are on welfare. The welfare explanation may have some force, but given the not enormous differences between the groups, this is unlikely to be the source of assimilation differences. Additionally, welfare is a negotiated benefit in the sense that to obtain welfare, one must apply and be approved by an agency. English speaking skills might be important in the acquisition of the benefits so the causal mechanism is confounded. (See table 3.4.)

There is some evidence, consistent with Borjas (1999), that immigrants from Mexico disproportionately go to states that have high welfare benefits. In table 3.5, column (1), a logit is run where the dependent variable is a dummy for whether the person in question is Mexican. The independent variables are the proportion of the native born population on welfare in the state in which the immigrant resides and the average level of welfare among the native born population in the state of immigrant's residence.

Table 3.4   **Summary statistics of welfare use**

	Non-Mexican		Mexican	
	Mean	Standard deviation	Mean	Standard deviation
On welfare	9.5	.29	13.1	.34
Dollar amount received if on welfare	3,584	3,826	3,595	3,566
No. with positive welfare values	4,271		2,042	

Table 3.5   **Welfare benefits and location decisions of Mexicans**

Variable	Logit dependent (variable = Mexican)	
	(1)	(2)
Proportion of native born in state who receive welfare (welfnatv)	6.99 (1.26)	
Average welfare received among native born in state (welfnave)		.0059 (.0002)
constant	−1.03 (.02)	−1.09 (.02)
Log likelihood	−168,454	−115,228
N	281,995	180,477

3.3.1   Immigration Policy

Concentration of individuals in enclaves explains some of the differences in the assimilation of Mexican and non-Mexican immigrants. But it is not the entire story. Welfare may account for a small fraction of the residual but cannot be the major issue. And even if welfare differences were pronounced, it is still necessary to explain why Mexicans and non-Mexicans differ in their use of welfare.

The facts suggest that U.S. immigration policy is the culprit. Mexico is a very large country, having over 100 million people. In 2003, the United States admitted (legally) about 115,000 immigrants from Mexico. In a country as large as Mexico, it is inconceivable that there are not a sufficient number of talented potential migrants who would not assimilate more slowly than other immigrants to the United States.

The United States admits more Mexicans than any other group, accounting for 16 percent of immigrants in 2003. This ignores the illegal immigrants entirely, who are more likely to come from Mexico. Because so many come from Mexico, it is not surprising that Mexican immigrants find it easier to locate in concentrated communities.

Also revealing is the effect of admission policy. The United States admits a far greater proportion of immigrants from Mexico on a family basis (sponsored or immediate relatives) than from any other country. Put differently, the proportion of Mexicans who are admitted on employment-based preferences is much lower than that for other immigrants. About 3 percent of Mexicans come in on employment (skills) preference, whereas 13 percent of non-Mexican immigrants come in through this channel. Some countries, like India, have a very high proportion of immigrants entering the United States on job-based visas. (See table 3.6.)

These differences might explain some of the differences between Mexicans and other groups, but probably not all. Among non-Mexicans, 13 per-

Table 3.6   2003 immigrants to the United States, by class of admission and country of origin

Country	Total immigrants	Employment based preference	Family sponsored	Immediate relatives	Other	Percent employment based
All	705,827	82,137	158,894	332,657	132,139	12
Mexico	115,864	3,261	29,664	78,782	4,157	3
Non-Mexico	589,963	78,876	129,230	253,875	127,982	13
India	50,372	20,560	15,359	12,693	1,760	41

cent of immigrants are employment based, whereas only 3 percent of Mexicans are admitted on an employment basis. Suppose that everyone who comes in on employment basis is fluent in English. It is also true that 49 percent of the Mexican immigrants, almost all of whom come in on a non-employment basis, are fluent in English. Converting another 10 percent of Mexican immigrants to employment based could at most raise the proportion fluent by $.10 \times .51$ or by about 5 percentage points, which would not close the gap between Mexican and non-Mexican fluency. To do that, other indirect mechanisms, involving spouses and children, would have to be important. That such factors are important is reasonable and could be examined by looking at the correlation between one immigrant's fluency and that of his family members.

The main point though seems plausible. Those who are admitted to the United States because they have desirable skills are more likely to speak English, have high levels of education, and obtain higher salaries than those who are admitted on a random or family basis. The fact that those who come in from Mexico do worse than those from other countries may reflect to a significant extent the admission policy of the United States rather than anything about country of origin. In fact, in an earlier study (Lazear 2000), it was found that the immigrants with the highest levels of education and English fluency came from North Africa. The reason is clear: it was so difficult to get into the United States from North Africa that the only individuals who succeeded in obtaining admission were those with very high skill sets.

3.4 Conclusion

Mexican immigrants assimilate more slowly than other immigrants as reflected in English fluency. They also have lower levels of education, lower wages, and live in more concentrated areas than other immigrants.

The source of the problem seems to be U.S. immigration policy. By admitting large numbers of Mexicans, relative to other groups on a family rather than job basis, the United States selects a group of immigrants from Mexico who are already at a disadvantage. The large numbers allow highly concentrated ethnic enclaves to form, which is not conducive to assimilation. Additionally, the fact that such a small proportion of Mexican immigrants are admitted on an employment preference basis means that the average level of skills of incoming Mexicans is lower than that for other immigrant groups.

Mexico is a large country with an abundant supply of highly skilled potential immigrants to the United States. Changes in U.S. immigration selection policy that moved in the direction of employment-based preferences for Mexican immigrants would likely close the gap between assimilation of Mexicans and other immigrants to the United States.

References

Borjas, George. 1985. Assimilation, changes in cohort quality, and the earnings of immigrants. *Journal of Labor Economics* 3:463–89.

———. 1999. Immigration and welfare magnets. *Journal of Labor Economics* 17 (4): 607–37.

Chiswick, Barry. 1978. The effect of Americanization on earnings of foreign-born men. *Journal of Political Economy* 86:897–921.

———. 1991. Speaking, reading, and earnings among low-skilled immigrants. *Journal of Labor Economics* 9 (2): 149–70.

———. 1993. Hebrew language usage: Determinants and effects on earnings among immigrants in Israel. University of Illinois at Chicago. Unpublished Manuscript.

Kalnins, Arturs, and Wilbur Chung. 2004. Social capital, geography and survival: Gujarti immigrant entrepreneurs in the U.S. lodging industry. University of Southern California. Unpublished Manuscript.

Kling, Jeffrey R., Jens Ludwig, and Lawrence F. Katz. 2004. Neighborhood effects on crime for female and male youth: Evidence from a randomized housing mobility experiment. *Quarterly Journal of Economics* 120:87–130.

Lazear, Edward P. 1983. Intergenerational externalities. *Canadian Journal of Economics* 16:212–28.

———. 1999. Culture and language. *Journal of Political Economy* 107 (6): S95–S126.

———. 2000. Diversity and immigration. In *Issues in the economics of immigration,* ed. George Borjas, 117–42. Chicago: University of Chicago Press.

McManus, Walter S., William Gould, and Finis Welch. 1983. Earnings of Hispanic men: The role of English language proficiency. *Journal of Labor Economics* 1 (2): 101–30.

Mexican Entrepreneurship
A Comparison of Self-Employment in Mexico and the United States

Robert W. Fairlie and Christopher Woodruff

4.1 Introduction

Mexico is one of the most entrepreneurial countries in the world. Self-employment or entrepreneurship rate estimates from the Organization for Economic Cooperation and Development (OECD; 2000) rank Mexico at the top of the list of twenty-eight member countries, the Global Entrepreneurship Monitor (Reynolds, Bygrave, and Autio 2003) ranks Mexico fourth in its listing of forty-one countries, and the International Labor Organization (ILO) rank Mexico in the 70th percentile of its list of seventy-four countries. Estimates from these sources and from the Mexico Census indicate that roughly one-fourth of Mexico's workforce is a self-employed business owner. Roughly 10 percent of individuals born in Mexico currently reside in the United States. In the United States, however, rates of self-employment among Mexican immigrants are low. The U.S. Mexican immigrant rate of self-employment is only 6 percent—a rate substantially lower than the national average of 11 percent. This difference between the U.S. and home-country self-employment rates for Mexican immigrants appears to be an outlier when examining the relationship across immigrant groups in the United States (see figure 4.1).[1]

Robert W. Fairlie is an associate professor of Economics at the University of California, Santa Cruz. Christopher Woodruff is an associate professor of Economics in the Graduate School of International Relations and Pacific Studies, University of California, San Diego.

We would like to thank Lori Kletzer, David Neumark, and seminar participants at the University of California at Davis and the NBER conference on Mexican immigration for helpful comments and suggestions. Daniel Beltran, Kuntal Das, and Jose Martinez provided excellent research assistance.

1. Previous research indicates that home-country–self-employment rates are either positively associated with self-employment rates in the United States (Yuengert 1995) or that the two are not significantly associated (Fairlie and Meyer 1996).

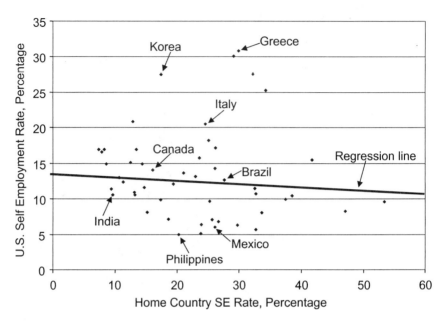

Fig. 4.1   Home country versus U.S. self-employment rate

The difference between the total self-employment rate in Mexico of approximately 25 percent and the total rate in the United States of approximately 11 percent is consistent with worldwide, cross-country evidence that shows a strong inverse relationship between income levels and self-employment (Gollin 2002). State-level data from the population census in Mexico are consistent with this pattern as well, showing an inverse relationship between average wage levels and self-employment rates. Gollin (2000) provides a theoretical motivation for this pattern with a version of the Lucas (1978) model, showing that self-employment rates in an economy are decreasing with the average productivity of the workforce. Given the higher income levels in the United States, the higher rate of self-employment in Mexico is consistent with this theory.

But why are self-employment rates among Mexican immigrants in the United States so much lower than those of non-Latino whites? This comparison creates somewhat of a puzzle because the likelihood of having previous experience in self-employment and the finding of a strong intergenerational link in business ownership suggest that Mexican immigrants should have high rates of self-employment, all else equal. In fact, individuals who had a self-employed parent are found to be roughly two to three times as likely to be self-employed as someone who did not have a self-employed parent (see Lentz and Laband 1990; Fairlie 1999; Dunn and

Holtz-Eakin 2000; Hout and Rosen 2000).[2] Immigrants are also generally more likely to be self-employed than are natives in the United States (Borjas 1986; Yuengert 1995; Fairlie and Meyer 2003). Estimates from the 2000 U.S. Census indicate that the total immigrant self-employment rate is 11 percent higher than the native self-employment rate.

Increasing the number and size of minority-owned businesses in the United States represents a major concern of policymakers. Although controversial, there exist a large number of federal, state, and local government programs providing set-asides and loans to minorities, women, and other disadvantaged groups.[3] In addition, many states and the federal government are promoting self-employment as a way for families to leave the welfare and unemployment insurance rolls (Vroman 1997; Kosanovich et al. 2001; Guy, Doolittle, and Fink 1991; Raheim 1997).

The interest in minority business development programs has been spurred by arguments from academicians and policymakers that entrepreneurship provides a route out of poverty and an alternative to unemployment (Glazer and Moynihan 1970; Light 1972, 1979; Sowell 1981; Moore 1983). Proponents also note that the economic success of earlier immigrant groups in the United States, such as the Chinese, Japanese, Jews, Italians, and Greeks, and more recent groups, such as Koreans, is in part due to their ownership of small businesses (see Loewen 1971; Light 1972; Baron, Kahan, and Gross 1985; Bonacich and Modell 1980; Min 1989, 1993). There also exists some recent evidence from longitudinal data indicating more upward mobility in the income distribution among low-income–self-employed workers than among low-income wage or salary workers (Holtz-Eakin, Rosen, and Weathers 2000), and business owners experience faster earnings growth on average than wage or salary workers after a few initial years of slower growth for some demographic groups (Fairlie 2004).

Another argument for promoting minority business ownership is job creation. For example, stimulating business creation in sectors with high growth potential (e.g., construction, wholesale trade, and business services) may represent an effective public policy for promoting economic development and job creation in poor neighborhoods (Bates 1993). Latino and other minority-owned firms are found to be substantially more likely to hire minority workers than are white-owned firms (U.S. Bureau of the Census 1997). Self-employed business owners are also unique in that they create jobs for themselves. Finally, whether self employment represents a path

2. Additional evidence indicates that business inheritances play only a minor role in contributing to the intergenerational link in business ownership, and previous work experience in a family member's business has a large positive effect on small business outcomes (Fairlie and Robb 2003).

3. See Bates (1993) for a description of programs promoting self-employment among minorities.

to economic progress or job creation for Mexicans in the United States, the data suggest that a substantial part of the gap in self-employment rates in the United States is caused by constraints on entry into a given worker's sector of choice. This implies some efficiency loss, although it is difficult to estimate the size of the loss using our data.

In this chapter, we explore several possible explanations of the lower rates of self-employment among Mexican immigrants in the United States. Self-employment rates of Mexican immigrants in the United States may be lower because the characteristics of migrants to the United States differ from those of Mexicans remaining in Mexico. Mexican immigrants, at least as measured using U.S. Census data, differ in age and education from the population resident in Mexico (Chiquiar and Hanson 2005). This may be important because age and education have been found to be important determinants of self-employment rates in the United States. Our estimates, however, indicate that age and education explain little of the gap between rates in Mexico and rates among Mexicans in the United States. We also examine the sectoral distribution of the workforce in the two countries. Although the distribution of workers across industries differs among Mexican immigrants in the United States, all workers in the United States, and the workforce in Mexico, these differences also do not account for much of the gap in self-employment.

Finally, we explore the potential causes of differences in rates of self-employment between Mexican immigrants in the United States and the national average. In contrast, we find that low levels of education and the youth of Mexican immigrants residing in the United States account for roughly half of the Mexican immigrant-U.S. total difference in self-employment rates for men and the entire difference for women. We then examine possible constraints on entry into self-employment among Mexicans working in the United States. We find that Mexican immigrant self-employment rates may be higher for those who reside in the United States legally and are fluent in English and, for men, those who live in ethnic enclaves. Data limitations require that we use different data sets to examine these various factors, so a precise estimate of what self-employment rates among Mexican immigrants would be in the absence of the constraints of language ability and legal status is difficult. However, the data suggest that these factors contribute to the low rate of self-employment among Mexican immigrants in the United States.

4.2   Data

Our data for the United States come from the 2000 Public Use Microdata 5-Percent Sample (PUMS), and our data for Mexico are a 50 percent random draw from the 10 percent extended survey sample of the 2000 Mexico Census. There are some differences in the two census surveys, which should be taken into account when interpreting the results. The U.S. Census asks individuals about average hours worked over the preceding year and annual income. The Mexican Census asks individuals if they worked in the week prior to the survey and what their earnings were that week. Additionally, categories of responses for questions sometimes differ; for example, the categories for marital status in Mexico include "live with partner without being married," whereas the U.S. Census does not include this possibility. However, overall the differences appear to be modest, and the data are roughly comparable.

In the U.S. Census, *self-employed workers* are defined as those individuals who identify themselves as mainly self-employed in their own not incorporated or incorporated business on the class-of-worker question.[4] Self-employed workers in the Mexico Census are those who report themselves as employers or workers for their own account in the week preceding the survey.

In our main sample, we include only individuals ages sixteen–sixty-four who usually worked at least thirty-five hours per week during the year and are employed in the survey week in the U.S. Census. For Mexico, we include individuals ages sixteen–sixty-four who worked at least thirty-five hours in the survey week. In some tables, we include nonworkers to address issues of labor force selection. We also create similar industry and education classifications using the two censuses. Both censuses use the North American Industry Classification System (NAICS) industry categories.

The important comparisons in the paper are made between Mexicans resident in Mexico, Mexican immigrants in the United States, and the overall population in the United States. For the U.S. sample of Mexican immigrants, we include only immigrants who arrived when they were at least twelve years old, representing 86 percent of all immigrants. This restriction ensures that our sample of Mexican immigrants was raised in Mexico and thus potentially exposed to the higher rates of business ownership in that country. These Mexican immigrants also participated in the Mexican educational system. In some cases, we also report estimates for U.S.-born Mexicans who are second- or higher-generation Mexicans.

4.3   Self-Employment Rates and Industry Composition Differences

Mexican immigrants in the United States have substantially lower rates of self-employment than Mexico residents. As reported in table 4.1, estimates from the Mexican Census indicate that 25.8 percent of the male, full-time labor force and 17.0 percent of the female labor force are self-employed business owners. In contrast, only 6.0 and 6.1 percent of male and female Mexican immigrants, respectively, are self-employed. The dis-

---

4. Unpaid family workers are not counted as self-employed.

Table 4.1   **Self-employment rates in Mexico and the United States**

	Mexico	Mexican immigrants in U.S.	Mexican natives in U.S.	U.S. total
Men				
Self-employment rate (nonagriculture)	22.1%	6.2%	6.0%	10.6%
Sample size	601,609	94,532	71,270	2,792,824
Self-employment rate (all industries)	25.8%	6.0%	6.0%	11.1%
Sample size	814,729	106,006	73,928	2,893,273
Women				
Self-employment rate (nonagriculture)	16.4%	6.2%	3.4%	5.5%
Sample size	268,259	33,987	55,095	2,079,656
Self-employment rate (all industries)	17.0%	6.1%	3.4%	5.6%
Sample size	285,377	35,980	55,582	2,096,007

Sources: Mexico Census (2000); U.S. Census 5% PUMS (2000).
Notes: The sample consists of individuals ages sixteen–sixty-four who work thirty-five or more hours per week. All estimates are calculated using sample weights provided by the Census.

parities in business ownership rates between Mexico residents and U.S. Mexican immigrants are somewhat smaller when we exclude agriculture. However, nonagricultural self-employment rates still differ by nearly 16 percentage points for men and slightly more than 10 percentage points for women. These differences are consistent with broader cross-country patterns.

Self-employment rates are notably higher in Mexico than in the United States. The U.S. male self-employment rate is 11.1 percent, and the U.S. female self-employment rate is 5.6 percent. The differences in rates raise the possibility that self-employment is a different phenomenon in the two countries. However, an examination of earnings distributions suggests that this is not the case. Figures 4.2 and 4.3 report nonzero log earnings distributions in the self-employed and wage or salary sectors in the United States and Mexico.[5] Although earnings are considerably lower in Mexico, the approximate shape and location of distributions are comparable. In both countries, the tails of the distribution are fatter for the self-employed than for wage workers, and the self-employment earnings distribution is slightly to the right of the wage or salary earnings distribution.[6] Although not reported, the comparison of earnings distributions is also similar for Mexican immigrants in the United States.

5. The shapes and comparisons of the distributions are similar if we include zero earnings observations.
6. Separate estimates by gender reveal a self-employment earnings distribution shifted more to the right relative to the wage or salary earning distribution for men and to the left for women in both countries.

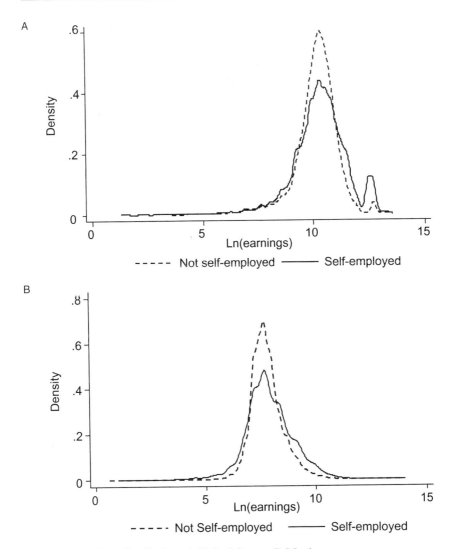

Fig. 4.2 Earnings distribution: *A*, United States; *B*, Mexico

Returning to rates and focusing on the U.S. experience, Mexican immi-grants have rates of business ownership that are notably lower than the national level for men but are slightly higher for women. The self-employment rate of Mexican immigrant men is 6.0 percent, compared to a U.S. total rate of 11.1 percent. Interestingly, Mexicans born in the United States have roughly similar rates of self-employment rates as Mexican immigrants for men, and native-born Mexicans have lower rates of

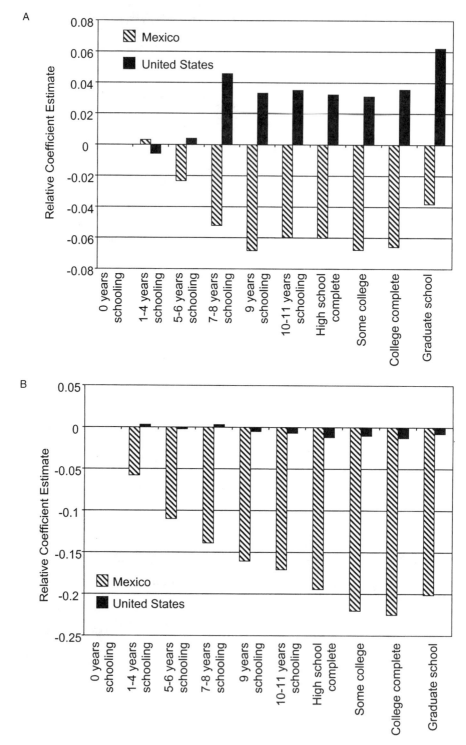

Fig. 4.3 Educational regression coefficients: *A*, **Men—includes agriculture;** *B*, **Women—includes agriculture**

self-employment than Mexican immigrants for women. These results are surprising because the native-born Mexican population in the United States is more educated and wealthier than the Mexican immigrant population. Overall, these estimates set the stage for the following analysis. We are interested in answering the question of whether factors other than the level of development of the economy contribute to the higher rates of self-employment in Mexico compared with rates for Mexican immigrants in the United States. We will first examine how much of this difference is explained by differences in the sectoral breakdown of the two economies, or differences in sectors in which Mexican immigrants are employed. Next, we consider the impact from differences in measurable characteristics—education, age, marital status, and the number of children—of the Mexican immigrant population compared to the population resident in Mexico.

4.3.1   Industry Comparison

Panels A and B of table 4.2 present the distribution of employment of males across fourteen major sectors of the economy as well as self-employment rates in each sector. The data are shown for the labor force by sector in Mexico, for Mexican immigrants in the United States, for Mexicans born in the United States, and for the entire U.S. labor force. We use fourteen major sectors based on U.S. Census classifications, though we combine armed forces and public administration and separate transportation from utilities. The top half of the table shows the employment distribution, and the bottom half the self-employment rates. A similar breakdown for females is shown in panels C and D of table 4.2.

Comparing first the structure of the male labor force in Mexico and in the United States (columns [1] and [4]), it is apparent that agriculture occupies a much larger part of the Mexican labor force (17.1 percent versus 2.6 percent in the United States), while finance, information, professional and education or health services occupy a larger part of the U.S. workforce (10.6 percent in Mexico versus 27.0 percent in the United States). But aside from these shifts, the most striking aspect of the data is the similarity of the structure of employment in Mexico and the United States. In construction, manufacturing, trade (retail and wholesale combined), and transportation, the percentage of the workforce employed in the two countries is quite similar.

Panel B of table 4.2 shows rates of self-employment at the sectoral level for the same four groups of workers. On the whole, rates of self-employment are much higher in Mexico than in the United States—25.8 percent versus 11.1 percent. The most important differences in self-employment rates between the two countries are in manufacturing; trade; other services; and the arts, entertainment, and recreation sector. The latter includes employment in hotels and restaurants, while other services includes domestic household workers. Rates of self-employment in the two

Table 4.2   **Industry shares and self-employment rates in Mexico and the United States (%)**

	Mexico	Mexican immigrants in U.S.	Mexican natives in U.S.	U.S. total
		Male		
A. Industry shares				
Agriculture/Mining	17.1	8.7	2.9	2.6
Construction	12.5	22.6	13.0	11.8
Manufacturing	22.2	22.7	17.5	19.8
Wholesale Trade	1.5	4.9	5.4	4.9
Retail Trade	13.2	6.1	11.2	9.8
Trans and Warehousing	6.6	3.1	6.6	6.1
Utilities	0.7	0.3	1.6	1.5
Information	1.0	0.7	2.9	3.2
FIRE	1.2	1.5	4.0	5.5
Prof Services	4.1	9.5	7.7	9.5
Educ/Health Services	4.3	2.0	8.1	8.8
Arts, Ent, Rec	4.2	12.5	6.1	5.4
Other Services	6.9	4.6	4.3	4.3
Public Admin/AF	4.5	0.6	8.7	6.8
Total	100.0	100.0	100.0	100.0
B. Self-employment rates				
Agriculture/Mining	43.5	4.3	7.0	32.5
Construction	24.0	8.3	13.3	22.7
Manufacturing	13.3	1.2	1.6	2.9
Wholesale Trade	24.3	3.7	3.6	8.9
Retail Trade	38.9	9.1	4.7	10.7
Trans and Warehousing	22.7	11.5	6.5	9.2
Utilities	2.0	0.0	0.0	0.0
Information	8.5	3.6	2.5	4.9
FIRE	15.7	7.4	8.4	14.7
Prof Services	26.1	12.1	13.8	20.7
Educ/Health Services	10.0	3.7	2.9	7.2
Arts, Ent, Rec	26.1	3.1	4.7	10.5
Other Services	34.7	13.6	15.6	19.9
Public Admin/AF	1.8	0.0	0.0	0.0
Total	25.8	6.0	6.0	11.1
Sample size	814,729	106,006	73,928	2,893,273
		Female		
C. Industry shares				
Agriculture/Mining	3.6	4.6	0.8	0.6
Construction	0.9	1.2	1.4	1.5
Manufacturing	23.4	29.1	10.5	11.7
Wholesale Trade	1.0	5.5	2.8	2.6
Retail Trade	20.1	8.2	12.1	10.3
Trans and Warehousing	1.1	1.5	2.5	2.5
Utilities	0.3	0.1	0.7	0.6
Information	1.3	1.0	3.3	3.4
FIRE	2.1	2.8	9.6	9.7

Table 4.2   (continued)

	Mexico	Mexican immigrants in U.S.	Mexican natives in U.S.	U.S. total
Prof Services	4.6	7.1	7.9	9.1
Educ/Health Services	14.4	13.4	30.0	31.4
Arts, Ent, Rec	8.2	16.4	7.1	6.3
Other Services	13.5	7.8	4.0	4.1
Public Admin/AF	5.6	1.3	7.4	5.9
Total	100.0	100.0	100.0	100.0
D. Self-employment rates				
Agriculture/Mining	33.1	2.9	4.8	25.0
Construction	10.7	10.0	7.3	14.0
Manufacturing	7.9	1.3	1.1	1.8
Wholesale Trade	11.8	2.8	1.5	4.8
Retail Trade	39.5	9.3	2.7	6.7
Trans and Warehousing	5.1	4.4	1.7	3.3
Utilities	1.5	0.0	0.0	0.0
Information	4.3	0.9	1.7	2.7
FIRE	5.4	4.0	3.1	4.8
Prof Services	11.9	9.3	6.2	11.4
Educ/Health Services	4.2	9.2	3.2	3.8
Arts, Ent, Rec	28.5	2.9	3.7	6.8
Other Services	15.1	25.4	17.4	22.1
Public Admin/AF	0.8	0.0	0.0	0.0
Total	17.0	6.1	3.4	5.6
Sample size	285,377	35,980	55,582	2,096,007

Sources: Mexico Census (2000); U.S. Census 5% PUMS (2000).
Note: See notes to table 4.1.

countries are much more similar in construction, and the higher-end service sectors (finance, professional, education or health).[7]

The data for females in table 4.2 show that the differences between the distribution of employment in Mexico and the United States (columns [1] and [4]) are much greater for females than for males. A much larger share of the female workforce in Mexico is found in manufacturing, trade and other services, and much less employment is found in education or health services as well as finance and professional services. As with males, the data in panel D of table 4.2 show that differences in self-employment rates

7. In the United States, the detailed industries with the largest concentrations of self-employed men are construction (31.4 percent), landscaping services (14.9 percent), auto repair (6.4 percent), restaurants (5.3 percent), truck transportation (4.3 percent), and crop production (4.2 percent). In Mexico, the most common detailed industries are crop production (37.5 percent), building construction (7.7 percent), retail sales of food products (6.7 percent), repair services (5.8 percent), and ground transportation (3.2 percent).

are notably higher in manufacturing; trade; and the art, entertainment, and recreation sectors. Notably, self-employment rates in other services are actually lower in Mexico than in the United States.[8]

How much of the difference between self-employment rates in Mexico and the United States is explained by sectors in which workers are employed? For example, does the relatively larger share of Mexican employment in agriculture, where self-employment rates are high even in the United States, explain a substantial part of the difference in self-employment rates between the two countries? The answer is that the sectoral composition explains only a small part of the overall difference in self-employment rates. Taking the rates of self-employment at the industry level in the United States and applying them to the sectoral distribution of the labor force in Mexico, we obtain a rate of self-employment of 14.4 percent for men. That is, if self-employment rates within each sector in Mexico were identical to the rates in the United States, we would expect a rate of self-employment in Mexico roughly 3 percentage points higher than that found in the United States because more employment is concentrated in high self-employment sectors.

Hence, only roughly 3 percentage points of the almost 15 percentage point difference in male self-employment rates is explained by differences in the allocation of labor across sectors. And, indeed, all of this is attributable to the larger share of employment in agriculture in Mexico. For nonagricultural employment, the rate of self-employment in the United States is 10.6 percent, while the projected rate of self-employment in the United States given the distribution of the labor force in Mexico is 10.7 percent. Thus, taking the U.S. rates of self-employment as a standard, we find that sectoral differences do little to explain the higher rates of self-employment in Mexico. Rather, the higher overall rate is driven by higher rates within given sectors, consistent with the models that focus on differences in the levels of workforce productivity.

The results for women are similar. Using the U.S. self-employment rates at the industry level and the sectoral distribution of the labor force in Mexico, we obtain a rate of self-employment of 7.6 percent for women. Thus, only 2 percentage points of the 9.4 percentage point gap in female self-employment rates is explained by differences in the allocation of labor across sectors.

The data in table 4.2 also allow us to say something about the process of assimilation of Mexican immigrants in to the U.S. economy. Column (2) of

8. The most common detailed industries for self-employed women in the United States are private households (24.0 percent), child day care services (16.9 percent), services to buildings (7.3 percent), restaurants (7.1 percent), and beauty salons (5.3 percent). In Mexico, the most common detailed industries are retail sales of food products (21.5 percent), food preparation (12.0 percent), crop production (9.9 percent), domestic service (7.8 percent), and retail sales of clothing (5.8 percent).

tables 4.2 shows the male and female sectoral division of labor and the rates of self-employment of first-generation Mexican immigrants in the United States, those born outside of the United States and arriving after reaching age twelve. Column (3) of the same table show the data for U.S. natives of Mexican descent. Among first-generation immigrants, the distribution of employment across sectors differs from both the distribution in Mexico and the distribution in the United States. Recent male migrants are much more likely to be employed in construction and arts, entertainment, and recreation (restaurants and hotels) than are either those residing in Mexico or the U.S. population as a whole. First-generation females are more likely to be employed in manufacturing and arts, entertainment, and recreation than are either females in Mexico or the entire female labor force in the United States. Compared with the U.S. labor force as a whole, males and especially females are much less likely to be found in education or health services. Somewhat surprisingly, the percentage of employment in professional services is as high among first-generation Mexicans as it is among the labor force as a whole.

Self-employment rates among first-generation Mexicans are far below those in Mexico and, for males at least, far below those for the population as a whole in the United States. The sectoral distribution of employment does not explain the gap between migrants and the population as a whole for males. Indeed, first-generation male migrants from Mexico tend to be concentrated in industries with high rates of self-employment overall in the United States. Given the industries in which they work, Mexican males would have an overall self-employment rate of 14.4 percent (12.8 percent if agriculture is excluded), compared to an overall rate in the United States of 11.1 percent (10.6 percent without agriculture). Recent female immigrants have rates of self-employment very similar to the females in the United States as a whole, though the data in table 4.2 suggest that this is due in part to their being overrepresented in the other services category, where rates of self-employment are high.

Among those of Mexican descent born in the United States, the sectoral distribution of employment is very similar to the United States as a whole for both males and females. Among this group, however, rates of self-employment are lower in every sector for both males and for females, compared to the U.S. labor force as a whole. Hence, while first-generation females have self-employment rates comparable to the overall U.S. population, females of Mexican descent born in the United States have markedly lower rates of self-employment.

4.4   Are Mexican Immigrants Different than Mexico Residents?

We next turn to an examination of the characteristics of Mexicans resident in Mexico and Mexican immigrants in the United States. Previous research using the 1990 and earlier Censuses (Feliciano 2001; Chiquiar and Hanson 2003) indicates that recent Mexican immigrants to the United States are more educated than residents of Mexico. The 2000 Census data reported in table 4.3 indicate a similar picture. We continue to report estimates for U.S. natives of Mexican descent and the entire U.S. population sixteen–sixty-four years old for comparison purposes, and we include the full sample of all individuals ages sixteen–sixty-four instead of conditioning on full-time employment. The median education levels is nine years for male Mexicans resident in Mexico and first-generation Mexican immigrants and twelve years for Mexicans born in the United States.[9] Despite the fact that a larger portion of Mexican immigrants have no schooling (10.0 percent versus 6.0 percent for males), Mexican immigrants are less likely to have nine years or less of schooling and more likely to have ten–fifteen years of schooling than are Mexicans resident in Mexico. This pattern holds for both males and females (see columns [1] and [2] of table 4.3). Male immigrants are less likely to have one–four years of schooling (6.5 percent versus 14.8 percent of the population of similar age in Mexico) and less likely to have seven–nine years of schooling (19.3 percent versus 26.3 percent). Among males, 38.9 percent of immigrants have ten–fifteen years of schooling, while only 22.4 percent of the population resident in Mexico has ten–fifteen years of schooling. However, Mexicans resident in Mexico are more likely to have a college or graduate degree (9.3 percent for males and 6.5 percent for females) than are Mexican immigrants in the United States (3.3 percent for males and 3.6 percent for females). Qualitatively, the same general patterns hold when the sample is limited to those in the labor force.

There are some differences in age distribution of Mexican residents and Mexican immigrants as well, with Mexican immigrants to the United States being somewhat older on average than Mexicans remaining in Mexico. Table 4.4 reports estimates for a comparison of age distributions in the two countries. The most notable difference between the age distribution of Mexicans resident in Mexico and Mexican immigrants in the United States is that the latter are much less likely to be sixteen–nineteen years of age. After accounting for the difference in the mass in this age range, there are essentially no differences in the proportion of the population in any of the five-year age ranges above age forty-five for either males or females. For both males and females, a larger part of the immigrant population is between the age of twenty-five and forty-five. On the whole, then, immigrants are slightly older than residents of Mexico, but this is driven entirely by under representation of the sixteen- to nineteen-year-old age group.

When the sample is limited to those participating full time in the labor

9. The U.S. Census data report education data by category, making it difficult to calculate mean education levels.

Table 4.3   Educational distributions in Mexico and the United States (%)

	Mexico	Mexican immigrants in U.S.	Mexican natives in U.S.	U.S. total
Men				
No schooling	6.0	10.0	1.7	1.2
1–4 years of school	14.8	6.5	0.8	0.6
5–6 years of school	21.3	22.0	2.0	1.7
7–8 years of school	5.8	9.0	3.4	2.3
9 years of school	20.5	10.3	5.3	3.3
10–11 years of school	7.4	15.3	23.6	13.4
High school graduate	10.2	15.8	28.1	26.9
Some college	4.8	7.8	26.4	27.8
College graduate	4.3	2.0	6.2	14.6
Graduate school	5.0	1.3	2.5	8.2
High school graduate or more	24.3	26.8	63.2	77.5
College graduate or more	9.3	3.3	8.7	22.8
Sample size	1,255,337	171,858	137,141	4,444,392
Women				
No schooling	8.2	10.5	1.4	1.0
1–4 years of school	15.8	6.9	0.7	0.5
5–6 years of school	23.5	22.0	1.8	1.3
7–8 years of school	4.4	8.9	3.2	1.8
9 years of school	19.0	9.9	4.9	2.8
10–11 years of school	6.8	13.9	20.9	11.9
High school graduate	11.2	16.0	27.5	26.9
Some college	4.6	8.3	29.9	31.4
College graduate	3.6	2.2	7.1	15.2
Graduate school	2.9	1.4	2.6	7.2
High school graduate or more	22.3	28.0	67.1	80.7
College graduate or more	6.5	3.6	9.7	22.4
Sample size	1,399,495	128,059	137,218	4,541,637

Sources: Mexico Census (2000); U.S. Census 5% PUMS (2000).

Notes: The sample consists of all individuals ages sixteen–sixty-four. All estimates are calculated using sample weights provided by the Census.

force, the age differences among males are slightly smaller, while those for females are slightly larger. For example, 23.5 percent of males in the labor force in Mexico are sixteen–twenty-four years of age, while 19.5 percent of Mexican immigrants are in that age range. For females, 30.5 percent of those in Mexican labor force and only 13.4 percent of immigrants in the labor force are sixteen–twenty-four years old.

The available data suggest there are no significant differences between migrant sending households and other households in Mexico with respect to the self-employment of household members. Data from the 2000 Mexican Population Census indicate that sending households are slightly more

Table 4.4   Age distributions in Mexico and the United States (%)

	Mexico	Mexican immigrants in U.S.	Mexican natives in U.S.	U.S. total
Men				
Ages				
16–19	14.9	6.0	17.6	9.0
20–24	16.1	15.5	18.2	10.7
25–29	14.4	18.0	14.2	10.7
30–34	12.6	16.7	11.3	11.3
35–39	11.2	14.6	10.8	12.7
40–44	9.3	10.9	9.1	12.5
45–49	7.2	7.7	7.0	11.0
50–54	6.0	5.1	5.5	9.4
55–59	4.5	3.4	3.6	7.1
60–64	3.9	2.3	2.8	5.7
Age (Mean)	33.5	34.2	32.2	37.9
Sample size	1,255,337	171,858	137,141	4,444,392
Women				
Ages				
16–19	14.1	4.2	17.2	8.5
20–24	16.5	12.6	17.2	10.2
25–29	14.8	16.9	13.6	10.4
30–34	12.8	16.5	11.2	11.0
35–39	11.4	15.0	11.1	12.7
40–44	9.2	11.8	9.5	12.5
45–49	7.1	8.7	7.5	11.2
50–54	5.9	6.4	5.8	9.7
55–59	4.5	4.5	3.8	7.6
60–64	3.8	3.5	3.2	6.2
Age (Mean)	33.5	35.9	32.7	38.5
Sample size	1,399,495	128,059	137,218	4,541,637

Sources: Mexico Census (2000); U.S. Census 5% PUMS (2000).
Note: See notes to table 4.3.

likely to have any member self-employed (34 percent versus 32 percent) but no more likely to be headed by someone who is self-employed (29 percent in either case). The census data do not contain information on households who moved in their entirety before the census was conducted.

4.5   The Determinants of Self-Employment in Mexico and the United States

Do the differences in the education and age patterns of migrants explain part of the higher self-employment rates in Mexico? We explore this question in two steps. First, we estimate regressions of self-employment status on worker characteristics in Mexico and the United States. We then combine the Mexican regressions with the characteristics of migrants in the United States to estimate what the self-employment rates of migrants would be were they working in Mexico. Table 4.5 shows regressions for self-employment status in Mexico and the United States for males and females from a linear probability model. The right-hand-side variables measure age (nine dummy variables with sixteen- to nineteen-year-olds being the base group), education (nine dummy variables with no schooling being the base group), the number of children under eighteen in the person's household, and a dummy variable indicating whether the individual is married.[10] The first two columns for each gender show results from the Mexico, and the third and fourth columns show results from the United States. For both countries, we first report results for the entire sample and then for the sample restricted to nonagricultural activities.

The industry breakdown in table 4.2 showed that for men agriculture absorbs a much larger share of the labor force in Mexico than in the United States. The differences between the determinants of self-employment status in agriculture and other activities are evident from comparing the two regressions for males. *Education,* defined as described in table 4.3, is negatively associated with self-employment beyond four years of schooling in the full sample. Males with high school complete are 6 percentage points less likely to be self-employed than males with no schooling. This relationship reflects the high rates of self-employment and low levels of schooling among the agricultural labor force. In the nonagricultural sector, the association between education and self-employment is very small and positive, at least over some ranges. Those with a high school education are 1.4 percentage points more likely to be self-employed than those without any schooling. For females, there is a very strong negative association between self-employment and education, even in nonagricultural activities. Females with high school complete are 19.5 percentage points more likely to be self-employed in the full sample and 18 percent more likely to be self-employed in the nonagricultural sector.

The effect of education on self-employment is markedly different in the United States, especially for females (see columns [3] and [4] for each gender). In the United States, the probability of being self-employed is increasing in education for males and decreasing very slowly for females through the high school-education level. While the effects of education in the United States appear very small in absolute terms, for males at least they are not so trivial relative to the overall self-employment rate of 11.1 percent. A male with a college degree is 3.5 percentage points more likely

10. The reported U.S. coefficients do not include ethnic, race, and immigrant dummies for comparability with the Mexico estimates. Estimates for the age, education, marriage, and children coefficients are fairly similar after including these controls.

Table 4.5   **Probability of self-employment regressions**

	Mexico		United States	
	With agriculture	Without agriculture	With agriculture	Without agriculture
A. Men				
Intercept	0.1362	0.0523	–0.01506	–0.01087
	(0.0009)	(0.0011)	(0.0026)	(0.0027)
Age				
20–24	0.0376	0.0405	0.00602	0.00635
	(0.0005)	(0.0005)	(0.0016)	(0.0016)
25–29	0.0889	0.099	0.02168	0.02173
	(0.0005)	(0.0005)	(0.0015)	(0.0015)
30–34	0.1372	0.1552	0.04239	0.04215
	(0.0006)	(0.0006)	(0.0015)	(0.0015)
35–39	0.1649	0.1873	0.06925	0.06773
	(0.0006)	(0.0006)	(0.0015)	(0.0015)
40–44	0.2026	0.2284	0.08796	0.0858
	(0.0007)	(0.0007)	(0.0015)	(0.0015)
45–49	0.2366	0.2575	0.10429	0.10072
	(0.0008)	(0.0008)	(0.0015)	(0.0015)
50–54	0.273	0.2897	0.11035	0.10629
	(0.0008)	(0.0009)	(0.0016)	(0.0016)
55–59	0.3112	0.3211	0.13432	0.12749
	(0.0010)	(0.0011)	(0.0016)	(0.0016)
60–64	0.3639	0.3632	0.16375	0.15197
	(0.0012)	(0.0014)	(0.0018)	(0.0018)
1–4 years schooling	0.0031	0.0167	–0.00578	–0.00241
	(0.008)	(0.0011)	(0.0035)	(0.0037)
5–6 years schooling	–0.0233	0.016	0.00395	0.00451
	(0.0008)	(0.0010)	(0.0027)	(0.0028)
7–8 years schooling	–0.0521	0.0175	0.04576	0.03453
	(0.0009)	(0.0011)	(0.0027)	(0.0027)
9 years schooling	–0.0683	–0.0023	0.03328	0.02771
	(0.0008)	(0.0010)	(0.0026)	(0.0027)
10–11 years schooling	–0.0599	0.0174	0.03518	0.03104
	(0.0009)	(0.0011)	(0.0023)	(0.0024)
High school complete	–0.0602	0.0138	0.03231	0.02318
	(0.0009)	(0.0011)	(0.0022)	(0.0023)
Some college	–0.0679	0.0068	0.03098	0.02498
	(0.0010)	(0.0012)	(0.0022)	(0.0023)
College complete	–0.0659	0.009	0.03562	0.03073
	(0.0010)	(0.0012)	(0.0022)	(0.0023)
Graduate school	–0.0381	0.0379	0.06213	0.06225
	(0.0010)	(0.0012)	(0.0023)	(0.0023)
Married	0.0092	0.0014	0.0195	0.0175
	(0.0003)	(0.0004)	(0.0004)	(0.0004)
No. of children	0.0063	0.0009	0.00548	0.00501
	(0.0001)	(0.0001)	(0.0002)	(0.0002)
R^2	0.058	0.055	0.024	0.023
Weighted observations	8,497,574	7,045,089	2,893,273	2,792,842
Dependent mean	0.2576	0.2209	0.111	0.106

Table 4.5 (continued)

	Mexico		United States	
	With agriculture	Without agriculture	With agriculture	Without agriculture
B. Women				
Intercept	0.1806	0.1654	0.02462	0.02499
	(0.0014)	(0.0016)	(0.0027)	(0.0027)
Age				
20–24	0.0313	0.0323	−0.0011	−0.0004866
	(0.0005)	(0.0005)	(0.0014)	(0.0014)
25–29	0.0723	0.0738	0.00623	0.00691
	(0.0006)	(0.0006)	(0.0014)	(0.0014)
30–34	0.103	0.107	0.01977	0.0203
	(0.0007)	(0.0007)	(0.0014)	(0.0014)
35–39	0.1273	0.1316	0.02853	0.02871
	(0.0008)	(0.0008)	(0.0014)	(0.0014)
40–44	0.1567	0.1623	0.03469	0.03458
	(0.0009)	(0.0009)	(0.0014)	(0.0014)
45–49	0.2042	0.2091	0.03967	0.03942
	(0.0011)	(0.0011)	(0.0014)	(0.0014)
50–54	0.2537	0.2577	0.04605	0.04567
	(0.0013)	(0.0013)	(0.0014)	(0.0014)
55–59	0.3183	0.3249	0.0574	0.0563
	(0.0018)	(0.0018)	(0.0015)	(0.0014)
60–64	0.4077	0.4171	0.06858	0.06667
	(0.0023)	(0.0024)	(0.0016)	(0.0016)
1–4 years schooling	−0.0579	−0.0532	0.00309	0.00771
	(0.0015)	(0.0017)	(0.0039)	(0.0040)
5–6 years schooling	−0.1099	−0.1023	−0.00217	−0.0005397
	(0.0014)	(0.0015)	(0.0030)	(0.0031)
7–8 years schooling	−0.1388	−0.1266	0.00313	0.00062506
	(0.0016)	(0.0017)	(0.0029)	(0.0029)
9 years schooling	−0.1604	−0.1479	−0.00491	−0.00586
	(0.0014)	(0.0015)	(0.0028)	(0.0028)
10–11 years schooling	−0.1707	−0.1566	−0.00683	−0.00762
	(0.0015)	(0.0016)	(0.0025)	(0.0025)
High school complete	−0.946	−0.1808	−0.01191	−0.01326
	(0.0014)	(0.0015)	(0.0024)	(0.0024)
Some college	−0.2203		−0.01005	−0.01108
	(0.0015)	(0.0016)	(0.0024)	(0.0024)
College complete	−0.2251	−0.2124	−0.01262	−0.01348
	(0.0015)	(0.0016)	(0.0024)	(0.0024)
Graduate school	−0.2012	−0.1883	−0.0076	−0.00754
	(0.0015)	(0.0016)	(0.0024)	(0.0024)
Married	0.0956	0.0937	0.01784	0.01677
	(0.0005)	(0.0005)	(0.0003)	(0.0003)
No. of children	0.0019	0.0015	0.00303	0.00299
	(0.0001)	(0.0001)	(0.0002)	(0.0002)
R^2	0.111	0.108	0.009	0.009
Weighted observations	3,307,417	3,189,182	2,096,007	2,076,656
Dependent mean	0.1698	0.164	0.056	0.055

to be self-employed than is a male without schooling; a female with a college degree is 1.3 percentage points less likely to be self-employed. The effect of education changes only very slightly when agriculture is excluded from the U.S. sample.

In all reported regressions, self-employment increases steadily in the age of the individual for males. For females, the rates are flat over the first two age ranges and then are increasing beyond age twenty-four. The effect of age on self-employment is larger in Mexico than in the United States in absolute terms. Relative to the overall levels of self-employment, age also has a much larger effect in Mexico among females and a slightly larger effect in Mexico among males. The strong positive relationship between age and self-employment, especially in Mexico, is evident in figure 4.4.

Being married and having more children make self-employment more likely for both genders in both countries. The effects are generally not large. Among females, the effect of being married is much larger in Mexico (about 10 percentage points), while among males the marriage effect is twice as large in the United States. Each additional child increases the likelihood of self-employment by a fifth to a half of a percent in Mexico and by a third to a half of a percent in the United States. Recall, however, that table 4.5 is measuring self-employment conditional on being in the labor force and hence indicates only a part of the effect being married with children has on self-employment. In Mexico, both being married and having children are associated with higher levels of labor force participation among males and lower levels of labor force participation among females.

The Mexican data allow us to separate self-employed workers working by themselves from employers. The majority of Mexican self-employed (88 percent of males and 89 percent of females) work by themselves. The percentage of the labor force that is an employer in Mexico (3.1 percent for males and 1.9 percent for females) is close to the percentage of the Mexican labor force that is self-employed in the United States (4.6 percent for males and 4.2 percent for females). In table 4.6, we explore differences in the association between education, age, marital status, and children on status as an own-account worker and an employer.

In the case of education, the regressions indicate very significant differences in these effects. While education is strongly negatively associated with being an own-account worker for both males and females, education is positively associated with being an employer for both genders. Relative to the proportion of the labor force that is an employer, the positive effect of education on being an employer is large. Males (females) with some college are almost 6 percent (3 percent) more likely to be an employer than males (females) without schooling. The U.S. Census data do not allow us to separate own-account workers from employers. But the Mexican employer regressions are similar to the U.S. self-employment status regressions, especially for males. Own-account status in Mexico appears to be

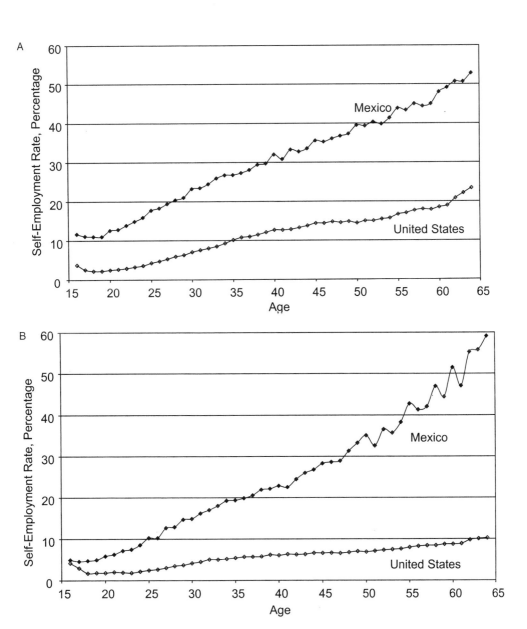

Fig. 4.4   Self-employment rates by age in Mexico and the United States: *A*, **Male;** *B*, **Female**

Table 4.6	Self-employment status regressions in Mexico			
	Males (with agriculture)		Females (with agriculture)	
	Own-account	Employer	Own-account	Employer
Intercept	0.1546	–0.0184	0.1978	–0.0172
	(0.0009)	(0.0002)	(0.0014)	(0.0003)
Age				
20–24	0.0403	–0.0027	0.0326	–0.0013
	(0.0005)	(0.0001)	(0.0005)	(0.0001)
25–29	0.0860	0.0029	0.0698	0.0025
	(0.0005)	(0.0002)	(0.0006)	(0.0002)
30–34	0.1244	0.0128	0.0956	0.0073
	(0.0006)	(0.0002)	(0.0007)	(0.0002)
35–39	0.1460	0.0189	0.1116	0.0157
	(0.0006)	(0.0002)	(0.0007)	(0.0003)
40–44	0.1760	0.0265	0.1359	0.0208
	(0.0007)	(0.0002)	(0.0008)	(0.0003)
45–49	0.2042	0.0325	0.1765	0.0276
	(0.0007)	(0.0003)	(0.0010)	(0.0004)
50–54	0.2310	0.0420	0.2172	0.0364
	(0.0008)	(0.0003)	(0.0013)	(0.0005)
55–59	0.2624	0.0487	0.2760	0.0424
	(0.0010)	(0.0004)	(0.0017)	(0.0007)
60–64	0.3105	0.0534	0.3613	0.0464
	(0.0012)	(0.0005)	(0.0023)	(0.0010)
1–4 years school	–0.0038	0.0068	–0.0662	0.0084
	(0.0008)	(0.0002)	(0.0015)	(0.0003)
5–6 years schooling	–0.0410	0.0176	–0.1257	0.0157
	(0.0008)	(0.0002)	(0.0014)	(0.0003)
7–8 years schooling	–0.0743	0.0222	–0.1582	0.0194
	(0.0009)	(0.0003)	(0.0016)	(0.0004)
9 years schooling	–0.0925	0.0242	–0.1809	0.0205
	(0.0008)	(0.0002)	(0.0014)	(0.0003)
10–11 years schooling	–0.0934	0.0335	–0.1931	0.0224
	(0.0009)	(0.0003)	(0.0015)	(0.0004)
High school complete	–0.1042	0.0440	–0.2204	0.0258
	(0.0008)	(0.0003)	(0.0014)	(0.0004)
Some college	–0.1254	0.0576	–0.2509	0.0306
	(0.0010)	(0.0005)	(0.0015)	(0.0005)
College complete	–0.1472	0.0813	–0.2586	0.0335
	(0.0009)	(0.0005)	(0.0014)	(0.0005)
Graduate school	–0.1295	0.0914	–0.2389	0.0377
	(0.0009)	(0.0005)	(0.0015)	(0.0005)
Married	0.0000	0.0092	0.0814	0.0142
	(0.0003)	(0.0001)	(0.0005)	(0.0002)
No. of children	0.0068	–0.0005	0.0020	–0.0001
	(0.0001)	(0.0000)	(0.0001)	(0.0000)
R^2	0.053	0.029	0.106	0.015
Weighted observations	8,497,574	8,497,574	3,307,417	3,307,417
Dependent mean	0.2263	0.0313	0.151	0.0188

Notes: Sample restricted to sixteen- to sixty-four-year-olds working thirty-five or more hours per week. Standard errors in parentheses.

driven by a different dynamic than either employer status in Mexico or self-employment in the United States.

Overall, we find both similarities and dissimilarities between the processes generating self-employment in Mexico and the United States. The differences are clearest among the own-account workers. The regressions on the determinants of self-employment status, then, are consistent with the cross-country pattern identified by Gollin (2002), suggesting that differences in income levels may be the primary driver of differences in self-employment rates between the United States and Mexico.

4.6   Predicted Self-Employment Rates in Mexico and the United States

4.6.1   Decomposition of the Mexico-U.S. Gap in Self-Employment

We now ask whether differences in the measured characteristics of workers in various groups explain differences in self-employment rates. We examine this question from three different perspectives. First, we ask whether characteristics of the workforce have any impact on the overall self-employment rates in the United States and Mexico. We next ask whether the characteristics of Mexican immigrants relative to those remaining in Mexico explain differences in self-employment rates of Mexican immigrants in the United States and Mexicans remaining in Mexico. Finally, we ask whether difference in characteristics of Mexican immigrants in the United States and other workers in the United States explain any part of the gap between Mexican and overall self-employment rate in the United States.

Table 4.7 reports estimates of predicted self-employment rates using coefficient estimates for Mexico and the United States reported in table 4.5 and average characteristics of workers in the United States and Mexico. For both men and women, predicted self-employment rates using the U.S. coefficients are substantially lower than those using the coefficients from Mexico. In fact, in every case, the difference between predicted self-employment rates in Mexico and the United States after switching characteristics of the working population is larger than the actual difference between Mexico and U.S. self-employment rates. This finding suggests that the large gaps between levels of self-employment in Mexico and the United States are entirely due to differences in the structures of the economy and would be even larger if not for the favorable characteristics of the U.S. population—mainly being older and more educated, on average.

4.6.2   Predicted Self-Employment Rates in Mexico

We next ask what the self-employment rate of Mexican immigrants would be if they had remained in Mexico. Using the regression coefficients for self-employment status in Mexico, we calculate the predicted probabil-

Table 4.7   Predicted self-employment rates for Mexico and the United States (%)

	Mean characteristics		
	Mexico	U.S. total	Difference
Male			
All industries			
Mexico	25.8	27.1	−1.3
U.S. total	8.4	11.1	−2.7
Difference	17.3	16.0	14.6
Nonagriculture			
Mexico	22.1	26.7	−4.6
U.S. total	8.2	10.6	−2.3
Difference	13.9	16.1	11.5
Female			
All industries			
Mexico	17.0	18.9	−1.9
U.S. total	4.9	5.6	−0.8
Difference	12.1	13.3	11.3
Nonagriculture			
Mexico	16.4	19.0	−2.6
U.S. total	4.9	5.5	−0.7
Difference	11.5	13.5	10.9

Notes: The sample consists of individuals ages sixteen–sixty-four who work thirty-five or more hours per week. All estimates are calculated using sample weights provided by the Census. Coefficient estimates are reported in table 4.5.

ity of self-employment for each immigrant and then take a weighted average of those predicted values. The results from this procedure are generally similar to those from the Blinder-Oaxaca decomposition, but this will allow us more easily to incorporate differences in labor force participation between residents of Mexico and the United States. We use the regressions reported in table 4.5 to estimate the probability of self-employment given some set of characteristics x. The level of self-employment in Mexico can then be written as a function of the determinants of self-employment and the distribution of those determinants:

$$g^{\text{Mex}}(\text{se}) = \int f(\text{se} \,|\, x) \, h \, (x \,|\, i = \text{Mex}) dx,$$

where x represents the characteristics determining entry into self-employment and $h \, (x \,|\, i = \text{Mex})$ the distribution of those characteristics over the population sixteen–sixty-four years of age resident in Mexico. Ignoring changes in the determinants of selection into self-employment that might be caused by the returning population, we can then substitute the characteristics of Mexican immigrants in the United States for those in Mexico:

$$g_{\text{US}}^{\text{Mex}}(\text{se}) = \int f(\text{se} \mid x)h(x \mid i = \text{US})dx.$$

This calculation presumes that individuals participating in the labor force in the United States would also participate in Mexico, and similarly for those not participating. Labor force participation rates appear to differ somewhat between the two countries, being higher in the United States for females born in Mexico and higher in Mexico for males born in Mexico.[11] For example, the female labor force participation rate among Mexican immigrants in the 2000 U.S. Census is 39.2 percent, compared with a rate of 33.0 percent among females in the Mexican Census. The *full-time participation rate,* defined as being in the labor force and working thirty-five hours or more per week, is 28.1 percent in the United States and 23.6 percent in Mexico for females. For males, the overall (full-time) rates for males are 70.4 percent (61.5 percent) in the United States and 77.8 percent (67.7 percent) in Mexico.[12] The lower rates in the United States for males may result from our defining *participation* as working in the week prior to the survey and their concentration in industries such as construction, where employment is more variable across time.

We can take into account differences in labor force participation rates by simply modeling entry into self-employment over the entire population, regardless of whether they participate in the labor force. Alternatively, given linear models, we can equivalently first model labor force participation and then model entry into self-employment conditional on being in the labor force. That is

$$g^{\text{Mex}}(\text{se}) = \int \int r(\text{lfp} \mid y)s(y \mid i = \text{Mex})dy \quad f(\text{se} \mid x)h(x \mid i = \text{Mex})dx,$$

where y represents the characteristics determining labor force participation and s $(y \mid i = \text{Mex})$ the distribution of those characteristics over the population sixteen–sixty-four years of age resident in Mexico. As in the preceding, we can project the self-employment rates of Mexican immigrants residing in the United States were they to return to Mexico by using the distribution of characteristics of immigrants in the United States:

$$g_{\text{US}}^{\text{Mex}}(\text{se}) = \int \int r(\text{lfp} \mid y)s(y \mid i = \text{US})dy \quad f(\text{se} \mid x)h(x \mid i = \text{US})dx.$$

In reporting the results of this exercise, we normalize the probabilities of entry into the labor force to 1 when estimating the expected self-employment rates so that the reported self-employment rates are compa-

---

11. Chiquiar and Hanson (2003) show much higher rates of labor force participation among Mexican immigrants in the United States using 1990 census data. It appears from their discussion that they do not condition on working in the week prior to the survey as we do here.

12. Some of the difference between U.S. and Mexican labor force participation rates may be due to differences in the survey questions. The Mexican Census asks about employment during the week before the survey. The U.S. Census asks about normal hours over the prior year and activity in the current week.

rable to those reported in table 4.1. That is, we estimate self-employment as a percentage of the labor force, using the projected labor force participation as a weight.

For males, the overall punch line is that the U.S. immigrants would be expected to have self-employment rates very similar to those in the Mexican labor force. Given the measured characteristics, Mexican immigrants residing in the United States would be expected to have slightly higher full-time labor force participation rates (71.1 percent versus 67.7 percent) but a slightly lower expected self-employment rate conditional on being in the labor force (24.9 percent versus 25.2 percent). Combining labor force participation and self-employment, we find that if immigrants in the United States were returned to Mexico, their self-employment rates would be almost identical to those of males actually in the labor force in Mexico, 25.7 percent.

The differences for females are slightly larger. Without conditioning on labor force participation, the immigrant population would be expected to have self-employment rates of 24.6 percent, higher than a projected rate of 22.1 percent for the entire female population resident in Mexico. Labor force participation rates would be expected to be lower given the characteristics of the immigrant population, however—21.7 percent compared with 23.6 percent among females resident in Mexico. Accounting for expected labor force participation, the projected self-employment rate for females with measured characteristics of immigrants resident in the United States would be 20.3 percent, significantly higher than the 17.0 percent rate among females resident in Mexico.[13]

Thus, for females, neither the lower labor force participation rates nor the higher self-employment rates are the result of differences in characteristics of the immigrant population. For males, the characteristics of immigrants suggest they would have even higher labor force participation rate in Mexico than the Mexican residents do.[14]

13. A part of the higher projected self-employment rate is due to the higher marriage rate among immigrant females (69 percent) compared with females in Mexico (50 percent). The Mexican Census includes a category of "live with spouse in free union." About 10 percent of females in Mexico give this response, which we have counted as unmarried. When we categorize these females as being married, the predicted self-employment rate of the immigrant population is 19.5 percent rather than 20.3 percent when this response is categorized as unmarried.

14. We also examined self-employment in the nonagricultural sector, conditional on working in the nonagricultural sector. We do this by defining *labor force participation* as participation in the nonagricultural workforce and taking this sample as the sample for the self-employment regression as well. The results are quite similar to those reported in the preceding. For males, the immigrants in the United States have characteristics that would result in higher levels of labor force participation (60.4 percent versus 56.2 percent) and quite similar expected self-employment rates (22.7 percent versus 22.9 percent). For females, the differences are equally modest, with the projected nonagricultural self-employment rate for females 19.8 percent compared with 16.4 percent among females employed in Mexico.

4.6.3   Predicted Self-Employment Rates of Mexican Immigrants in the United States

In the previous section, we compared the characteristics of Mexican immigrants with residents of Mexico, using the structure of labor markets in Mexico. To understand how self-employment rates among Mexican immigrants compare to what would be expected given the characteristics of the U.S. labor market, we now turn to a comparison of Mexican immigrants with other participants in the U.S. labor market. Mexican immigrants may possess characteristics that are associated with even lower levels of self-employment in the United States than those possessed by the U.S. populations as a whole. A younger and less-educated Mexican immigrant working population may explain why self-employment rates for this group, at least for men, are lower than the U.S. total.

To investigate this issue further, we calculate predicted self-employment rates for Mexican immigrants using the U.S. coefficients reported in table 4.5. Estimates are reported in table 4.8. Mexican immigrants are predicted to have self-employment rates of roughly 8 percent for men and 6 percent for women. The estimates do not differ much when agriculture is excluded.

The findings have contrasting implications for men and women. For men, Mexican immigrants are predicted to have lower self-employment rates than the U.S. total, suggesting that low levels of education and youth contribute to the lower rates of self-employment. The comparison of predicted self-employment rates indicates that from 2.6 to 2.8 percentage points (or 55.4 to 58.3 percent) of the gaps in self-employment rates are due to differences in measurable characteristics between Mexican immigrants and the U.S. total.[15] The self-employment rate gaps in the United States are 4.4 and 5.1 percentage points for the nonagriculture and total workforce, respectively.

Among the individual characteristics, roughly 40 percent of the gap is explained by the relatively young Mexican immigrant workforce. As expected, education differences are also important. Low levels of education among Mexican immigrants explain 23.2 to 24.1 percent of the gap in self-employment rates. Finally, Mexican immigrants have more children on average than the U.S. total, which is associated with higher levels of self-employment, suggesting that the self-employment rate gap would be 0.4 percentage points larger.

The predicted self-employment rates are higher for Mexican immigrant women than for the U.S. total. This finding suggests that Mexican immigrant women have favorable characteristics, in terms of predicting self-employment, compared to the total U.S. workforce. The similarities be-

---

15. The estimate is equal to $\hat{\beta}^{US}(\overline{X}^{US} - \overline{X}^{MI})$, which is the familiar explained component of the gap in a Blinder-Oaxaca decomposition.

Table 4.8   Predicted self-employment rates in the United States (%)

	Specification			
Explanatory variables	(1)	(2)	(3)	(4)
Sample	Men	Men	Women	Women
Industries	All	Nonagriculture	All	Nonagriculture
U.S. self-employment rate	11.1	10.6	5.6	5.5
Mexican immigrants				
Actual self-employment rate	6.0	6.2	6.1	6.2
Predicted self-employment rate	8.3	8.0	6.1	6.1

Source: U.S. Census (2000).
Note: See notes to table 4.7.

tween the predicted rates and the actual rates for women also indicate that differences in measurable characteristics are responsible for roughly the entire Mexican immigrant–U.S.-total gap in levels of self-employment. The negative relationship between self-employment and education for U.S. women and relatively low levels of education among Mexican immigrant women contribute to self-employment rates that are higher for this group than the national average. Having more children and a slightly higher probability of being married among Mexican immigrant women than the U.S. population as a whole also contributes to the gap, but this is roughly offset by the relative youth of Mexican immigrant women.

Returning to our comparison of self-employment rates in Mexico and among Mexican immigrants in the United States, we can use these estimates to calculate a rough estimate of the contribution from Mexico-U.S. differences. The difference in predicted self-employment rates in Mexico and the United States for this group approximates the effect of leaving a country that supports relatively high levels of self-employment to one that does not. Using estimates for all industries, we find that the predicted self-employment for male Mexican immigrants drops from 25.7 percent in Mexico to 8.3 percent in the United States. Female Mexican immigrants are predicted to have a self-employment rate of 20.3 percent in Mexico and 6.1 percent in the United States. These findings confirm that the large difference in self-employment rates between Mexico and Mexican immigrants in the United States are primarily due to country-level differences in self-employment. A large part of the difference appears to be due to the fact that the U.S. economy supports a lower level of self-employment than does the Mexican economy.

In sum, the evidence suggests that the difference in the rates of self-employment in the United States and Mexico overall are not explained by the characteristics of the work forces in the two countries. The analysis suggests that the differences are consistent with the Lucas-Gollin thesis that self-employment rates are decreasing in the per capita income of a country. In contrast to these results, the standard measured characteristics of workers, such as age, education, and family status, explain roughly half of the gap between the self-employment rate of Mexican immigrants and others in the U.S. economy for men and the entire gap for women. We turn now to an analysis of additional factors that might contribute to differences between Mexican immigrant and U.S. total self-employment rates.

4.7   Some Additional Evidence on Low Self-Employment Rates in the United States

In this section, we provide evidence on several factors that might constrain entry into self-employment among Mexican immigrants in the United States. We address three issues closely related to migration: enclave effects, English language ability, and legal status. We measure enclave effects as the percentage of individuals residing in a Public Use Microsample Area (PUMA) who were born in Mexico. English language ability is self-reported in the census. To examine legal status, we use data from the Legalized Population Survey (LPS).

Using a measure of enclave at the standard metropolitan statistical area (SMSA) level, Borjas (1986) finds that self-employment among Mexican, Cubans, and "other Hispanics" is increasing in the percentage of Hispanics in an SMSA. The effect is larger among the immigrant population than among the population born in the United States. English language ability has been found to affect earnings in wage labor markets (McManus, Gould, and Welch 1983; Dustmann and van Soest 2002; Bleakley and Chin 2003). Fairlie and Meyer (1996) find that better command of the English language associated with more self-employment among males, while the opposite holds among females.

The raw data suggest that enclave effects are important. Self-employment rates among Mexican-born males and females are higher in PUMAs where a larger percentage of the population is of Latino descent. To see this, we rank the PUMAs according to the percentage of their population that is of Latino origin. The lower quartile of PUMAs have a less than 1.8 percent Latino-origin population. The cutoffs for the second and third quartiles are 4.5 percent and 15 percent, respectively. The PUMA at the 90th percentile has an almost 34 percent population of Latino descent. For males, the self-employment rate among the Mexican-born population living in the PUMAs in the three lower quartiles is around 4.4 percent. There is no clear trend in the rate within the three lower quartiles. The rate among those in the top quartile of PUMAs according to Latino population is 6.6 percent. Moreover, the self-employment rates are clearly increasing even within the last quartile. Among the Mexican-born residing in PUMAs in the top decile, the rate is 7.3 percent; among those in the top percentile (more than

79 percent Latino population), the rate is 10.8 percent. Females have a pattern which is similar in the direction of the trend, but less pronounced. Those living in PUMAs in the lower three quartiles of Latino-origin population have self-employment rates of around 4.4 percent. Those in the top quartile of PUMAs have self-employment rates of 5.8 percent. Within the top decile (percentile) of PUMAs by Latino-origin population, the female self-employment rate is 5.8 percent (6.2 percent).

English language ability is also associated with self-employment rates among males, but not among females. The census asks member of households where a language other than English is spoken whether they speak English "very well," "well," "not well," or "not at all." We group the last two categories together as indicating difficulty with English language and compare people in this group to those who either report that they speak only English or report that they speak English very well or well. Among those with lower English language ability, male self-employment rates are 4.7 percent; the comparable number among those who speak English well or fluently are 7.3 percent. The raw differences among females are much smaller. Females with lower language ability have self-employment rates of 5.4 percent; those with fluency or near fluency have self-employment rates of 5.7 percent.

To see if these raw differences hold up to controlling for other factors such as age and education, we ran probits on self-employment status. The regressions include the same basic controls as those reported earlier: education and age categories, marital status, and number of children. Table 4.9 reports results for the English language and enclave variables. The sample for the regression is limited to Mexican immigrants.[16] For males (column [1]), the data from the 2000 Census are consistent with the earlier findings of Borjas (1986) and Fairlie and Meyer (1996). For females (column [3]), we find that neither enclave nor command of the English language are associated with higher rates of self-employment, results consistent with those reported by Fairlie and Meyer (2000). Relative to the gap between actual and expected self-employment rates, the language and enclave effects are large for males. A 1 standard deviation increase in the percentage of the Latino-origin population in the PUMA (16 percentage points) is associated with an increase in the self-employment rate by 0.9 percentage points; fluency or near fluency in English is associated with an increase in self-employment rates of 2.0 percentage points.

Language ability and enclave effects are likely to interact with one an-

---

16. We also looked at English language ability in the sample of all foreign born. For males, the coefficient on English language ability is of a very similar magnitude. Among females, the language coefficient in the larger sample of all immigrants is actually negative and marginally significant, indicating that better English language ability is associated with a 0.7 percent lower probability of self-employment.

Table 4.9   **Language and enclave effects**

	Males		Females	
	(1)	(2)	(3)	(4)
English language ability	0.0196	0.0278	0.00083	0.00877
	(0.0017)	(0.0026)	(0.0027)	(0.0041)
Percentage Latino-origin population,	0.00058	0.00087	–0.00011	0.00016
PUMA	(0.0001)	(0.0002)	(0.0001)	(0.0002)
Language · percent Latino population		–0.00053		–0.00053
		(0.0001)		(0.00002)
Pseudo R^2	0.036	0.036	0.016	0.017
Weighted observations	2,644,810	2,644,810	991,715	991,715
Dependent mean	0.061	0.06	0.055	0.055

Source: U.S. Census (2000).

other. In particular, we might expect language ability to be less important for individuals residing in enclaves. Indeed, we find this is the case. The interaction term for the enclave measure and language ability is negative when included in the regressions (columns [2] and [4]). For males, inclusion of the interaction term increases the effect of English language fluency to 2.5 percentage points for males evaluated at the median Latino population (4.4 percent) and the effect of a standard deviation increase in the Latino population in the PUMA to 1.4 percentage points. Among those fluent in English, the enclave effect is cut by two-thirds. For females, including the interaction effects makes the language effect marginally significant. English fluency is associated with a 0.65 percentage point increase in self-employment rates at the median Latino density. The effect is smaller in PUMAs with more Latino-origin population and disappears in the upper quartile of those PUMAs. While these results suggest a correlation between English language ability and self-employment, the direction of causation and whether the relationship is driven by an unobserved factor, such as entrepreneurial ability, are difficult to ascertain.[17]

The final explanation we explore here is the legal status of Mexican immigrants. The U.S. Bureau of the Census estimates that 3.9 million of the 7.8 million Mexican-born residents of the United States are not registered with immigration authorities (Costanzo et al. 2001). Included in this num-

17. One instrument for language ability that has been suggested in the literature is the age of arrival in the United States (Bleakley and Chin 2003). Because migration to the United States might also be seen as a decision endogenous to entrepreneurial ability, this instrument is valid only among a sample of those arriving in the United States at a young age—that is, as dependents. Among the sample of those arriving at age fourteen or younger, the language and enclave effects are not significant in both linear probability and IV regressions. Hence, we report the language and enclave results as associations rather than causal factors.

ber are many residents who are in the United States legally but not yet reported in official immigration statistics.[18] The Immigration and Naturalization Service places the number of undocumented Mexican born in 2000 at 4.8 million and Passel, Capps, and Fix (2004) at 5.3 million. These estimates suggest that half or more of the Mexican-born population resides in the United States without legal documentation. Legal status may affect the self-employment decision through its affect on the ability to access institutions important to entrepreneurs. For example, legal status helps ensure that immigrants have access to the court system, should disputes arise with employees or customers. Legal migrants are more likely to own property that might be used as collateral and hence have access to credit. On the other hand, legal status may increase employment opportunities and earnings in the wage and salary sector (Kossoudji and Cobb-Clark 2002).

To see whether legal status affects self-employment rates, we use data from the 1990 Census and the Legalized Population Survey (LPS). The LPS interviewed immigrants applying for legal status through the Immigration Reform and Control Act of 1986 (IRCA) in 1988 and again in 1992. The LPS asked about employment the week before applying for legal status, generally in 1987 or 1988, and again in 1992. The sample includes 892 males and 500 females born in Mexico. The LPS data indicate that the self-employment rate of immigrants increased markedly after they were legalized through IRCA. For the full sample of male (female) immigrants, the rate of self-employment increased from 4.6 percent (3.6 percent) in 1989 to 8.3 percent (5.1 percent) in 1992. Among the Mexican-born males, self-employment increased over the same period from 3.0 percent to 5.6 percent; among females, self-employment increased from 2.2 percent to 3.2 percent. Thus, if half of the resident Mexican-born population lacks legal status, and legal status is associated with a 2.3 percentage point increase in self-employment, then rates of self-employment among the Mexican-born population might be expected to increase by 1.2 percentage points with legalization of the resident population. The data suggest, then, that legal status may be an important factor in explaining the lower self-employment rates among the Mexican-born population.

4.8   Conclusions

We have started with the large difference between self-employment rates in Mexico and among Mexican immigrants in the United States and have examined the separate components of this difference. The male and female self-employment rates in Mexico are 25.8 and 17.0 percent, respectively. In comparison, male and female Mexican immigrants in the United States

---

18. The 3.9 million estimate is part of the "residual foreign-born population." See Costanzo et al. (2001) for details on the estimation.

have self-employment rates of only 6.0 and 6.1 percent, respectively. The composition of industries in Mexico and the United States explains very little of the difference in self-employment rates. Agriculture, a sector with high rates of self-employment, occupies a much larger share of the male labor force in Mexico. But large differences in self-employment rates remain in the nonagricultural sector. For males, 22.1 percent of the labor force in Mexico is self-employed, compared with only 6.2 percent of the immigrant labor force in the United States. We find that none of this difference is explained by the sectoral composition of the nonagricultural labor force. Rather, the difference is explained by higher rates of self-employment within sectors in Mexico compared to the United States.

We also compared the determinants of self-employment in the two countries and found some interesting differences. One example is that the positive relationship between self-employment and age is stronger in Mexico than in the United States. Calculating predicted self-employment rates, we also find that the large gaps between levels of self-employment in Mexico and the United States are entirely due to differences in the structures of the economy and would be even larger if not for the favorable characteristics of the U.S. population—mainly being older and more educated, on average. These differences may be due to country-level differences in institutions, production technologies, tax rates, and other economic factors between the two countries.

We next turn to differences in the characteristics of Mexican immigrants in the United States compared with the population remaining in Mexico. Consistent with previous research, we show that Mexican immigrants are more likely to have ten–fifteen years of schooling and less likely to have levels of schooling lower or higher than this range. We also show that immigrants are older than residents of Mexico. Using a linear model to estimate self-employment status in Mexico, however, we find that these differences explain very little of the difference in self-employment rates for males and actually increase the differences for females. That is, based on measured characteristics, female immigrants would be expected to have higher rates of self-employment than females resident in Mexico, were they to return.

We also calculate predicted self-employment rates for Mexican immigrants using U.S. coefficients and find contrasting results for men and women. For men, Mexican immigrants are predicted to have lower self-employment rates than the U.S. total, suggesting that low levels of education and youth contribute to why self-employment is relatively low among Mexican immigrants. We find that more than 50 percent of the U.S. total-Mexican immigrant gap is due to differences in measurable characteristics. In contrast, predicted self-employment rates are higher for Mexican immigrant women than for the U.S. total. This finding suggests that Mexican immigrant women have favorable characteristics, in terms of predicting self-employment, compared to the total U.S. workforce and that roughly the entire Mexican immigrant-U.S. total gap in levels of self-employment is explained by differences in measurable characteristics. We also find some evidence suggesting that for both men and women, Mexican immigrant self-employment rates may be higher for those who reside in the United States legally and are fluent in English, and for men, those who live in ethnic enclaves.

References

Baron, Salo W., Arcadius Kahan, and Nachum Gross. 1985. *Economic history of the Jews.* New York: Schocken Books.

Bates, Timothy. 1993. *Assessment of state and local government minority business development programs.* Report to the U.S. Department of Commerce Minority Business Development Agency. Washington, DC: U.S. Department of Commerce.

Bleakley, Hoyt, and Aimee Chin. 2003. Language skills and earnings: Evidence from childhood immigrants. University of California at San Diego, Working Paper.

Bonacich, Edna, and John Modell. 1980. The economic basis of ethnic solidarity in the Japanese American community. Berkeley: University of California Press.

Borjas, George. 1986. The self-employment experience of immigrants. *Journal of Human Resources* 21 (4): 487–506.

Chiquiar, Daniel, and Gordon Hanson. 2005. International migration, self-selection, and the distribution of wages: Evidence from Mexico and the United States. University of California at San Diego, Working Paper.

Costanzo, Joe, Cynthia Davis, Caribert Irazi, Daniel Goodkind, and Roberto Ramirez. 2001. Evaluating components of international migration: The residual foreign born. http://www.census.gov/population/documentation/twps0061.html.

Dunn, Thomas A., and Douglas J. Holtz-Eakin. 2000. Financial capital, human capital, and the transition to self-employment: Evidence from intergenerational links. *Journal of Labor Economics* 18 (2): 282–305.

Dustmann, Christian, and Arthur van Soest. 2002. Language and the earnings of immigrants. *Industrial and Labor Relations Review* 55 (3): 473–92.

Fairlie, Robert W. 1999. The absence of the African-American owned business: An analysis of the dynamics of self-employment. *Journal of Labor Economics* 17 (1): 80–108.

———. 2000. Trends in self-employment among black and white men: 1910–1990. *Journal of Human Resources* 35 (4): 643–69.

———. 2004. Does business ownership provide a source of upward mobility for blacks and Hispanics? *Entrepreneurship and public policy,* ed. Doug Holtz-Eakin, 153–80. Cambridge, MA: MIT Press.

Fairlie, Robert W., and Bruce D. Meyer. 1996. Ethnic and racial self-employment differences and possible explanations. *Journal of Human Resources* 31:757–93.

———. 2003. The effect of immigration on native self-employment. *Journal of Labor Economics* 21 (3): 619–50.

Fairlie, Robert W., and Alicia Robb. 2003. Families, human capital, and small businesses: Evidence from the Characteristics of Business Owners Survey. Economic Growth Center Discussion Paper no. 871. New Haven, CT: Yale University.

Feliciano, Zadia. 2001. The skill and economic performance of Mexican immigrants from 1910 to 1990. *Explorations in Economic History* 38:386–409.

Glazer, Nathan, and Daniel P. Moynihan. 1970. *Beyond the melting pot: The Negroes, Puerto Ricans, Jews, Italians, and Irish of New York.* 2nd ed. Cambridge, MA: MIT Press.

Gollin, Douglas. 2000. Nobody's business but my own: Self-employment and small enterprise in economic development. Williams College.

———. 2002. Getting income shares right. *Journal of Political Economy* 100 (2): 458–74.

Guy, Cynthia, Fred Doolittle, and Barbara Fink. 1991. *Self-employment for welfare recipients: Implementation of the SEID Program.* New York: Manpower Demonstration Research Corporation.

Holtz-Eakin, Douglas, Harvey S. Rosen, and Robert Weathers. 2000. Horatio Alger meets the mobility tables. *Small Business Economics* 14:243–74.

Hout, Michael, and Harvey S. Rosen. 2000. Self-employment, family background, and race. *Journal of Human Resources* 35 (4): 670–92.

Kosanovich, William T., Heather Fleck, Berwood Yost, Wendy Armon, and Sandra Siliezar. 2001. *Comprehensive assessment of self-employment assistance programs.* U.S. Department of Labor Report. Washington, DC: U.S. Department of Labor.

Kossoudji, Sherrie A., and Deborah A. Cobb-Clark. 2002. Coming out of the shadows: Learning about legal status and wages from the legalized population. *Journal of Labor Economics* 20 (3): 598–628.

Lentz, Bernard, and David Laband. 1990. Entrepreneurial success and occupational inheritance among proprietors. *Canadian Journal of Economics* 23 (3): 563–79.

Light, Ivan. 1972. *Ethnic enterprise in America.* Berkeley: University of California Press.

———. 1979. Disadvantaged minorities in self-employment. *International Journal of Comparative Sociology* 20 (1–2): 31–45.

Loewen, James W. 1971. *The Mississippi Chinese: Between black and white.* Cambridge, MA: Harvard University Press.

Lucas, Robert E. 1978. On the size distribution of firms. *The Bell Journal of Economics* 9 (2): 508–23.

McManus, Walter S., William Gould, and Finis Welch. 1983. Earnings of Hispanic men: The role of English language proficiency. *Journal of Labor Economics* 1 (2): 101–30.

Min, Pyong Gap. 1989. *Some positive functions of ethnic business for an immigrant community: Koreans in Los Angeles.* Final report submitted to the National Science Foundation. Washington, DC: National Science Foundation.

———. 1993. Korean immigrants in Los Angeles. In *Immigration and entrepreneurship: Culture, capital, and ethnic networks,* ed. Ivan Light and Parminder Bhachu, 185–204. New Brunswick, NJ: Transaction Publishers.

Moore, Robert L. 1983. Employer discrimination: Evidence from self-employed workers. *Review of Economics and Statistics* 65:469–501.

Organization for Economic Cooperation and Development. 2000. *Self-employment rates.* Paris: OECD.

Passel, Jeffrey, Randy Capps, and Michael Fix. 2004. Undocumented immigrants: Facts and figures. Urban Institute, Working Paper.

Raheim, Salome. 1997. Problems and prospects of self-employment as an economic independence option for welfare recipients. *Social Work* 42 (1): 44–53.

Reynolds, Paul D., William D. Bygrave, and Erkko Autio. 2003. *Global Entrepre-*

neurship Monitor: 2003 executive report. Babson Park, MA: Global Entrepreneurship Monitor.

Sowell, Thomas. 1981. *Markets and minorities.* New York: Basic Books.

U.S. Bureau of the Census. 1997. *1992 Economic Census: Characteristics of business
owners.* Washington, DC: Government Printing Office.

Vroman, Wayne. 1997. *Self-employment assistance: Revised report.* Washington,
DC: Urban Institute.

Yuengert, Andrew M. 1995. Testing hypotheses of immigrant self-employment.
Journal of Human Resources 30 (1): 194–204.

5

Mexican Immigration and Self-Selection
New Evidence from the 2000 Mexican Census

Pablo Ibarraran and Darren Lubotsky

5.1   Introduction

We use data from the 2000 Mexican and U.S. Censuses to examine how the educational attainment of Mexican migrants to the United States compares to the educational attainment of those who remain in Mexico. We present a version of the standard economic model of migration that predicts lower-educated Mexicans have a greater incentive to migrate to the United States than higher-educated Mexicans. Moreover, we expect there to be substantial variation in the degree of migrant selectivity throughout Mexico: areas within Mexico that have high returns to education will tend to attract more highly educated Mexicans and provide a greater incentive for low-educated Mexicans to move to the United States. By contrast, lower-educated Mexicans will tend to remain in those areas within Mexico that have a relatively lower return to education. Migration from these areas will tend to be more balanced between higher- and lower-educated Mexicans or may even favor highly educated Mexicans.

Alternative theories of migration posit that wage differences between countries may not be important determinants of the magnitude and skill composition of migratory flows. Instead, factors such as migration costs, community social capital, migration networks, and access to credit markets may be more important. Some of these theories predict that Mexican

Pablo Ibarraran is an Evaluation Economist in the Office of Evaluation and Oversight at the Inter-American Development Bank. Darren Lubotsky is an Assistant Professor of Economics and Labor and Industrial Relations at the University of Illinois at Urbana-Champaign.

For useful feedback, we thank numerous seminar participants as well as Gadi Barlevy, George Borjas, Ilana Redstone Akresh, Richard Akresh, John DiNardo, Todd Elder, Kevin Hallock, Gordon Hanson, Roger Koenker, Justin McCrary, Craig Olson, Cordelia Reimers, and an anonymous referee. We are naturally responsible for any remaining errors.

migrants will be positively selected; that is, they will be more skilled than nonmigrants. Our primary goal is to accurately assess whether migrants are in fact positively or negatively selected as a first step in determining the relative importance of wage differences, returns to human capital, and other influences on Mexico-U.S. migration patterns.

Knowing whether Mexicans tend to come from the bottom or the top of the Mexican skill distribution has important implications for a number of research and policy questions. Perhaps most important, migration may have profound effects on the Mexican labor force and, through remittances, on the economic well-being of families in Mexico. In one view, if migration responds to differences in the return to skills between countries and migrants are largely composed of less-skilled Mexicans, then migration will tend to reduce the relative scarcity of high-skilled labor in Mexico and reduce earnings disparities between high- and low-skilled workers. Inequality across Mexican families will be further reduced by remittance income from abroad. Moreover, if economic development and rising educational attainment in Mexico are accompanied by a reduction in the return to skills, then over time there may be a reduction in the size of migrant flows from Mexico to the United States and an increase in the skill composition of future Mexican migrants. On the other hand, if household wealth or access to credit markets are important preconditions for migration, migrants will tend to be drawn from the upper half of the Mexican skill distribution, and economic development may lead to increased migration and increased inequality within Mexico.[1]

U.S. immigration policy is routinely criticized for encouraging too many low-skilled immigrants and too few high-skilled immigrants. A better understanding of the determinants of the stock of migrants to the United States is critical for evaluating the likely effects of alternative policies. For example, the fear that increased welfare generosity or increases in the U.S. minimum wage will encourage low-skilled migration is more realistic if low-skilled Mexicans indeed do respond to earnings differences between Mexico and the United States. On the other hand, English language programs and other policies that may increase the returns to skills may be more likely to increase migration among higher-skilled Mexicans.

Finally, studies of immigrants' performance in the U.S. labor market typically compare immigrants' earnings to that of native-born workers.[2] While this comparison is certainly interesting and important, it does not tell us the extent to which the well-being of immigrants improved as a result of their migration. A better understanding of the socioeconomic status of Mexican migrants and their families back in Mexico will help us to put the

---

1. McKenzie and Rapoport (2004) find that migration tends to reduce inequality within rural Mexican communities.

2. For example, Trejo (1997) studies the earnings of Mexicans in the U.S. labor market.

immigrant labor market experience in the United States in a wider perspective.

Our main finding is that low-skilled Mexicans are more likely than higher-skilled Mexicans to migrate to the United States. Moreover, consistent with the predictions of the theoretical model, the degree of negative selection among migrants is larger in counties within the Mexican states where migrants typically originate that have higher returns to education. We also find that Mexican immigrants in the 2000 U.S. Census are older and significantly better-skilled than migrants in the 2000 Mexican Census. Though part of this discrepancy is likely caused by the particular sampling procedure of the Mexican Census, part is also likely caused by an undercount of young, largely illegal Mexican immigrants and overreporting of education in the U.S. Census.

The paper proceeds as follows: in the next section we discuss the standard theoretical framework to analyze migration and selection, and we review the literature on education and self-selection of Mexican migrants. In section 5.3 we describe the 2000 Mexican Census and compare its coverage of migrants with that in the 2000 U.S. Census. Section 5.4 compares the level of education among migrants and nonmigrants. Section 5.5 investigates the relationship between the degree of migrant selection and local returns to education. Section 5.6 concludes.

5.2   Theory and Existing Evidence

We begin with a standard migration model in which Mexicans compare their potential earnings in Mexico with their potential earnings in the United States net of moving costs.[3] Let the log earnings of individual i who lives in Mexican county c be given by

(1a) $$\log(w_{ic}) = \alpha_c + \beta_c S_{ic},$$

where S_{ic} is the level of schooling completed by the individual, β_c is the return to schooling in county c, and α_c captures differences in the level of earnings across counties. If the individual were to move to the United States, his log earnings would be determined by

(1b) $$\log(w_{iu}) = \alpha_u + \beta_u S_{ic},$$

where β_u is the return to education faced by Mexican immigrants in the United States. Our formulation of the model assumes there is variation at the county level in the average level of earnings and the returns to schooling within Mexico, but there is a single rate of return in the United States.

3. This is a single-index model of skill, similar to that in Chiquiar and Hanson (2005). Borjas (1987, 1991, 1999) presents a two-index model that allows the rank ordering of workers by skill to be different across countries. All of these models ignore the possibility of back-and-forth migration between Mexico and the United States.

We assume these rates of return are exogenously given. We also assume that all schooling is completed in Mexico, prior to the migration decision.

A person migrates to the United States if the wage gain plus any nonpecuniary gains outweigh the costs of migration. Denote by C_{ic} the migration costs net of any nonpecuniary gains for person i moving from county c to the United States. The person migrates if $\log(w_{iu} - C_{ic}) \approx \log(w_{iu}) - \pi_{ic} > \log(w_{ic})$, where $\pi_{ic} = C_{ic}/w_{ic}$ is the time-equivalent net cost of migration. The wage gain to individual i were he to move to the United States from county c is given by

$$(2) \qquad G_{ic} = (\alpha_u + \beta_u S_{ic}) - (\alpha_c + \beta_{cu} S_{ic})$$
$$= (\alpha_u - \alpha_c) + S_{ic}(\beta_u - \beta_c).$$

The migration decision can therefore be expressed as a comparison of the wage gain G_{ic} to the time-equivalent net migration costs π_{ic}. The person migrates if $G_{ic} > \pi_{ic}$, which is equivalent to

$$(3) \qquad (\alpha_u - \alpha_c - \pi_{ic}) + S_{ic}(\beta_u - \beta_c) > 0.$$

Equation (3) highlights the important role of differences in the rates of return to education between Mexico and the United States in influencing the types of Mexicans that migrate. Theory and evidence support the notion that the return to schooling acquired in Mexico is considerably higher in Mexico than in the United States. Because education and human capital more generally is a relatively more scarce resource in Mexico than in the United States, it stands to reason that the rate of return is higher in Mexico. Mexicans who acquire their schooling in Mexico and, in particular, in Spanish, may have skills that are not as highly rewarded in, or easily transmittable to, the U.S. labor market. Finally, language barriers may mean that better-educated Mexicans are not able to reap the full benefits of their skills in the U.S. labor market, where English is the predominant language, especially in more highly skilled occupations. While there are a number of empirical challenges in computing comparable rates of return to education for Mexicans in Mexico and in the United States, the difference in the order of magnitude is clear: the coefficient on years of education from an ordinary least squares regression of the log hourly wage on education and a quartic in age is 0.098 in the 2000 Mexican Census and is 0.011 for recent Mexican immigrants in the U.S. Census.[4]

Because the return to education is higher in Mexico than in the United

---

4. Both estimates use samples of men aged eighteen to fifty-four in the respective censuses. The U.S. data include migrants who arrived in the United States between 1995 and 2000 or who lived in Mexico in April 1995 and do not have allocated data for their place of birth, migration date, schooling, or wage and salary income. A continuous measure of years of schooling is created from the education categories in the census according to the scheme described in Jaeger (1997). Conditioning on a quartic in potential experience instead of age delivers estimates that are slightly larger than those reported in the text.

States, $(\beta_u - \beta_c) < 0$, the wage gain from migrating to the United States is larger for lower-educated Mexicans than it is for higher-educated Mexicans. That is, the relationship between schooling and migrating to the United States should be negative.

Equation (3) also shows that the relationship between schooling and migration should be stronger (i.e., more negative) in areas within Mexico that have relatively larger rates of return to schooling. By contrast, there should be little relationship between schooling and migration in areas with low rates of return. An extreme example would be an area with a rate of return equal to that in the United States, in which case migration and schooling should be unrelated.

The predictions about migrant selectivity are driven by wage differences between Mexico and the United States that result from differences in the return to skill across countries. These predictions may not hold if time-equivalent migration costs tend to be lower for highly skilled Mexicans, as suggested by Chiquiar and Hanson (2005). For example, fixed costs of migrating will translate into a smaller time-equivalent cost for high-wage migrants than for low-wage migrants. There may also be higher borrowing costs among low-income Mexican families than among high-income families. The presence of these factors may lead migrants to be positively selected even if the wage gain is relatively larger for low-skilled Mexicans. But there are also reasons to believe migration costs may be higher for better-skilled workers. For example, highly skilled workers may require legalized status to practice their profession in the United States, or they may require an extended stay in the United States to acquire U.S. or firm-specific skills. In any event, little is known about the source or magnitude of migration costs.

Though the model captures the essential idea behind wage differences as a driving force behind migration incentives, it contains a number of simplifications that may influence the interpretation of our results. Perhaps most important, the rate of return to education in a Mexican county is not necessarily exogenous to the migration process, as we have assumed. Instead, it is likely to be jointly determined with the skill composition of migrants moving from the county to the United States and with the skill composition of internal migration within Mexico. The model also ignores aspects of skills besides education. Finally, recent work stresses the importance of networks and social capital in the migration process.[5] One can view these institutions as either influencing the net costs of migration, C_{ic}, the level of earnings in the United States, α_u, or the return to education in the United States, β_u, for some migrants more than others. Our paper does not address the role of these factors in influencing migrant selectivity.

5. For example, see Durand, Massey, and Zenteno (2001); de Janvry, Sadoulet, and Winters (2001); Massey and Singer (1998); and Munshi (2003).

Though the literature on Mexican immigration is vast, there is very little that focuses on the selectivity of migration. Chiquiar and Hanson (2005) compare Mexicans in the 1990 and 2000 U.S. Censuses to nonmigrant Mexicans in the 1990 and 2000 Mexican Censuses. They conclude that migrants, if they were to return to Mexico, would tend to fall in the middle or upper part of the Mexican wage distribution, which suggests that factors other than wage differences play an important role in shaping Mexican migration. In a similar type of analysis, Cuecuecha (2003) compares Mexicans in the 1994 U.S. Current Population Survey with Mexicans in the 1994 Encuesta Nacional de Ingreso y Gasto de los Hogares, an income and consumption survey, and also concludes that positive selection takes place within Mexico.

A primary source of data on both Mexican residents and migrants to the United States, especially prior to the release of the 2000 Mexican Census, is the Mexican Migration Project. Orrenius and Zavodny (2005) use these data to examine how various factors influence the selectivity of migrants over time. Among their findings are that improvements in U.S. and Mexican economic conditions lead to increased negative selection of migrants, but stricter border enforcement, coupled with deteriorating conditions within Mexico, lead to increased positive selection. Their descriptive statistics suggest that, overall, migrants come from the middle of the distribution of education.

In the remainder of the paper we use data from the 2000 Mexican Census and the 2000 U.S. Census to compare the educational attainment of migrants and nonmigrants. In doing so, we also attempt to shed light on how coverage of Mexican immigrants differs across the two data sources.

5.3   Description of the Mexican Census Data and Its Coverage of Mexican Migrants

With the right data, comparing the skills of migrants to nonmigrants in Mexico is straightforward: the ideal data set would contain information on all Mexicans at a point in time, indicators for which Mexicans moved to the United States during some subsequent time period, and a set of exogenous measures of each individual's skill and the return to skill in their local area. Because this ideal data set does not exist, past researchers have relied on the alternative data sources described in section 5.2. We take a new approach and use the 2000 Mexican Census to compare the characteristics of Mexican migrants and nonmigrants. In doing so, we lay out the potential problems and biases associated with both censuses.

The Mexican Census was conducted in February 2000 by the Instituto Nacional de Estadística Geografía e Informática (INEGI), the Mexican statistical agency. Household heads were asked to list all current members of the household and to also list any current or past household member who had lived abroad during the preceding five years.[6] A relatively large amount of economic and demographic information was collected about current household members. A much more limited amount of information was collected on the migrants, including their age, gender, Mexican state of origin, month and year of most recent departure, destination country, and current country of residence. About 16 percent of migrants had returned to Mexico, and the census records the month and year of their return.[7] The data consist of a 10 percent sample of the Mexican population. Like the U.S. Census, the Mexican Census includes household weights that account for nonresponse. There are 2,312,035 Mexican households in the sample, containing a total of 10,099,182 persons who live in Mexico.

Although the Mexican Census allows us to shed light on some of the limitations of other data sources, the data also have important limitations relative to our ideal data set: first, we do not have key socioeconomic information about the migrants themselves. In particular, we do not know their educational attainment or labor market success in Mexico prior to moving to the United States. We also do not know migrants' relationship to the household members in Mexico. Second, we do not have any information about households in which all members moved to the United States. We return to this sampling issue below.

The major advantages of these data compared to the sample of Mexican migrants in the U.S. Census are, first, that we can compare migrants and nonmigrants using the same data source and thus avoid complications stemming from comparing educational attainment measured in the U.S. Census with attainment measured from a different question in the Mexican Census. Second, we can link migrants to their original place of residence in Mexico. This allows us to examine the influence of the local return to education on the decision to migrate among Mexicans from different points in the skill distribution. Third, there is widespread concern that the U.S. Census undercounts Mexican immigrants, and the undercount is likely to be most severe among illegal migrants and the least-skilled migrants (Bean et

---

6. In Spanish, the census question is "¿Durante los últimos 5 años, esto es, de enero de 1995 a la fecha, alguna persona que vive o vivía con ustedes (en este hogar) se fue a vivir a otro país?" We translate this as "During the last five years, that is, from January 1995 to today, has any person that lives or lived with you (in this household) gone to live in another country?" The instructions for Mexican Census enumerators defines a *household,* according to our translation, as an "Entity formed by one or more individuals, with or without kinship bonds, that regularly reside in the same dwelling and that rely on common consumption of food." The enumerator instructions also make clear that migrants are only counted if they moved abroad directly from the Mexican household. Mexicans that moved from one household to another and then abroad are only included in the migrant roster of the latter Mexican household.

7. Thus, a household member could be listed as both a current household member and as an international migrant if he or she had moved abroad during the past five years and had returned to the same household in Mexico. Unfortunately, the data do not directly link return migrants with current household members or even identify if return migrants currently live in the household. At best, one could match return migrants with current household members by age and gender.

al. 1998, 2001). Costanzo et al. (2001) suggest that the undercount rate appears to be smaller in the 2000 U.S. Census than it was in the 1990 Census. Clearly, neither the Mexican nor U.S. Censuses provide a fully representative sample of all recent Mexican migrants, and they probably provide samples with different sources of bias compared to the universe of all Mexican migrants.

Nonresponse to census questions in both data sources also poses a problem for comparing the migrant populations. The U.S. Census Bureau allocates responses for missing values in most cases by imputing a valid response from another respondent in the data. The characteristics used to match "donor" responses to the missing values depend on the particular variable being allocated, but typical characteristics are age, gender, race, and, in some cases, Hispanic ethnicity. It does not appear that ethnicity or migration status is used in the allocation procedure for education, so imputed values for migrants could be coming from American-born respondents.[8] Of all people recorded in the U.S. Census as being born in Mexico, approximately 13.4 percent have allocated data for their country of birth; 23.5 percent have an allocated year of arrival in the United States, 18.9 percent have allocated education; and 9.9 percent have an allocated age. The Mexican Census does not include indicators for allocated data, though unlike most variables in the U.S. Census, there are missing values in the data. For example, 2.3 percent of migrants in the Mexican Census are missing a value for their age. As we note below, in some cases our conclusions depend on how we handle missing values in both censuses.

In addition to the sources of discrepancy identified previously between the U.S. and Mexican Census counts and between the censuses and the universe of all Mexican migrants in the United States, there are two other sources of discrepancy in coverage. First, the U.S. Census was taken on April 1, two months after the Mexican Census. Migrants who moved in February or March of 2000 may be in the U.S. Census but not show up as migrants in the Mexican Census. If the migration flow during these two months is equal to the average flow between 1995 and 2000, this discrepancy will lead to an increase in the U.S. Census count of about one thirtieth or 3.033 percent, over five years, relative to the Mexican Census count. This source of discrepancy could of course be larger if migration to the United States was larger than average during February and March of 2000. Second, a back-and-forth migrant could be listed as both someone in the Mexican Census who returned to Mexico and also in the U.S. Census as a current household member. Without knowing the size of this group, it is not clear whether the focus should be on all migrants identified in the Mexican

---

8. Hirsch and Schumacher (2004) discuss biases that result from using allocated data in wage regressions. Crease, Ramirez, and Spencer (2001) discuss the quality of the country of birth and Hispanic ethnicity variables in the 2000 Census.

Census or only those who are reported not to have returned to Mexico. Although this distinction is important for assessing the overall level of coverage in the Mexican Census, it turns out not to be important for our conclusions regarding migrant selectivity.

To shed light on the relative coverage of recent Mexican immigrants enumerated in the 2000 U.S. and Mexican Censuses, we begin in table 5.1 and figures 5.1 and 5.2 with a comparison of estimated population counts of Mexican migrants in the Mexican and U.S. Censuses. Panel A of table 5.1 shows estimates of the migrant population taken from the Mexican Census. There are 137,910 male migrants aged sixteen or older and 38,538 female migrants of that age. The average age of the migrants is about twenty-

Table 5.1   **Estimates of the Mexican immigrant population in the United States**

A. Migrant population estimates from 2000 Mexican Census

	All migrants age 16 and older			All migrants age 16 and older, excluding migrants that returned to Mexico		
	All	Male	Female	All	Male	Female
No. of observations	176,448	137,910	38,538	149,276	115,760	33,516
Population estimate	1,454,690	1,111,895	342,795	1,221,598	925,587	296,011
	(3,328)	(3,220)	(2,174)	(3,054)	(2,018)	(2,944)
Fraction of U.S. population estimate (%)	66.0	83.9	38.9	55.4	69.9	33.6
Percent female	23.6			24.2		
	(0.1)			(0.2)		
Age	26.7	26.6	27.0	26.0	26.0	26.2
	(0.03)	(0.04)	(0.08)	(0.04)	(0.04)	(0.08)

B. Migrant population estimates from 2000 U.S. Census

	All migrants age 16 and older			All migrants age 16 and older, excluding those married with spouse present		
	All	Male	Female	All	Male	Female
No. of observations	103,812	62,409	41,403	70,752	49,048	21,704
Population estimate	2,205,356	1,324,762	880,594	1,492,111	1,033,060	459,051
	(3,776)	(4,500)	(4,060)	(3,149)	(3,722)	(3,077)
Percent female	40.0			30.8		
	(0.2)			(0.2)		
Age	28.7	27.8	30.0	27.2	26.4	29.1
	(0.04)	(0.05)	(0.07)	(0.05)	(0.05)	(0.10)

Notes: Population estimates are computed as the sum of the population weights in the respective surveys. Standard errors of estimates in parentheses. U.S. Census sample includes people who report they came to the United States between 1995 and April 2000 or reported that they lived in Mexico in April 1995. Individuals with missing or allocated age data are included in tabulations.

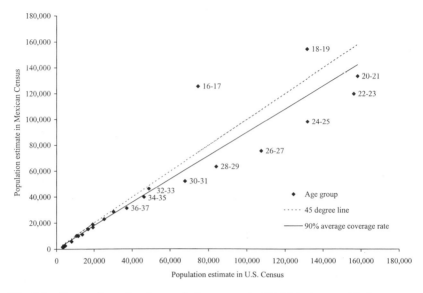

Fig. 5.1   Comparison of male population counts in 2000 Mexican and U.S. Censuses by age

seven years old for both genders. Using the household weights provided by the Mexican Census, these observations correspond to population estimates of 1,111,895 males and 342,795 females. About 15 percent of Mexican migrants are reported to have returned to Mexico by February 2000. Excluding these individuals leaves 115,760 male migrants and 33,516 female migrants aged sixteen or older, corresponding to population estimates of 925,587 males and 296,011 females. These population estimates include migrants with missing values for age.

In panel B we show analogous estimates of the Mexican immigrant population in the United States from the 5 percent sample of the 2000 United States Public Use Microdata Sample. This sample includes all people who report that they came to the United States between 1995 and April 2000 or report that they lived in Mexico in April 1995. There are 62,409 males and 41,403 females in the data. Using the person weights provided in the census, these sample counts correspond to population estimates of 1,324,762 and 880,594. The average male is twenty-eight years old, and the average female is thirty years old. Thus, the total male and female migrant populations in the Mexican Census are about 84 and 39 percent of the size of the populations in the U.S. Census. Excluding return migrants, the populations in the Mexican Census are 70 and 34 percent of the size of the populations in the U.S. Census. These tabulations include respondents in the U.S. Census with allocated data for country of birth, year of migration, age, or education.

The right side of panel B presents population estimates from the U.S.

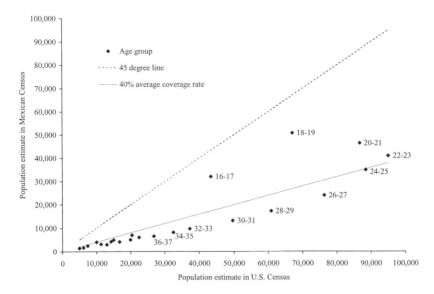

Fig. 5.2   Comparison of female population counts in 2000 Mexican and U.S. Censuses by age

Census that exclude migrants who report themselves as married with spouse present. Because Mexican married couples in the United States seem most likely to have migrated as a whole household, they are most likely to be missing from the migrant population in the Mexican Census. The population estimates for the remaining migrants in the U.S. Census are 1,033,060 men and 459,051 women. Excluding return migrants, the population estimates from the Mexican Census correspond to 90 and 64 percent of these population estimates.

These aggregate population comparisons hide important differences in coverage between the Mexican and U.S. Censuses across age groups. Figure 5.1 is a plot of the population estimate from the Mexican Census against the estimate from the U.S. Census for men in two-year age groups from sixteen to fifty, five-year age groups from fifty to seventy, and men over seventy. Figure 5.2 is the analogous plot for women.[9] The dashed 45-degree line represents an equal population estimate in the two data sources. The solid line shows the average coverage rate of 90 percent.[10] These comparisons among men are summarized in table 5.2. These tabulations

9. The population estimates of children under age sixteen are smaller in the Mexican Census than in the U.S. Census, almost certainly because most children move only when the whole household moves and because of births to Mexicans that occur while in the United States. We thus exclude children from our population comparisons.

10. This average coverage rate of 90 percent in figure 5.1 and 40 percent in figure 5.2 are higher than the coverage rates of 84 percent and 39 percent reported in table 5.1 because the data in table 5.1 include respondents with missing or allocated age data, while the data underlying figures 5.1 and 5.2 do not.

Table 5.2   Differences in coverage of male Mexican migrants in the United States and Mexican Censuses

Data source	Population estimate		Age distribution of migrants (%)		Mexican Census population as a percentage of U.S. Census population	HS graduation rate (%)	Migration rate (%)
	U.S. Census	Mexican Census	U.S. Census	Mexican Census		U.S. Census	Mexican Census
Age group							
16 to 19	206,095	280,036	17.0	25.8	135.9	15.0	7.2
20 to 31	705,201	543,085	58.3	50.0	77.0	27.3	5.7
32 to 54	267,378	241,715	22.1	22.2	90.4	26.0	2.2
55 to 65	19,602	15,878	1.6	1.5	81.0	10.0	0.7
Over 65	11,606	5,773	1.0	0.5	49.7	9.2	0.3
Age 16 and older	1,209,882	1,086,487	100.0	100.0	89.8	24.5	3.7
HS graduation rate using age distribution from Mexican Census =						23.5	

Notes: Samples exclude individuals with missing or allocated age data. Population estimates are computed as the sum of population weights in each census. High school graduation rate is tabulated from the U.S. Census, excluding individuals with allocated education data. Migration rate is calculated as the estimated population of male migrants divided by the estimated population of nonmigrants in the relevant age group. Both figures are computed from the Mexican Census.

exclude respondents in the U.S. Census with allocated age data and also exclude respondents in the Mexican Census with missing age data.

Figure 5.1 and table 5.2 show that young migrant men are actually undersampled in the U.S. Census, in contrast to the pattern for older migrants. There are 36 percent more migrant men aged sixteen to nineteen in the Mexican Census than in the U.S. Census. Men aged twenty to thirty-one are underrepresented in the Mexican Census by 77 percent relative to the U.S. Census. In fact, the two data sets disagree over which age group comprises the largest segment of the Mexican migrant population: according to the U.S. Census, it is those aged twenty to twenty-one, with those aged twenty-two to twenty-three a close second. But according to the Mexican Census, the largest group is those eighteen to nineteen. Men aged thirty-two and older are also underrepresented in the Mexican Census, and the degree of underrepresentation tends to rise with age. The undercount of sixteen- to nineteen-year-old Mexican migrants in the U.S. Census is likely caused by the fact they are more likely than older migrants to be in the United States illegally and less likely to have established permanent roots in the United States. For example, we examined the likelihood of being in the United States illegally using data from the migration module of the 2002 National Employment Survey and found that about 86 percent of migrants aged sixteen to nineteen are in the United States illegally, compared to 78 percent among migrants aged twenty to fifty-four.[11]

Although the coverage rate for women as a whole is lower than that of men, figure 5.2 shows that younger women have higher than average coverage compared to older migrants. The lower average coverage rate among women is probably a result of a large number of women only migrating as part of a whole household and thus not being enumerated in the Mexican Census.

The relative undersample of young migrants in the U.S. Census is likely to lead users of those data to overstate the age and skill level of male Mexican migrants. To gauge the magnitude of these differences, the right-hand column in table 5.2 shows how high school graduation rates of Mexican immigrants in the U.S. Census vary by age. The overall high school graduation rate of Mexicans in the U.S. Census is 24.5 percent, but is only 15.0 percent among migrants aged sixteen to nineteen. When we reweight the Mexican immigrants in the U.S. Census to reflect the same distribution across the five age categories as migrants in the Mexican Census, the high school graduation rate falls by 1 percentage point, to 23.5 percent. In unreported tabulations, we also find that the average annual wage of employed Mexican migrants in the U.S. Census falls by about 8 percent when we reweight migrants in different age groups.

11. Like the Mexican Census, the National Employment Survey asks household members in Mexico whether any other members have recently moved to the United States. Migrants' legal status is reported by the household respondent in Mexico.

To summarize, migrants in the Mexican Census make up a fairly representative sample of the large group of men who migrate to the United States, and for this reason we focus most of the remainder of our analysis on men's migration decisions. Both the United States and Mexican Censuses understate the size of the Mexican migration flow, but they have different shortcomings. The U.S. Census tends to have a greater undersample of migrants aged sixteen to nineteen, who make up about a quarter of all migrants and tend to be less educated than older migrants. The Mexican Census is less well-equipped to provide data on entire households that move to the United States, a group that may be more educated than the typical Mexican migrant. In the following we discuss how the relative skills of these unenumerated migrants may affect our conclusions about migrant selectivity. Finally, the last column of table 5.2 shows the migration rate of different age groups in Mexico. Since the migration rate is below 1 percent for Mexicans aged fifty-five and older and such migrants make up only 2 percent of all migrants, we focus the remainder of our analysis on migrants aged sixteen to fifty-four.

5.4   Differences in Educational Attainment between Migrants and Nonmigrants

A direct comparison of the educational attainment of migrants and nonmigrants in the Mexican Census is not possible because education of the migrants was not recorded. We instead pursue several alternative strategies: first, we compare educational attainment of nonmigrants in the Mexican Census to migrants in the 2000 U.S. Census. We next turn to two comparisons of educational attainment using only the Mexican Census. First, we compare the educational attainment of nonmigrant Mexicans who live in households that had a migrant to the education of nonmigrants that live in households without any migrants. Second, we use other information available in the Mexican Census to develop a predicted level of education for both migrants and nonmigrants in Mexico.

Most Mexicans have six, nine, twelve, sixteen, or seventeen years of education, corresponding to finishing primary school, secondary school, high school, and college. The Mexican Census has a degree-based question and individual degrees (such as primary and secondary) are converted by INEGI into a variable measuring the number of years of schooling, which range from zero to twenty-two years. Table 5.3 shows the distribution of education among nonmigrant men sampled in the Mexican Census and migrant men sampled in the U.S. Census. Column (1) shows that 44.8 percent of Mexican men aged sixteen to fifty-four have eight or fewer years of schooling; 21.9 percent have nine years of schooling; and 25.4 percent have a high school degree or more education. The next four columns show the distribution of education by age and indicate that younger generations are

Table 5.3 Educational attainment of Mexican-born men in Mexico and the United States, by age group (%)

Years of completed education	Distribution among nonmigrant Mexicans in the 2000 Mexican Census					Distribution among Mexican migrants in the 2000 U.S. Census				
	16 to 54	16 to 17	18 to 25	26 to 35	36 to 54	16 to 54	16 to 17	18 to 25	26 to 35	36 to 54
0 to 4	17.6	8.5	11.2	13.8	28.5	12.6	7.5	10.5	12.3	23.0
5 to 8	27.2	32.6	25.5	26.0	28.5	32.8	32.2	33.3	31.0	35.3
9	21.9	29.9	26.2	24.4	14.1	13.6	21.5	15.2	12.0	7.9
10 to 12 without degree	7.8	26.3	10.0	5.9	3.0	16.4	29.9	17.7	14.4	10.0
12 with degree	10.8	2.8	13.9	13.3	8.0	16.2	8.3	17.8	17.6	10.7
13 or more	14.6	0.0	13.1	16.6	17.8	8.4	0.7	5.5	12.7	13.2
Unweighted sample size	2,406,595	210,044	693,078	686,496	816,977	42,372	2,813	20,946	12,638	5,975
Fraction of sample	100.0	8.3	28.8	28.8	34.1	100.0	6.2	49.6	30.1	14.1

Notes: All estimates and the distribution of each sample across age categories use appropriate population weights. Mexican migrants in the U.S. Census are defined as those who reported that they migrated between 1995 and 2000 or who reported living in Mexico in April 1995. Mexicans with allocated data for country of birth, year of arrival in the United States, age, or education are excluded from the sample. The category of ten to twelve years without a high school degree includes people in the Mexican Census who have ten or eleven years of education and people in the U.S. Census who report completing tenth, eleventh, or twelfth grade but did not receive a high school diploma.

more likely to get a secondary or high school degree than are people aged thirty-five or older.

The right side of table 5.3 shows the distribution of educational attainment among recent Mexican immigrant men in the 2000 U.S. Census. We restrict our sample in this table to those without allocated place of birth, year of arrival, age, or education; this excludes 30 percent of those who would otherwise appear in this table. The U.S. Census also has a grade and degree-based question, but naturally the categories are different than in the Mexican Census. Over 45 percent of Mexican migrant men report they have completed eighth grade or fewer years of schooling; 13.6 percent report they have completed ninth grade; 16.4 percent report they completed tenth through twelfth grade and do not have a high school degree; and 24.6 percent have a high school degree or more education.[12]

Allocated values of education tend to be higher than the actual reported values of education among Mexican migrants, a problem we suspect may be caused by the use of American-born respondents as "donors" for missing data. In any case, including Mexicans with allocated data in the U.S. Census tabulations tend to raise reported education. For example, in unreported tabulations we find that the fraction of sixteen to fifty-four year olds with zero to eight years of education falls from 45.4 percent to 42.8 percent when the 18,074 sample members with allocated data are included. Including allocated data raises the fraction of Mexicans with 10 or more years of education from 41.0 percent to 44.4 percent.

The tabulations in table 5.3 suggest that Mexican migrants in the U.S. Census come from the upper middle of the Mexican educational distribution, which echoes the findings of Chiquiar and Hanson (2005). Forty-five percent of both the U.S. and Mexico samples have between zero and eight years of education. Nonmigrant Mexicans are more likely than Mexicans in the U.S. Census to have nine years of education (a secondary school degree), while migrants are more likely to have between ten years of education and a high school degree. Interestingly, nonmigrants are more likely than migrants to have thirteen or more years of education. In unreported tabulations, we also find that nonmigrants are more likely than migrants to have a college degree or more education. This general pattern is not altered if we included Mexicans in the U.S. Census who have allocated data.

Attempting to credibly compare educational attainment in the U.S. and Mexican Censuses raises several important concerns. First, migrants in the U.S. Census may tend to overreport their education, possibly due to a mistranslation or misunderstanding of the grade and degree choices in the U.S.

12. Unlike the Mexican Census, the U.S. Census has a category for someone who completed twelve years of schooling but does not have a high school degree; 7.8 percent of Mexican migrants are in this category, which is nearly half the number of people who report having a high school degree. The high school degree category in the U.S. Census includes those who passed a high school equivalency exam.

Census.[13] We do not have a method to directly test for a reporting bias among Mexican immigrants in the U.S. Census, but a suggestive piece of evidence that Mexican immigrants in the United States may overstate their educational attainment (or understate their age) is that 9.0 percent of sixteen- and seventeen-year-old Mexicans claim to have a high school degree or more education, compared to 3.6 percent of American-born sixteen- and seventeen-year-olds. In both countries a person would typically be in their third and final years of high school at ages sixteen and seventeen.[14]

A second potential problem is that the migrants in the U.S. Census are a nonrandom subsample of all migrants. We have detailed in the previous section differences in the age distribution of migrants in the two censuses that indicate the U.S. Census undercounts younger migrants. A related worry is that the U.S. Census significantly undercounts illegal and low-skilled migrants of all ages. A final problem is the high prevalence of imputed values among Mexican immigrants in the U.S. Census: A full 30 percent of the migrants in the U.S. Census did not give valid responses to key variables, such as place of birth, year of migration, age, and education. The U.S. Census Bureau provides imputed values for all missing data and the values imputed for migrants' education tend to be higher than the average actual reported values. For example, the fraction of Mexican migrants with a high school degree or more rises from 24.6 percent to 27.1 when individuals with allocated data are included. This increase may result from the U.S. Census Bureau using higher-educated native-born American respondents to impute education to Mexican immigrants. Thus researchers are faced with a choice of using imputed values that are potentially too large or dropping individuals with imputed values and using a sample with an unknown selection bias.

To alleviate some of the difficulties in comparing Mexicans in two different national censuses, with different sampling schemes and different questions, we next turn to an analysis of educational attainment using only the Mexican Census. We begin in table 5.4 with a comparison of the educational attainment of the highest-educated nonmigrant in households that contain at least one migrant to the highest educated member of nonmigrant households. Migrants themselves are not included in this tabulation because we do not observe their level of education. Migrant households are those that had at least one migrant during the past five years, including those in which migrants returned to Mexico. Higher education among

13. For example, a high school degree in Mexico is sometimes referred to as a *bachillerato*, while a bachelor's degree in the United States signifies college completion. Mexicans filling out the U.S. Census may also indicate they have a high school degree when they in fact have a secondary school degree in Mexico, which requires nine years of schooling.

14. Most sixteen- and seventeen-year-old Mexican men in the U.S. Census are the children or relatives of the head of household; less than 3 percent are recorded as the head or spouse. Thus, a parent may be reporting on behalf of sixteen- and seventeen-year-old children. The census does not record which household member filled out the form.

Table 5.4   Comparison of educational attainment between migrant and nonmigrant households

Actual years of education	Highest educated nonmigrant in household		Highest educated female nonmigrant in household		
	Nonmigrant	Migrant	Nonmigrant	Migrant	Only male migrants in households
0 to 4	10.7	10.5	18.5	19.6	19.7
5 to 8	23.1	31.9	28.2	35.1	37.5
9	21.9	24.1	20.0	20.5	21.0
10 to 11	7.8	8.0	6.7	6.3	6.1
12	14.8	11.7	12.8	9.6	8.8
13 or more	21.8	13.9	13.9	9.0	7.0
Average	9.7	8.9	8.3	7.6	7.4
25th percentile	6	6	6	6	6
Median	9	9	9	8	7
75th percentile	12	12	12	9	9
No. of households	2,148,425	137,667	2,014,849	133,025	96,699

Note: A migrant household is a household that contains at least one migrant.

nonmigrant family members is associated with higher family income and is likely associated with higher education among migrant members of the same family. If migrants' family members tend to be better educated than nonmigrant Mexicans, one might have more confidence in the evidence of positive selection of migrants, presented previously. But the tabulations in the left-hand columns of table 5.4 do not bear this out: members of migrant families are more likely than nonmigrant families to have nine years of education or less, while nonmigrant families are more likely to have twelve or more years of education. Members of nonmigrant families have, on average, about 0.8 years more schooling than those in migrant families.

Although these tabulations suggest that migrants come from less-educated households in Mexico, there are two important problems. First, migrants tend to be men aged sixteen to thirty-five, a group that tends to have high educational attainment within Mexico. Thus, migrant households are likely to be missing their most highly educated members, while nonmigrant households contain them. This would lead us to understate the education of migrant households. Second, if children tend to be the highest educated member of migrant households, while adults tend to be the highest educated member of nonmigrant households, then the maximal education in the household may be a poor barometer of the overall economic well-being of the household.

One simple way to address these concerns is to compare the highest educated women across households. Because about 75 percent of migrants are men, measurement of household educational attainment of women in Mexico is much less affected by the absence of migrants. The right-hand columns in table 5.4 compare the educational attainment of the highest educated woman in nonmigrant households, in migrant households, and in migrant households where all migrants are men. The highest educated woman in 55 percent of migrant families has eight or fewer years of education, while only 47 percent of nonmigrant families fall in that range. Women in nonmigrant families are more likely than their counterparts in migrant families to have twelve or more years of education. These conclusions are not altered when we restrict the sample of migrant households to just those with male migrants, shown in the final column. In unreported tabulations, we also find similar conclusions when we restrict attention to women aged sixteen to thirty-five, so the higher educational attainment among nonmigrant families is not driven by higher education solely among children. In sum, our comparison of educational attainment among nonmigrants in Mexico indicates that migrants tend to come from households with lower-educated members.

Our final and preferred method to compare the relative educational attainment of male migrants and nonmigrants is to generate a predicted level of education for each migrant and nonmigrant male Mexican based on their household characteristics and location. We then compare the predicted education of migrants to the predicted education of nonmigrants.

To predict education, we use an ordered logit framework to model the number of years of schooling, S_{ic}, of individual i who lives in county c as a function of indicator variables for age (A_{ic}), six indicator variables for individuals' town size (T_{ic}), indicator variables for the number of children in the household aged zero to eight (Kid_{1ic}), indicators for the number of children nine to sixteen years old (Kid_{2ic}), indicators for the number of men aged seventeen to thirty-five (Man_{1ic}), indicators for the number of men aged thirty-six and older (Man_{2ic}), indicators for the number of women aged seventeen to thirty-five (Woman_{1ic}), and indicators for the number of women aged thirty-six and older (Woman_{2ic}). Formally, we specify a model for a continuous latent schooling index, S_{ic}^*, and run a separate ordered logit model in each county using all men aged twelve and over who are not migrants and who, furthermore, do not live in a migrant household:

$$(4) \quad S_{ic}^* = \delta_{1c} + \delta_{2c}A_{ic} + \delta_{3c}T_{ic} + \delta_{4c}\text{Kid}_{1ic} + \delta_{5c}\text{Kid}_{2ic} + \delta_{6c}\text{Man}_{1ic}$$
$$+ \delta_{7c}\text{Man}_{2ic} + \delta_{8c}\text{Woman}_{1ic} + \delta_{9c}\text{Woman}_{2ic} + \varepsilon_{ic},$$

where each δ_{kc} is a vector of coefficients that vary by county, and ε_{ic} is the error term. The age indicators include single-year indicators for ages twelve to thirty, indicators for three-year groups from thirty-one to seventy, an indicator for people in their seventies, and an indicator for people over eighty. The town-size indicators correspond to towns with less than 2,500 people; 2,500 to 14,999; 15,000 to 19,999; 20,000 to 49,999; 50,000 to 99,999; 100,000 to 499,999; and a half-million or more people. The indicator variables for the number of children, adult men, and adult women include indicators that the household contains one, two, three, or more than three of each type of person. Equation (4) is only estimated on nonmigrants who live in nonmigrant households because the educational attainment of the migrants' family members may be affected by remittances from migrants living abroad (see Hanson and Woodruff 2003).[15]

Next, we use the coefficient estimates to compute the predicted education for all Mexicans in the data, which includes out-of-sample predictions for nonmigrants who live in migrant households and for migrants themselves. The probability that education is equal to j years is given by $\hat{S}_{ic}(j) = P(S_{ic} = j \mid x_{ic}) = \Lambda(\hat{\alpha}_j - x_{ic}\hat{\delta}_c) - \Lambda(\hat{\alpha}_{j-1} - x_{ic}\hat{\delta}_c)$, where Λ is the logit function, x_{ic} is the set of covariates, and $\hat{\alpha}_j$ is the estimated cut point between schooling level j and $j + 1$.[16] Thus, for each person we have twenty-three probabilities, corresponding to the probability of having zero through twenty-two years of education. We also compute the expected number of years of education, given by

$$(5) \qquad \hat{S}_{ic} = E(\hat{S}_{ic} \mid x_{ic}) = \sum_{j=0}^{22} j\hat{S}_{ic}(j).$$

These measures of predicted education can be interpreted as an index of educational attainment or socioeconomic status more generally. The model in equation (4) and the prediction are based only on the individuals' county, age, and household-level characteristics as these are the only variables available for the migrants. Another way to view this procedure is that we are assigning to migrants the average educational attainment of nonmigrants who live in towns of the same size in their county, who are the same age, and who have a similar family structure. If there are systematic unobserved differences between migrants and nonmigrants in these narrow cells, we may over- or underpredict migrant education. For example, the theory in section 5.2 predicted that migrants will tend to be less educated than nonmigrants from across Mexico as a whole. If this prediction holds even within narrow geography, age, and family structure cells, then we are likely overstating the education of migrants. Similarly, if migrants were more likely to work when young and thus attended fewer class sessions, then we are again likely to be overstating the relative skills of migrants. Although we cannot directly test the identifying assumption underlying this procedure that there are no unobserved differences between migrants and nonmigrants within the narrow geography, age, and family

---

15. An earlier version of this paper used a linear regression to estimate equation (4); (Ibarraran and Lubotsky 2005). The results are nearly identical to those based on the ordered logit model here.

16. The predicted probability of zero years of education is $P(S_{ic} = 0 \mid x_{ic}) = \Lambda(\hat{\alpha}_1 - x_{ic}\hat{\delta}_c)$, and the probability of twenty-two years of education is $P(S_{ic} = 22 \mid x_{ic}) = 1 - \Lambda(\hat{\alpha}_{22} - x_{ic}\hat{\delta}_c)$. More details on the ordered logit model are given in Woolridge (2002).

Table 5.5   **Comparison of actual and predicted education**

	Actual education		Predicted education		
Years of education	Men in nonmigrant households (1)	Nonmigrant men in migrant households (2)	Men in nonmigrant households (3)	Nonmigrant men in migrant households (4)	Migrant men (5)
0 to 4	17.3	23.3	15.4	23.0	17.8
5 to 8	27.0	31.5	31.7	35.1	36.2
9	21.9	20.9	20.9	18.2	19.8
10 to 11	7.9	6.9	7.4	5.7	6.1
12	11.0	8.1	10.1	7.6	8.4
13 or more	14.9	9.3	14.6	10.5	11.7
Mean	8.5	7.5	8.5	7.5	8.0
25th percentile	6	5	7.0	5.7	6.3
Median	9	7	9.0	7.7	8.0
75th percentile	12	9	10.3	9.5	9.7
Sample size	2,276,862	129,733	2,276,862	129,733	134,743

Note: Data include men aged sixteen to fifty-four in the 2000 Mexican Census.

structure cells, we provide suggestive evidence below that it may be reasonable.[17]

Table 5.5 and figure 5.3 compare the distribution of actual and predicted education. For ease of exposition, in table 5.5 the twenty-three levels of education are grouped into six bins. A comparison of actual and predicted education at all levels is shown in figure 5.3. Column (1) of table 5.5 shows the distribution of actual years of education among nonmigrant men aged sixteen to fifty-four who do not live in a migrant household. Column (3) shows the distribution of predicted education for this group. In the table and figure, the predicted frequency of education level j is given by the average predicted probability of education being equal to j. The distribution of actual and predicted education match closely, and there is no systematic pattern in the differences between the two across the levels of education. The mean education of these nonmigrants is eight and a half years and matches the average predicted education, computed according to equation (5).

The model also does well in making out-of-sample predictions of the education of nonmigrants who live in households that also contain migrants. The distribution of actual education, shown in column (2) of table 5.5, closely matches the distribution of predicted education, shown in column (4), for these nonmigrants. The actual and predicted means are both equal to seven and a half years of education. An informal way to assess the ac-

17. One might also be concerned that as migrants are more likely to come from rural areas, they may also attend lower-quality schools. Thus simply comparing completed years of schooling may understate the relative skills of migrants.

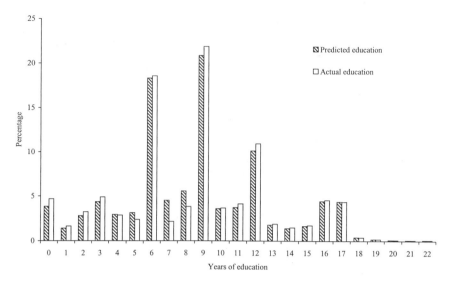

Fig. 5.3   Comparison of predicted and actual education for nonmigrants

Note: Sample excludes nonmigrants who live in households that also contain migrants, as described in the text.

curacy of the model for nonmigrants in migrant households is to note that the root mean square error is 3.57 for the model using nonmigrants who live in nonmigrant households and is 3.66 in the out-of-sample prediction for nonmigrants who live in migrant households.[18] The good fit of the model in predicting education for nonmigrants in migrant households indicates there are not systematic differences in unmeasured determinants of schooling between nonmigrants who live in migrant households and those who do not. We take this as suggestive evidence that the identifying assumption underlying our method of comparing predicted education between nonmigrants and migrants is reasonable.

Column (5) of table 5.5 shows the distribution of predicted education among Mexican migrants. Figures 5.4 and 5.5 compare the distributions of predicted education between migrants and nonmigrants in nonmigrant households and show quite clearly that migrants tend to be less educated than nonmigrants. This is most clearly seen in figure 5.5, which graphs the difference between the height of the distribution of nonmigrants' predicted education and the height of the distribution among migrants. Migrants are more likely than nonmigrants to have between zero and seven years of education. Nonmigrants, by contrast, are more likely to have eight or more years of education. On average, the predicted education of migrants is a

---

18. The root mean square error is given by $[(1/N)\Sigma_N (S_{ic} - \hat{S}_{ic})^2]^{1/2}$, where i indexes the sample from 1 to N.

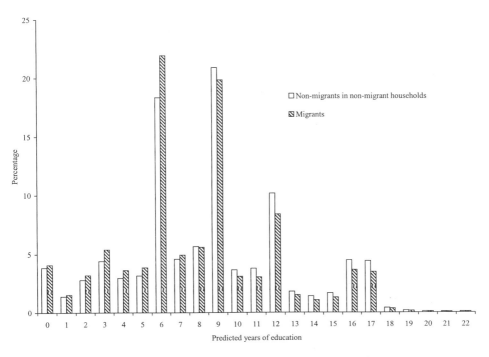

Fig. 5.4   Comparison of predicted education of migrants and nonmigrants
Note: Nonmigrant sample excludes nonmigrants who live in households that also contain migrants, as described in the text.

half year less than the predicted education of nonmigrants who live in non-migrant households and is a half year more than the predicted education of nonmigrants coming from their same households. If the lack of a discrepancy between actual and predicted education among nonmigrants who live with migrants is any guide, the actual education of migrants is likely to also be less than the actual education of nonmigrants.[19] The bottom panel of table 5.5 shows the 25th, median, and 75th percentiles of the distributions of actual and predicted education. The lower predicted education of migrants we see at the mean is also evident throughout the distribution. The predicted education of the median migrant would put him at the 36th percentile in the distribution of predicted education among nonmigrants.

The three panels of table 5.6 show differences in predicted education by age, by region within Mexico, and by town size. One might worry that our

19. Note that another way we could test the assumption underlying our use of predicted education is to construct predicted education for Mexican migrants in the U.S. Census. Unfortunately, we cannot do this because we do not have their Mexican household or geographic information.

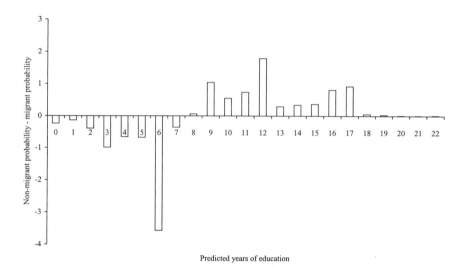

Fig. 5.5   Difference in distribution of predicted education between nonmigrants and migrants

Note: Nonmigrant sample excludes nonmigrants who live in households that also contain migrants, as described in the text.

finding of lower predicted education among migrants may be driven by differences in the average age of migrants and nonmigrants. The tabulations in panel A of table 5.6 show evidence of negative selection within four age groups, and the degree of negative selection is, in fact, larger among older Mexicans than among younger ones. Interestingly, the magnitude of negative selection among migrants within age groups is larger than the negative selection among migrants of all ages. Because overall educational attainment is considerably lower among those aged forty-six to fifty-four and very few of them are migrants, including them in an aggregate analysis reduces the overall gap in education between migrants and nonmigrants.

Panel B shows that two-thirds of Mexican migrant men aged sixteen to fifty-four originate in one of fourteen states in Central Mexico, and the migration rate in this region is 7.5 percent. Interestingly, the nationwide gap in predicted education is entirely driven by the difference in this region. Migrants from the southern states of Mexico are slightly more educated than nonmigrants, while predicted education is approximately equal among migrants and nonmigrants in Mexico City and the state of Mexico and the seven northern border states.

Mexican migrants to the United States tend to come from smaller towns within Mexico. Panel C of table 5.6 shows differences in selection by town size: 42.5 percent of migrants come from towns with populations less than 2,500, but the remaining 57.5 percent of migrants are fairly equally dis-

Table 5.6   **Differences in predicted education between migrants and nonmigrants by age, region, and town size**

	Sample size	Migration rate (%)	Fraction of all migrants (%)	Average predicted education of nonmigrants	Average predicted education of migrants	Difference
			A. Differences by age			
Age group						
16 to 25	985,227	6.7	59.0	8.89	8.20	0.69
26 to 35	720,191	4.0	26.4	8.97	8.24	0.72
36 to 45	529,494	2.3	11.0	8.22	6.89	1.33
46 to 54	306,426	1.3	3.6	6.53	5.27	1.26
Total	2,541,338	4.3	100.0	8.47	7.96	0.51
			B. Differences by region of origin			
Region						
Central Mexico	963,705	7.5	63.5	8.01	7.55	0.46
Southern states	680,742	3.0	15.1	7.41	7.59	−0.18
Northern border states	395,079	2.2	9.3	9.06	9.09	−0.03
Mexico City and state	501,812	2.2	12.1	9.65	9.68	−0.04
Total	2,541,338	4.3	100.0	8.47	7.96	0.51
			C. Differences by town size			
Town size						
Less than 2,500	964,661	8.0	42.5	5.78	6.41	−0.63
2,500 to 14,999	435,627	6.0	18.0	7.43	7.81	−0.38
15,000 to 99,999	273,048	4.3	13.6	8.52	8.70	−0.18
100,000 to 499,999	393,062	2.2	11.2	9.84	10.14	−0.30
500,000 or more	474,940	2.3	14.7	9.92	10.28	−0.37
Total	2,541,338	4.3	100.0	8.47	7.96	0.51

Notes: Sample includes men aged sixteen to fifty-four. The sample size is unweighted; all other estimates use the population weights. Predicted education is defined in the text. Central Mexico includes the states of Aguascalientes, Colima, Durango, Guanajuato, Hidalgo, Jalisco, Michoacán de Ocampo, Morelos, Nayarit, Puebla, Querétaro de Arteaga, San Luis Potosí, Sinaloa, and Tlaxcala. The northern border states include Baja California, Baja California Sur, Coahuila de Zaragoza, Chihuahua, Nuevo León Sonoora, and Tamaulipas. The southern states include Campeche, Chiapas, Guerrero, Oaxaca, Quintana Roo, Tabasco, Veracruz-Llave, and Yucatán.

tributed among towns with populations of 2,500 and larger. The migration rate is 7.8 percent among all towns with a population of less than 2,500, and the rate tends to fall as town size increases. At the same time, average education of both migrants and nonmigrants tends to rise with town size. Conditional on town size, migrants tend to be more educated than nonmigrants. Negative selection overall is driven by the fact that migrants tend to come from small towns, where educational attainment is very low, while the average nonmigrant lives in a larger city, where educational attainment tends to be higher. These patterns may reflect a process in which better-educated individuals tend to migrate from smaller towns in Mexico to both larger cities and to the United States, and only the least educated people remain in small towns.

The results in this section show that Mexican migrants enumerated in the 2000 Mexican Census come from less-educated households than nonmigrants and also have characteristics associated with being less educated, consistent with the predictions of our theoretical model. This evidence of negative selection is at odds with results from the U.S. Census. However, an important limitation of the Mexican Census is that it does not contain migrants whose whole household moved to the United States. The degree to which our results would be affected if we were able to include this group depends on the size of the missing group and on the degree of positive or negative selection among them. Clearly, our general conclusion about negative selection will not change if the educational attainment of nonsampled migrants is similar to the educational attainment of sampled migrants or the fraction of migrants not sampled is very small. Our tabulations in table 5.1 indicate that the estimated population of Mexican immigrants in the Mexican Census is about 84 percent of the size of the estimated population in the U.S. Census, corresponding to a 16 percent undercount. To the extent that the U.S. Census undercounts migrants as well, the size of the undercount in the Mexican Census may be larger than indicated by the preceding numbers. Because the migrants missing from the Mexican Census are those whose whole household moved to the United States, another way to approximate the magnitude of the undercount is to note that there are about 292,000 Mexican men in the U.S. Census who are classified as married with spouse present in the household. If each of these men were missing from the Mexican Census, it would correspond to a 26 percent undercount of men.

Table 5.7 investigates the degree to which our results would be affected by positive selection among migrants not enumerated in the Mexican Census. The left-hand column shows alternative hypothetical undercount rates among Mexican migrants, ranging from 0 percent (i.e., the Mexican Census actually contains a full random sample of Mexican migrants) to 50 percent (i.e., the Mexican Census contains a random sample of 50 percent of the Mexican migrant population and contains none of the other 50 percent). The next five columns of the table correspond to alternative assumptions about the degree of positive or negative selection among the nonsampled group. The first column assumes that 100 percent of the missing migrants would have predicted education above 8.9 years, which is the median predicted education among all nonmigrant Mexicans. This is an unrealistically large degree of positive selection, but it gives a lower bound on how large the undercount would have to be for there to be negative selection among the enumerated migrants and positive selection overall. The remaining columns correspond to 75 percent, 50 percent, 36 percent, and 25 percent of the missing migrants having predicted education above 8.9

Table 5.7   Estimates of how the undercount in the Mexican Census influences conclusions about migrant self-selection

	Fraction of missing migrants with predicted education above the median among nonmigrant Mexicans				
	100%	75%	50%	36%	25%
Fraction of Mexican migrants missing from 2000 Mexican Census	Fraction of all Mexican migrants with predicted education above the median Mexican nonmigrant				
0	36.0	36.0	36.0	36.0	36.0
5	39.2	38.0	36.7	36.0	35.5
10	42.4	39.9	37.4	36.0	34.9
15	45.6	41.9	38.1	36.0	34.4
20	48.8	43.8	38.8	36.0	33.8
22	50.1	44.6	39.1	36.0	33.6
25	52.0	45.8	39.5	36.0	33.3
30	55.2	47.7	40.2	36.0	32.7
40	61.6	51.6	41.6	36.0	31.6
50	68.0	55.5	43.0	36.0	30.5

Notes: The entries in the left column are alternative measures of the fraction of male Mexican migrants who are not enumerated in the 2000 Mexican Census. The columns to the right give the fraction of all male Mexican migrants with predicted education above 8.9 years (the median predicted education among all nonmigrant men) based on alternative assumptions about the predicted education of the missing migrants.

years. The column corresponding to 36 percent is significant because it is the same degree of negative selection that we estimate for migrants who are enumerated in the Mexican Census. The entries in the table give the fraction of all Mexican migrants (among both the sampled and missing groups) who would predict education above 8.9 years. Hence, an entry larger than 50 percent indicates overall positive selection of migrants, and an entry smaller than 50 percent indicates overall negative selection.[20]

The results indicate the undercount rate among Mexican migrants would have to be greater than 22 percent to overturn the degree of negative selection that we find among sampled Mexican migrants, and at this undercount rate the predicted education of all nonsampled migrants would have to be greater than the median predicted education of nonmigrant men. However, this degree of positive selection is certainly unrealistic. If only 75 percent of nonsampled migrants had predicted education above the median, then the undercount would have to be nearly 40 percent. Finally, if there was no selection among nonsampled migrants relative to nonmigrants—which still corresponds to nonsampled migrants being significantly better educated than sampled migrants—then there would still be significant negative selection among all Mexican migrants.

20. Specifically, the entries in the table are computed as $(1 - \alpha) \cdot 36\% + \alpha \cdot \beta$, where α is the fraction of Mexican migrants not represented in the Mexican Census, and β is the fraction of that group that has predicted education above 8.9 years.

We conclude from these tabulations that although negative selection among sampled migrants may overstate the overall degree of negative selection, the undercount rate would have to be very large, and there would have to be a significantly large degree of positive selection among nonsampled migrants for there to, in fact, be positive selection among Mexican migrants as a whole. It seems likely that the small degree of positive selection found by comparing migrants in the U.S. Census with nonmigrants in the Mexican Census is driven by a combination of an undersample of young and lower-skilled migrants and overreporting of education by Mexican migrants. But clearly more research is needed to definitively reconcile these two data sources.

5.5   The Returns to Schooling and Migrant Self-Selection

In this section we test the prediction that the degree of selection will be larger in regions within Mexico that have relatively higher returns to schooling. Recall that in our earlier model the wage gain from migrating to the United States for a person with schooling level S_{ic} who lives in Mexican county c is given by

$$(6) \qquad G_{ic} = (\alpha_u - \alpha_c) + S_{ic}(\beta_u - \beta_c),$$

where β_u is the return to schooling in the United States, and β_c is the return to schooling in Mexican county c. A person migrates if the wage gain plus any nonpecuniary gains outweigh the costs of migration. Formally, define the indicator variable M_{ic} to equal one if person i migrates to the United States and zero otherwise. Then $M_{ic} = 1$ if $G_{ic} > \pi_{ic}$, where π_{ic} are time-equivalent migration costs net of any nonpecuniary gains. Alternatively, $M_{ic} = 1$ if

$$(7) \qquad (\alpha_u - \alpha_c - \pi_{ic}) + S_{ic}(\beta_u - \beta_c) > 0.$$

Lacking data on migration costs, we approximate the term $(\alpha_u - \alpha_c - \pi_{ic})$ as a function of indicators for an individual's age and either county or state of residence and model the migration probability as

$$(8) \qquad \mathrm{Pr}(M_{ic} = 1) = A_{ic} + d_c + \lambda_1 \hat{S}_{ic} + \lambda_2 \hat{\beta}_c + \lambda_3 \hat{\beta}_c \hat{S}_{ic} + v_{ic},$$

where A_{ic} is a full set of indicators for each age from sixteen to fifty-four, and d_c is either a set of state or county indicators.[21] $\hat{S}_{ic}$ is the predicted schooling level, computed according to equation (5). $\hat{\beta}_c$ is an estimate of the returns to schooling in county c, as described below.

---

21. The main effect of the county rate of return to schooling, λ_2, is not identified when county-fixed effects are included in the model, but the interaction effect λ_3 is identified. Both the main and interaction effects are identified when the county-fixed effects are replaced with state-fixed effects.

Our main parameter of interest is λ_3, the coefficient on the interaction between an individual migrant's education and the return to education in his county of origin. If $\beta_u - \beta_c < 0$, then according to equation (6), schooling should have a negative influence on the wage gain to migrating, and this effect should be more negative in areas with higher returns to schooling. That is, we expect λ_3 to be negative.

We estimate the county-level returns to schooling, $\hat{\beta}_c$, by estimating a regression of the log monthly wage on years of completed schooling and a quartic in age among men aged eighteen to fifty-four. We run this model separately by county and weight each observation by the Mexican Census population weight. One clear problem is that our estimated return to education at the county level may be influenced by the relative skill levels of past migrants. If less-educated Mexicans tend to leave a county, the return to education in the county should fall. If this is an important feature of the data, it would tend to bias our regression estimates of equation (8) toward finding a positive effect of the interaction between migrants' predicted education and their local return to schooling. More generally, it will lead our ordinary least squares estimates to understate the negative interaction between schooling and the local return to education. Lacking any credible instruments for the local return to schooling, we proceed with our ordinary least squares models.

Our estimates of the return to schooling may also be influenced by the lack of earnings data for workers in the informal sector. Missing earnings data may be particularly problematic in rural areas and among those working in a family business. Typically, these workers have low levels of schooling and low earnings. The exclusion of these workers from our sample will likely lead us to understate the return to education in general, but may also affect the relative returns to education across areas.

We estimate equation (8) separately by region using a linear probability model.[22] The results are shown in table 5.8 and, at least for the central and southern regions of Mexico, are consistent with our theoretical predictions. We estimate the model without any geographic-fixed effects (model 1), with state-fixed effects (model 2), and with county-fixed effects (model 3). In Central and Southern Mexico, the origin of nearly 80 percent of migrants, the interaction between individuals' predicted education and their county return to education has a negative and statistically significant effect on the probability of migrating to the United States.[23] The predictions are not supported by the results from Northern Mexico or from Mexico City and the state of Mexico. The parameter estimate for the interaction effect is positive and, in the latter group, statistically significant.

22. Linear probability models were considerably quicker to estimate, particularly when we included county-fixed effects. We find essentially similar results using probit models.

23. The standard errors in table 5.8 adjust for clustering at the county level but are not adjusted for the fact that predicted education and the country return to schooling are themselves estimated variables.

Table 5.8   Regression estimates of migration propensity, by region

	Central Mexico			Southern states			Northern border states			Mexico City and state		
	(1)	(2)	(3)	(1)	(2)	(3)	(1)	(2)	(3)	(1)	(2)	(3)
County rate of return to schooling	0.520**	0.366*		0.055	0.004		-0.078	-0.236		-0.652***	-0.639**	
	(0.232)	(0.198)		(0.069)	(0.065)		(0.247)	(0.255)		(0.254)	(0.248)	
Years of predicted education	-0.002	0.000	0.006***	0.006***	0.002*	0.006***	-0.003	-0.002	0.001	-0.005*	-0.005*	0.001
	(0.002)	(0.002)	(0.002)	(0.001)	(0.001)	(0.001)	(0.002)	(0.002)	(0.002)	(0.003)	(0.003)	(0.002)
Rate of return · years of predicted education	-0.111***	-0.113***	-0.085***	-0.073***	-0.035***	-0.059***	0.011	0.019	0.042**	0.054**	0.058**	0.035**
	(0.029)	(0.025)	(0.026)	(0.013)	(0.012)	(0.011)	(0.024)	(0.026)	(0.021)	(0.024)	(0.023)	(0.017)
Age indicators	Yes	Yes	Yes	Yes	Yes	Yes	Yes	Yes	Yes	Yes	Yes	Yes
State indicators	No	Yes	No	No	Yes	No	No	Yes	No	No	Yes	No
County indicators	No	No	Yes	No	No	Yes	No	No	Yes	No	No	Yes
Sample size	963,705	963,705	963,705	670,657	670,657	670,657	395,079	395,079	395,079	501,812	501,812	501,812
R^2	0.030	0.039	0.079	0.015	0.026	0.066	0.005	0.007	0.028	0.006	0.006	0.024

Notes: Each column is a separate regression, as described in the text. Standard errors in parentheses are adjusted for clustering at the county level. All models use population weights. Sample includes all Mexican men aged sixteen to fifty-four. Regions are given in the note to panel B in table 5.6.

***Significant at the 1 percent level.

**Significant at the 5 percent level.

*Significant at the 10 percent level.

It is difficult to know why the regression results support the predictions of the theoretical model within Central and Southern Mexico but do not support the predictions in the northern states or Mexico City and the state of Mexico. Central Mexico is the source of most migrants, and has been for some time. Migration networks may be developed in this area to the point that migration costs are generally low for most families, and migration decisions largely reflect wage differences. More generally, a potentially interesting avenue for future research is to explore differences in the level and source of migration costs between Mexican regions as well as differences in migration propensities.

To help interpret the magnitude of our regression results, in table 5.9 we show predicted migration probabilities derived from our regressions. These rates refer to twenty-five-year-old Mexicans and show how migration differs between those with six and ten years of predicted education living in Mexican counties with returns to education of either 0.06 or 0.10. In Central Mexico these levels of predicted education correspond to approximately the 30th and 85th percentiles, and the returns to education correspond to approximately the 30th and 90th percentiles. At the top of this table, we show the migration rate in each region, the fraction of migrants that originate in each region, and the average rate of return to education in

Table 5.9   **Predicted migration propensities, by region, predicted education, and return to education**

	Central Mexico		Southern states		Northern border states		Mexico City and state	
Migration rate	7.5%		3.0%		2.2%		2.2%	
Fraction of total migrants	63.5%		15.1%		9.3%		12.1%	
Average return to education	0.074		0.087		0.084		0.100	
	Model specification							
	(1)	(2)	(1)	(2)	(1)	(2)	(1)	(2)
State indicators	No	Yes	No	Yes	No	Yes	No	Yes
Predicted migration rate with return to education = 0.06								
Predicted education								
6 years	12.2%	11.9%	5.1%	4.6%	3.7%	3.6%	4.7%	4.3%
10 years	8.8%	9.4%	5.6%	4.7%	2.9%	3.1%	3.8%	3.5%
Predicted migration rate with return to education = 0.10								
Predicted education								
6 years	11.6%	10.7%	3.5%	3.8%	3.6%	3.2%	3.3%	3.2%
10 years	6.4%	6.3%	2.9%	3.3%	3.0%	3.0%	3.3%	3.3%

Note: The predicted migration rates are calculated from the parameter estimates in table 5.8 for a twenty-five-year-old person.

each region. Counties in Central Mexico with a rate of return to education of 0.6 would tend to have a migration rate of 12.2 percent among Mexicans with six years of education, based on our results from model 1. The migration rate falls by 3.4 percentage points to 8.8 percent among those with ten years of education who live in the same area. Areas in Central Mexico with a rate of return to schooling of 0.10 are predicted to have a 5.2 percentage point difference in migration propensities between higher- and lower-educated Mexicans. In this scenario, migration rates are 11.6 percent and 6.4 percent for the lower- and higher-educated Mexicans. Our findings are similar when we use models 2 and 3 from table 5.8 to generate the predicted migration rates.

In Central Mexico, the gap in migration rates between low- and high-educated Mexicans is significant even in areas with low returns to education, but the gap is considerably larger in areas that have relatively high returns to education. We view this evidence as indicating strong support for the idea that local variation in the wage gap between the United States and counties throughout this part of Mexico generates economically significant variation in the incentives for different types of Mexicans to migrate to the United States. In southern Mexico, which accounts for 15.1 percent of migration, migrants in areas with returns to education of 0.06 are slightly positively selected. Using the estimates from specification 1, the migration rate is predicted to be 5.1 percent among those with six years of predicted education and 5.6 percent among those with ten years of predicted education. However, migration becomes negatively selected as the rate of return to education rises. In areas with a return of 0.10, we predict a migration of 3.5 percent among lower-educated Mexicans and 2.5 percent among higher-educated Mexicans. Echoing our regression results in table 5.8, higher returns to education in the northern border states or in Mexico City and state do not generate an increase in the magnitude of negative selection.

5.6 Conclusions

We use the 2000 Mexican Census to examine the educational attainment of Mexican migrants to the United States and their families. Our primary conclusion is that migrants tend to be less educated than nonmigrants. This is consistent with the idea that the greater return to skills in Mexico provides an incentive for better-skilled Mexicans to remain in Mexico and for lower-skilled Mexicans to migrate to the United States. We also find that the degree of negative selection is magnified in Mexican counties that have relatively higher returns to skills. Finally, we find that Mexican migrants in the 2000 U.S. Census are better educated than migrants in the Mexican Census. Although part of this discrepancy may be caused by an undercount of Mexican migrants whose whole household moved to the

United States and were therefore not sampled in the Mexican Census, part may also be due to an undercount of younger, illegal, and low-skilled Mexicans in the U.S. Census.

References

Bean, Frank D., Rodolfo Corona, Rodolfo Tuirán, and Karen A. Woodrow-Lafield. 1998. The quantification of migration between Mexico and the United States. In *Migration between Mexico and the United States: Bi-National study,* 1–88. Mexican Ministry of Foreign Affairs and U.S. Commission on Immigration Reform. Austin, TX: Morgan Printing.

Bean, Frank D., Rodolfo Corona, Rodolfo Tuirán, Karen A. Woodrow-Lafield, and Jennifer van Hook. 2001. Circular, invisible, and ambiguous migrants: Components of difference in estimates of the number of unauthorized Mexican migrants in the United States. *Demography* 38 (3): 411–22.

Borjas, George. 1987. Self-selection and the earnings of immigrants. *American Economic Review* 77 (4): 531–53.

———. 1991. Immigration and self-selection. In *Immigration, trade, and the labor market,* ed. John M. Abowd and Richard B. Freeman, 29–76. Chicago: University of Chicago Press.

———. 1999. The economic analysis of immigration. In *Handbook of labor economics.* Vol. 3A, ed. Orley C. Ashenfelter and David Card, 1697–1760. Amsterdam: North-Holland.

Chiquiar, Daniel, and Gordon Hanson. 2005. International migration, self-selection, and the distribution of wages: Evidence from Mexico and the United States. *Journal of Political Economy* 113 (2): 239–81.

Costanzo, Joe, Cynthia Davis, Caribert Irazi, Daniel Goodkind, and Roberto Ramirez. 2001. Evaluating components of international migration: The residual foreign born. U.S. Census Bureau Population Division Working Paper Series no. 61. Washington, DC: U.S. Census Bureau, December.

Crease, Arthur, Roberto Ramirez, and Gregory Spencer. 2001. Evaluating components of international migration: Quality of foreign-born and Hispanic population data. U.S. Census Bureau Population Division Working Paper Series no. 65. Washington, DC: U.S. Census Bureau, December.

Cuecuecha, Alfredo. 2003. The educational characteristics of the immigrants from Mexico to the U.S. Instituto Technológico Autónomo de México-Centro de Investigacion Economica, Working Paper.

de Janvry, Alain, Elisabeth Sadoulet, and Paul Winters. 2001. Family and community networks in Mexico-U.S. migration. *Journal of Human Resources* 36 (1): 159–84.

Durand, Jorge, Douglas Massey, and Rene Zenteno. 2001. Mexican immigration to the United States: Continuities and changes. *Latin American Research Review* 36 (1): 107–27.

Hanson, Gordon, and Christopher Woodruff. 2003. Emigration and educational attainment in Mexico. University of California at San Diego, Department of Economics, Working Paper.

Hirsch, Barry T., and Edward J. Schumacher. 2004. Match bias in wage gap estimates due to earnings imputation. *Journal of Labor Economics* 22 (3): 689–722.

Ibarraran, Pablo, and Darren Lubotsky. 2005. Mexican immigration and self-selection: New evidence from the 2000 Mexican Census. NBER Working Paper no. 11456. Cambridge, MA: National Bureau of Economic Research, June.

Jaeger, David A. 1997. Reconciling the old and new Census Bureau education questions: Recommendations for researchers. *Journal of Business and Economic Statistics* 15 (3): 300 309.

Massey, Douglas, and Audrey Singer. 1998. The social process of undocumented border crossing among Mexican migrants. *International Migration Review* 32: 561–92.

McKenzie, David, and Hillel Rapoport. 2004. Network effects and the dynamics of migration and inequality: Theory and evidence from Mexico. Bureau for Research and Economic Analysis of Development Working Paper no. 063. Cambridge, MA: BREAD, April.

Munshi, Kaivan. 2003. Networks in the modern economy: Mexican migrants in the U.S. labor market. *Quarterly Journal of Economics* 118 (2): 549–97.

Orrenius, Pia, and Madeline Zavodny. 2005. Self-selection among undocumented immigrants from Mexico. *Journal of Development Economics* 78 (1): 215–40.

Trejo, Stephen. 1997. Why do Mexican Americans earn low wages? *Journal of Political Economy* 105 (6): 1235–68.

Woolridge, Jeffrey M. 2002. *Econometric analysis of cross section and panel data.* Cambridge, MA: MIT Press.

6

The Diffusion of Mexican Immigrants during the 1990s
Explanations and Impacts

David Card and Ethan G. Lewis

During the 1990s the number of Mexican immigrants living in the United States rose by nearly five million people. This rapid growth is illustrated by the solid line in figure 6.1, which shows the number of working-age Mexican immigrants recorded in the 2000 Census by year of arrival in the United States.[1] At the time of the census, Mexican immigrants represented 4.1 percent of the working-age population, nearly double their proportion in 1990. The surge in arrivals from Mexico was accompanied by a remarkable shift in their residence patterns. In previous decades, nearly 80 percent of Mexican immigrants settled in either California or Texas. Over the 1990s, however, this fraction fell rapidly. As shown by the dotted line in figure 6.1, less than one-half of the most recent Mexican immigrants were living in California or Texas in 2000. Many cities that had very few Mexican immigrants in 1990—including Atlanta, Raleigh-Durham, Portland, and Seattle—gained significant Mexican populations. The inflow of Mexican immigrants to Southeastern cities is particularly significant because of the potential impact on the labor market prospects of less-skilled African Americans.

In this paper we explore potential explanations for the widening geo-

David Card is Class of 1950 Professor of Economics at the University of California at Berkeley, and a research associate of the National Bureau of Economic Research. Ethan G. Lewis is an economist in the research department of the Federal Reserve Bank of Philadelphia.

We are grateful to Elizabeth Cascio and Christian Dustmann for helpful discussions and to George Borjas, Lawrence Katz, Gordon Hanson, and other seminar participants for comments and suggestions. Card's research was supported by a grant from the National Institute of Child Health and Development.

1. The jagged nature of the line reflects the tendency of census respondents to report that they arrived five, ten, fifteen, . . . years ago.

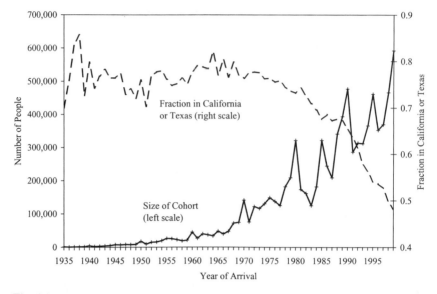

Fig. 6.1   Number and location of Mexican immigrants, by arrival year

graphic distribution of Mexican immigrants and examine the effects of Mexican immigration on local labor markets across the country. We begin with a descriptive overview of the location choices and other characteristics of recent Mexican immigrants. Post-1990 Mexican immigrants have about the same education and English-speaking ability as those who arrived in earlier decades. They differ mainly in their destinations: those who arrived in the 1990s were less likely to move to Los Angeles (the traditional destination of about one-third of all Mexican immigrants) and more likely to move to cities in the Southeast, Northwest, and Mountain states. The geographic shift was associated with some change in industry concentration, with fewer of the recent arrivals working in agriculture and more in construction (for men) and retail trade (for women).

We then go on to a more formal analysis of the role of supply-push and demand-pull factors in explaining the diffusion of Mexican immigrants across U.S. cities in the 1990s. Supplies of potential immigrants were rising over the decade, driven by population growth, falling real wages, and persistently weak economic conditions in Mexico.[2] Historically, new immigrants tend to follow earlier immigrants from the same country. Thus, we use information on the fraction of Mexican immigrants in a city in 1980 and 1990 as predictors of the supply-push component of immigrant flows.

2. Real wages in Mexico were about 20 percent lower in 2000 than in 1990. See Organization for Economic Cooperation and Development (OECD; 2000, 32).

On the demand side, we use predicted county-level employment growth over the 1990s, extrapolated from trends in the 1980s, as a measure of exogenous employment demand growth. Both factors are significant predictors of Mexican immigrant inflows, with supply-push factors explaining 75 percent of the intercity variation in inflow rates over the 1990s and demand-pull factors explaining another 10 percent.[3] By comparison, the relative wages and employment rates of Mexican immigrants in a city in 1990 are uncorrelated with subsequent inflows.

The remainder of the paper is focused on understanding how inflows of Mexican immigrants have affected local labor market conditions. We begin by showing that higher inflows of recent Mexican immigrants are associated with increases in the relative supply of less-educated labor in the local economy. Offsetting movements of previous immigrants and natives with low levels of education appear to be relatively small. We then examine the role of changing industry structure in explaining the absorption of relatively unskilled population inflows. The Hecksher-Olin (HO) model of trade suggests that shifts in the relative supply of unskilled labor can be absorbed by the expansion of low-skill-intensive industries, with little or no change in relative wages of unskilled workers. We develop a simple decomposition that allows us to characterize the fraction of the excess supply of dropout labor in a local market that has been absorbed by HO-style industry shifts. Our analysis suggests that between-industry shifts account for only a small fraction of the overall absorption of the extra dropout labor created by Mexican inflows.

In view of this finding, we turn to the impact of Mexican immigration on the relative wage structure. We construct estimates of the wage gap in each city between native men with exactly twelve years of schooling and those who did not complete high school and relate this gap to the relative supply of dropouts in the local market. Consistent with most of the existing literature (see, e.g., the review in Card 2005) we find that increases in the relative supply of dropouts induced by Mexican immigration inflows have small effects on relative wages of less-educated natives. The absence of a discernable effect on relative wages is especially puzzling given that most of the absorption of the excess supply of dropout labor created by Mexican immigrant inflows arises within narrowly defined (three-digit) industries. Evidently, the adjustments needed to accommodate differences in the relative supply of dropout labor in different markets occur without the intervening mechanism of relative wage changes. The data do not allow us to tell whether this is because high school dropouts and high school graduates are highly substitutable in production or as a result of other adjustment processes, such as endogenous technical change.

---

3. The two components are almost orthogonal so their contributions add up.

6.1   An Overview of Mexican Immigration in the 1990s

6.1.1   Census Data

Our empirical analysis is based on public use data from the 1980, 1990, and 2000 Censuses. The primary advantages of these data files are sample size and geographic coverage. For example, the 1980 Census includes 109,628 Mexican immigrants (72 percent of whom are between the ages of sixteen and sixty-five) and identifies more than 300 separate Metropolitan Statistical Areas (MSAs). A serious disadvantage is undercoverage of Mexican immigrants. Calculations by Borjas, Freeman, and Lang (1991) suggest that the 1980 Census missed approximately 40 percent of unauthorized Mexican immigrants, leading to a 25 percent undercount in the overall Mexican immigrant population.[4] Van Hook and Bean (1998) use a similar method to estimate a 30 percent undercount rate of unauthorized Mexicans in the 1990 Census and a 20 percent undercount of all Mexicans.[5] Analysts believe that the 2000 Census was substantially more successful in counting unauthorized immigrants (Citro, Cork, and Norwood 2004), with net undercount rates on the order of 10 percent (U.S. Department of Citizenship and Immigration Services 2003). This suggests an undercount rate for all Mexican immigrants of about 6–8 percent.[6] Based on these estimates, we believe that problems caused by the undercount of unauthorized Mexicans are likely to be relatively modest in our 2000 data, but more of an issue in interpreting the 1980 and 1990 data.

With these caveats in mind, we turn to table 6.1, which presents information on the characteristics of working-age Mexican immigrants in the 1980, 1990 and 2000 Censuses.[7] The demographic characteristics are fairly stable over time, though the average age of Mexican immigrants and their number of years in the United States are rising over time, reflecting the accumulating stock of previous migrants. There is also a modest upward trend in average education. Even in 2000, however, 70 percent report having less than a high school education, and more than one-half report low

---

4. Estimates of the overall census undercount rates (based on sets of households that were identified and interviewed in two separate counts) are 1.2 percent for the 1980 Census, 1.6 percent for 1990, and 0.1 to 1.1 percent for 2000. Estimated undercount rates are higher for Hispanics (e.g., around 5 percent in the 1990 Census (Hogan and Robinson 1993), and 1–4 percent in the 2000 Census (Elliot and Little 2005). Estimates of undercount rates for the unauthorized population are based on comparisons of birth or death rates to population estimates.

5. Van Hook and Bean (1998) show the sensitivity of their estimates to various assumptions. The 30 percent undercount rate is based on relatively conservative assumptions. Other assumptions lead to lower undercount rates, on average.

6. Passel (2002) estimates that 80 percent of all Mexican immigrants who arrived in the 1990s were unauthorized.

7. We define *Mexican immigrants* as census respondents who report that they are either naturalized citizens or noncitizens and who report that their place of birth is Mexico.

Table 6.1   Characteristics of Mexican immigrants in 1980, 1990, and 2000

	1980	1990	2000
Percent female	46.5	44.2	43.7
Age distribution			
Percent under 30	47.2	45.5	39.9
Percent 31–50	40.9	44.2	49.2
Percent 51–65	11.9	10.3	10.9
Distribution of years in United States			
0–5 years	30.0	26.3	25.0
6–10 years	25.2	20.0	19.1
10 or more years	44.7	53.6	55.9
Education			
Percent <12 years schooling	76.7	74.6	70.2
Mean years of schooling	7.4	8.1	8.4
Percent low English ability	54.6	50.3	52.3
Geographic distribution			
Percent in California	58.0	58.4	44.9
Percent in Texas	22.2	21.2	19.5
Percent in MSA	92.8	91.3	90.1
Labor market outcomes			
Percent employed last year			
Men	85.9	85.7	83.9
Women	49.4	53.7	52.9
Mean hourly wage (1999$)			
Men	14.22	11.61	12.89
Women	11.06	9.68	11.07
Mean log wage gap relative to other workers ($\times$ 100)			
Men	−30.6	−42.6	−41.2
Women	−17.0	−29.5	−33.2
Percent of total population (age 16–65)	1.13	2.16	4.11
Sample size	83,628	174,364	373,909

Note: Based on tabulations of individuals age sixteen–sixty-five in 1980–2000 U.S. and Mexico Censuses.

or very low English ability.[8] The fraction of Mexican immigrants living in either California or Texas was stable between 1980 and 1990, but fell sharply in the 1990s. Roughly 90 percent of Mexican immigrants lived in a larger urban area (i.e., in a metropolitan area or consolidated metropolitan area) in 1980, and this rate has not changed much over the past two decades. Finally, the employment rates of Mexican immigrants have been relatively stable, whereas average real wages show a decline between 1980 and 1990 and a modest rebound by 2000. The hourly wage gap between

8. Based on observation at an English instruction class for immigrant parents, we suspect that Mexican immigrants tend to overreport their education. Many immigrants from rural areas attended ungraded schools with interruptions for work at home, so "years of school" may overstate actual years of full-time learning.

Mexican workers and all other workers expanded between 1980 and 1990 and was fairly stable between 1990 and 2000.

6.1.2   Intercohort Comparisons

Comparisons across the populations in different census years potentially mask differences between newly arriving and earlier cohorts of Mexicans. Figures 6.2–6.8 compare Mexican immigrants by years of residence in the United States in 1990 and 2000. A caveat in the interpretation of these figures is that many Mexican immigrants enter and leave the United States multiple times, leading to some ambiguity in the "arrival year" responses in the census. Moreover, some migrants enter and then leave permanently (Lubotsky 2000). To the extent that these factors are stable over time, however, comparisons by years since arrival in the different census years are informative.

Figure 6.2 plots the fractions of Mexican immigrants living in California and Texas by years in the country. In 1990, the probabilities of living in California or Texas were fairly similar for different arrival cohorts. In the 2000 data, however, recent arrivals are much less likely to live in California than earlier cohorts. This contrast suggests that the widening geographic diffusion of Mexican immigrants during the 1990s was driven by the locational choices of new immigrants—a conclusion that is reinforced by further analysis in the following.

Figures 6.3 and 6.4 compare the fractions of Mexican immigrants with less than a high school degree and with low English ability. Female immigrants from Mexico have about the same probability of below-high school

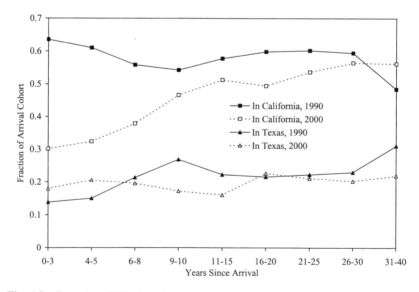

Fig. 6.2   Location of Mexican immigrants, by years since arrival

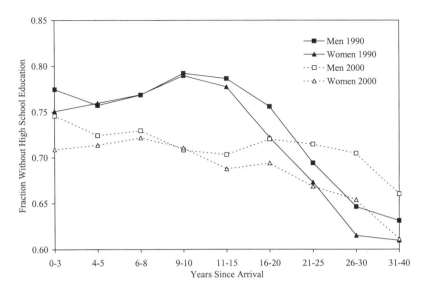

Fig. 6.3   Fraction of Mexican immigrants with less than high school education, by years since arrival

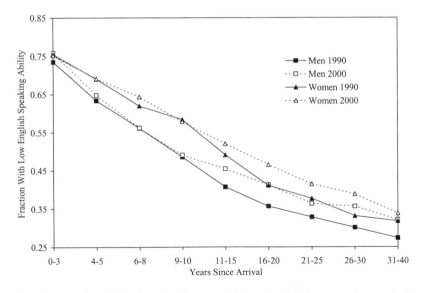

Fig. 6.4   Fraction of Mexican immigrants with low English, by years since arrival

education as males, but report lower English-speaking abilities. Recent arrivals of either gender in the 2000 Census have a slightly lower probability of below-high school education than their counterparts in 1990, perhaps reflecting gains in education for younger cohorts in Mexico. The levels of low English ability, on the other hand, are very similar in 1990 and

2000.[9] Although we do not present them here, the marital status profiles for men and women are also remarkably similar in the two censuses.

Figure 6.5 shows mean log hourly wages (in 1999 dollars) by gender and time in the United States. There was a modest rise in real wages for more recent arrivals over the 1990s, but not much gain for longer-term residents. Overall, the wage profiles are quite similar in 1990 and 2000. We have also constructed profiles of employment probabilities (based on the likelihood of reporting positive weeks of work in the past year). For men, the 1990 and 2000 profiles are very close together, while for women there is a slightly lower employment rate in 2000 for those who have been in the United States for six–ten years and not much difference elsewhere.[10]

Finally, figures 6.6–6.8 show the fractions of Mexican workers employed in agriculture, construction, and retail trade. In 1990, the data in figure 6.6 show that recently arrived Mexicans of either gender were more likely to work in agriculture than earlier arrivals. (Of course, this could have been driven by the presence of many short-term migrant workers in agriculture in 1990.) By 2000, however, the profiles by time in the United States are much flatter. Looking across major industry groups, we found that the decline in agricultural employment among recent immigrants was offset by rises in the fraction of employment in construction (for men) and retail trade (for women). In 2000, nearly a quarter of recent male Mexican immigrants was working in construction (see figure 6.7), while about one-sixth of recent females were working in retail trade (figure 6.8). The rises in Mexican employment in these industries are striking because both sectors also employ relatively large fractions of low-skilled native workers, raising the obvious concern about labor market competition.

6.1.3   Distribution across Cities

As we have noted, one of the most important changes for Mexican immigrants between 1990 and 2000 was the move out of California. Further information on this phenomenon is provided in table 6.2, which shows the changing fractions of Mexican immigrants in the fifteen traditional destination cities that had the largest numbers of Mexicans in 1980.[11] In 1980, nearly one-third of all working-age Mexicans were living in Los Angeles.

---

9. To the extent that the immigrants who are most likely to be undercounted in the census are recent arrivals with low education and language ability, there may be more reporting bias in the 1990 Census data than the 2000 data. This would tend to mask any actual gains in education or English ability that actually occurred over the 1990s.

10. As with education and language, there may be some correlation between wages and the probability of underreporting, especially for recent Mexican immigrants. Assuming this was a bigger problem in 1990, the observed mean wage trends for recent arrival groups may understate the actual growth that occurred.

11. Throughout this paper, we use as *cities* individual MSAs and the constituent PMSA's in consolidated metropolitan areas. Thus, we treat Los Angeles and Orange County California as separate *cities*.

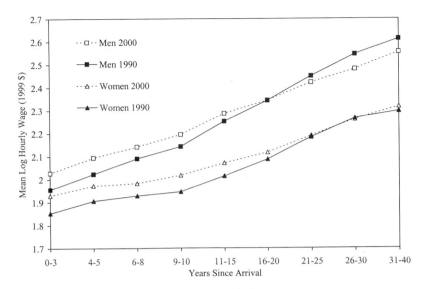

Fig. 6.5   Mean log hourly wages of Mexican immigrants, by years since arrival

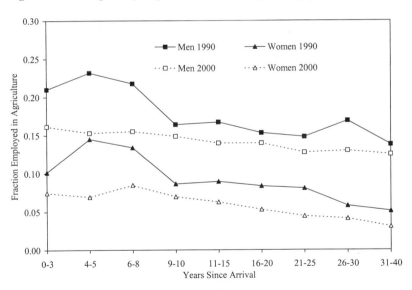

Fig. 6.6   Fraction of Mexican immigrants in agriculture, by years since arrival

Another 8 percent were living in Chicago, and roughly 4 percent were living in each of Houston, Orange County, San Diego, and El Paso. Over the 1980s, the shares in Los Angeles and Chicago fell slightly, but as of 1990 the top five cities still accounted for nearly one-half of all Mexican immigrants. Between 1990 and 2000, however, the share of Mexican immigrants

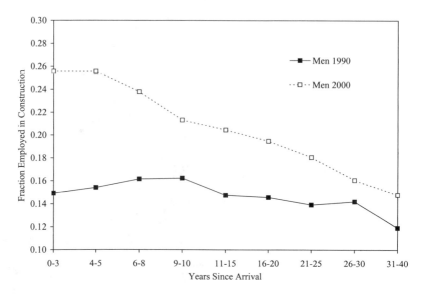

Fig. 6.7   Fraction of Mexican immigrants in construction, by years since arrival

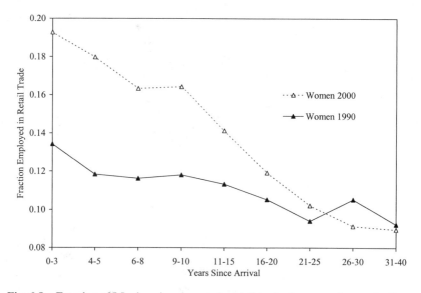

Fig. 6.8   Fraction of Mexican immigrants in retail trade, by years since arrival

living in Los Angeles dropped by 10 percentage points, accounting for most of the fall in the total California share noted in figure 6.1 and table 6.1. The total share in Texas fell by much less, although this stability masks a sizeable (2.8 percentage point) loss in shares for San Antonio and the smaller border cities (El Paso, McAllen, and Brownsville) coupled with gains for Houston and Dallas.

Table 6.2   **Geographic concentration of Mexican immigrants**

	1980	1990	2000
Percent of Mexican immigrants (age 16–65) living in:			
Los Angeles	31.7	27.9	17.4
Chicago	7.9	5.4	5.5
Houston	4.4	4.1	4.4
Orange County, CA	4.1	6.0	4.7
San Diego	3.9	4.1	3.1
El Paso	3.9	2.7	1.6
San Francisco/Oakland	2.5	2.3	2.4
Dallas/Fort Worth	2.3	3.3	4.7
McAllen	2.1	1.7	1.5
San Antonio	2.0	1.5	1.1
San Jose	1.7	1.7	1.5
Brownsville	1.6	1.9	0.8
Ventura County, CA	1.6	1.4	1.1
Fresno	1.4	1.6	1.6
Riverside/San Bernardino, CA	1.3	4.1	4.1
Share of Top 5	51.9	47.5	35.1
Share of Top 15	72.3	69.7	55.5

Note: Based on tabulations of 1980–2000 U.S. and Mexico Censuses.

Where did the rapidly growing population of Mexican immigrants settle in the 1990s? To answer this question, we calculated the increase in the number of Mexican immigrants in each MSA between 1990 and 2000 and then tabulated the cities by their shares of the total increase in Mexican immigrants. The results for the top forty cities, which together account for about 80 percent of the overall growth in the Mexican population, are presented in table 6.3.

The first three columns of the table show the total working-age population of each city in 1990, the number of Mexican immigrants in 1990, and the fraction of Mexican immigrants in the local working-age population. The remaining five columns present information on the changes in each city between 1990 and 2000, including the total population growth rate (for sixteen- to sixty-five-year-olds), the growth rate of the Mexican immigrant population, the absolute increase in the total number of Mexican immigrants living in the city, the fraction of the national increase in the Mexican population "absorbed" in the city, and, finally, the number of post-1990 immigrants living in the city in 2000.

Although Los Angeles's share of Mexican immigrants was falling over the 1990s, the first row of table 6.3 shows that the city still absorbed the largest number of Mexicans (over 300,000). In fact, the Mexican population of Los Angeles grew by 34 percent between 1990 and 2000. Because the total population of Mexican working-age immigrants grew by 114 percent over the decade, however, Los Angeles would have had to absorb

Table 6.3   Growth in overall and Mexican immigrant populations, 1990 to 2000

	Working age population in 1990				Changes from 1990 to 2000			
	Total	Mexican immigrants	Percent Mexican immigrants	Adult population growth (%)	Mexican immigrant growth (%)	Growth in no. Mexican immigrants	Cumulative percent of total rise	No. of post-1990 Mexican immigrants
1 Los Angeles	5,785,200	973,120	16.8	5.8	33.5	326,260	9.5	413,140
2 Chicago	4,170,420	186,800	4.5	9.8	119.8	223,800	15.9	182,560
3 Phoenix	1,268,280	52,400	4.1	62.1	363.9	190,700	21.5	135,640
4 Dallas	1,693,060	85,320	5.0	36.6	215.6	183,960	26.8	153,240
5 Houston	1,908,400	137,320	7.2	26.2	131.3	180,300	32.0	147,220
6 Riverside/San Bernardino, CA	1,444,480	142,620	9.9	27.8	112.6	160,560	36.6	89,860
7 Orange County	1,687,500	208,000	12.3	13.1	69.7	144,900	40.8	139,200
8 Las Vegas	470,200	15,240	3.2	113.4	615.8	93,840	43.6	52,360
9 San Diego	1,603,060	144,440	9.0	11.1	63.0	90,980	46.2	74,960
10 Atlanta	1,757,700	7,320	0.4	41.7	1,076.5	78,800	48.5	66,180
11 New York City	4,520,040	28,140	0.6	13.8	270.2	76,020	50.7	67,040
12 Denver	1,018,560	12,620	1.2	25.5	585.4	73,880	52.8	54,260
13 Oakland	1,379,320	46,500	3.4	13.7	152.2	70,780	54.9	52,780
14 Fresno	396,560	54,320	13.7	41.4	113.7	61,780	56.7	45,260
15 Fort Worth	920,880	30,240	3.3	10.6	178.3	53,920	58.2	41,700
16 Austin, TX	518,400	16,060	3.1	60.9	322.0	51,720	59.7	36,900
17 San Jose	1,048,420	59,660	5.7	8.0	86.0	51,280	61.2	49,380
18 McAllen, TX	202,860	60,960	30.1	45.5	84.1	51,240	62.7	35,900
19 Tulare County, CA	171,560	31,800	18.5	67.4	154.3	49,080	64.1	28,800

20	Monterey County, CA	224,860	36,000	16.0	43.2	131.5	47,340	65.5	31,420
21	Bakersfield	318,120	32,480	10.2	22.4	124.8	40,540	66.6	25,060
22	Portland	885,080	9,320	1.1	35.1	424.3	39,540	67.8	30,820
23	Ventura County, CA	437,260	48,200	11.0	9.3	76.8	37,020	68.9	28,920
24	San Francisco	1,030,900	32,720	3.2	12.6	91.0	29,760	69.7	28,740
25	Raleigh-Durham	469,180	880	0.2	78.0	3,156.8	27,780	70.5	23,360
26	San Antonio	841,060	51,400	6.1	4.2	53.4	27,420	71.3	26,240
27	El Paso	351,640	93,900	26.7	5.2	28.3	26,580	72.1	32,140
28	Greensboro, NC	729,680	1,140	0.2	8.8	2,287.7	26,080	72.8	21,420
29	Salt Lake City	575,160	3,700	0.6	23.4	670.3	24,800	73.6	18,960
30	Sacramento	941,920	22,040	2.3	6.6	112.4	24,780	74.3	19,200
31	Santa Barbara	251,580	27,460	10.9	15.5	88.1	24,200	75.0	21,640
32	Tucson	399,780	23,880	6.0	28.7	100.8	24,060	75.7	16,900
33	Seattle	1,204,960	3,360	0.3	18.0	695.8	23,380	76.4	17,140
34	Washington, DC	2,610,900	7,860	0.3	25.1	271.3	21,320	77.0	18,260
35	Stockton, CA	298,380	26,380	8.8	19.5	79.9	21,080	77.6	18,800
36	Charlotte, NC	785,040	900	0.1	12.7	2,313.3	20,820	78.2	17,660
37	Yuma, AZ	59,120	12,920	21.9	59.5	158.5	20,480	78.8	10,600
38	Modesto, CA	231,440	21,460	9.3	22.0	91.4	19,620	79.3	13,420
39	Santa Rosa	224,040	8,840	4.0	40.2	217.7	19,240	79.9	13,700
40	Vallejo, CA	302,080	11,560	3.8	10.2	159.2	18,400	80.4	13,500

nearly a million Mexicans to maintain its share. In contrast to Los Angeles, Chicago's Mexican immigrant population grew at about the national average rate, implying a near doubling of the Mexican immigrant share over the 1990s. Dallas and Houston had even faster growth rates in their Mexican populations, together absorbing nearly 10 percent of the national rise. Phoenix and Las Vegas—two very rapidly growing cities—also experienced rapid growth in their Mexican immigrant populations.

More surprising than these figures are the large numbers of Mexican immigrants absorbed in Atlanta, New York, and Denver (the cities ranked numbers 10–12 in table 6.3). All three cities are far from the Mexican border and had very low Mexican population densities in 1990, yet together these cities absorbed over 9 percent of the total increase in the Mexican immigrant population. Looking further down the table, Portland Oregon (22), Salt Lake City (29), Seattle (32), Washington, D.C. (34) and three cities in North Carolina—Raleigh-Durham (25), Greensboro (28), and Charlotte (36)—also stand out as cities with historically small Mexican immigrant populations that experienced very rapid inflows over the 1990s. Together these ten cities accounted for 412,000 of the rise in the adult Mexican population between 1990 and 2000, or 12 percent of the national total.

A key feature of table 6.3 is the high correlation across cities between the growth in the total number of working age Mexican immigrants (column [6]) and the number of post-1990 Mexican immigrants present in 2000 (column [8]). This correlation has two implications. On one hand, it suggests that the arrival of new Mexican immigrants had little displacement effect on previous Mexican immigrants. On the other, it also implies that most of the growth in the number of Mexicans in new destination cities was attributable to the arrival of recent immigrants. These impressions are confirmed by the patterns in figure 6.9, which plots the change in the total number of adult Mexican immigrants living in each city between 1990 and 2000 (as a percent of the city's population in 1990) against the inflow rate of new Mexican immigrants, which we define as the number of post-1990 Mexican immigrants in the city in 2000 divided by the city population in 1990. The points for all but two cities lie on or above the 45-degree line, implying that in most cities new Mexican inflows led to equivalent or larger increases in the total Mexican population.[12] Only in Los Angeles and El Paso is there any evidence of displacement of older Mexican immigrants by new arrivals. In the labeled cities above the 45-degree line, net inflows of older immigrants complemented the inflows of post-1990 arrivals, amplifying the impact on local population growth.

12. The same conclusion emerges when we plot the data for the 150 largest cities in the United States. Over this broader set, only three cities have notably smaller growth in the total Mexican population than in new Mexican inflows: Los Angeles; El Paso; and Laredo, Texas.

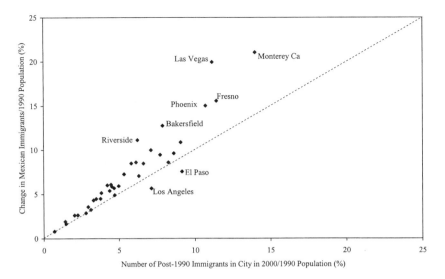

Fig. 6.9   Growth in Mexican Immigrant population: Recent arrivals and total change

6.2   Modeling the Diffusion of Recent Mexican Immigrants

In light of this descriptive evidence, we turn to the task of modeling the flows of recent Mexican immigrants to different cities between 1990 and 2000. Our dependent variable is the inflow rate of new Mexican immigrants, defined as the number of post-1990 working age Mexican immigrants observed in a city in the 2000 Census, divided by the working age population of the city in 1990. Following the traditional taxonomy, we develop a framework for measuring the contribution of supply push and demand pull to total immigrant inflows. We measure demand-pull factors by total employment growth in the MSA between 1990 to 2000, derived from County Business Patterns (CBP) data.[13] There is a potential endogeneity problem with this variable as immigrant arrivals may stimulate employment growth. Exploiting the persistence in city-specific employment trends, however, we use employment levels from 1982 to 1990 as instruments for the 1990–2000 employment growth rate. Thus, our demand-pull measure is the predicted component of overall employment growth in the city, based on employment trends in the preceding decade.

On the supply side, numerous studies have shown that new immigrants tend to go to cities where earlier waves of immigrants from the same source

---

13. Except in New England, MSAs consist of complete counties, so MSA employment is the sum of employment in the constituent counties. For consistency, we use fixed 2000 MSA-county definitions.

country have settled (e.g., Bartel 1989; Card 2001). Thus, we use the density of Mexican immigrants in a city in 1980 and 1990 as proxies for the magnitude of supply-push immigration flows from Mexico over the 1990–2000 period.

Estimation results from a series of alternative specifications of the model are presented in table 6.4. The models are estimated on a sample of 142 larger MSAs that can be consistently defined on a county basis in the 1980, 1990, and 2000 Censuses.[14] The first column of the table reports a specification that includes only the lagged Mexican immigrant density variables. These supply-push proxies are highly significant and together explain 78 percent of the variation across cities in the recent Mexican immigrant inflow rate. The second column reports a model that includes only the employment growth variable. This is also a significant determinant of new immigrant inflows, explaining about 10 percent of the intercity variation. A parallel model estimated by instrumental variables is presented in column ([5]; using log employment levels in 1984–1990 as instruments). Interestingly, the point estimate of the effect of employment growth is slightly *larger* in the IV model, contrary to what might have been expected under the assumption that the ordinary least squares (OLS) estimate is upward biased by the presence of unobserved factors that contribute to both overall employment growth and Mexican inflows.[15] Finally, the models in columns (3) and (6) include both the lagged density and employment growth variables. Together the demand-pull and supply-push variables explain 86 percent of the intercity variation in new Mexican immigrant inflows. Again, the point estimates of the models are not much different between the OLS and IV specifications.[16]

Given the large fraction of Mexican immigrants who traditionally migrated to Los Angeles and the sharp decline in this fraction over the 1990s, an interesting challenge for our model is to predict the changing flows to Los Angeles. To address this challenge, we reestimated the model in column (3), adding a dummy for the Los Angeles observation. The estimated Los Angeles dummy is –0.025, with a standard error of 0.013, while the point estimates of the other coefficients are virtually the same as those reported in column (3). Thus, our baseline model overpredicts the inflow rate

14. Copies of the computer programs that process the 1980, 1990, and 2000 Census data and construct the city-level variables are available on request.
15. The OLS estimate is probably downward biased by measurement errors in the CBP data. The CBP data are based on counts of people paying Social Security contributions and missing uncovered employment. Errors can also arise because of changes in the boundaries of MSAs between 1990 and 2000 and because of the fact that we measure population changes by place of residence, whereas CBP measures employment changes by place of work. It appears that the downward bias dominates any upward endogeneity bias.
16. The OLS estimate of the demand coefficient in column (3) is 0.0748, with a standard error of 0.008. The corresponding IV estimate in column (6) is 0.0675, with a standard error of 0.012.

Table 6.4   **Regression models for growth in recent Mexican immigrant population**

	Estimated by OLS				Estimated by IV		
	(1)	(2)	(3)	(4)	(5)	(6)	(7)
Mexican population share, 1990	1.33		1.34	1.34		1.34	1.34
	(0.12)		(0.09)	(0.09)		(0.09)	(0.09)
Mexican population share, 1980	−1.16		−1.18	−1.18		−1.18	−1.18
	(0.18)		(0.14)	(0.14)		(0.14)	(0.14)
Employment growth, 1990–2000		0.09	0.07	0.08	0.12	0.07	0.07
		(0.02)	(0.01)	(0.01)	(0.03)	(0.01)	(0.01)
Mean log wage of Mexican men in 1990 ($\times$100)				0.47			0.35
				(0.43)			(0.45)
Relative employment rate of Mexican men in 1990 ($\times$100)				−0.12			−0.06
				(1.10)			(1.16)
R^2	0.78	0.11	0.86	0.86	0.10	0.86	0.86
First stage F-statistic (9 d.f.)					13.40	14.81	13.06

Notes: All models estimated on sample of 142 larger cities with census data for 1980–2000 and matching employment data from county business patterns for 1982–2000. Dependent variable is number of recent (post-1990) adult Mexican immigrants in city in 2000, divided by population in 1990. Mean and standard deviation of dependent variable are 0.023 and 0.033, respectively. Instruments for employment growth 1990–2000 are log employment levels in 1982–1990. Mean log wage and relative employment rate for city in 1990 are regression adjusted for characteristics of Mexican male workers in the city.

of new Mexican immigrants to Los Angeles (predicted inflow rate = 0.096; actual = .071), though the magnitude of the prediction error is just on the margin of statistical significance. Moreover, the Los Angeles observation is not a large enough outlier to have any affect on the coefficient estimates. The model in column (3) predicts that Los Angeles would have attracted about 558,000 new Mexican immigrants over the 1990s, compared to the actual inflow of 413,000. By comparison, if Los Angeles had maintained its 1990 share of Mexican immigrants, it would have attracted 961,000 new Mexican immigrants (an inflow rate of 0.165).[17] Thus, the decline in the share of Mexican immigrants moving to Los Angeles in the 1990s is largely explained by a combination of slow employment growth in the city and the pattern of the coefficients on lagged immigrant shares, which indicate a tendency for all cities with a longer history of Mexican immigration to have slower growth in new arrivals in the 1990s. An interesting question that we leave unanswered is whether this pattern could have been predicted by observing settlement patterns over the 1980s or whether it is a "new" phenomenon.

Although the simple supply-push and demand-pull proxies used in the models in columns (3) and (6) explain much of the variation in new Mexi-

17. Los Angeles had 27.9 percent of all working-age Mexican immigrants in 1990. According to the 2000 Census, there were 3,445,000 working age Mexicans who arrived after 1990 in the United States in 2000.

can immigrant inflow rates, other factors may also affect the destination choices of potential migrants. An obvious consideration is the labor market success of earlier cohorts of Mexican immigrants in a particular city. We used 1990 Census data to estimate the average employment rate and mean log wage of Mexican male immigrants in each city in 1989 (adjusted for the characteristics of the Mexican workers in each city).[18] We then included these as additional explanatory variables in the models in columns (4) and (7) of table 6.4. The results suggest that new immigrants tend to go to cities where Mexicans earned higher wages in 1990, although the estimated effects small in magnitude and insignificantly different from 0.[19] The estimated employment effects are also very small in magnitude and insignificantly different from 0. Overall these variables add little to our basic specification.

The models in table 6.4 are estimated using unweighted OLS and IV methods. We have also estimated the same specifications using weighted OLS and IV, with the MSA population in 1990 as a weight. The estimated coefficients from the weighted models are similar to the estimates from the unweighted models and lead to very similar conclusions about the explanatory power of the supply-push and demand-pull variables. As in the unweighted models, the weighted IV estimates of the employment growth effect are very close to the weighted OLS estimates, giving no indication of an endogeneity problem.

We conclude that a simple model that includes demand-pull and supply-push factors provides a relatively good description of the destination choices of new Mexican immigrants over the 1990s. A model with just three parameters explains 86 percent of the observed intercity variation in new Mexican immigrant inflow rates. The model cannot fully explain the sharp downturn in the share of Mexican inflows to Los Angeles in the 1990s, but it predicts about 75 percent of the observed decline.

6.3   Impacts of Mexican Inflows

6.3.1   Effects on the Relative Supply of Low-Education Labor

Having documented the relatively large inflows of Mexican immigrants to many cities in the 1990s, we now turn to analyzing the effects of these inflows. A first question is whether inflows of Mexican immigrants lead to any shift in the skill mix of local populations. Many models of local labor

---

18. To estimate these adjusted outcomes, we fit models for log hourly wages and the event of working last year, which included education, age, years in the United States, an indicator for low English ability, and unrestricted city dummies. We then use the city dummies as measures of relative wages and employment probabilities.

19. For example, the 0.47 coefficient for wages in the model in column (4) implies that cities where Mexican men earned 10 percent higher wages in 1989 had an inflow rate 0.0005 points higher in the 1990s.

market equilibrium have a constant-returns-to-scale feature that implies that population inflows only affect wages and employment to the extent that they shift the relative supply of different skill groups.[20]

As a starting point, figure 6.10 plots the change in the fraction of dropouts in the population of each major MSA between 1990 and 2000 against the inflow rate of new Mexican immigrants to the city. If 70 percent of recent Mexican arrivals have less than a high school education and Mexican inflows are orthogonal to all other characteristics in a city, then one would expect the points in figure 6.10 to lie along a line with slope slightly below 0.7.[21] For reference, we have graphed a line with this slope in the figure. While there is considerable variation in the scatter of points, there is a strong positive relation between Mexican inflows and the change in the dropout share, with a slope that is a little flatter than the reference line.

Table 6.5 presents a series of regression models that examine more formally the link between Mexican immigrant inflows and the share of low-education workers in a city. The dependent variable for the models in the first two columns is the fraction of dropouts among adult residents of a city in 2000, while in columns (3)–(5) the dependent variable is the *change* in the share of dropouts between 1990 and 2000. Looking first at the simple model in column (1), each percentage point increase in the inflow rate of new Mexican immigrants over the 1990s is estimated to raise the fraction of dropouts by 1.29 percentage points. This estimate is too large to represent a causal effect of the Mexican inflow. The problem is that inflows tend to be larger in cities that had larger inflows of Mexican immigrants in the past. This is illustrated by the model in column (2), which also includes the Mexican inflow rate over the 1980s. The 0.69 coefficient on the 1980s inflows suggest that Mexican arrivals have a highly persistent impact on the fraction of dropouts present in the labor market in 2000. Controlling for these flows, the marginal impact of inflows in the 1990s is about 0.9.

A potentially better specification relates the *change* in the dropout share to the inflow rate of new Mexican immigrants (as in figure 6.10). As shown by the models in columns (3) and (4), in such a specification each percentage point increase in the inflow rate of new Mexican immigrants is estimated to raise the fraction of dropouts in a city by 0.5 points. This estimate

20. Strictly speaking, such a feature requires perfectly elastic supplies of capital to different cities and no shortage of land within a city. Arguably both features are true for many MSAs, though not necessarily for high density MSAs like Los Angeles or New York.

21. Let D_t represent the number of working age dropouts in a city in 2000, let N_t represent total working age population, let D_{t-1} and N_{t-1} represent the same concepts for 1990, and let M_t represent the number of new Mexican immigrants present in 2000. If 70 percent of new Mexican immigrants are dropouts, then $(D_t - D_{t-1})/N_{t-1} = .7\, M_t/N_{t-1} + \Delta/N_{t-1}$, where Δ represents the net change in the number of dropouts from all other sources (net flows of natives or previous immigrants). If Δ/N_{t-1} is orthogonal to the *inflow rate* of new Mexican immigrants, then a regression of $(D_t - D_{t-1})/N_{t-1}$ on M_t/N_{t-1} will have a coefficient of 0.7. The y-axis in the graph is $D_t/N_t - D_{t-1}/N_{t-1} = (D_t - D_{t-1})/N_{t-1} - (D_t/N_t) \times (N_t - N_{t-1})/N_{t-1}$. The second term in this sum is negatively correlated with the inflow rate of new Mexicans, leading to the prediction of a slope under 0.7.

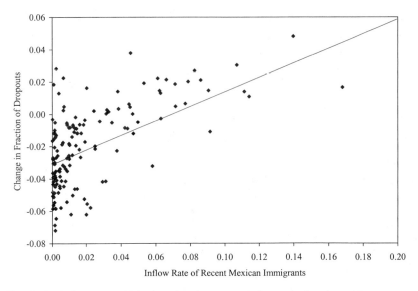

Fig. 6.10   **Inflow rate of Mexican immigrants and change in fraction of dropouts**

suggests that any offsetting migration of earlier immigrants or native dropouts induced by the inflow of new Mexican immigrants is relatively small. Interestingly, the inflow rate of immigrants in the 1980s has no effect on the change in dropout shares between 1990 and 2000, providing a simple specification check for the first-differenced model.

A concern with the models in columns (3) and (4) is that Mexican immigrants may be attracted to cities where there is an unusually high rate of growth in demand for less-educated labor. If that is the case and if less-educated natives (or less-educated immigrants from other countries) are attracted by the same demand factors, then the measured effect of Mexican inflows on the change in the dropout share may overstate their true net impact. Such a bias can be reduced or eliminated by using the supply-push variables (i.e., the historical fractions of Mexican immigrants in the city) as instruments for the inflow rate of new Mexican immigrants over the 1990s. We implement this procedure in the model in column (5). At the same time, we instrument employment growth in the city with the lagged employment variables used in table 6.4. The resulting coefficient estimates are not very different from the OLS estimates and provide no evidence that endogeneity of Mexican immigrant inflows leads to an overstatement of the effect of these flows on the relative fraction of dropout labor in a city. Overall, we conclude there is robust evidence that inflows of Mexican labor increase the share of dropouts in a city, with each percentage point increase in the inflow rate of recent immigrants leading to about a .5 percentage point higher dropout share in 2000.

Table 6.5   **Regression models for level or change in fraction of dropouts in local population**

	Models for fraction of dropouts in 2000: Estimated by OLS		Models for change in fraction of dropouts between 1990 and 2000: Estimated by OLS		IV
	(1)	(2)	(3)	(4)	(5)
Growth in "new" (post-1990) Mexican immigrants (1990–2000), divided by population in 1990	1.29 (0.11)	0.89 (0.19)	0.49 (0.04)	0.49 (0.10)	0.52 (0.05)
Growth in "new" (post-1980) Mexican immigrants (1980–1990), divided by population in 1980		0.69 (0.20)		0.01 (0.10)	
Employment growth, 1990–2000		−0.09 (0.03)		0.00 (0.01)	0.02 (0.01)
R^2	0.51	0.64	0.44	0.44	0.41

Notes: All models estimated on sample of 144 larger cities with census data for 1980–2000 and matching employment data from county business patterns for 1982–2000. Dependent variable is fraction of dropouts in adult population in city in 2000 (columns [1]–[2]) or the change in the fraction of dropouts in the adult population from 1990 to 2000 (columns [3]–[5]). Model in column (5) is estimated by instrumental variables, using as instruments the fraction of Mexicans in the city in 1980 and 1990 and the log of employment in the MSA in 1982–1990.

6.3.2 Industry Structure and the Absorption of Mexican Labor

Because inflows of Mexican labor increase the pool of less-educated labor in a city, it is interesting to ask how these workers are absorbed by local employers. One possibility, suggested by the HO model of international trade, is that the industry structure in a city adapts to the relative supply conditions in the local labor market. Indeed, under certain conditions, changes in industry structure can fully accommodate differences in the relative supply of different skill groups in a given city with no change in the relative wage structure. In this section, we use the decomposition method of Lewis (2003) to evaluate the role of HO-style adjustments in absorbing differences in the fraction of low-education workers in different cities.

The decomposition starts with an identity that expresses the overall fraction of dropouts employed in a given city, $s^d(c)$, as a weighted sum of the industry shares in the city, times the dropout intensity in each industry:

$$(1) \qquad s^d(c) = \frac{1}{N(c)} \sum_i N_i^d(c)$$

$$= \sum_i \frac{N_i(c)}{N(c)} \frac{N_i^d(c)}{N_i(c)}$$

$$= \sum_i \lambda_i(c) s_i^d(c),$$

where $N(c)$ is total employment in city c, $N_i^d(c)$ is the number of dropouts employed in industry i in city c, $N_i(c)$ is total employment in industry i in city c, $\lambda_i(c) \equiv N_i(c)/N(c)$ is the employment share of industry i in city c, and $s_i^d(c) = N_i^d(c)/N_i(c)$ is the share of dropout workers in industry i in city c. It follows that the gap between $s^d(c)$ and the national average fraction of dropouts, s^d, can be written as the sum of a "between industry component" B representing shifts in the relative employment shares of different industries in the city, a "within industry component" W, representing shifts in the relative fraction of dropout workers in each industry, and an interaction component I:

(2) $$s^d(c) - s^d = B(c) + W(c) + I(c),$$

where

$$B(c) = \sum_i s_i^d[\lambda_i(c) - \lambda_i]$$

$$W(c) = \sum_i \lambda_i[s_i^d(c) - s_i^d]$$

$$I(c) = \sum_i [\lambda_i(c) - \lambda_i] \times [s_i^d(c) - s_i^d].$$

Under the idealized conditions of the Heckscher-Olin model, *all* of the variation in the share of dropout labor across cities can be absorbed by expansion or contraction of high-dropout-intensity industries (i.e., via the $B[c]$ term), with no city-level variation in relative wages or the dropout intensity of any particular industry.[22]

We use 2000 Census data on employment classified by three-digit industry to compute the terms in equation (2) for each of 150 larger MSAs. We then performed a series of cross-city regressions of the form:

(3a) $$B(c) = a_B + b_B[s^d(c) - s^d] + e_B(c)$$

(3b) $$W(c) = a_w + b_W[s^d(c) - s^d] + e_w(c)$$

(3c) $$I(c) = a_I + b_I[s^d(c) - s^d] + e_I(c).$$

Because equation (2) holds as an identity, the coefficients b_B, b_W, and b_I sum to 1. A strict version of the HO model implies $b_B = 1$.

Figure 6.11 plots the between-industry component $B(c)$ against the excess fraction of dropouts in each of the 150 larger MSAs. For reference, note that if changing industry structure accounted for the absorption of dropouts in cities with high dropout shares the points would lie along a line with slope 1. Although the points suggest an upward-sloping relationship, the slope is relatively modest, suggesting that changing industry structure

22. These conditions include infinitely elastic supplies of capital, perfectly integrated product markets, and the existence of at least one industry that produces a tradeable good or service that has a dropout intensity that exceeds the maximum dropout share in any city.

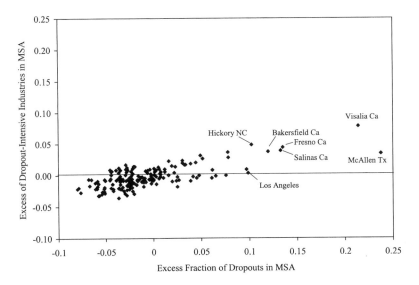

Fig. 6.11   Contribution of between-industry component to absorption of dropouts

accounts for only a small share of the absorption of dropouts. Indeed, the OLS estimate of b_B, reported in the first column of table 6.6, is 0.22, and is significantly below 1. By contrast, figure 6.12 plots the within-industry component $W(C)$ against the excess fraction of dropouts in each city. This component is more highly correlated with the dropout share, and many of the city observations are tightly clustered along the 45-degree line. The estimate of b_w, shown in column (2) of table 6.6, is 0.76. Though not shown in a figure, the interaction terms are relatively small and essentially uncorrelated with differences across cities in the share of dropout workers. Consistent with this, the estimate of b_I in column (3) of table 6.4 is 0.02 (with a very small R-squared = 0.03).

The MSAs that show some evidence of significant between-industry adjustment are labeled in figures 6.11 and 6.12. Interestingly, most of these MSAs represent counties in California with substantial agricultural employment.[23] The framework of equation (2) can be used to examine the contribution of specific industries to the absorption of local supplies of dropout labor. The contribution of industry i to the between-industry effect is $s_i^d[\lambda_i(c) - \lambda_i]$, which is the excess employment share of the industry in city c relative to its national average share, multiplied by the average dropout intensity of the industry. Columns (4)–(6) of table 6.6 show estimates of models similar to equation (3a), focusing on the absorption contributions of agriculture, textiles, apparel and footwear industries, and a set of

23. Hickory, North Carolina is an exception. This city is a major center for the furniture industry.

Table 6.6 Regression models measuring cross-city absorption of excess dropout workers or Mexican immigrants

	Absorption of excess fraction of dropout workers						Absorption of excess fraction of Mexican immigrants					
				Sector-specific absorption						Sector-specific absorption		
	Between industry (1)	Within industry (2)	Interaction (3)	Agriculture (4)	Textiles apparel (5)	Low-skill services (6)	Between industry (7)	Within industry (8)	Interaction (9)	Agriculture (10)	Textiles apparel (11)	Low-skill services (12)
Excess fraction of dropouts or Mexican immigrants	0.22 (0.02)	0.76 (0.02)	0.02 (0.01)	0.09 (0.02)	0.05 (0.01)	0.03 (0.01)	0.06 (0.01)	0.92 (0.01)	0.01 (0.01)	0.04 (0.01)	0.01 (0.00)	0.01 (0.00)
R^2	0.37	0.84	0.03	0.17	0.24	0.33	0.25	0.96	0.01	0.14	0.13	0.41

Notes: All models estimated across 150 larger cities, using 264 industry cells per city. Regressions are weighted by city size.

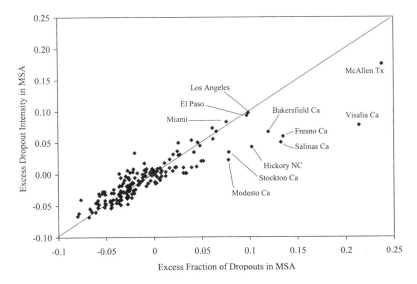

Fig. 6.12   Contribution of within-industry component to absorption of dropouts

low-skilled service industries.[24] The estimates suggest that these three industry clusters account for most of the between industry effect observed in column (1): agriculture alone accounts for nearly one-half.

Figure 6.13 plots the between-industry component of absorption of dropout labor in different cities *excluding agriculture,* while figure 6.14 shows the absorption contributions of agriculture industries and textiles and apparel industries. Overall, though there is some evidence that textiles and apparel manufacturing tends to cluster in cities with moderately high dropout shares and that agricultural employment is higher in cities with very high dropout shares, the results in table 6.6 and figure 6.14 suggest that most of the absorption of unskilled labor across cities occurs within industries rather than between.

Similar conclusions were reached by Lewis (2003), who examined changes in the absorption of workers in four education groups over the 1980–1990 period. Lewis used census data to estimate first-differenced versions of equation (3a) for each skill group. He also compared OLS estimates to IV estimates that used immigrant inflows based on historical immigration patterns as instruments for the changes in the relative shares of each skill group.[25] A potential advantage of a first-differenced approach is

24. We include textiles, apparel, knitting mills, footwear, and leather industries as apparel and the following as "low-skilled services": building services, landscaping services, carwashes, landscaping, dry cleaning and laundry services, private household services, and other personal services.
25. One difference is that Lewis regresses the between-industry effects on the population share of the skill group in the local labor market, rather than the employment share.

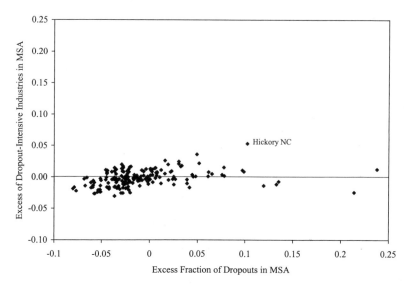

Fig. 6.13   Contribution of between-industry component to absorption of dropouts, excluding agriculture

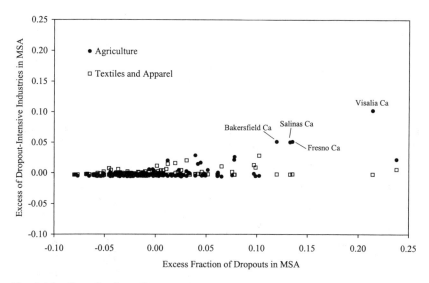

Fig. 6.14   Contribution of between-industry component to absorption of dropouts, agriculture and textiles or apparel industries

that it eliminates any MSA-specific factors that are constant over time and affect the attractiveness of the MSA to different industries (such as the amount of agricultural land available). Consistent with the pure cross-sectional results here, however, Lewis finds that changes in the scale of different industries are only weakly related to changes in the relative supply of different skill groups. Lewis's estimates of b_B for manufacturing industries (which can readily expand their sales beyond the local market) are very close to 0, while his estimates for all industries range from 0 to 0.08. He also reports parallel specifications in which the dependent variable is the within-industry relative employment term. These are much more strongly correlated with relative population growth, accounting for 90 percent of the adjustment to skill-group specific relative supply shocks.

As a final exercise, we conducted a parallel analysis focusing on the absorption of Mexican immigrants. The relation between the within-industry absorption component and the share of Mexican workers in the local labor market is plotted in figure 6.15, while regression models similar to the models for dropout workers are reported in columns (7)–(12) of table 6.6. The results reinforce our conclusions based on an analysis of total dropout labor. In particular, over 90 percent of the adjustment to differences in the local availability of Mexican labor is explained by differences in the utilization of Mexican labor *within* three-digit industries. Surprisingly, there is almost no evidence that availability of Mexican immigrant labor stimulates low-skill service employment.

Taken as a whole, the results in this section suggest that HO-style changes in industry structure play a relatively small role in explaining how cities have been able to absorb inflows of relatively unskilled Mexican immigrants over the 1990s. Contrary to our initial expectations, most of the inflows appear to be absorbed by city-specific–within-industry increases in use of unskilled labor.

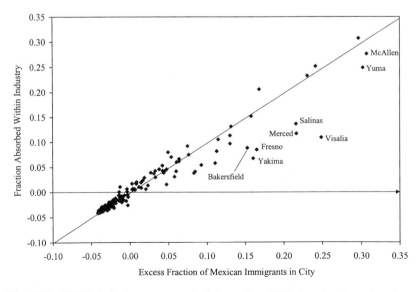

Fig. 6.15   Within-industry component of absorption of Mexican immigrant workers

6.3.3 Relative Wage Adjustments

The observation that variation in the relative supply of dropout labor is mainly absorbed by changes in utilization within industries points to the potential importance of relative wage adjustments in response to inflows of Mexican labor. We analyze relative wages in the framework of a conventional constant elasticity of substitution (CES) production function. The results in the last section suggest that we can ignore differences across industries and focus on a one industry model. Specifically, consider a production function for a single local output good:

$$y = \left[\sum_j (e^j N^j)^{(\sigma-1)/\sigma} \right]^{\sigma/(\sigma-1)}$$

where N^j is the number of people employed in skill group j, e^j is a relative productivity shock, and σ is the elasticity of substitution between labor types. Given a set of wage rates w^j for different skill groups, the relative labor demand curve between any two skill groups, say d = dropout labor and H = high school graduate labor, can be written as

$$\log\left(\frac{N^d}{N^H}\right) = -\sigma \log\left(\frac{w^d}{w^H}\right) + (\sigma - 1)\log\left(\frac{e^d}{e^H}\right).$$

This equation shows that employers can be induced to increase the relative utilization of dropout labor by reducing the relative wage of dropout workers. Inverting the relative demand curve leads to a simple estimating equation that relates the relative wage gap between high school graduates and dropouts in a city to the relative supply of the two types of workers:

$$(4) \qquad \log\left(\frac{w^H}{w^d}\right) = \frac{-1}{\sigma} \log\left(\frac{N^H}{N^d}\right) - \frac{(\sigma-1)}{\sigma} \log\left(\frac{e^H}{e^d}\right).$$

As has been recognized in the immigration literature, a problem for the estimation of a model like (4) is that local relative demand shocks may raise relative wages *and* attract differential inflows of skilled versus unskilled workers. To address this concern, we consider a first-differenced version of (4) that abstracts from any permanent characteristics of a city that may affect the relative demand for less-skilled labor. We also consider IV estimates of the first-differenced model in which we use the supply-push variables (lagged Mexican immigrant densities in the city) to instrument the change in the relative supply of dropout labor in a city.

Table 6.7 presents estimation results for equation (4), based on data for 145 larger MSAs. We measure the dependent variable as the difference between regression-adjusted mean log wages for native male workers in a city with exactly twelve years of schooling and those with less than twelve years of schooling. Following the recent inequality literature (e.g., Katz and Murphy 1992) we measure the supply of high school workers in a city by

Table 6.7   **Regression models for wage gap between high school and dropout native male workers**

	Estimated by OLS				Estimated by IV—Change: 1990–2000	
			Change: 1990–2000			
	2000	1990				
	(1)	(2)	(3)	(4)	(5)	(6)
Log relative supply (high school vs. dropout labor)	0.01 (0.01)	−0.03 (0.01)	−0.04 (0.04)	−0.05 (0.04)	0.00 (0.07)	−0.04 (0.06)
Employment growth, 1990–2000				−0.06 (0.04)		−0.01 (0.05)
F-statistics for first-stage models:						
Model for log relative supply					26.8	10.68
Model for employment growth						19.02
R^2	0.00	0.04	0.01	0.02	0.00	0.00

Notes: All models estimated on sample of 145 larger cities with census data for 1980–2000 and matching employment data from county business patterns for 1982–2000. Dependent variable is gap between regression adjusted mean log wage of high school male natives in city and regression adjusted mean log wage of dropout male natives in city. Models are estimated by weighted OLS or IV using 1990 population counts of working age adults as weights. Instruments in column (5) are fraction Mexican immigrants in adult population of city in 1980 and 1990. Instruments in column (6) are fraction of Mexican immigrants in adult population in 1980 and 1990 and log of city-level employment in 1982–1990.

the number of people with a high school diploma, plus half of the number who have between thirteen and fifteen years of completed schooling. We similarly measure the supply of dropout workers as a simple count of the number with less than a high school education. The models are estimated by weighed OLS and IV, using 1990 population counts as weights.

The results for the OLS models in columns (1)–(3) suggest that there is not a large or statistically significant relationship between the relative wages of high school dropouts and their relative supply in different cities, although the point estimate of the relative supply effect in the first-differenced model is negative. We also consider a specification in column (4) that adds employment growth in the city as an additional explanatory variable. This has a modest negative effect on the wage gap, suggesting that relative wages of dropouts are higher in rapidly growing cities, though the coefficient is not significant at conventional levels. Adding this variable has little impact on the estimated supply effect.

The IV estimates in columns (5) and (6) use the shares of Mexican immigrants in the city in 1980 and 1990 as instruments for the change in the log relative supply of high school versus dropout labor. Before discussing these results, it is instructive to look at the data in figures 6.16 and 6.17,

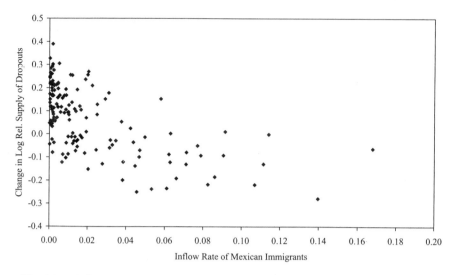

Fig. 6.16   Inflow rate of Mexican immigrants and change in relative supply of dropout labor

which illustrate the relationship between inflows of new Mexican immigrants to a city and the relative supply (figure 6.16) and relative wages (figure 6.17) of dropout labor. Figure 6.16 establishes that there is a strong impact of Mexican inflows on the relative supply of dropout versus high school labor. Given the models in table 6.4 suggesting that 75 percent or more of the variation in Mexican inflows can be explained by supply-push factors, it is clear that our IV strategy has a powerful first stage. (Indeed, the F-statistic for the first stage underlying the results in column [5] of table 6.7 is 26.8, with 2 and 142 degrees of freedom.) Figure 6.17, on the other hand, suggests that there is not much correlation between high school-dropout wage gap and the inflow rate of Mexican immigrants. The overall scatter of the points is slightly positively sloping (consistent with the idea that an increase in the relative supply of dropouts lowers their relative wages), but close inspection suggests that only a handful of points contribute to the slope.

The simple IV specification in column (5) of table 6.7 yields an estimate of the effect of relative supply that is somewhat less precise than the corresponding OLS model but no more negative in magnitude. The same conclusion emerges from the model in column (6), in which we treat both the change in relative supply and employment growth as endogenous.[26] It does

26. In this model, both the change in relative supply and employment growth from 1990 to 2000 are treated as endogenous, and the fractions of Mexican immigrants in the city in 1980 and 1990 and the log of employment in 1984–1990 are used as instrumental variables. The

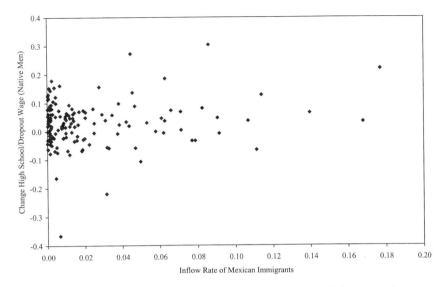

Fig. 6.17   Inflow rate of Mexican immigrants and change in relative wage of native male dropouts

not appear that increasing supplies of dropout labor arising from the predictable component of inflows of Mexican immigrants have much effect on the relative wage structure in a city.

We have also estimated a number of variants of the models in table 6.7. In one variant, we added a control for the change in the relative number of college versus high school-educated workers to the first-differenced specification in column (4). This variable has a marginally significant positive effect on the high school dropout wage gap (coefficient = 0.15, standard error = 0.07), but its addition does not have any impact on the coefficient of the variable measuring the relative supply of dropouts or on the employment growth effect. We also estimated the models using unweighted OLS and IV. The coefficient estimates from the unweighted models are somewhat less precise but show a similar pattern to the results in table 6.7. For example, the estimated relative supply effect from the first-differenced specification in column (4) is –0.07 (with a standard error of 0.05). Finally, we considered a specification in which the supply of high school workers was narrowly defined to include only those with exactly twelve years of schooling. This leads to a slightly bigger coefficient on the relative supply variable. For example, the estimate corresponding to the specification in column (4) is –0.06, with a standard error of 0.04. Overall, there is not

---

F-statistic for the first-stage model explaining the change in relative supply is 10.68 (with 11 and 133 degrees of freedom). The F-statistic for the first-stage model explaining the change in employment is 19.02 (with 11 and 133 degrees of freedom).

much evidence that the relative supply of dropout labor in a city has much impact on dropout relative wages.

6.3.4   Interpretation

Our findings with respect to the impacts of Mexican immigration present a puzzle. Inflows of Mexican immigrants appear to raise the relative supply of low-education labor in a city. Contrary to a simple trade-style model, however, shifts in the relative supply of low-education labor across cities do not lead to systematic expansions or contractions in dropout-intensive industries. Rather, most of the variation in the relative supply of dropout labor is absorbed by changes in dropout intensity within narrowly defined industries. Even more surprisingly, differences in dropout intensity of employment do not seem to be strongly related to the relative wages of dropout workers. Thus, it is hard to explain the variation in dropout intensity across cities as variation along a relative demand curve.

We believe there are a number of possible explanations for these findings. One is that high school dropouts are highly substitutable with high-school educated workers. Under this assumption, the share of dropouts relative to high school graduates employed in a given city will vary with local supply, but the relative wage gap between the two groups will be roughly constant. The near-perfect substitutes assumption is consistent with the fact that the aggregate wage gap between high school graduates and dropouts has been constant since 1980 (Card 2005). It is also potentially consistent with the very imprecise estimates of the inverse elasticity of substitution across education groups obtained by Borjas (2003) and Borjas and Katz (2005) using national data from the past four decades.[27] If dropouts and high school graduates are close to perfect substitutes, Mexican immigration may be depressing the relative wages of *all* workers with low and medium levels of education (e.g., up to fourteen years of schooling) relative to college graduates. Nevertheless, the proportional impact of Mexican inflows on the relative supply of workers with up to fourteen years of schooling is considerably smaller than their impacts on the relative supply of dropout labor, so if this hypothesis is true, concerns over the negative impacts of Mexican immigrants on low-wage natives are overstated.

A second possibility is that local industry structure responds to relative factor supplies as predicted by the HO model but that changes occur *within* narrowly defined industries (i.e., below the three-digit industry level). For example, if an industry consists of subsectors that use different relative

---

27. For example, the estimate of the inverse elasticity of substitution across four education groups (including dropouts, high school graduates, people with some college, and people with a bachelor's degree or more) obtained by Borjas and Katz (2005) using a nested CES structure is 0.41 with a standard error of 0.31. (Revised estimate and standard error reported in personal communication from Larry Katz.) This relatively imprecise estimate does not rule out perfect substitution across different education groups.

fractions of dropout workers, then the relative supply of dropout workers in a city may determine the relative size of the dropout-intensive subsector, with little or no affect on the overall size of the combined industry. This hypothesis is observationally equivalent to the model proposed by Beaudry and Green (2005) in which output is produced by two coexistent technologies, one of which is relatively more intensive in low-skilled labor. This class of models may be useful in describing certain industries but seems less appealing for other industries, like locally traded services.

A final (closely related) hypothesis is that employers adapt to the relative supply of different skill groups in their local market without the signals of relative wage changes. Acemoglu's (1998) model of endogenous technological change, for example, suggests that firms will innovate in a direction to take advantage of more readily available factors, even in the absence of relative wage changes. Lewis (2004) presents some direct evidence for an endogenous technological change mechanism, using data on the number of advanced technologies adopted by manufacturing plants in the late 1980s and early 1990s. He finds that controlling for very detailed (four-digit) industry effects, the adoption of advanced technologies by individual plants is significantly slowed by the presence of a greater relative supply of unskilled labor in the local labor market. More work is needed to understand how firms choose which technologies to use and whether the choice is influenced by the relative availability of different skill groups, particularly low-skilled immigrants.

6.4   Conclusions

Mexicans are the largest single group of immigrants in the United States, representing about one-third of all immigrants and more than 4 percent of the country's working-age population. Until the last decade, Mexican immigrants were geographically clustered in a relatively small number of cities. In 1990, nearly one-half of all working-age Mexicans were living in just five U.S. cities, and 70 percent were living in only fifteen cities. During the 1990s, however, arrivals from Mexico established sizeable immigrant communities in many new cities, including Atlanta, Denver, Portland, and Raleigh-Durham. These immigrants are changing the face of the new destination cities and setting the stage for many years of future inflows.

In this paper we present some simple evidence on the causes and consequences of the widening geographic diffusion of Mexican immigrants. A combination of demand-pull and supply-push factors explains 85 percent of the variation across major cities in the rate of Mexican inflows during the 1990s and helps illuminate the single most important trend in the destination choices of new Mexican immigrants—the move away from Los Angeles.

Like their predecessors, recent Mexican immigrants have relatively low levels of education. We show that inflows of Mexican immigrants lead to systematic shifts in the relative supply of low-education labor in a city, opening up the question of how different local labor markets are adopting to substantial differences in relative supply. One possibility—suggested by the conventional Heckscher Olin model of international trade—is that these differences are accommodated by shifts in industry composition. Despite the theoretical appeal of this hypothesis, we find it has limited empirical relevance: most of the differences across cities in the relative supply of low-education labor (or Mexican labor) are absorbed by changes in skill intensity *within* narrow industries. Such adjustments could be readily explained if Mexican immigrant inflows had large effects on the relative wage structures of different cities. As has been found in previous studies of the local impacts of immigration, however, our analysis suggests that relative wage adjustments are small. Thus, we are left with the puzzle of explaining the remarkable flexibility of employment demand in different cities to local variation in supply. Given the continuing pace of Mexican immigration, the next decade should provide even more evidence on the ways that local economies adjust to shifts in relative supply.

References

Acemoglu, Daron. 1998. Why do new technologies complement skills? Directed technical change and wage inequality. *Quarterly Journal of Economics* 114:1055–89.
Bartel, Anne. 1989. Where do the new U.S. immigrants live? *Journal of Labor Economics* 7:371–91.
Beaudry, Paul, and David A. Green. 2005. Changes in U.S. wages, 1976–2000: Ongoing skill bias or major technological change? *Journal of Labor Economics* 23:609–48.
Borjas, George J. 2003. The labor demand curve *is* downward sloping: Reexamining the impact of immigration on the labor market. *Quarterly Journal of Economics* 118:1335–74.
Borjas, George J., Richard B. Freeman, and Kevin Lang. 1991. Undocumented Mexican-born workers in the United States: How many, how permanent? In *Immigration, trade, and the labor market,* ed. John M. Abowd and Richard B. Freeman, 77–100. Chicago: The University of Chicago Press.
Borjas, George J., and Lawrence F. Katz. 2005. The evolution of the Mexican-born workforce in the United States. NBER Working Paper no. 11281. Cambridge, MA: National Bureau of Economic Research, April.
Card, David. 2001. Immigrant inflows, native outflows and the local labor market impacts of higher immigration. *Journal of Labor Economics* 19:22–64.
———. 2005. Is the new immigration really so bad? *Economic Journal* 115:F300–F323.
Citro, Constance F., Daniel L. Cork, and Janet L. Norwood. 2004. *Counting under adversity: Panel to review the 2000 Census.* Washington, DC: National Academies Press.
Elliot, Michael R., and Roderick J. A. Little. 2005. A Bayesian approach to 2000

Census evaluation using survey data and demographic analysis. *Journal of the American Statistical Association* 100:380–88.

Hogan, Howard, and Gregory Robinson. 1993. What the Census Bureau's coverage evaluation programs tell us about differential undercount. In *Proceedings of the 1993 Research Conference on Undercounted Ethnic Populations,* 9–28. Washington, DC: U.S. Department of Commerce, Bureau of the Census.

Katz, Lawrence, and Kevin M. Murphy. 1992. Changes in relative wages, 1963–1987: Supply and demand factors. *Quarterly Journal of Economics* 107:35–78.

Lewis, Ethan G. 2003. Local open economies within the U.S.: How do industries respond to immigration? Federal Reserve Bank of Philadelphia Working Paper. Philadelphia: Federal Reserve Bank of Philadelphia.

———. 2004. The effect of local skill mix on new technology adoption in U.S. manufacturing. Federal Reserve Bank of Philadelphia. Unpublished Manuscript.

Lubotsky, Darren. 2000. Chutes or ladders? A longitudinal analysis of immigrant earnings. University of Illinois at Urbana-Champaign. Unpublished Manuscript.

Norwood, Janet, et al. 2004. *The 2000 Census: Counting under adversity.* Washington, DC: National Academy of Sciences.

Organization for Economic Cooperation and Development. 2000. *OECD economic surveys 1999–2000: Mexico.* Paris: OECD.

Passel, Jeffrey. 2002. New estimates of the undocumented population in the United States. *Migration Information Source.* Washington, DC: Migration Policy Institute, May. http://www.migrationinformation.org/USfocus/display.cfm?id=19.

U.S. Department of Citizenship and Immigration Services. 2003. Estimates of the unauthorized immigrant population residing in the United States: 1990 to 2000. Unpublished Manuscript. http://www.uscis.gov/graphics/shared/aboutus/statistics/Ill_Report_1211.pdf.

Van Hook, Jennifer, and Frank D. Bean. 1998. Estimating underenumeration among unauthorized Mexican migrants to the United States: Applications of mortality analyses. In *Migration between Mexico and the United States: Research reports and background materials,* 551–69. Washington, DC: U.S. Commission on Immigration Reform.

7

Ethnic Identification, Intermarriage, and Unmeasured Progress by Mexican Americans

Brian Duncan and Stephen J. Trejo

7.1 Introduction

One of the most important and controversial questions in U.S. immigration research is whether the latest wave of foreign-born newcomers (or their U.S.-born descendants) will ultimately assimilate into the mainstream of American society and whether the pace and extent of such assimilation will vary across immigrant groups. In terms of key economic outcomes such as educational attainment, occupation, and earnings, the sizeable differences by national origin that initially persisted among earlier European immigrants have largely disappeared among the modern-day descendants of these immigrants (Neidert and Farley 1985; Lieberson and Waters 1988; Farley 1990). There is considerable skepticism, however, that the processes of assimilation and adaptation will operate similarly for the predominantly nonwhite immigrants who have entered the United States in increasing numbers over the past thirty years (Gans 1992; Portes and Zhou 1993; Rumbaut 1994). In a controversial new book, Huntington (2004) voices a particularly strong version of such skepticism with regard to Hispanic immigration.

Mexicans assume a central role in current discussions of immigrant inter-

Brian Duncan is an associate professor of economics at the University of Colorado at Denver. Stephen J. Trejo is an associate professor of economics at the University of Texas at Austin.

For helpful comments and advice, we are grateful to Jorge Chapa, Alfredo Cuecuecha, Alberto Davila, Dan Hamermesh, Harry Holzer, Bob Hummer, Evelyn Lehrer, Marie Mora, Gerald Oettinger, Art Sakamoto, Adela de la Torre, two anonymous reviewers, and participants in the NBER conference on Mexican immigration, the 2005 Institute for the Study of Labor (IZA) annual migration meeting, and the 2005 Instituto Technológico Autónomo de México (ITAM)–University of Texas conference. We thank the Russell Sage Foundation for initial support of this research.

generational progress and the outlook for the so-called *new second generation,* not just because Mexicans make up a large share of the immigrant population, but also because most indications of relative socioeconomic disadvantage among the children of U.S. immigrants vanish when Mexicans are excluded from the sample (Perlmann and Waldinger 1996, 1997). Therefore, to a great extent, concern about the long-term economic trajectory of immigrant families in the United States is concern about Mexican American families.

Several recent studies compare education and earnings across generations of Mexican Americans (Trejo 1997, 2003; Fry and Lowell 2002; Farley and Alba 2002; Grogger and Trejo 2002; Livingston and Kahn 2002; Blau and Kahn 2005; Duncan, Hotz, and Trejo 2006). Table 7.1 illustrates the basic patterns that emerge for men.[1] Between the first and second generations, average schooling rises by almost three and one-half years, and average hourly earnings grow by about 30 percent for Mexicans. The third generation, by contrast, shows little or no additional gains, leaving Mexican American men with an educational deficit of 1.3 years and a wage disadvantage of about 25 percent, relative to whites. Similar patterns emerge for women and also when regressions are used to control for other factors such as age and geographic location (Grogger and Trejo 2002; Blau and Kahn 2005; Duncan, Hotz, and Trejo 2006).

The apparent lack of socioeconomic progress between second and later generations of Mexican Americans is surprising. Previous studies have consistently found parental education to be one of the most important determinants of an individual's educational attainment and ultimate labor market success (Haveman and Wolfe 1994; Mulligan 1997). Through this mechanism, the huge educational gain between first- and second-generation Mexican Americans should produce a sizable jump in schooling between the second and third generations because, on average, the third generation has parents who are much better educated than those of the second generation. Yet the improvement in schooling we expect to find between the second and third generations is largely absent.

The research summarized in table 7.1 suggests that intergenerational progress stalls for Mexican Americans after the second generation. As noted by Borjas (1993) and Smith (2003), however, generational comparisons in a single cross-section of data do a poor job of matching immigrant

---

1. These averages are calculated from March 1998–2002 Current Population Survey data, with standard errors shown in parentheses. The samples for the earnings data are limited to individuals who worked during the calendar year preceding the survey. The "white" ethnic group is defined to exclude Hispanics, as well as blacks, Asians, and Native Americans. The first generation consists of immigrants: foreign-born individuals whose parents were also born outside the United States. The second generation denotes U.S.-born individuals who have at least one foreign-born parent. The so-called "third generation," which really represents the third and all higher generations, identifies U.S. natives whose parents are also natives.

Table 7.1   **Average years of education and log hourly earnings, men ages 25–59**

	Mexicans			
	1st generation	2nd generation	3rd+ generation	3rd+ generation whites
Years of education	8.8	12.2	12.3	13.6
	(.04)	(.06)	(.04)	(.007)
Log hourly earnings	2.244	2.560	2.584	2.837
	(.006)	(.015)	(.010)	(.002)

Source: March 1998–2002 Current Population Survey data.

Notes: Standard errors are in parentheses. Sampling weights were employed in these calculations. The samples for the hourly earnings data are limited to individuals who worked during the calendar year preceding the survey. The "white" ethnic group is defined to exclude Hispanics, as well as blacks, Asians, and Native Americans. The first generation consists of immigrants: foreign-born individuals whose parents were also born outside the United States. The second generation denotes U.S.-born individuals who have at least one foreign-born parent. The third generation identifies U.S. natives whose parents are also natives. Excluded from the samples are foreign-born individuals who have at least one U.S.-born parent, as well as individuals for whom generation cannot be determined because birthplace data are missing for themselves or either parent.

parents and grandparents in the first generation with their actual descendants in later generations. Indeed, Smith (2003) finds evidence of more substantial gains between second- and third-generation Mexicans when he combines cross-sectional data sets from successive time periods in order to compare second-generation Mexicans in some initial period with their third-generation descendants twenty-five years later. Yet even Smith's analysis shows signs of intergenerational stagnation for Mexican Americans. In his table 4, for example, five of the six most recent cohorts of Mexicans experience no wage gains between the second and third generations. Moreover, all studies conclude that large education and earnings deficits (relative to whites) remain for third- and higher-generation Mexicans.[2]

These findings—that the economic disadvantage of Mexican Americans persists even among those whose families have lived in the United States for more than two generations and that the substantial progress observed between the first and second generations seems to stall thereafter—raise doubts whether the descendants of Mexican immigrants are enjoying the same kind of intergenerational advancement that allowed previous groups of unskilled immigrants, such as the Italians and Irish, to eventually enter the economic mainstream of American society. Such conclusions could have far-reaching implications, but the validity of the intergenerational comparisons that underlie these conclusions rests on assumptions about ethnic identification that have received relatively little scrutiny for Mexican Americans. In particular, analyses of intergenerational change typically

2. Borjas (1994) and Card, DiNardo, and Estes (2000) investigate patterns of intergenerational progress for many different national origin groups, including Mexicans.

assume, either explicitly or implicitly, that the ethnic choices made by the descendants of Mexican immigrants do not distort outcome comparisons across generations.

Ethnic identification is to some extent endogenous, especially among people at least one or two generations removed from immigration to the United States (Alba 1990; Waters 1990). Consequently, the descendants of Mexican immigrants who continue to identify themselves as Mexican in the third and higher generations may be a select group. For example, if the most successful Mexican Americans are more likely to intermarry or, for other reasons, cease to identify themselves or their children as Mexican, then available data may understate human capital and earnings gains between the second and third generations.[3] In other words, research on intergenerational assimilation among Mexicans may suffer from the potentially serious problem that the most assimilated members of the group under study eventually fade from empirical observation as they more closely identify with the group they are assimilating toward.[4]

For other groups, selective ethnic identification has been shown to distort observed socioeconomic characteristics. American Indians are a particularly apt example because they exhibit very high rates of intermarriage, and fewer than half of the children of such intermarriages are identified as American Indian by the census race question (Eschbach 1995). For these and other reasons, racial identification is relatively fluid for American Indians, and changes in self-identification account for much of the surprisingly large increase in educational attainment observed for American Indians between the 1970 and 1980 U.S. Censuses (Eschbach, Supple, and Snipp 1998). In addition, Snipp (1989) shows that those who report American Indian as their race have considerably lower schooling and earnings, on average, than the much larger group of Americans who report a non-Indian race but claim to have some Indian ancestry.

To cite another example, Waters (1994) observes selective ethnic identification among the U.S.-born children of New York City immigrants from the West Indies and Haiti. The teenagers doing well in school tend to come from relatively advantaged, middle-class families, and these kids identify most closely with the ethnic origins of their parents. In contrast, the teenagers doing poorly in school are more likely to identify with African Americans. This pattern suggests that self-identified samples of second-generation Caribbean blacks might overstate the socioeconomic achievement of this population, a finding that potentially calls into question the

3. For groups such as Mexicans with relatively low levels of schooling, Furtado (2006) shows that assortative matching on education in marriage markets can create a situation whereby individuals who intermarry tend to be the more highly educated members of these groups.

4. Bean, Swicegood, and Berg (2000) raise this possibility in their study of generational patterns of fertility for Mexican-origin women in the United States.

practice of comparing outcomes for African Americans and Caribbean blacks as a means of distinguishing racial discrimination from other explanations for the disadvantaged status of African Americans (Sowell 1978).

Using microdata from the U.S. Census and from recent years of the Current Population Survey (CPS), we begin to explore these issues for Mexican Americans. In particular, we investigate what factors influence whether individuals choose to identify themselves (or their children) as Mexican-origin, and how these ethnic choices may affect inferences about the intergenerational progress of Mexican Americans. To date, analyses of ethnic responses and ethnic identification employing large national surveys have focused primarily on whites of European descent (Alba and Chamlin 1983; Lieberson and Waters 1988, 1993; Farley 1991), and, therefore, much could be learned from a similar analysis that highlights ethnic choices among the Mexican-origin population.

Existing studies (Stephan and Stephan 1989; Eschbach and Gomez 1998; Ono 2002) demonstrate that the process of ethnic identification by Mexican Americans is fluid, situational, and at least partly voluntary, just as has been observed for non-Hispanic whites and other groups. These studies, however, do not directly address the issue that we will focus on: the selective nature of Mexican identification and how it affects our inferences about intergenerational progress for this population. Though previous research has noted the selective nature of intermarriage for Hispanics overall (Qian 1997, 1999) and for Mexican Americans in particular (Fu 2001; Rosenfeld 2001), this research has not examined explicitly the links between intermarriage and ethnic identification, nor has previous research considered the biases that these processes might produce in standard intergenerational comparisons of economic status for Mexican Americans. Closer in spirit to our analysis is recent work by Alba and Islam (2005) that tracks cohorts of U.S.-born Mexicans across the 1980–2000 Censuses and uncovers evidence of substantial declines in Mexican self-identification as a cohort ages. In contrast with our work, however, Alba and Islam (2005) are able to provide only limited information about the socioeconomic selectivity of this identity shift, and they focus on the identity shifts that occur within rather than across generations of Mexicans.

Ideally, if we knew the family tree of each individual, we could identify which individuals are descended from Mexican immigrants and how many generations have elapsed since that immigration took place. It would then be a simple matter to compare outcomes for this "true" population of Mexican descendants with the corresponding outcomes for a relevant reference group (e.g., non-Hispanic whites) and also with those for the subset of Mexican descendants who continue to self-identify as Mexican-origin.[5]

5. Detailed ancestry information of this sort would raise complicated issues about how to define ethnic groups. For example, should calculations for the Mexican American population

Such an analysis would provide an unbiased assessment of the relative standing of the descendants of Mexican immigrants in the United States, and it would show the extent to which selective ethnic identification distorts estimated outcomes for this population when researchers are forced to rely on standard, self-reported measures of Mexican identity.

Following the 1970 Census, unusually detailed information of this sort was collected for a small sample of individuals with ancestors from a Spanish-speaking country. After each decennial U.S. Census, selected respondents to the Census long form are reinterviewed in order to check the accuracy and reliability of the Census data. The 1970 Census was the first U.S. Census to ask directly about Hispanic origin or descent, and therefore a primary objective of the 1970 Census Content Reinterview Study (U.S. Bureau of the Census 1974) was to evaluate the quality of the responses to this new question. For this purpose, individuals in the reinterview survey were asked a series of questions regarding any ancestors they might have who were born in a Spanish-speaking country. Among those identified by the reinterview survey as having Hispanic ancestors, table 7.2 shows the percent who had previously responded on the 1970 Census long form that they were of Hispanic "origin or descent."[6]

Overall, 76 percent of reinterview respondents with ancestors from a Spanish-speaking country had self-identified as Hispanic in the 1970 Census, but the correspondence between Hispanic ancestry in the reinterview and Hispanic identification in the census fades with the number of generations since the respondent's Hispanic ancestors arrived in the United States. Virtually all (99 percent) first-generation immigrants born in a Spanish-speaking country identified as Hispanic in the census, but the rate of Hispanic identification dropped to 83 percent for the second generation, 73 percent for the third generation, 44 percent for the fourth generation, and all the way down to 6 percent for higher generations of Hispanics. Interestingly, intermarriage seems to play a central role in the loss of Hispanic identification. Almost everyone (97 percent) with Hispanic ancestors on both sides of their family identified as Hispanic in the census,

---

differentially weight individuals according to their "intensity" of Mexican ancestry? In other words, among third-generation Mexicans, should those with four Mexican-born grandparents count more than those with just one grandparent born in Mexico? The answer might depend on the question of interest. For the questions of intergenerational assimilation and progress that we study here, our view is that all descendants of Mexican immigrants should count equally, regardless of how many branches of their family tree contain Mexican ancestry. This conceptualization allows intermarriage to play a critical role in the process of intergenerational assimilation for Mexican Americans, as it did previously for European immigrants (Gordon 1964; Lieberson and Waters 1988). As we note in the following, however, our data and analyses can shed light on the direction, but not the ultimate magnitude, of measurement biases arising from selective intermarriage and ethnic identification by Mexican Americans. Our conclusions about the direction of these measurement biases require only that persons of mixed ancestry—that is, the products of Mexican intermarriage—be included with some positive weight in whatever definition is adopted for the Mexican American population.

6. The information in table 7.2 is reproduced from table C of U.S. Bureau of the Census (1974, 8).

Table 7.2   Hispanic identification of individuals with ancestors from a Spanish-speaking
country, as reported in the 1970 U.S. Census Content Reinterview Study

Hispanic ancestry classification in reinterview	Percent who identified as Hispanic in the census	Sample size
Most recent ancestor from a Spanish-speaking country		
Respondent (1st generation)	98.7	77
Parent(s) (2nd generation)	83.3	90
Grandparent(s) (3rd generation)	73.0	89
Great grandparent(s) (4th generation)	44.4	27
Further back (5th+ generations)	5.6	18
Hispanic ancestry on both sides of family	97.0	266
Hispanic ancestry on one side of family only	21.4	103
Father's side	20.5	44
Mother's side	22.0	59
All individuals with Hispanic ancestry	75.9	369

Source: Table C of U.S. Bureau of the Census (1974, 8).

Note: Information regarding the generation of the most recent ancestor from a Spanish-speaking country was missing for sixty-eight respondents who nonetheless indicated that they had Hispanic ancestry on one or both sides of their family.

whereas the corresponding rate was only 21 percent for those with Hispanic ancestors on just one side of their family. Given the small number of Hispanics in the reinterview sample (369 individuals reported having at least one ancestor from a Spanish-speaking country), the percentages in table 7.2 should be regarded with caution, especially those for the very small samples of Hispanics who are fourth generation or higher. Nonetheless, these data do suggest that self-identified samples of U.S. Hispanics might omit a large proportion of later-generation individuals with Hispanic ancestors and that intermarriage could be a fundamental source of such intergenerational ethnic "attrition."

Unfortunately, the microdata underlying table 7.2 no longer exist, so we cannot use these data to examine in a straightforward manner how selective ethnic attrition affects observed measures of intergenerational progress for Mexican Americans.[7] Out of necessity, we instead adopt much

7. Starting in 1980, the Census has included an open-ended question asking for each person's "ancestry" or "ethnicity," with the first two responses coded in the order that they are reported (Farley 1991). For the purposes of identifying individuals with Mexican or Hispanic ancestors, however, the census ancestry question is not a good substitute for the detailed battery of questions included in the 1970 Census Content Reinterview Study. Indeed, many 1980–2000 Census respondents who identified as Hispanic in response to the Hispanic origin question failed to list an Hispanic ancestry in response to the ancestry item that comes later on the census long-form questionnaire, perhaps because they thought it redundant and unnecessary to indicate their Hispanic ethnicity a second time. Comparatively few respondents listed an Hispanic ancestry after identifying as non-Hispanic when answering the Hispanic-origin question, so the ancestry question actually produces a lower overall count of Hispanics than does the Hispanic-origin question (Lieberson and Waters 1988; del Pinal 2004).

less direct strategies for trying to shed light on this issue. First, we use the presence of a Spanish surname as an objective, though imperfect, indicator of Mexican ancestry. Second, we analyze the extent and selectivity of intermarriage by Mexican Americans. Third, we study the links between Mexican intermarriage and ethnic identification, focusing on the children produced by these intermarriages. Finally, we explore how intermarriage and ethnic identification vary across generations of U.S.-born Mexicans. Throughout, we analyze the same four outcome variables. The first two—educational attainment and English proficiency—are important measures of human capital. The other two—employment and average hourly earnings—are key indicators of labor market performance.

7.2   Spanish Surname

Our first set of analyses exploits the information about Spanish surnames that was made available most recently in the 1980 Census. The microdata file indicates whether an individual's surname appears on a list of almost 12,500 Hispanic surnames constructed by the Census Bureau. This information, however, is provided only for those individuals who reside in the following five southwestern states: California, Texas, Arizona, Colorado, and New Mexico.

Though the surname list constructed for the 1980 Census is more extensive and accurate than those used with previous censuses, as a tool for identifying Hispanics the list suffers from sins of both omission and commission. Indeed, both types of errors are introduced by the common practice of married women taking the surname of their husbands, as Hispanic women can lose and non-Hispanic women can gain a Spanish surname through intermarriage. The surname list also errs by labeling as Hispanic some individuals of Italian, Filipino, or Native Hawaiian descent who have names that appear on the list (Bean and Tienda 1987; Perkins 1993).

For our purposes, another weakness of the surname list is that it cannot distinguish Mexicans from other Hispanic national origin groups. This weakness is minimized, however, by limiting the sample to the aforementioned five southwestern states. In 1980, the Puerto Rican and Cuban populations in these states were still quite small, and large-scale immigration from Central and South America had not yet begun. As a result, the overwhelming majority of Hispanics in these southwestern states are Mexican-origin. Indeed, in the samples of U.S.-born individuals analyzed in the following, 88 percent of those who self-report as being of Hispanic origin indicate Mexican as their national origin, and almost all remaining self-reported Hispanics fall into the "Other Hispanic" category. Individuals in this "Other Hispanic" category are especially prevalent in the states of New Mexico and Colorado, where some Hispanics whose families have lived in these regions for many generations prefer to call themselves "Hispanos," emphasizing their roots to the Spaniards who settled the new world over their Mexican and Indian ancestry (Bean and Tienda 1987).

The Spanish surname information provided in the 1980 Census is in addition to the race and Hispanic origin questions typically employed to identify racial or ethnic groups. Our hope is that, particularly for men, the presence of a Spanish surname in the five southwestern states provides an objective, albeit imperfect, indicator of Mexican ancestry that allows us to identify some individuals of Mexican descent who fail to self-report as Hispanic and who are therefore missed by subjective indicators such as the Hispanic origin question in the census. If so, then perhaps differences in human capital and labor market outcomes between Spanish-surnamed individuals who do and do not self-identify as Hispanic can reveal something about the selective nature of ethnic identification for Mexican Americans.

To pursue this idea, we extracted from the 1980 Census five-percent microdata sample all individuals between the ages of twenty-five and fifty-nine who reside in the states of California, Texas, Arizona, Colorado, and New Mexico. We focus on individuals in this age range because they are old enough that virtually all of them will have completed their schooling, yet they are young enough that observed labor market outcomes reflect their prime working years. Given our interest in ethnic identification, we exclude from our sample anyone whose information about race, Hispanic origin, or country of birth was allocated by the Census Bureau. To increase the accuracy of the Spanish surname indicator, individuals whose race is American Indian or Asian are also excluded, as is anyone else with a race other than white or black who neither has a Spanish surname nor self-reports as being of Hispanic origin.

In our data, there are two different ways for individuals to be identified as Hispanic. They can self-report being Hispanic in response to the Hispanic origin question, and they can possess a Spanish surname. Based on these two Hispanic indicators, we define three mutually exclusive types of Hispanic identification: those identified as Hispanic *both* by self-report and by surname, those identified as Hispanic by self-report *only* (and not by surname), and those identified as Hispanic by surname *only* (and not by self-report). Remaining individuals in our sample are non-Hispanic whites and blacks (i.e., persons of white or black race who do not self-report as being of Hispanic origin and also do not possess a Spanish surname). We conduct all analyses separately for men and women.

Table 7.3 shows the ethnic distribution of our sample separately for U.S. natives and three different groups of foreign-born individuals: those born in Mexico, those born in another Hispanic country, and those born in a non-Hispanic foreign country. For now, let us focus on the data for men in the top panel of the table. As might be expected, almost everyone born in Mexico is identified as Hispanic, and very few men born in non-Hispanic foreign countries are identified as Hispanic. Just over 85 percent of men

Table 7.3   Ethnic distributions, by country of birth, 1980 (%)

| | Country of birth | | | |
	United States	Mexico	Other Hispanic country	Non-Hispanic foreign country
Men				
Identified as Hispanic by:				
Self-report and surname	10.3	91.9	64.4	.7
Self-report only	1.6	7.0	20.4	1.0
Surname only	.5	.5	1.0	1.1
Non-Hispanic				
White	79.9	.5	9.0	95.0
Black	7.7	.02	5.1	2.2
	100.0	100.0	100.0	100.0
Sample size	373,700	23,719	6,124	15,675
Women				
Identified as Hispanic by:				
Self-report and surname	9.4	87.0	54.0	.6
Self-report only	3.0	11.6	31.5	1.0
Surname only	1.8	.6	1.2	2.9
Non-Hispanic				
White	77.3	.7	8.7	94.7
Black	8.5	.1	4.7	.8
	100.0	100.0	100.0	100.0
Sample size	378,873	22,163	7,045	18,560

Source: 1980 U.S. Census data.

Notes: The samples include individuals ages 25–59 who reside in the states of California, Texas, Arizona, Colorado, and New Mexico. Individuals whose race is American Indian or Asian are excluded, as is anyone else with a race other than white or black who neither has a Spanish surname nor self-reports as being of Hispanic origin. The category "other Hispanic country" refers to individuals born in a Hispanic country other than Mexico. The following countries are included in this category: Puerto Rico, Cuba, Dominican Republic, El Salvador, Guatemala, Honduras, Nicaragua, Costa Rica, Panama, Colombia, Peru, Ecuador, Argentina, Chile, Venezuela, Bolivia, Uruguay, Paraguay, and Spain.

born in Hispanic countries other than Mexico are identified as Hispanic. The Spanish surname indicator does not capture all Hispanics, as substantial numbers of men born in Mexico and other Hispanic countries are identified as Hispanic by self-report only. But note that few men born in Mexico and other Hispanic countries are identified as Hispanic by surname only. Of men identified as Hispanic, only 0.5 percent of those born in Mexico and 1.2 percent of those born in other Hispanic countries are identified by surname only. Among U.S.-born men identified as Hispanic, however, the corresponding rate is about 4 percent—still low, but noticeably higher. The higher rate of surname-only identification for U.S.-born Hispanics compared to foreign-born Hispanics is what we might expect if this group in part captures men of Hispanic descent who are choosing not to self-identify as Hispanic because ethnicity is likely to be more fluid and malleable for U.S.-born Hispanics than for Hispanic immigrants. The patterns are similar for women in the bottom panel of the table, except that for all countries of birth women show more inconsistency between self-reported and surname-based indicators of Hispanicity than men do, presumably because of errors sometimes introduced when married women take their husband's surname.

Henceforth we limit the analysis to U.S.-born individuals because issues of ethnic identification are most relevant for this group. Table 7.3 indicates that, even among the U.S.-born, men with a Spanish surname usually also self-report being of Hispanic origin. As noted previously, just 4 percent of the U.S.-born men that we label as Hispanic are so identified only by their Spanish surname. A larger share of Hispanic men, 13 percent, self-identify as Hispanic but do not possess a surname on the census list of Spanish surnames. The vast majority, 83 percent, identifies as Hispanic through both self-report and surname. For U.S.-born Hispanic women, the corresponding proportions are 13 percent identify as Hispanic by surname only, 21 percent by self-report only, and 66 percent through both indicators.

For each type of Hispanic identification, as well as for non-Hispanic whites and blacks, table 7.4 displays averages for the following measures of human capital and labor market performance: completed years of schooling, percent deficient in English, percent employed, and the natural logarithm of average hourly earnings. Here, we define someone to be "deficient" in English if they speak a language other than English at home and they report speaking English worse than "very well."[8] The employment and earnings measures pertain to the calendar year preceding the census. We compute average hourly earnings as the ratio of annual earnings to annual hours of work, where annual earnings are the sum of wage and salary income and self-employment income, and annual hours of work are the product of weeks worked and usual weekly hours of work. The samples for the earnings data are limited to those who were employed.[9] Standard errors are shown in parentheses.

In general, the top panel of table 7.4 shows that men identified as Hispanic by self-report only or by surname only have more human capital and better labor market outcomes than men identified as Hispanic by both indicators. Men with inconsistent responses to the Hispanic indicators have at least a year and a half more schooling and over 10 percent higher wages

---

8. The census asks individuals whether they "speak a language other than English at home," and those who answer affirmatively then are asked how well they speak English, with possible responses of "very well," "well," "not well," or "not at all."

9. In addition, observations in the 1980 Census data with computed hourly earnings below $1 or above $200 are considered outliers and excluded.

Table 7.4 **Average outcomes by type of Hispanic identification, 1980, U.S.-born individuals only**

	Years of education	Deficient English	Percent employed	Log hourly earnings
Men				
Identified as Hispanic by:				
Self-report and surname	10.6	28.8	90.7	1.900
	(.02)	(.23)	(.15)	(.003)
Self-report only	12.1	14.4	90.8	2.008
	(.05)	(.46)	(.38)	(.009)
Surname only	12.2	7.0	91.8	2.083
	(.08)	(.61)	(.66)	(.017)
All types of Hispanics	10.8	26.1	90.8	1.921
	(.02)	(.20)	(.13)	(.003)
Non-Hispanic				
White	13.6	.6	94.1	2.163
	(.005)	(.01)	(.04)	(.001)
Black	12.0	.8	84.1	1.926
	(.02)	(.05)	(.22)	(.004)
Women				
Identified as Hispanic by:				
Self-report and surname	9.7	33.3	59.6	1.476
	(.02)	(.26)	(.26)	(.004)
Self-report only	11.7	13.0	67.9	1.624
	(.03)	(.32)	(.44)	(.007)
Surname only	12.3	3.2	67.7	1.626
	(.03)	(.21)	(.56)	(.009)
All types of Hispanics	10.5	25.1	62.4	1.531
	(.02)	(.19)	(.21)	(.003)
Non-Hispanic				
White	13.0	.5	68.7	1.679
	(.005)	(.01)	(.09)	(.001)
Black	12.1	.6	70.8	1.649
	(.02)	(.04)	(.25)	(.004)

Source: 1980 U.S. Census data.

Notes: Standard errors are in parentheses. The samples include U.S.-born individuals ages 25–59 who reside in the states of California, Texas, Arizona, Colorado, and New Mexico. Individuals whose race is American Indian or Asian are excluded, as is anyone else with a race other than white or black who neither has a Spanish surname nor self-reports as being of Hispanic origin. The samples for the hourly earnings data are further limited to individuals who were employed at some time during the calendar year preceding the census. The sample sizes for men are 373,700 for the full sample and 339,272 for the employed sample, and the sample sizes for women are 378,873 for the full sample and 247,111 for the employed sample.

than Hispanic men with consistent responses,[10] and rates of English deficiency are lower for men with inconsistent responses. The bottom panel of table 7.4 shows patterns for women that are qualitatively similar but even stronger, with a substantial advantage in the employment rate now evident for women with inconsistent Hispanic indicators.

The least squares regression coefficients reported in table 7.5 illustrate more clearly these comparisons and also show how the comparisons change after conditioning on the influence of various controls. The dependent variables are the four outcomes introduced in table 7.4. The key independent variables are dummies indicating the type of Hispanic identification and a dummy identifying non-Hispanic blacks so that the reference group consists of non-Hispanic whites. The first regression specification—the columns labeled (1) in table 7.5—includes only the ethnic dummy variables, and therefore these coefficients reproduce the mean comparisons from table 7.4. The second specification—the columns labeled (2)—adds controls for geographic location and age. The controls for geographic location are dummy variables identifying the five states included in the sample and whether the individual resides in a metropolitan area. The controls for age are dummy variables identifying five-year age intervals. Finally, for the employment and earnings outcomes, there is a third specification—the columns labeled (3)—that also conditions on the human capital variables that measure educational attainment and English proficiency.

Table 7.5 indicates that, for both men and women and for all outcomes, controlling for geographic location and age has little effect on the patterns just described. The coefficients change only slightly as we move from specification (1) to specification (2). For the labor market outcomes, however, controlling for human capital has a large effect. Moving from specification (2) to specification (3) dramatically shrinks the employment and earnings differences associated with the type of Hispanic identification, and it also reduces the labor market disadvantage of Hispanics relative to non-Hispanic whites.[11] These findings reveal that differences in labor market

---

10. For expositional convenience, throughout the paper we will treat log wage differences as representing percentage wage differentials, although we recognize that this approximation becomes increasingly inaccurate for log differences on the order of .25 or more in absolute value. In such instances, one can calculate the implied percentage wage differential as $e^x - 1$, where x represents the estimated log wage difference.

11. One surprise in table 7.5 is that the specification (3) earnings regression for women yields a positive and statistically significant coefficient for the dummy variable indicating deficient English. This counterintuitive result arises from the strong correlation, for Hispanics, between education and English proficiency and from the fact that the regression restricts the returns to education to be the same for Hispanics and non-Hispanics. Either dropping education from this regression or allowing its effect to vary by ethnicity produces the expected negative coefficient for deficient English. Allowing the impact of education to differ for Hispanics and non-Hispanics does not, however, alter the pattern of earnings differences by type of Hispanic identification or the conclusion that most of these earnings differences derive from human capital differences.

Table 7.5 Regression-adjusted outcome differences by type of Hispanic identification, 1980, U.S.-born individuals only

					Dependent variable						
	Education		Deficient English		Employment			Log hourly earnings			
Regressor	(1)	(2)	(1)	(2)	(1)	(2)	(3)	(1)	(2)	(3)
Men											
Identified as Hispanic by:											
Self-report and surname	-3.02	-3.03	.282	.280	-.034	-.040	.003	-.263	-.227	-.075
	(.02)	(.02)	(.001)	(.001)	(.001)	(.001)	(.002)	(.004)	(.004)	(.004)
Self-report only	-1.49	-1.67	.138	.141	-.033	-.039	-.015	-.154	-.129	-.048
	(.04)	(.04)	(.002)	(.002)	(.003)	(.003)	(.003)	(.009)	(.008)	(.008)
Surname only	-1.34	-1.39	.064	.065	-.024	-.022	-.003	-.080	-.007	-.010
	(.08)	(.07)	(.004)	(.004)	(.006)	(.006)	(.006)	(.016)	(.015)	(.015)
Non-Hispanic black	-1.58	-1.60	.002	-.0004	-.101	-.106	-.087	-.237	-.231	-.167
	(.02)	(.02)	(.001)	(.001)	(.002)	(.002)	(.002)	(.004)	(.004)	(.004)
Years of education							.012			.046
							(.0001)			(.0004)
Deficient English							-.021			-.074
							(.002)			(.006)
Women											
Identified as Mexican by:											
Self-report and surname	-3.30	-3.30	.328	.326	-.091	-.097	.014	-.203	-.176	-.013
	(.02)	(.02)	(.001)	(.001)	(.003)	(.003)	(.003)	(.004)	(.004)	(.005)
Self-report only	-1.27	-1.48	.125	.130	-.007	-.026	.024	-.055	-.061	.014
	(.03)	(.03)	(.002)	(.002)	(.004)	(.004)	(.004)	(.007)	(.007)	(.007)
Surname only	-.66	-.96	.026	.033	-.009	-.035	-.005	-.053	-.069	-.016
	(.03)	(.03)	(.002)	(.002)	(.006)	(.006)	(.005)	(.009)	(.009)	(.009)

Non-Hispanic black	-.91	-.94	.0008	-.001	.022	.009	.037	-.030	-.028	.018
	(.02)	(.02)	(.001)	(.001)	(.003)	(.003)	(.003)	(.004)	(.004)	(.004)
Years of education							.029			.064
							(.0003)			(.0005)
Deficient English							-.042			.035
							(.004)			(.008)
Controls for:										
Geographic location	No	Yes	No	Yes	No	Yes	Yes	No	Yes	Yes
Age	No	Yes	No	Yes	No	Yes	Yes	No	Yes	Yes

Source: 1980 U.S. Census data.

Notes: The reported figures are estimated coefficients from ordinary least squares regressions run separately for men and women. Standard errors are in parentheses. The samples include U.S.-born individuals ages 25–59 who reside in the states of California, Texas, Arizona, Colorado, and New Mexico. Individuals whose race is American Indian or Asian are excluded, as is anyone else with a race other than white or black who neither has a Spanish surname nor self-reports as being of Hispanic origin. The samples for the hourly earnings regressions are further limited to individuals who were employed at some time during the calendar year preceding the Census. The sample sizes for men are 373,700 for the full sample and 339,272 for the employed sample, and the sample sizes for women are 378,873 for the full sample and 247,111 for the employed sample. For the dummy variables indicating ethnicity, the reference group consists of non-Hispanic whites. The controls for geographic location are dummy variables identifying the five states included in the sample and whether the individual resides in a metropolitan area. The controls for age are dummy variables identifying five-year age intervals.

outcomes across Hispanic groups and between Hispanics and whites are largely driven by the corresponding differences in schooling and English proficiency.

How should we interpret these patterns? If the group of Hispanic men identified by surname only captures some Hispanics who are choosing to loosen their ethnic attachment, then we have found evidence that such individuals are positively selected in terms of human capital and labor market outcomes. The small size of this group, however, argues against regarding these results as anything more than suggestive. Note that we also found evidence of positive selection for Hispanic men identified by self-report only. These men may be Hispanics who lost their Spanish surname through intermarriage as could occur if they have an Hispanic mother or grandmother who married a non-Hispanic man and took his surname. Therefore, the results for the "Hispanic by self-report only" group are consistent with the results on the selectivity of Mexican intermarriage that we present in the next section. Finally, the patterns for women are similar to those for men but cannot necessarily be interpreted in the same way because the "Hispanic by surname only" group includes some non-Hispanic women who acquired a Spanish surname through marriage.

7.3   Mexican Intermarriage

Intermarriage has always been a fundamental source of ethnic flux and leakage in American society (Lieberson and Waters 1988). For Mexican Americans, Rosenfeld (2002, table 1) shows that intermarriage increased substantially between 1970 and 1980 and even more sharply between 1980 and 1990. Indeed, Perlmann (2003) argues that the proclivity for intermarriage by second-generation Mexicans today is similar to what was observed for second-generation Italians in the early 1900s. This argument has potentially provocative implications for intermarriage by future generations of Mexican Americans because intermarriage became so commonplace for subsequent generations of Italian Americans that Alba (1986) characterized this group as entering the "twilight of ethnicity." Accordingly, our second set of analyses examines the extent and selectivity of Mexican American intermarriage.

Because intermarriage is probably the predominant source of leakage from the population of self-identified Mexican Americans (through the ethnic choices made by the children and grandchildren of these intermarriages), knowing the magnitude of Mexican American intermarriage is important for evaluating the potential bias that such leakage could produce in intergenerational comparisons. One important limitation, however, of census (and CPS) data for investigating the frequency of intermarriage is that these data measure prevalence rather than incidence. In other words, these data show the marriages that exist at a given point in time rather than all marriages that took place over a given span of time. Prevalence measures of intermarriage may differ from incidence measures if, for example, intermarriages have a higher risk of divorce than do endogamous marriages. For our purposes, prevalence measures of intermarriage that capture both marital incidence and duration may actually be preferable as longer-lasting marriages are more likely to produce children and have the influence on ethnic identification in succeeding generations that is the focus of our interest.

For these analyses, we employ microdata from the 2000 Census. The sample includes marriages that meet the following conditions: both spouses are between the ages of twenty-five and fifty-nine, the couple currently lives together, and at least one spouse is a U.S.-born individual identified as Mexican by the census question regarding Hispanic origin. Furthermore, we exclude marriages in which either spouse has allocated information about Hispanic origin. These restrictions yield a sample of 62,734 marriages.

For the U.S.-born Mexican husbands and wives involved in these marriages, table 7.6 shows the nativity/ethnicity distributions of their spouses. Intermarriage is widespread in our samples of Mexican American husbands and wives. The first column indicates that just over half (51 percent) of U.S.-born husbands of Mexican descent have wives of the same nativity and ethnicity, and another 14 percent are married to Mexican immigrants. Therefore, the remaining 35 percent of Mexican American husbands have wives that are neither Mexican nor Mexican American, with the bulk of these wives (27 percent) being U.S.-born non-Hispanic whites. The nativity/ethnicity distribution of Mexican American wives is quite similar, except for a somewhat higher rate of marriage to Mexican immigrants and a correspondingly lower rate of marriage to U.S.-born Mexicans.

Table 7.6 suggests that, in terms of nativity and ethnicity, the marital choices of U.S.-born Mexicans can be classified into three main categories of spouses: U.S.-born Mexicans, foreign-born Mexicans, and non-Mexicans. Based on this simplification, table 7.7 proposes a typology of marriages involving U.S.-born Mexicans that also indicates, for marriages in which only one spouse is a U.S.-born Mexican, whether the other spouse is the husband or the wife. Note that the unit of analysis in table 7.7 is the marriage, rather than the U.S.-born Mexican husband or wife as in table 7.6. This shift in focus is consistent with our interest in how Mexican intermarriage may impact the ethnic identification and observed socioeconomic characteristics of subsequent generations because children are a product of the marriage. Table 7.7 demonstrates the potential for ethnic leakage among the children of Mexican Americans as almost half (48 percent) of Mexican American marriages involve a non-Mexican spouse.

Using this same typology of Mexican American marriages, table 7.8 presents averages of the human capital and labor market variables for the

Table 7.6   **Nativity/ethnicity distributions of the spouses of U.S.-born Mexicans, 2000 (%)**

Nativity/ethnicity of spouse	U.S.-born Mexican Husbands	U.S.-born Mexican Wives
U.S.-born		
Mexican	50.6	45.3
Other Hispanic	2.7	2.3
Non-Hispanic:		
White	26.7	28.1
Black	.6	1.5
Asian	.4	.3
Other race	.8	.6
Multiple race	1.0	1.0
Foreign-born		
Mexican	13.6	17.4
Other Hispanic	1.5	1.8
Non-Hispanic:		
White	1.1	1.2
Black	.04	.06
Asian	.7	.3
Other race	.06	.03
Multiple race	*.2*	*.2*
	100.0	100.0

Source: 2000 U.S. Census data.

Notes: The sample includes marriages that meet the following conditions: both spouses are between the ages of 25–59, the couple currently lives together, and at least one spouse is a U.S.-born individual identified as Mexican by the census question regarding Hispanic origin. For the U.S.-born Mexican husbands and wives involved in these marriages, the table shows the nativity/ethnicity distributions of their spouses. There are 62,734 such marriages, and these marriages involve 38,911 U.S.-born Mexican husbands and 43,527 U.S.-born Mexican wives.

Table 7.7   **Types of marriages involving U.S.-born Mexicans, 2000**

Type of marriage	Percent of sample
Both spouses U.S.-born Mexican	31.4
Husband foreign-born Mexican (wife U.S.-born Mexican)	12.0
Wife foreign-born Mexican (husband U.S.-born Mexican)	8.4
Husband non-Mexican (wife U.S.-born Mexican)	25.9
Wife non-Mexican (husband U.S.-born Mexican)	22.2
	100.0

Source: 2000 U.S. Census data.

Notes: The sample includes marriages that meet the following conditions: both spouses are between the ages of 25–59, the couple currently lives together, and at least one spouse is a U.S.-born individual identified as Mexican by the census question regarding Hispanic origin. There are 62,734 such marriages.

Table 7.8   Average outcomes by type of marriage, 2000

	Years of education	Deficient English	Percent employed	Log hourly earnings
Husbands				
Type of marriage				
Both spouses U.S.-born Mexican	12.0	14.1	91.9	2.692
	(.02)	(.25)	(.19)	(.005)
Husband foreign-born Mexican	9.6	53.3	92.8	2.544
	(.05)	(.57)	(.30)	(.007)
Wife foreign-born Mexican	11.5	24.4	91.8	2.621
	(.04)	(.59)	(.38)	(.009)
Husband non-Mexican	13.5	4.0	95.1	2.919
	(.02)	(.15)	(.17)	(.005)
Wife non-Mexican	13.1	5.1	94.9	2.845
	(.02)	(.19)	(.19)	(.005)
All husbands	12.3	15.0	93.5	2.763
	(.01)	(.14)	(.10)	(.003)
Wives				
Type of marriage				
Both spouses U.S.-born Mexican	12.1	14.2	73.3	2.415
	(.02)	(.25)	(.32)	(.005)
Husband foreign-born Mexican	11.4	18.8	69.8	2.355
	(.03)	(.45)	(.53)	(.009)
Wife foreign-born Mexican	10.3	53.5	60.0	2.289
	(.05)	(.69)	(.67)	(.012)
Husband non-Mexican	13.1	6.0	79.2	2.565
	(.02)	(.19)	(.32)	(.006)
Wife non-Mexican	13.3	4.4	79.6	2.579
	(.02)	(.17)	(.34)	(.006)
All wives	12.4	13.7	74.7	2.480
	(.01)	(.14)	(.17)	(.003)

Source: 2000 U.S. Census data.

Notes: Standard errors are in parentheses. The samples include husbands and wives in marriages that meet the following conditions: both spouses are between the ages of 25–59, the couple currently lives together, and at least one spouse is a U.S.-born individual identified as Mexican by the census question regarding Hispanic origin. The samples for the hourly earnings data are further limited to individuals who were employed at some time during the calendar year preceding the census. The sample sizes are 62,734 husbands and 62,734 wives for the full samples, and 58,003 husbands and 45,857 wives for the employed samples.

husbands and wives in each type of marriage.[12] These calculations include *all* husbands or wives in the relevant marriages, not just the Mexican American husbands or wives. Therefore, we can observe not only the selectivity of U.S.-born Mexicans who intermarry, but also the characteris-

12. As before, the samples for the earnings data are limited to employed individuals. In addition, observations in the 2000 Census data with computed hourly earnings below $2.50 or

tics of their spouses. For example, wife outcomes for the marriage type "Husband non-Mexican" provide information about Mexican American women who marry non-Mexicans, whereas husband outcomes for this same marriage type provide information about the spouses of these women. For both husbands and wives, outcomes for the marriage type "Both spouses U.S.-born Mexican" provide information about Mexican Americans involved in endogamous marriages.

Table 7.8 reveals striking differences in human capital and labor market outcomes between Mexican Americans married to Mexicans and those married to non-Mexicans. U.S.-born Mexicans married to non-Mexicans have much higher education, English proficiency, employment, and earnings than those with spouses that are also U.S.-born Mexicans,[13] whereas U.S.-born Mexicans married to Mexican immigrants have lower outcomes than any other group of Mexican Americans. Table 7.8 also shows that non-Mexican spouses of Mexican Americans have the best outcomes of any group considered and that Mexican immigrant spouses of Mexican Americans have the worst outcomes.

The magnitudes of these differences are easier to see in table 7.9, which displays regression-adjusted outcome differences constructed in a similar fashion as those shown previously in table 7.5. Here, the key independent variables are dummies indicating the type of marriage, with the reference group consisting of endogamous marriages in which both spouses are U.S.-born Mexicans. In addition, the controls for geographic locations are now dummy variables identifying the nine census divisions, the individual states of California and Texas, and whether the respondent resides in a metropolitan area.

Among Mexican American husbands, for example, those with non-Mexican wives average a year more schooling than those with U.S.-born Mexican wives. Compared to their counterparts in endogamous marriages, intermarried Mexican American men also have a 9 percentage point lower rate of English deficiency, a 3 percentage point higher rate of employment, and a 15 percent wage advantage. These unadjusted differences, from regression specification (1), narrow only slightly after controlling for geographic location and the husband's age in specification (2). The non-Mexican husbands of intermarried Mexican American women have even better outcomes than intermarried Mexican American men, particularly in terms of education and hourly earnings, but these differences are

---

above $500 are considered outliers and excluded. Beginning in 1990, the census questions about educational attainment were changed to ask specifically about postsecondary degrees obtained rather than years of schooling. We follow Jaeger's (1997) recommendations for how to construct a completed years of schooling variable from the revised education questions.

13. Consistent with our results, White and Sassler (2000) find that Mexican Americans married to non-Hispanic whites tend to live in neighborhoods with higher socioeconomic status than do endogamously married Mexican Americans.

Table 7.9 Regression-adjusted outcome differences by type of marriage, 2000

					Dependent variable							
	Education		Deficient English		Employment			Log hourly earnings				
Regressor	(1)	(2)	(1)	(2)	(1)	(2)	(3)	(1)	(2)	(3)		
Husbands												
Type of marriage												
Husband foreign-born Mexican	-2.46	-2.53	.392	.401	.009	.0001	.030	-.148	-.147	.027		
	(.04)	(.04)	(.004)	(.004)	(.003)	(.003)	(.004)	(.009)	(.009)	(.009)		
Wife foreign-born Mexican	-.53	-.57	.104	.108	-.001	-.006	.001	-.071	-.065	-.028		
	(.04)	(.04)	(.005)	(.005)	(.004)	(.004)	(.004)	(.010)	(.010)	(.010)		
Husband non-Mexican	1.42	1.35	-.101	-.089	.032	.028	.013	.227	.199	.115		
	(.03)	(.03)	(.003)	(.004)	(.003)	(.003)	(.003)	(.007)	(.007)	(.007)		
Wife non-Mexican	1.05	.98	-.090	-.077	.031	.026	.015	.153	.125	.064		
	(.03)	(.03)	(.004)	(.004)	(.003)	(.003)	(.003)	(.007)	(.007)	(.007)		
Years of education							.010			.060		
							(.0003)			(.001)		
Deficient English							-.010			-.056		
							(.003)			(.008)		
Wives												
Type of marriage												
Husband foreign-born Mexican	-.70	-.81	.046	.057	-.035	-.042	-.011	-.061	-.075	-.015		
	(.04)	(.04)	(.004)	(.004)	(.006)	(.006)	(.006)	(.010)	(.010)	(.010)		
Wife foreign-born Mexican	-1.76	-1.86	.393	.400	-.134	-.139	-.043	-.126	-.138	.003		
	(.04)	(.04)	(.005)	(.005)	(.007)	(.007)	(.007)	(.012)	(.012)	(.012)		
Husband non-Mexican	1.08	.95	-.082	-.064	.059	.046	.010	.150	.130	.061		
	(.03)	(.03)	(.003)	(.003)	(.005)	(.005)	(.005)	(.008)	(.008)	(.007)		

(*continued*)

Table 7.9   (continued)

	Education		Deficient English		Employment			Log hourly earnings		
Regressor	(1)	(2)	(1)	(2)	(1)	(2)	(3)	(1)	(2)	(3)
Wife non-Mexican	1.21	1.08	−.098	−.079	.063	.049	.007	.164	.144	.062
	(.03)	(.03)	(.004)	(.004)	(.005)	(.005)	(.005)	(.008)	(.008)	(.008)
Years of education							.032			.081
							(.0006)			(.001)
Deficient English							−.091			−.038
							(.005)			(.009)
Controls for:										
Geographic location	No	Yes	No	Yes	No	Yes	Yes	No	Yes	Yes
Age	No	Yes	No	Yes	No	Yes	Yes	No	Yes	Yes

Source: 2000 U.S. Census data.

Notes: The reported figures are estimated coefficients from ordinary least squares regressions run separately for husbands and wives. Standard errors are in parentheses. The samples include husbands and wives in marriages that meet the following conditions: both spouses are between the ages of 25–59, the couple currently lives together, and at least one spouse is a U.S.-born individual identified as Mexican by the census question regarding Hispanic origin. The samples for the hourly earnings regressions are further limited to individuals who were employed at some time during the calendar year preceding the census. The sample sizes are 62,734 husbands and 62,734 wives for the full samples, and 58,003 husbands and 45,857 wives for the employed samples. For the dummy variables indicating the type of marriage, the reference group consists of endogamous marriages in which both spouses are U.S.-born Mexicans. The controls for geographic location are dummy variables identifying the nine Census divisions, the individual states of California and Texas, and whether the individual resides in a metropolitan area. The controls for age are dummy variables identifying five-year age intervals.

not nearly as great as the corresponding differences just described between Mexican American men in endogamous versus exogamous marriages. Similar patterns are evident for women, except that employment differences associated with intermarriage are larger than they are for men, and outcome differences between Mexican Americans with non-Mexican spouses and non-Mexicans with Mexican American spouses tend to be smaller for women than for men.

For both husbands and wives, a comparison of specifications (2) and (3) shows that controlling for education and English proficiency dramatically shrinks employment and earnings differences across marriage types. Evidently, the human capital selectivity associated with intermarriage generates most of the labor market differences observed along this same dimension.

Our finding of positive educational and economic selectivity for intermarried Mexican Americans is not unexpected (Qian 1999). First of all, opportunities for meeting and interacting with people from other racial or ethnic groups are better for more educated Mexican Americans because highly-educated Mexican Americans tend to live, study, and work in less segregated environments. Second, given the sizeable educational deficit of the average Mexican American, better-educated Mexican Americans are likely to be closer in social class to the typical non-Mexican (Furtado 2006). Third, attending college is an eye-opening experience for many students that may work to diminish preferences for marrying within one's own racial or ethnic group. Finally, the theory of "status exchange" in marriage formulated by Davis (1941) and Merton (1941) predicts that members of lower-status minority groups (such as Mexican Americans) would tend to need higher levels of socioeconomic attainment to attract spouses who are members of higher-status majority groups.

7.4 Mexican Identification of Children

We next investigate the link between intermarriage and ethnic identification by examining what determines whether the children of Mexican Americans are identified as Mexican.[14] We start with the same sample of Mexican American marriages from the 2000 Census used in the intermarriage analyses of the preceding section, but henceforth we further restrict the sample to those marriages that have produced at least one child under age nineteen currently residing in the household. We continue to exclude marriages in which either spouse has allocated information about Hispanic origin, and we now impose this condition for the relevant children as well.

---

14. Along the same lines, Xie and Goyette (1997) use 1990 Census data to study the determinants of Asian identification among children produced by intermarriages between an Asian and a non-Asian.

Table 7.10   **Mexican identification of youngest child by type of marriage, 2000**

	Percent with youngest child identified as Mexican
Type of marriage	
Both spouses U.S.-born Mexican	98.2
	(.12)
Husband foreign-born Mexican	97.9
	(.20)
Wife foreign-born Mexican	97.8
	(.24)
Husband non-Mexican	63.5
	(.51)
Wife non-Mexican	71.1
	(.51)
All types of marriages	84.4
	(.19)

Source: 2000 U.S. Census data.

Notes: Standard errors are in parentheses. The sample includes marriages that meet the following conditions: both spouses are between the ages of 25–59, the couple currently lives together, at least one spouse is a U.S.-born individual identified as Mexican by the census question regarding Hispanic origin, and the marriage has produced at least one child under age nineteen that resides in the household. There are 37,921 such marriages.

Finally, to the extent possible with the information available in the census, we exclude families in which any of the children are suspected of being stepchildren. These restrictions produce a sample of 37,921 families.

Using the same typology of Mexican American marriages introduced earlier, table 7.10 reports for each type of marriage the percent in which the youngest child is identified as Mexican by the Hispanic origin question in the census.[15] Of primary interest for our purposes is how this percentage varies with the nativity and ethnicity of the parents. Overall, the youngest child is identified as Mexican in 84 percent of these families, which raises the possibility of substantial ethnic attrition among the children of Mexican Americans. The crucial determinant of a child's Mexican identification is whether both parents are Mexican-origin. In marriages between two U.S.-born Mexicans or between a U.S.-born Mexican and a Mexican immigrant, Mexican identification of the child is virtually assured (i.e., the relevant rates are 98 percent). In marriages between a U.S.-born Mexican

15. Because Mexican identification varies little across children within a given family, we report results using only information for the *youngest* child. Instead using information for the *oldest* child produces similar results, as would using indicators for whether *any* or *all* of the children in the family are identified as Mexican. In census data, note that parents are likely to be responding for their children. An important question is how these children will respond to survey questions about ethnic identification when they become adults and answer for themselves. See Portes and Rumbaut (2001, chapter 7) for a discussion of parental and other influences on the evolving ethnic identities of second-generation adolescents.

and a non-Mexican, however, the likelihood that the child is identified as Mexican drops to 64–71 percent, with the precise figure depending on which parent is non-Mexican, the father or the mother.[16]

Tables 7.11 and 7.12 show how measures of the human capital and labor market performance of parents correlate with whether their youngest child is identified as Mexican. Table 7.11 presents mean outcomes, by the Mexican identification of the child, and table 7.12 reports regression-adjusted differences relative to the reference group consisting of parents whose youngest child is *not* identified as Mexican. In these marriages involving at least one Mexican American spouse, parents with children not identified as Mexican average about a year more schooling and have approximately a 10 percentage point lower rate of English deficiency than do their counterparts with children designated as Mexican. Parents with children not identified as Mexican also exhibit advantages in employment (2 percentage points for men and 3 percentage points for women) and earnings (16 percent for men and 8 percent for women). Conditioning on geographic location and the parent's age reduces these outcome differences, but modestly (compare the estimates in specifications [1] and [2] of table 7.12).

Specification (3) of table 7.12 adds as regressors the dummy variables indicating the type of marriage, and this change has a dramatic impact on the results, eliminating the outcome disadvantages previously associated with the youngest child's Mexican identification. To understand what this means, recall from table 7.10 that virtually all families with two Mexican-origin parents identify their children as Mexican. Therefore, in specification (3), the dummy variable for the youngest child's Mexican identification essentially becomes an interaction term between the child's Mexican identification and a dummy variable identifying marriages involving a non-Mexican spouse. Because the type of marriage dummies capture the main effect of intermarriage (i.e., marriages involving a non-Mexican spouse), the estimated effect of the child's Mexican identification now represents outcome differences between intermarried parents whose youngest child *is* identified as Mexican and intermarried parents whose youngest child *is not* identified as Mexican. The generally small and statistically insignificant coefficients estimated on the child's Mexican identification dummy in specification (3) reveal that, *within* the group of marriages involving a non-Mexican spouse, parents' outcomes do not vary with the Mexican identification of their children.[17] In other words, intermarriage is the crucial link between the ethnic identification of Mexican American children and the

16. In regressions not reported here, we find that the impact of intermarriage on the Mexican identification of children does not change when controls are included for the age and gender of the child, the number of additional children in the family, geographic location, and various characteristics of the parents (age, education, and English proficiency).

17. Not surprisingly, this same conclusion emerges from comparing mean outcomes for the relevant groups.

Table 7.11   Average parental outcomes by Mexican identification of youngest child, 2000

| | Parental outcomes | | | |
	Years of education	Deficient English	Percent employed	Log hourly earnings
Fathers				
Youngest child identified as:				
Mexican	12.1	18.0	94.3	2.733
	(.02)	(.21)	(.13)	(.004)
Not Mexican	13.2	6.2	96.2	2.888
	(.03)	(.31)	(.25)	(.009)
All fathers	12.3	16.1	94.6	2.757
	(.02)	(.19)	(.12)	(.003)
Mothers				
Youngest child identified as:				
Mexican	12.3	15.8	73.0	2.454
	(.02)	(.20)	(.25)	(.004)
Not Mexican	13.1	6.5	75.9	2.535
	(.03)	(.32)	(.56)	(.010)
All mothers	12.4	14.4	73.4	2.467
	(.01)	(.18)	(.23)	(.004)

Source: 2000 U.S. Census data.

Notes: Standard errors are in parentheses. The samples include fathers and mothers in marriages that meet the following conditions: both spouses are between the ages of 25–59, the couple currently lives together, at least one spouse is a U.S.-born individual identified as Mexican by the census question regarding Hispanic origin, and the marriage has produced at least one child under age nineteen that resides in the household. The samples for the hourly earnings data are further limited to individuals who were employed at some time during the calendar year preceding the census. The sample sizes are 37,921 fathers and 37,921 mothers for the full samples, and 35,496 fathers and 27,227 mothers for the employed samples.

human capital and labor market performance of their parents. The strong correlation observed between parental skills and whether the child is identified as Mexican arises because of the intense selectivity of Mexican American intermarriage, especially in terms of human capital, and the powerful influence of intermarriage on the ethnic identification of children.

Despite the apparent strength of intermarriage selectivity and its close link to the Mexican identification of children, one could use our data to argue that these factors ultimately produce little bias in observed outcomes for Mexican Americans. For example, table 7.11 shows that, in families with at least one Mexican American parent, fathers average 1.1 years more schooling (and mothers average 0.8 years more schooling) if their youngest child is not identified as Mexican. This pattern reflects the educational selectivity of Mexican intermarriage, but the impact of such selectivity is attenuated by the small overall incidence of non-Mexican affiliation among

Table 7.12 Regression-adjusted parental outcome differences by Mexican identification of youngest child, 2000

	Dependent variable (parental outcomes)											
	Education			Deficient English			Employment			Log hourly earnings		
Regressor	(1)	(2)	(3)	(1)	(2)	(3)	(1)	(2)	(3)	(1)	(2)	(3)
Fathers												
Youngest child Mexican	-1.11	-1.01	-.005	.118	.107	.002	-.019	-.018	-.002	-.155	-.126	-.004
	(.04)	(.04)	(.04)	(.005)	(.005)	(.005)	(.003)	(.003)	(.004)	(.009)	(.009)	(.010)
Type of marriage												
Husband foreign-born Mexican			-2.35			.400			.004			-.135
			(.05)			(.005)			(.004)			(.010)
Wife foreign-born Mexican			-.57			.120			-.005			-.049
			(.05)			(.006)			(.004)			(.012)
Husband non-Mexican			1.30			-.079			.030			.211
			(.04)			(.005)			(.003)			(.010)
Wife non-Mexican			1.02			-.075			.030			.147
			(.04)			(.005)			(.003)			(.010)
Mothers												
Youngest child Mexican	-.86	-.74	.04	.093	.080	-.001	-.030	-.022	.013	-.081	-.066	.026
	(.04)	(.04)	(.04)	(.005)	(.005)	(.005)	(.006)	(.006)	(.007)	(.011)	(.010)	(.011)
Type of marriage												
Husband foreign-born Mexican			-.72			.063			-.034			-.057
			(.04)			(.005)			(.007)			(.012)
Wife foreign-born Mexican			-1.77			.405			-.146			-.126
			(.05)			(.005)			(.008)			(.015)

(continued)

Table 7.12   (continued)

	Dependent variable (parental outcomes)											
	Education			Deficient English			Employment			Log hourly earnings		
Regressor	(1)	(2)	(3)	(1)	(2)	(3)	(1)	(2)	(3)	(1)	(2)	(3)
Husband non-Mexican			.96			-.065			.028			.140
			(.04)			(.005)			(.007)			(.011)
Wife non-Mexican			1.09			-.077			.041			.167
			(.04)			(.005)			(.007)			(.011)
Controls for:												
Geographic location	No	No	Yes	No	No	Yes	No	No	Yes	No	No	Yes
Age of parent	No	Yes	Yes	No	Yes	Yes	No	Yes	Yes	No	Yes	Yes

Source: 2000 U.S. Census data.

Notes: The reported figures are estimated coefficients from ordinary least squares regressions run separately for fathers and mothers. Standard errors are in parentheses. The samples include fathers and mothers in marriages that meet the following conditions: both spouses are between the ages of 25–59, the couple currently lives together, at least one spouse is a U.S.-born individual identified as Mexican by the census question regarding Hispanic origin, and the marriage has produced at least one child under age nineteen that resides in the household. The samples for the hourly earnings data are further limited to individuals who were employed at some time during the calendar year preceding the census. The sample sizes are 37,921 fathers and 37,921 mothers for the full samples, and 35,496 fathers and 27,227 mothers for the employed samples. The dummy variable "youngest child Mexican" indicates parents whose youngest child is identified as Mexican by the census question regarding Hispanic origin; the reference group consists of parents whose youngest child is not identified as Mexican. The controls for geographic location are dummy variables identifying the nine census divisions, the individual states of California and Texas, and whether the family resides in a metropolitan area. The controls for age of the parent are dummy variables identifying five-year age intervals.

children with at least one Mexican American parent (i.e., from the bottom row of table 7.10, just 16 percent of these children fail to identify as Mexican). As a result, in table 7.11, restoring to our samples the potentially "missing" families with children not identified as Mexican only raises the average schooling of fathers from 12.1 to 12.3 years (and of mothers from 12.3 to 12.4 years). Moreover, estimates of intergenerational correlations suggest that less than half of any educational gains for parents get transmitted to their children (Couch and Dunn 1997; Mulligan 1997; Card, DiNardo, and Estes 2000). Therefore, our census analyses can directly substantiate only a tiny amount of "hidden" progress for these children of Mexican Americans: less than 0.1 years of education and similarly small amounts for the other outcomes.

We think it premature, however, to conclude that the measurement issues and potential biases that motivated this paper can be safely ignored. In our census samples, for us to know that a child is of Mexican descent, at least one of his U.S.-born parents must continue to self-identify as Mexican. We therefore miss completely any Mexican-origin families in which the relevant Mexican descendants no longer identify as Mexican. Data from the 1970 Census Content Reinterview Study, presented earlier in table 7.2, indicate that we could be missing a large share of later-generation–Mexican-origin families (e.g., well over half of Mexican descendants beyond the third generation). For this reason, we believe that our results show the direction, but not the magnitude, of measurement biases arising from selective intermarriage and ethnic identification by Mexican Americans. Estimating the magnitude of such biases would require either microdata with more detailed information about ancestors' national origins (such as that collected in the now-extinct 1970 Census Content Reinterview Study), or a complicated simulation model that starts with a cohort of Mexican immigrants and analyzes how selective intermarriage interacts with the parent-child transmission of skills and ethnic identification to produce the joint distributions of outcomes and Mexican identity across generations.[18] The census and CPS results reported here could provide some of the inputs for a simulation model of this type.

7.5 Generational Patterns

Our final set of analyses use recent CPS data to explore how patterns of intermarriage and ethnic identification vary by generation for U.S.-born Mexicans. To the extent that Mexican intermarriage or the selectivity of such intermarriage increases with generation, or that ethnic attachment declines with generation, the potential becomes greater for existing data to

18. Brito (2004) provides an initial attempt at using simulation techniques to analyze this problem.

give an inaccurate representation of the intergenerational progress of Mexican Americans.

Beginning in 1980, the Decennial Census stopped asking respondents where their parents were born. Starting in 1994, the CPS began collecting this information on a regular basis from all respondents. As a result, the CPS is currently the best large-scale U.S. data set for investigating how outcomes vary by immigrant generation. Using the CPS information on the nativity of each individual and his parents, we define three broad categories of immigrant generation for Mexicans. The first generation consists of immigrants: foreign-born individuals whose parents were also born outside of the United States. The second generation includes U.S.-born individuals who have at least one foreign-born parent. The designation "third and higher generation" applies to U.S. natives whose parents are also natives. For ease of exposition, we will often refer to this last group as the "3rd+ generation" or simply the third generation. Compared to the census data analyzed earlier, the main advantage of the CPS is this ability to distinguish between the second and higher generations of U.S.-born Mexicans. For our purposes, important drawbacks of the CPS data are the smaller sample sizes and the absence of information about English proficiency.

We analyze microdata from the March CPS files for the years 1996, 1998, 2000, and 2002.[19] Our CPS samples and variables are created using the same procedures that we employed with the 2000 Census data. In the CPS data, these procedures yield a sample of 4,407 marriages for our intermarriage analyses.

Table 7.13 shows the nativity/ethnicity distributions of the spouses of the U.S.-born Mexican husbands and wives in our CPS sample of marriages. This table is comparable to table 7.6 presented earlier for the 2000 Census data, except that the current table distinguishes between second- and third-generation Mexicans. Intermarriage by Mexican Americans rises between the second and third generations, driven by increased marriage to U.S.-born, non-Hispanic whites. Among Mexican American husbands, the proportion married to non-Mexicans grows from 31 percent for the second generation to 34 percent for the third generation. Among Mexican American wives, the corresponding increase is from 28 percent to 34 percent. The biggest difference between generations, however, is in the composition of endogamous Mexican marriages. For both husbands and wives, the rate of marriage to third-generation Mexicans doubles between the second and the third generation, and simultaneously the rate of marriage to Mexican immigrants is cut to a third of its initial level. All told,

---

19. The CPS sample rotation scheme implies that about half of the households will be the same in any two March surveys from adjacent years, so to obtain independent samples we skip odd-numbered years.

Table 7.13   Nativity/ethnicity distributions of the spouses of U.S.-born Mexicans,
                      by generation (%)

| | U.S.-born Mexican | | | |
| | 2nd generation | | 3rd+ generation | |
Nativity/ethnicity of spouse	Husbands	Wives	Husbands	Wives
U.S.-born				
2nd generation Mexican	21.9	19.4	9.7	10.3
3rd+ generation Mexican	24.9	18.9	49.2	44.4
Other Hispanic	2.0	1.9	1.6	1.3
Non-Hispanic				
White	23.4	19.3	28.8	28.3
Black	.5	1.6	.3	1.2
Asian	.6	.5	.5	.6
Other race	.9	.5	.6	.8
Foreign-born				
Mexican	22.5	34.1	6.8	11.1
Other Hispanic	1.5	1.8	.8	.7
Non-Hispanic				
White	1.1	1.5	1.5	1.1
Black	0.0	0.0	0.0	.1
Asian	.8	.5	.4	.1
Other race	0.0	0.0	0.0	.1
	100.0	100.0	100.0	100.0

Source: March 1996–2002 CPS data.

Notes: The sample includes marriages that meet the following conditions: both spouses are between the ages of 25–59, the couple currently lives together, and at least one spouse is a U.S.-born individual identified as Mexican by the CPS question regarding Hispanic origin. For the U.S.-born Mexican husbands and wives involved in these marriages, the table shows the nativity/ethnicity distributions of their spouses. There are 4,407 such marriages. These marriages involve 2,819 U.S.-born Mexican husbands (882 from the 2nd generation and 1,937 from the 3rd+ generation) and 3,141 U.S.-born Mexican wives (996 from the 2nd generation and 2,145 from the 3rd+ generation).

around half of second-generation Mexican husbands and wives have spouses who are first- or second-generation Mexicans, whereas the same is true for only about a fifth of third-generation Mexicans. In this sense, intergenerational assimilation in marriage occurs for Mexican Americans not just through increased intermarriage with non-Mexicans, but also through sharply higher rates of marriage to later-generation Mexicans.

For our CPS sample of marriages, table 7.14 applies the typology introduced previously in table 7.7. In table 7.14, the column labeled "2nd generation" shows the distribution by type for all sample marriages that involve a second-generation Mexican, and the "3rd+ generation" column reports the same distribution for all marriages that involve a third-generation Mexican. Consequently, there exists some overlap between the

Table 7.14   Types of marriages involving U.S.-born Mexicans, by generation

	Percent of sample	
Type of marriage	2nd generation	3rd+ generation
Both spouses U.S.-born Mexican	35.7	43.5
Husband foreign-born Mexican (wife U.S.-born Mexican)	20.2	7.6
Wife foreign-born Mexican (husband U.S.-born Mexican)	11.8	4.2
Husband non-Mexican (wife U.S.-born Mexican)	16.3	23.5
Wife non-Mexican (husband U.S.-born Mexican)	16.1	21.2
	100.0	100.0

Source: March 1996–2002 CPS data.

Notes: The sample includes marriages that meet the following conditions: both spouses are between the ages of 25–59, the couple currently lives together, and at least one spouse is a U.S.-born individual identified as Mexican by the CPS question regarding Hispanic origin. There are 4,407 such marriages, with 1,685 of these marriages involving at least one 2nd generation Mexican and 3,130 involving at least one 3rd+ generation Mexican (408 marriages are between a 2nd generation Mexican and a 3rd+ generation Mexican).

two columns because marriages between a second-generation Mexican and a third-generation Mexican will be counted in the first row of both columns. Between the second and third generations, table 7.14 shows that Mexican American marriages undergo a marked increase in the involvement of non-Mexicans and a large decline in the involvement of Mexican immigrants. Given our earlier finding that marriages to non-Mexicans are particularly susceptible to ethnic leakage (see table 7.10), the increased prevalence of intermarriage across generations raises the potential for intergenerational attrition of Mexicans in standard data sources.

For the CPS data, table 7.15 replicates the Census analysis presented earlier in table 7.8. In terms of the outcome variables available in the CPS—education, employment, and hourly earnings—the patterns of intermarriage selectivity are similar to those found in the census data. Moreover, the CPS data show these patterns to be similar for second- and third-generation Mexicans. Although the extent of intermarriage selectivity for Mexicans does not appear to increase between the second and later generations, neither does it appear to diminish. Given this stability in intermarriage selectivity, the rising rate of Mexican intermarriage across generations could by itself produce biased intergenerational comparisons for this population.

Finally, table 7.16 reproduces with CPS data the analysis from table 7.10 of how the youngest child's Mexican identification varies with intermarriage. Once again, we find that a child is almost certain to be identified as Mexican when both his parents are Mexican-origin. Moreover, this pattern does not weaken across generations. Overall, the rate at which the youngest child is identified as Mexican in the CPS data falls from 82 percent for mar-

Table 7.15   **Average outcomes by type of marriage and generation**

	Years of education		Percent employed		Log hourly earnings	
	2nd	3rd+	2nd	3rd+	2nd	3rd+
Husbands						
Type of marriage						
Both spouses U.S.-born Mexican	12.1	12.0	94.8	93.1	2.642	2.612
	(.11)	(.07)	(.90)	(.69)	(.024)	(.017)
Husband foreign-born Mexican	10.0	9.6	95.3	92.8	2.484	2.454
	(.22)	(.27)	(1.15)	(1.68)	(.031)	(.045)
Wife foreign-born Mexican	11.3	12.1	98.0	90.2	2.499	2.542
	(.22)	(.24)	(1.00)	(2.60)	(.041)	(.054)
Husband non-Mexican	13.6	13.7	94.5	96.5	2.901	2.859
	(.13)	(.09)	(1.37)	(.68)	(.039)	(.024)
Wife non-Mexican	13.2	13.1	95.9	95.2	2.810	2.808
	(.13)	(.09)	(1.20)	(.83)	(.036)	(.022)
All husbands	12.0	12.4	95.4	94.2	2.662	2.699
	(.08)	(.05)	(.51)	(.42)	(.015)	(.011)
Wives						
Type of marriage						
Both spouses U.S.-born Mexican	12.2	12.0	76.5	74.3	2.348	2.282
	(.10)	(.07)	(1.73)	(1.18)	(.026)	(.018)
Husband foreign-born Mexican	11.7	11.5	72.1	69.2	2.288	2.234
	(.15)	(.16)	(2.44)	(3.01)	(.037)	(.052)
Wife foreign-born Mexican	10.5	10.9	58.6	56.8	2.180	2.187
	(.25)	(.30)	(3.51)	(4.33)	(.050)	(.062)
Husband non-Mexican	13.4	13.2	80.4	77.6	2.512	2.460
	(.12)	(.07)	(2.40)	(1.54)	(.043)	(.025)
Wife non-Mexican	13.2	13.4	79.0	77.9	2.534	2.511
	(.13)	(.08)	(2.48)	(1.61)	(.041)	(.029)
All wives	12.2	12.5	74.5	74.7	2.381	2.370
	(.07)	(.04)	(1.06)	(.78)	(.017)	(.013)

Source: March 1996–2002 CPS data.

Notes: Standard errors are in parentheses. The samples include husbands and wives in marriages that meet the following conditions: both spouses are between the ages of 25–59, the couple currently lives together, and at least one spouse is a U.S.-born individual identified as Mexican by the census question regarding Hispanic origin. The samples for the hourly earnings data are further limited to individuals who were employed at some time during the calendar year preceding the CPS. For the marriages involving a 2nd generation Mexican, the sample sizes are 1,685 husbands and 1,685 wives for the full samples, and 1,581 husbands and 1,220 wives for the employed samples. For the marriages involving a 3rd+ generation Mexican, the sample sizes are 3,130 husbands and 3,130 wives for the full samples, and 2,899 husbands and 2,262 wives for the employed samples.

riages involving a second-generation Mexican to 73 percent for marriages involving a higher-generation Mexican. This decline arises primarily from the changing composition of marriage types across generations, in particular, the increased prevalence in later generations of intermarriage between Mexican Americans and non-Mexicans.

Table 7.16   **Mexican identification of youngest child by type of marriage and generation**

	Percent with youngest child identified as Mexican	
	2nd generation	3rd+ generation
Type of marriage		
Both spouses U.S.-born Mexican	99.3	98.9
	(.41)	(.33)
Husband foreign-born Mexican	98.2	97.7
	(.79)	(1.12)
Wife foreign-born Mexican	99.4	98.0
	(.62)	(1.41)
Husband non-Mexican	48.2	47.4
	(3.59)	(2.23)
Wife non-Mexican	40.1	34.3
	(3.46)	(2.20)
All types of marriages	81.7	73.3
	(1.09)	(.95)

Source: March 1996–2002 CPS data.

Notes: Standard errors are in parentheses. The sample includes marriages that meet the following conditions: both spouses are between the ages of 25–59, the couple currently lives together, at least one spouse is a U.S.-born individual identified as Mexican by the CPS question regarding Hispanic origin, and the marriage has produced at least one child under age nineteen that resides in the household. There are 3,174 such marriages, with 1,261 of these marriages involving at least one 2nd generation Mexican and 2,193 involving at least one 3rd+ generation Mexican (280 marriages are between a 2nd generation Mexican and a 3rd+ generation Mexican).

7.6   Conclusion

In this paper, we look for evidence on whether selective intermarriage and selective ethnic identification might bias observed measures of socio-economic progress for later generations of Mexican Americans. Ideal data for this purpose would allow us to identify which individuals are descended from Mexican immigrants and how many generations have elapsed since that immigration took place. We could then simply compare outcomes for this "true" population of Mexican descendants with the corresponding outcomes for the subset of Mexican descendants who continue to self-identify as Mexican-origin. Unfortunately, we do not have access to microdata of this sort, so we instead adopt much less direct strategies for trying to shed light on this issue.

We begin by examining 1980 Census data that provide an indicator for Spanish surnames in addition to the information about Hispanic origin typically used to identify Mexican ethnics. Our hope is that, particularly for men, the presence of a Spanish surname in the five southwestern states provides an objective, albeit imperfect, indicator of Mexican ancestry that allows us to identify some individuals of Mexican descent who fail to self-report as Hispanic and who are therefore missed by subjective indicators such as the Hispanic-origin question in the census. If so, then differences in human capital and labor market outcomes between Spanish-surnamed individuals who do and do not self-identify as Hispanic might reveal something about the selective nature of ethnic identification for Mexican Americans. We find that U.S.-born men identified as Hispanic by surname only have more human capital and better labor market outcomes than U.S.-born men identified as Hispanic by both self-report and surname. The same pattern holds for women, though in this case interpretation is clouded by the common practice of married women taking the surname of their husbands. Overall, the results are consistent with the notion that individuals of Mexican descent who no longer self-identify as Hispanic are positively selected in terms of socioeconomic status. Relatively few individuals with Spanish surnames fail to self-identify as Hispanic, however, so it would be unwise to regard these results as anything more than suggestive.

Using data from the 2000 Census and recent March Current Population Surveys, we then investigate the extent and selectivity of Mexican intermarriage and how such intermarriage influences the Mexican identification of children. We show that U.S.-born Mexican Americans who marry non-Mexicans are substantially more educated and English proficient, on average, than are Mexican Americans who marry coethnics (whether they be Mexican Americans or Mexican immigrants). In addition, the non-Mexican spouses of intermarried Mexican Americans possess relatively high levels of schooling and English proficiency, compared to the spouses of endogamously married Mexican Americans. The human capital selectivity of Mexican intermarriage generates corresponding differences in the employment and earnings of Mexican Americans and their spouses. Moreover, the children of intermarried Mexican Americans are much less likely to be identified as Mexican than are the children of endogamous Mexican marriages. These forces combine to produce strong negative correlations between the education, English proficiency, employment, and earnings of Mexican American parents and the chances that their children retain a Mexican ethnicity.

Despite the apparent strength of intermarriage selectivity and its close link to the Mexican identification of children, our analyses cannot *directly* substantiate significant biases in measuring the intergenerational progress of Mexican Americans. The data used here are inadequate, however, because they overlook families descended from Mexican immigrants in which neither parent self-identifies as Mexican. Indeed, data from the 1970 Census Content Reinterview Study indicate that we could be missing a large share of later-generation–Mexican-origin families (e.g., well over half of Mexican descendants beyond the third generation). For this reason, we believe that our results show the direction, but not the magnitude, of measurement biases arising from selective intermarriage and ethnic identification by Mexican Americans. Estimating the magnitude of such biases would require either microdata with more detailed information about ancestors' national origins (such as that collected in the now-extinct 1970 Census Content Reinterview Study), or a complicated simulation model that starts with a cohort of Mexican immigrants and analyzes how selective intermarriage interacts with the parent-child transmission of skills and ethnic identification to produce the joint distributions of outcomes and Mexican identity across generations. The empirical results reported here could provide some of the inputs for a simulation model of this type.

References

Alba, Richard D. 1986. *Italian Americans: Into the twilight of ethnicity.* Englewood Cliffs, NJ: Prentice-Hall.
———. 1990. *Ethnic identity: The transformation of white America.* New Haven, CT: Yale University Press.
Alba, Richard D., and Mitchell B. Chamlin. 1983. A preliminary examination of ethnic identification among whites. *American Sociological Review* 48 (2): 240–47.
Alba, Richard D., and Tariqul Islam. 2005. The case of the disappearing Mexican Americans: An ethnic-identity mystery. State University of New York at Albany. Unpublished Manuscript.
Bean, Frank D., C. Gray Swicegood, and Ruth Berg. 2000. Mexican-origin fertility: New patterns and interpretations. *Social Science Quarterly* 81 (1): 404–20.
Bean, Frank D., and Marta Tienda. 1987. *The Hispanic population of the United States.* New York: Russell Sage Foundation.
Blau, Francine D., and Lawrence M. Kahn. 2005. Gender and assimilation among Mexican Americans. NBER Working Paper no. 11512. Cambridge, MA: National Bureau of Economic Research, August.
Borjas, George J. 1993. The intergenerational mobility of immigrants. *Journal of Labor Economics* 11 (1): 113–35.
———. 1994. Long-run convergence of ethnic skill differentials: The children and grandchildren of the great migration. *Industrial and Labor Relations Review* 47 (4): 553–73.
Brito, Dagobert L. 2004. Education and asymmetric Hispanic assimilation: A preliminary exploration. Rice University. Unpublished Manuscript.
Card, David, John DiNardo, and Eugena Estes. 2000. The more things change: Immigrants and the children of immigrants in the 1940s, the 1970s, and the 1990s. In *Issues in the economics of immigration,* ed. George J. Borjas, 227–69. Chicago: University of Chicago Press.
Couch, Kenneth A., and Thomas A. Dunn. 1997. Intergenerational correlations in labor market status: A comparison of the United States and Germany. *Journal of Human Resources* 32 (1): 210–32.
Davis, Kingsley. 1941. Intermarriage in caste societies. *American Anthropologist* 43 (3, part 1): 376–95.

del Pinal, Jorge H. 2004. *Race and ethnicity in Census 2000.* U.S. Bureau of the Census, Census 2000 Testing, Experimentation, and Evaluation Program: Topic Report no. 9. Washington, DC: Government Printing Office.

Duncan, Brian, V. Joseph Hotz, and Stephen J. Trejo. 2006. Hispanics in the U.S. labor market. In *Hispanics and the future of America,* ed. Marta Tienda and Faith Mitchell, 228–90. Washington, DC: National Academies Press.

Eschbach, Karl. 1985. The enduring and vanishing American Indian: American Indian population growth and intermarriage in 1990. *Ethnic and Racial Studies* 18 (1): 89–108.

Eschbach, Karl, and Christina Gomez. 1998. Choosing Hispanic identity: Ethnic identity switching among respondents to high school and beyond. *Social Science Quarterly* 79 (1): 74–90.

Eschbach, Karl, Khalil Supple, and C. Matthew Snipp. 1998. Changes in racial identification and the educational attainment of American Indians, 1970–1990. *Demography* 35 (1): 35–43.

Farley, Reynolds. 1990. Blacks, Hispanics, and white ethnic groups: Are blacks uniquely disadvantaged? *American Economic Review* 80 (2): 237–41.

———. 1991. The new Census question about ancestry: What did it tell us? *Demography* 28 (3): 411–29.

Farley, Reynolds, and Richard Alba. 2002. The new second generation in the United States. *International Migration Review* 36 (3): 669–701.

Fry, Richard, and B. Lindsay Lowell. 2002. *Work or study: Different fortunes of U.S. Latino generations.* Pew Hispanic Center Report. Washington, DC: Pew Hispanic Center.

Fu, Vincent Kang. 2001. Racial intermarriage pairings. *Demography* 38 (2): 147–59.

Furtado, Delia. 2006. Human capital and interethnic marriage decisions. IZA Discussion Paper no. 1989. Bonn, Germany: Institute for the Study of Labor, February.

Gans, Herbert J. 1992. Second-generation decline: Scenarios for the economic and ethnic futures of the post-1965 American immigrants. *Ethnic and Racial Studies* 15 (2): 173–92.

Gordon, Milton M. 1964. *Assimilation in American life: The role of race, religion, and national origins.* New York: Oxford University Press.

Grogger, Jeffrey, and Stephen J. Trejo. 2002. *Falling behind or moving up? The intergenerational progress of Mexican Americans.* San Francisco: Public Policy Institute of California.

Haveman, Robert, and Barbara Wolfe. 1994. *Succeeding generations: On the effects of investments in children.* New York: Russell Sage Foundation.

Huntington, Samuel P. 2004. *Who are we?: The challenges to America's identity.* New York: Simon and Schuster.

Jaeger, David A. 1997. Reconciling the old and new Census Bureau education questions: Recommendations for researchers. *Journal of Business and Economics Statistics* 15 (3): 300–309.

Lieberson, Stanley, and Mary C. Waters. 1988. *From many strands: Ethnic and racial groups in contemporary America.* New York: Russell Sage Foundation.

———. 1993. The ethnic responses of whites: What causes their instability, simplification, and inconsistency? *Social Forces* 72 (2): 421–50.

Livingston, Gretchen, and Joan R. Kahn. 2002. An American dream unfulfilled: The limited mobility of Mexican Americans. *Social Science Quarterly* 83 (4): 1003–12.

Merton, Robert K. 1941. Intermarriage and the social structure: Fact and theory. *Psychiatry* 4:361–74.

Mulligan, Casey B. 1997. *Parental priorities and economic inequality.* Chicago: University of Chicago Press.

Neidert, Lisa J., and Reynolds Farley. 1985. Assimilation in the United States: An analysis of ethnic and generation differences in status and achievement. *American Sociological Review* 50 (6): 840–50.

Ono, Hiromi. 2002. Assimilation, ethnic competition, and ethnic identities of U.S.-born persons of Mexican origin. *International Migration Review* 36 (3): 726–45.

Perkins, R. Colby. 1993. Evaluating the Passel-Word Spanish surname list: 1990 Decennial Census Post Enumeration Survey Results. Population Division Working Paper no. 4. Washington, DC: U.S. Bureau of the Census, Population Division, August.

Perlmann, Joel. 2003. Mexicans now, Italians then: Intermarriage patterns. Jerome Levy Economics Institute Working Paper no. 376. Annandale-on-Hudson, NY: Jerome Levy Economics Institute, April.

Perlmann, Joel, and Roger Waldinger. 1996. The second generation and the children of the native born: Comparisons and refinements. Jerome Levy Economics Institute Working Paper no. 174. Annandale-on-Hudson, NY: Jerome Levy Economics Institute, November.

———. 1997. Second generation decline? Children of immigrants, past and present—A reconsideration. *International Migration Review* 31 (4): 893–922.

Portes, Alejandro, and Ruben G. Rumbaut. 2001. *Legacies: The story of the immigrant second generation.* Berkeley, CA: University of California Press.

Portes, Alejandro, and Min Zhou. 1993. The new second generation: Segmented assimilation and its variants among post-1965 immigrant youth. *Annals of the American Academy of Political and Social Science* 530:74–96.

Qian, Zhenchao. 1997. Breaking the racial barriers: Variations in interracial marriage between 1980 and 1990. *Demography* 34 (2): 263–76.

———. 1999. Who intermarries? Education, nativity, region, and interracial marriage, 1980 and 1990. *Journal of Comparative Family Studies* 30 (4): 579–97.

Rosenfeld, Michael J. 2001. The salience of pan-national Hispanic and Asian identities in U.S. marriage markets. *Demography* 38 (2): 161–75.

———. 2002. Measures of assimilation in the marriage market: Mexican Americans 1970–1990. *Journal of Marriage and Family* 64 (1): 152–62.

Rumbaut, Ruben G. 1994. The crucible within: Ethnic identity, self-esteem, and segmented assimilation among children of immigrants. *International Migration Review* 28 (4): 748–94.

Smith, James P. 2003. Assimilation across the Latino generations. *American Economic Review* 93 (2): 315–19.

Snipp, C. Matthew. 1989. *American Indians: The first of this land.* New York: Russell Sage Foundation.

Sowell, Thomas. 1978. Three black histories. In *Essays and data on American ethnic groups,* ed. Thomas Sowell, 7–64. Washington, DC: Urban Institute.

Stephan, Cookie White, and Walter G. Stephan. 1989. After intermarriage: Ethnic identity among mixed-heritage Japanese-Americans and Hispanics. *Journal of Marriage and the Family* 51 (2): 507–19.

Trejo, Stephen J. 1997. Why do Mexican Americans earn low wages? *Journal of Political Economy* 105 (6): 1235–68.

———. 2003. Intergenerational progress of Mexican-origin workers in the U.S. labor market. *Journal of Human Resources* 38 (3): 467–89.

U.S. Bureau of the Census. 1974. *1970 Census of Population and Housing, Evaluation and Research Program: Accuracy of data for selected population characteristics as measured by reinterviews.* Washington, DC: Government Printing Office.

Waters, Mary C. 1990. *Ethnic options: Choosing identities in America.* Berkeley, CA: University of California Press.

———. 1994. Ethnic and racial identities of second-generation black immigrants in New York City. *International Migration Review* 28 (4): 795–820.

White, Michael J., and Sharon Sassler. 2000. Judging not only by color: Ethnicity, nativity, and neighborhood attainment. *Social Science Quarterly* 81 (4): 997–1013.

Xie, Yu, and Kimberly Goyette. 1997. The racial identification of biracial children with one Asian parent: Evidence from the 1990 Census. *Social Forces* 76 (2): 547–70.

8

Impacts of Policy Reforms
on Labor Migration from Rural
Mexico to the United States

Susan M. Richter, J. Edward Taylor,
and Antonio Yúnez-Naude

Immigrant workers from Mexico are a critical component of the supply of labor to agriculture and many nonagricultural sectors in the United States. They constitute 3.5 percent of U.S. labor force but are heavily concentrated into two types of sectors: 25 percent are in services, and 29 percent are involved in production and transportation occupations (Grieco and Ray 2004). The majority of U.S. farmworkers are Mexican-born. According to the National Agricultural Worker Survey (NAWS), Mexican-born persons represented an estimated 77 percent of the U.S. farm workforce in 1997–1998 (up from 57 percent in 1990; U.S. Department of Labor 2000, 1991). Since the late 1990s, most farm workers have been unauthorized (Martin, Fix, and Taylor 2006). An overwhelming majority originate from households in rural Mexico (U.S. Commission on Immigration Reform 1997).

Two major policy changes, the North American Free Trade Agreement (NAFTA) and the 1986 Immigration Reform and Control Act (IRCA), together with intensified enforcement along the southern U.S. border, were aimed wholly or partially at curtailing the flow of unauthorized Mexico-to-U.S. migration. The curtailment of unauthorized migration had the potential to reduce the supply of labor to these U.S. economic sectors. But the policies had potentially counteracting effects. The overall impact of

Susan M. Richter and J. Edward Taylor are PhD candidate and professor, respectively, in the Department of Agricultural and Resource Economics at the University of California at Davis, and Antonio Yúnez-Naude is professor at the Center for Economic Studies at El Colegio de México. Taylor is a member of the Giannini Foundation of Agricultural Economics.

We gratefully acknowledge support from the William and Flora Hewlett Foundation, the U.S. Department of Agriculture (USDA/NRI), Mexico's Consejo Nacional de Ciencia y Tecnología (CONACYT), and the University of California Institute for Mexico (UCMEXUS), without which this research would not have been possible, and valuable insights from Aaron Smith and an anonymous referee.

NAFTA, IRCA, and increased border enforcement on migration is theoretically ambiguous and therefore must be estimated econometrically.

In this paper, we estimate a dynamic econometric model to test the effect of these policy changes on the flow of migrant labor from rural Mexico to the United States. Recognizing that policy changes may have differential effects on male and female labor migration, we estimate the effects of policy changes by the gender of migrant flows as well. The models are estimated using retrospective data from the 2003 Mexico National Rural Household Survey.

8.1   Conceptual Framework

We isolate the impact of three policies: IRCA, NAFTA, and increased expenditure on enforcement along the U.S.-Mexican border. Each of these policies has counteracting effects on migration, making the overall impact on migration ambiguous.

The IRCA had two main components. First, it made employers who hired illegal aliens subject to fines or imprisonment. These penalties were meant to discourage the hiring of unauthorized immigrants and reduce migration by dampening the employment expectations of migrants. Second, IRCA provided amnesty to illegal aliens who had lived in the United States continually since 1982 if they applied before 1988. This policy legalized U.S. migration contacts for households throughout rural Mexico. In so doing, it may have encouraged migration by family members of newly legalized migrants, while also sending a signal to rural Mexicans that future amnesty deals might be forthcoming. Therefore, these two components of IRCA potentially have counteracting effects on immigration.

The North American Free Trade Agreement was only partially motivated by migration concerns but was expected to have far-reaching impacts on migration flows. In the long run, trade liberalization policies open North American markets to Mexico, encouraging export of goods and decreasing migration pressures.[1] That is, in the long run, trade and migration may be substitutes. After Mexico joined NAFTA, Mexican agricultural exports to the United States did, indeed, increase. However, in the short run, NAFTA could displace rural workers as production shifts from importables to exportables and labor markets adjust to new market realities. Computable general equilibrium models predicted that the increase in labor demand generated by exports to the United States would be insufficient to absorb workers displaced from agricultural activities that had been protected by government policies prior to NAFTA. This, in turn, would stimulate out-migration from rural Mexico (Levy and van Wijnbergen 1992; Robinson et al. 1991).

---

1. Presidents Salinas and Bush (senior) argued this point to gain support for NAFTA.

The process of dismantling protectionist agrarian policies, which began just prior to NAFTA, was also expected to displace agricultural workers throughout Mexico. Mexico phased out price supports for eleven agricultural field crops and the processing, storing, and marketing activities of the state-run National Company of Popular Subsistence (CONASUPO; Yúnez-Naude 2003). Agricultural credit subsidies were also reduced sharply (Yúnez-Naude and Barceinas 2004). For rural workers displaced by policies related to NAFTA, migration may have been a vehicle to overcome short-term financial shocks.

The third policy that we evaluate is the increase in enforcement along the U.S.-Mexico border. Increases in border enforcement were meant to curtail unauthorized immigration. However, they could have the opposite effect by discouraging unauthorized immigrants from returning to their home countries and thus extending their stays in the United States. Increased border enforcement raises smuggler fees, but family members may be willing to pay the increased cost in order to reunite with relatives who have extended their stays in the United States.

The possible impacts of these three policies on migration are complex and theoretically ambiguous. The net effects of these policy shocks on the migration of labor from rural Mexico to the United States can only be determined empirically. However, in order to isolate the effects of policy changes on migration, we also need to control for the plethora of individual, household, and community variables influencing migration decisions over time as well as macroeconomic shocks that affect the migration decision.

Individual, household, and community variables affect the costs and benefits of migrating relative to staying at home and thus the propensity to migrate. The propensity to migrate and obtain employment in the United States is partly a function of migration networks and sending-area characteristics. Sending-area characteristics and community-level heterogeneity are controlled for econometrically via fixed effects, while migration networks or contacts with employed migrants in the United States are represented by lagged stocks of employed villagers in the United States. Networks may be gender-specific. For example, females may base their migration decision on the knowledge that other females in the village have succeeded in crossing the border and obtaining employment in the United States. In order to evaluate gender-specific network effects, we include separately the lagged stocks of male and female villagers employed in the United States.

Several macroeconomic variables also may influence the benefits and costs of international migration. These variables include changes in the peso-dollar exchange rate and in per capita gross domestic products (GDPs) of both countries. Mexican currency devaluations increase the purchasing power of dollars remitted to Mexico. Changes in U.S. GDP are included as a proxy for the availability of jobs in the United States. They are expected to be positively related to migration. The impact of an increase in Mexico's GDP is ambiguous. On one hand, it could reflect employment growth that discourages migration. On the other hand, higher income in Mexico could provide households with the liquidity to finance investments, including investments in international migration, that is, the costs associated with crossing the U.S.-Mexico border and establishing oneself in a foreign labor market. Our econometric analysis controls explicitly for these variables in order to isolate the impact of our three policy variables.

8.2 Theoretical Model

At the micro level, international migration is only observed for households and family members that choose to participate in migration, which is a discrete decision. Migrants are individuals for whom the expected benefits of migration, R, exceed the (unobserved) migration "reservation wage," ω. The migration reservation wage depends on local opportunities on and off the farm. Following Mincer (1974), the local wage is a function of human capital that affects the marginal productivity of labor. Let $\mathbf{X_W}$ denote a vector of human capital characteristics influencing wage income in the local labor market. The productivity of family members' in household farm and non-farm activities is shaped both by these human capital variables and by family assets $\overline{K}$. Remittances are a function of migrants' human capital, which affects earnings, as well as migrants' motivations to remit, which may be influenced by both human capital and family assets (Lucas and Stark 1985; Taylor 1987). Contacts at migrant destinations, MK, are a form of migration capital that can enhance the labor-market prospects of migrants (Munshi 2003). Migration networks can be defined as "sets of interpersonal ties that connect migrants, former migrants, and nonmigrants in origin and destination areas through . . . kinship, friendship, and shared community origin" (Massey 1988, 396). These ties are predominately formed with contacts from one's own village and not across villages. As we shall investigate later in the chapter, $\overline{MK}$ can vary according to gender, and the effects of networks on migration appear to be gender-specific.

Migrant remittances and reservation wages have both deterministic and stochastic components; thus, $R = R(X_R) + u$ and $\omega = \omega(X_\omega) + v$, where $X_\omega = (\mathbf{X_W}, \overline{K})$, $X_R = (\mathbf{X_W}, \overline{K}, \overline{MK})$, and u and v are stochastic errors. Letting $\delta = 1$ if a household member migrates and 0 otherwise, the migration participation decision becomes

$$(1) \qquad \delta = \begin{cases} 1 & \text{if } \eta < R(X_R) - \omega(X_\omega), \\ 0 & \text{otherwise} \end{cases}$$

where $\eta = v - u$. Total migration is simply the sum of individuals who migrate; that is, $M = \Sigma \, \delta$. Let θ_t represent the joint distribution of variables X_R and X_ω in community j at time t. Then

$$(2) \qquad\qquad M_{jt} = M(\theta_{jt}, Z_{jt}),$$

where Z_{jt} is a vector of community variables influencing the productivity of labor in local activities and remittances. In the econometric model, we control for the influences of θ_{jt} and Z_{jt} by including lagged migration $(M_{j,t-1})$, fixed effects for communities, and a time trend.

8.3   Data

The data used to estimate the model are from a nationwide rural household survey carried out jointly by El Colegio de Mexico and the University of California, Davis. The Mexico National Rural Household Survey (Encuesta Nacional a Hogares Rurales de Mexico [ENHRUM]) provides retrospective data on migration by individuals from a sample of rural households that is both nationally and regionally representative (see http://precesam.colmex.mx). Past studies of Mexican labor supply to the United States used proxies including border apprehensions (e.g., Torok and Huffman 1986) or data from surveys of small numbers of villages. Usually, surveys do not collect migration flows over extended periods of time and thus are unable to evaluate policies' long-term impact on the dynamics and trends of migration.

The ENHRUM was carried out in January and February 2003 in all five of Mexico's census regions. The Instituto Nacional de Estadística, Geografía e Informática (INEGI), Mexico's national census office, designed the sampling frame to provide a statistically reliable characterization of Mexico's population living in rural areas, defined by INEGI as communities with fewer than 2,500 inhabitants. The survey was designed to be representative both nationally and regionally. Rural households were selected via a three-tiered stratified random sampling method involving states, communities, and households randomly drawn within each community. This method generated a sample of 1,782 households in eighty villages and fourteen Mexican states. For reasons of cost and tractability, individuals in hamlets or disperse populations with fewer than 500 inhabitants were not included in the survey. The sample is representative of more than 80 percent of the population that the Mexican census office considers to be rural.

The ENHRUM survey assembled complete migration histories from 1980 through 2002 for (a) the household head, (b) the spouse of the head, (c) all individuals who lived in the household three months or more in 2002, and (d) a random sample of sons and daughters of either the head or his or her spouse who lived outside the household longer than three months in

2002. In theory, the ENHRUM survey collected retrospective information only about labor migrants.[2] However, data on place of residence of all family members were gathered for 2002, regardless of employment status. For 2002, virtually all migrants were considered by family members in the village to be labor migrants. If the same is true for earlier years, our counts of labor migrants will also reflect total migration. For each year, the survey provides information on the migrant's sector of employment, agricultural or nonagricultural, and the state in which he or she worked. The survey provides the most reliable longitudinal data on migration from rural Mexican communities to the United States.

The survey asked individuals to recall employment information for each migrant from 1980 to 2002. Individuals may be unable to remember their (or their migrant sons' and daughters') employment histories for twenty-two years. However, when employment is coupled with a life event such as international migration, there is a smaller likelihood that data will be misreported. A study by Smith and Thomas (2003) showed that when respondents are asked to recall information linked to salient events, such as marriage or birth of a child, misreporting is insignificant. Also, individuals asked to recall labor or migration histories reported more accurately moves that involved either a long distance or extended stays.

To implement the survey, Mexico was divided into five regions, reflecting INEGI's standard regionalization of the country: Center, South-Southeast, Center-West, Northwest, and Northeast.[3] Table 8.1 summarizes migration from households in rural Mexico. Sixteen percent of all households in the sample had a family member living in the United States at the start of 2002, the year of the survey, and 26 percent had a family member living in another part of Mexico. Many households had more than one migrant. The number of U.S. migrants per household ranged from 0 to 9, while the number of internal migrants ranged from 0 to 10. The average household in the sample had 0.35 U.S. migrants and 0.71 internal migrants in 2002—or 1.06 migrants in total.

As indicated in the table, there are sharp differences in migration experience among the five rural regions. West-Central Mexico traditionally has been the largest sender of migrants to the United States, with far and away the highest current participation in international migration and the most international migration experience. In this region, nearly 28 percent

2. The questions asked in the survey were: "¿Qué años trabajó _____ en los E.U. desde 1980? ¿En qué trabajó y en qué estado? ¿Por un salario o por cuenta propia?" ("In what years did _____ work in the U.S. since 1980? In what job and which state? For a salary or self-employed?").

3. The high-migration West-Central region was the focus of Mexico Migration Project (MMP) surveys (Population Studies Center, University of Pennsylvania, Philadelphia [producer and distributor], http://www.pop.upenn.edu/mexmig/welcome.html). The MMP surveyed a random sample of households within communities, but the sample of MMP communities was not random.

Table 8.1   Migration summary statistics for rural Mexico, by region

Region/Variable	Percentages	Sample mean	Standard deviation
South-south east			
Households with U.S. migrants (%)	7.53		0.26
U.S. migrants per household		0.10	0.42
Household sample size		372	
Center			
Households with U.S. migrants (%)	14.52		0.35
U.S. Migrants per household		0.27	0.89
Household sample size		365	
Center-west			
Households with U.S. migrants (%)	27.75		0.45
U.S. migrants per household		0.62	1.29
Household sample size		346	
Northwest			
Households with U.S. migrants (%)	12.09		0.33
U.S. migrants per household		0.23	0.79
Household sample size		339	
Northeast			
Households with U.S. migrants (%)	19.72		0.40
U.S. migrants per household		0.54	1.43
Household sample size		360	
Total			
Households with U.S. migrants (%)	16.22		0.37
U.S. migrants per household		0.35	1.04
Household sample size		1,782	

Source: 2003 ENHRUM survey.

of all households have at least one family member in the United States, and the average household had .62 U.S. migrants. By contrast, 7.5 percent of households in the south-southwest have U.S. migrants, with an average of .10 U.S. migrants per household.

8.4   Econometric Model

We econometrically estimate the impact of policy reforms on three dependent variables: (a) the share of villagers employed in the United States; (b) the share of female villagers employed in the United States; and (c) the share of male villagers employed in the United States.

For the first dependent variable, we estimate two fixed effects panel data models for all employed immigrants.

8.4.1   Model I

Model I is intended to capture the basic dynamics of rural Mexico-to-U.S. migration. The share of village population observed as labor migrants in the United States at time t, M_t, is regressed on the same share lagged one year (M_{jt-1}) and a time trend (t), controlling for a vector of village fixed effects, α_j:[4]

(3a) $M_{jt} = \alpha_j + \gamma t + \delta M_{jt-1} + u_{jt}$

Equation (3a) is a basis to estimate the dynamic structure of employed migration and to evaluate the role of networks and the inertia of employed migration over time. The time trend, t, captures unobserved time-varying variables that effect multiple villages, such as changes in U.S. attitudes about immigrants. Village fixed effects, α_j, control for unobserved community-specific characteristics that vary across villages but not over time. Village fixed effects allow each village to have its own migration trajectory. The village fixed effects model makes it possible to isolate the underlying migration trend (t) and influence of networks and inertia (the lagged-migration variable) from policy and macroeconomic variables shaping migration. We assume that networks from other villages have little or no impact on the migration propensity of a given village. This assumption is plausible, inasmuch as the communities in the survey are rural and isolated from one another. In the event that migration from a village is influenced by the presence of networks from another village throughout the period, which our field work indicates as rare, this effect would become part of the village fixed effect.[5]

8.4.2   Model II

Model II includes three policy variables: dummy variables for IRCA (1 for all time periods beginning in 1986, the year of IRCA's implementation), NAFTA (1 beginning in 1994, 0 before), and a continuous variable measuring the percentage change in border enforcement expenditures (ΔBE_t). The 1980–2002 period witnessed large year-to-year increases in border enforcement expenditures. On one hand, an increase in enforcement from one year to the next might deter new border crossings. Nevertheless, in rural Mexico it is rare to find individuals who tried but did not succeed at crossing the border, perhaps after multiple attempts. On the other hand, as noted by the U.S. Commission on Immigration Reform (1997) and the Public Policy Institute of California (2002), heightened border enforcement can also have the perverse effect of deterring return migration by individuals who realize that reentering the United States will be more diffi-

---

4. We use the percentage rather than the sum of villagers who migrated because of our concern that the size of village populations in the synthetic cohorts created using retrospective data is biased downward as one goes back in time, as individuals are removed from the population due to death (and thus are not available to be counted in 2003).

5. For example, our field work reveals that in almost no instance did an individual make his or her first trip assisted by someone from another village. The benefits of international migration networks are concentrated first in families and next in the community of which the family is part.

cult in the future. It is not clear which of these effects will dominate, particularly in the short run. We also include macroeconomic variables: the percentage changes between time t and $t-1$ in the peso-dollar exchange rate (ΔER_t) and the U.S. and Mexico GDP's ($\Delta USGDP_t$, $\Delta MGDP_t$). The U.S. GDP changes are used as a proxy for employment growth, which would be expected to stimulate immigration. Increases in Mexico's GDP could deter migration as a result of a similar employment effect. However, they could also provide households with the income to finance relatively costly and risky international moves, as has been noted by some other studies (e.g., Schiff 1996).

$$(3b) \quad M_{jt} = \alpha_j + \gamma t + \delta M_{jt-1} + \beta_1 IRCA_t + \beta_2 NAFTA_{it} + \beta_3 \Delta BE_t$$
$$+ \theta_1 \Delta ER_t + \theta_2 \Delta USGDP_t + \theta_3 \Delta MGDP_t + u_{jt}$$

Our use of dummy variables to evaluate the impact of NAFTA and IRCA warrants some explanation. Other methods are possible, including controls for trade flows or changes in real wages in Mexico and the United States; however, these variables may not be exogenous to migration. For example, changes in real agricultural wages in the United States are likely related to the supply of migrant labor from rural Mexico. The inclusion of policy dummy variables in the regressions makes it possible to evaluate the long-run impact of exogenous policy shocks on the rate and dynamic of labor migration. Inclusion of the lagged-migration variable allows for the impacts of policy shocks to unfold gradually over time.

The vector of fixed effects, α_j, γ, δ, β_k, $k = 1, \ldots, 3$ and θ_l, $l = 1, \ldots, 3$ are parameters to be estimated, and the u_{jt} are stochastic errors. The use of migration shares (M_{jt}) instead of differences in migration shares between periods ($M_{jt} - M_{jt-1}$) as the dependent variable allows for the possibility that $\delta \neq 1$. Under the null hypothesis of no policy impacts on migration, the coefficients $\beta_k = 0 \; \forall \; k$.

We estimate three types of dynamic fixed effects models for labor migration by gender ($g = m, f$). The first model is similar to equation (3a). We estimate the share of males (females) in employed migration as a function of a time trend (t) and the lagged share of male (female) migrants in village populations:

$$(4a) \quad M_{jgt} = \alpha_j + \gamma t + \delta M_{jgt-1} + u_{jt}$$

We reestimated each equation including the lagged stock of other-gender migrants to evaluate the gender sensitivity of network effects:

$$(4b) \quad M_{jgt} = \alpha_j + \gamma t + \delta_1 M_{jmt-1} + \delta_2 M_{jft-1} + u''_{jt}$$

If both male and female networks shape female migration, then both δ_1 (lagged-female migration) and δ_2 (lagged-male migration) will be significant, and conversely for the male migration regression.

In the final estimation we include in each gender-specific migration equation all of the policy and enforcement and macroeconomic-change variables. This model is similar to equation (3b) except that it includes the lagged stock of other gender's participation in employed migration:

$$(4c) \quad M_{jgt} = \alpha_j + \gamma t + \delta_1 M_{jmt-1} + \delta_2 M_{jft-1} + \beta_1 \Delta IRCA_t + \beta_2 \Delta NAFTA_t$$
$$+ \beta_3 \Delta BE_t + \theta_1 \Delta ER_t + \theta_2 \Delta USGDP_t + \theta_3 \Delta MGDP_t + u_{jt}$$

8.5   Estimation and Results

M_{jgt}, the dependent variable, is calculated for each of the eighty villages in each of the twenty-three (from 1980 to 2002) years of observations. However, one year (eighty observations) is lost due to the inclusion of lagged right-hand-side variables. Thus, for each village we have twenty-two annual observations, for a total sample size of 1,760 (twenty-two years $\times$ eighty villages). The variability in migration and other variables both across villages and over time contribute to identifying the effects of networks and policy shocks on international migration.

The series of models given by (3a)–(3b) and (4a)–(4c) was estimated using the standard least square dummy variable (LSDV) method. This method results in a downward bias in the estimate of δ; however, this bias diminishes as the number of observations in the time dimension (T) increases (Judson and Owen 1999). Judson and Owen show that the bias becomes negligible as T approaches 30. In our data set, $T = 23$ (1980–2002, inclusive), which indicates that there will be some bias, but it will be small. Judson and Owen also conclude that when T is greater than 20 the bias in the other parameter estimates is negligible. The key hypotheses that we wish to test involve not δ but, rather, the other parameters in the model (i.e., the effects of policy variables).

Figure 8.1 presents estimated shares of populations from the surveyed villages in U.S. farm and nonfarm jobs from 1980 to 2002. It shows an upward trend in migration to the United States for both males and females. However, the trend is steeper for males.[6] Female migration is lower than male migration and has a steady increase over the twenty-three-year period. Table 8.2 presents variable definitions and means for variables used in the econometrics.

Table 8.3 reports the econometric results for the village labor-migrant shares using ordinary least squares, controlling for fixed effects. The first column of table 8.3 shows results from the model that only controls for the lagged stock of migration. The time trend is significant and positive. The

6. The surge in migration to the United States in the 1990s is mirrored in U.S. Census 2000 data. The U.S. Census does not provide information on where migrants originate in Mexico (e.g., from rural or urban areas). However, they show an unexpectedly large increase in Mexican-born persons living in the United States.

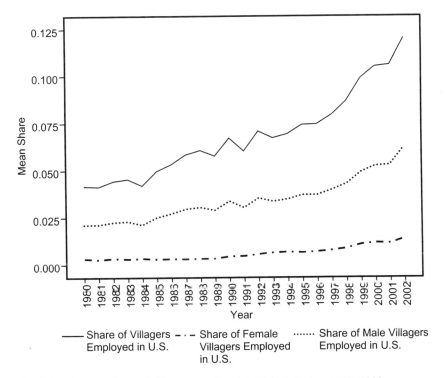

Fig. 8.1   Average share of villagers employed in United States: 1980–2002

coefficient on lagged migration is also significant and positive, indicating that networks created through past migration influence current migration.

Macroeconomic variables and policies, such as NAFTA and IRCA, can change the overall trend and influence of migration rates. Results from Model II, which includes these variables, are reported in column (2) of table 8.3.[7] The time trend and coefficient on lagged migration remain positive, large, and significant. The dummy variables for NAFTA and IRCA have a significant and negative impact on migration. Therefore, the supply of migrant labor from rural Mexico to the United States decreases after the implementation of IRCA in 1986, and it decreases once again following NAFTA in 1994. While the effect of NAFTA may seem large (a decrease of .75 in its year of implementation), NAFTA's main effect is to slow down the upward trend in migration. In the year following NAFTA's implementation and thereafter, the positive coefficients on the time trend and lagged migration once again increase migration. These findings support the

7. Trends in migration may also be influenced by regional dynamics. When separate regressors are estimated for Mexico's five census regions, there were no differences in the signs of significant variables among regions for all of the models presented in this paper.

Table 8.2 **Variable definitions and means**

Variable	Description	Mean
T	Time trend	11
USMIG	Share of villagers employed in U.S.	4.03
Female migration	Share of female villagers employed in U.S.	1.2
Male migration	Share of male villagers employed in U.S.	6.84
% change ER	% change in Peso-Dollar exchange rate from previous year	1.31
% change border control	% change in INS border enforcement budget from previous year	13.14
NAFTA	Dummy variable = 1 beginning in 1994	0.39
IRCA	Dummy variable = 1 beginning in 1986	0.74
% change MGDP	% change Mexico GDP	2.4
% change US GDP	% change U.S. GDP	2.9

Table 8.3 **OLS coefficients for three dynamic models—Participation in migration ($USMIG_t$)**

	All regions	
Variable	Model I	Model II
Constant	−.006	−1.28
	(.304)**	(.352)**
T	.054	.117
	(.006)**	(.018)**
$USMIG_{t-1}$	.846	.845
	(.015)**	(.015)**
NAFTA		−.750
		(.0154)**
IRCA		−.299
		(.132)**
% change border control		.011
		(.003)**
% change ER		.015
		(.004)**
% change MGDP		.034
		(.016)**
% change US GDP		.051
		(.022)**
R^2		.948

Notes: Dependent variable: Weighted total of international workers in village. All models were estimated with village fixed effects. Standard errors are in parentheses. $N = 1,760$.
**Significant at the 5 percent level.

hypothesis that NAFTA relieved migration pressures. The IRCA also temporarily reduced migration, but to a smaller degree than NAFTA.[8]

In contrast, increases in border enforcement are associated with an *increase* in the share of villagers working in the United States. This finding supports the hypothesis that most migrants eventually succeed in crossing the border and increased border enforcement discourages return migration. There is a negative correlation in the data between border expenditures and return migration (not shown in the tables).

The macroeconomic variables are all significant. The devaluation of the peso increases the rate of migration, echoing Massey and Espinosa (1997). This effect is of the expected sign, inasmuch as the devaluation raises the returns to international migration (remittances) in pesos. Changes in both countries' GDPs increase migration. Economic expansion in the United States pulls rural Mexicans into the country. The finding that GDP growth in Mexico encourages migration is consistent with the argument by Schiff (1996) that income growth enables households in sending areas to finance the cost of crossing the border and establishing migrants abroad.

Gender-specific regression results appear in table 8.4, for female migration, and table 8.5, for male migration. The column labeled "Model I" in each table shows results for the basic dynamic regression model. When we estimate the migration model by gender, the trend remains significant and positive. The lagged migration participation rate is both statistically and quantitatively significant. When the lagged migration rate of males is added to the estimate of female migration (Model II in table 8.4), it has only a small significant impact. A 1 percentage point increase in the share of male migrants increases female migration by only .014. The effect of lagged female migration on male migration (table 8.5) likewise is positive and significant but quantitatively small. A 1 percentage point increase in the share of village females working in the United States, other things being equal, is associated with a .08-percentage point increase in male participation in international migration. This finding suggests that labor migration networks are gender-specific. That is, estimates of a gender's participation in labor migration do not improve appreciably when the other gender's migration network is included in our regressions.

Macroeconomic and policy variables (Model II in tables 8.4 and 8.5) significantly increase the predicative power of the migration models for both genders.[9] Qualitatively, policy changes have similar effects on male and female migration, with the exception of GDP growth. However, quantita-

---

8. Boucher, Smith, and Taylor (2006) examine migration from rural Mexico to U.S. farm jobs, which constitutes a relatively small share of *total* migration and appears to have been affected differently by the policy shocks.

9. An *F*-test of restricted versus unrestricted regressions for both male and female migration shares rejected the joint hypothesis that the macroeconomic and policy variables were jointly zero.

Table 8.4   OLS coefficients for three dynamic models—Female participation in migration (female USMIG$_t$)

| | All regions | |
Variable	Model I	Model II
Constant	−.263	−.527
	(.194)	(.226)**
T	.023	.053
	(.003)**	(.012)**
Female USMIG$_{t-1}$	.889	.878
	(.014)**	(.015)**
Male USMIG$_{t-1}$		.014
		(.006)**
NAFTA		−.387
		(.131)**
IRCA		−.160
		(.085)*
% change border control		.003
		(.001)**
% change ER		.006
		(.003)**
% change MGDP		.021
		(.010)**
% change US GDP		.018
		(.014)
R^2	.882	.884

Notes: Dependent variable: Weighted total of female international workers in village. All models were estimated with village fixed effects. Standard errors are in parentheses. N = 1,760.
**Significant at the 5 percent level.
*Significant at the 10 percent level.

tively the results differ according to gender. The decrease in the male migrant share after NAFTA is three times greater than the drop in the female share. This suggests that female migration was more resilient to NAFTA-related policy changes. The decrease in migration shares after implementation of IRCA is twice as large for males as females. Other things being equal, a 1 percent increase in U.S. border enforcement has a larger positive percentage effect on male migration than on female migration (.015 and .003, respectively). This indicates either that border enforcement increases male stays more than female stays or, perhaps more plausibly, that border controls are more of a deterrent to border crossings by females than by males.

The effects of changes in Mexico's GDP are significant only for female migration. By contrast, changes in U.S. GDP are significant only for male migration. These findings may suggest that female migration is more sen-

Table 8.5   OLS coefficients for three dynamic models—Male participation in migration (male USMIG$_t$)

	All regions	
Variable	Model I	Model II
Constant	−1.02	−1.89
	(.540)*	(.625)**
T	.089	.163
	(.010)**	(.033)**
Male USMIG$_{t-1}$	.804	.796
	(.016)**	(.016)**
Female USMIG$_{t-1}$		.082
		(.042)*
NAFTA		−.964
		(.362)**
IRCA		−.317
		(.236)
% change border control		0.015
		(.005)**
% change ER		.012
		(.008)**
% change MGDP		.043
		(.029)
% change US GDP		.075
		(.038)*
R^2	.948	.948

Notes: Dependent variable: Weighted total of male international workers in village. All models were estimated with village fixed effects. Standard errors are in parentheses. $N = 1,760$.
**Significant at the 5 percent level.
*Significant at the 10 percent level.

sitive to liquidity constraints that can be loosened by income growth in Mexico, while female migrant labor demand is robust to U.S. GDP growth. Male migration, on the other hand, appears to be sensitive to U.S. economic growth.

8.6   Limitations and Caveats

Reliance on policy dummy variables and retrospective data to test for effects of policy changes on migration raises some questions and concerns that should be kept in mind when interpreting the findings presented here.

It might be argued that policy changes were endogenous responses to increasing migration in the period covered by our analysis. However, the build up to IRCA was gradual and commenced several years prior to the period covered by our analysis. Sanctions were enacted by the U.S. House of Representatives twice in the early 1970s but subsequently blocked in the

Senate. President Carter proposed sanctions against employment of unauthorized immigrants and legalization in 1977. Following several years of debate and the establishment of the Select Commission on Immigration Reform, IRCA was finally passed in 1986. It might also be argued that IRCA was a response to economic recession, which in turn could be correlated with immigration. However, by the time IRCA was passed, the early 1980s recession was largely over. There was more unauthorized Mexico-to-U.S. migration after the 1982–1983 recession, and migration accelerated in the 1990s (Martin 2003, chapter 7).

Our analysis uses fixed effects to control for unobserved village characteristics on migration. It might be argued, however, that the effects of IRCA and NAFTA on migration probabilities varied across regions. IRCA's effects may have been different in rural areas in which the prevalence of migration was high prior to the policy's implementation. The North American Free Trade Agreement's influence on migration may have been different in regions with high agricultural potential or high levels of industrialization. How these regional characteristics might have influenced migration is not clear a priori. For example, the influence of a large manufacturing sector on NAFTA's migration effects could be positive (in the case of internationally competitive industries) or negative (in the case of industries that were protected by Mexican trade policies prior to NAFTA). A high prevalence of migration prior to IRCA could reflect a region's vulnerability to immigration reforms or an enhanced ability to adapt to reforms, for example, through amnesty programs. A rich agricultural base could reflect opportunities for expanding agro-exports post-NAFTA; however, labor-saving technological change is concentrated on high-potential lands. To explore the sensitivity of policy findings to regional conditions, we reestimated the model including, as explanatory variables, interactions between the following:

- IRCA and the share of villagers who were international labor migrants in 1980
- NAFTA and the share of cultivated land that was irrigated in 1980
- NAFTA and the share of manufacturing in state GDPs in 1980

We chose 1980 values for these variables to minimize possible endogeneity bias. In no case was an interaction term significant in explaining migration probabilities. Inclusion of these interactions did not qualitatively alter the effects of the policy variables presented earlier.

A number of other economic and policy changes were more or less coincident with IRCA and NAFTA. Foremost among these were the peso devaluation of late 1994 and 1995 and enactment of a major welfare reform in the United States in 1996.

We attempt to disentangle the effects of currency devaluations from those of policy shocks by including changes in the peso-dollar exchange rates in our regression. The 1994–1995 period saw a sharp increase in this exchange rate. However, this was not the only period of significant devaluation in our time series. We believe that there is sufficient variation in our exchange-rate variable from 1980 to 2002 to control for currency effects.

Other policies that could have affected immigration were enacted within several years of IRCA and NAFTA. Foremost among these was the Personal Responsibility and Work Opportunity Reconciliation Act of 1996 (PL 104-193; PRWORA), which singled out immigrants. Most legal immigrants arriving after August 22, 1996 are not eligible for federal welfare assistance until they have been in the United States for at least five years, and many legal immigrants receiving assistance when PRWORA was enacted lost their eligibility for benefits. Enacted only two years after NAFTA, PRWORA's effects could conceivably contaminate our findings if restricting immigrants' access to benefits created a deterrent to immigration. In a study of agricultural counties in California, Green, Martin, and Taylor (2003) found that PRWORA reduced the number of adults receiving cash assistance; however, controlling for employment and other variables, the estimated effect of the policy change was not large. Borjas (2002) concluded that much of the potential impact of welfare reform on immigrants outside of California was undone by the actions of state governments. Many states—particularly those with large immigrant populations—chose to offer state-provided benefits to otherwise ineligible immigrants. Empirical studies overwhelmingly point to employment and wages as the primary economic drivers of immigration. These considerations raise doubts about the extent to which welfare reform influenced immigration.

Due to mortality, some (mostly older) individuals disappear from our synthetic cohorts of migrants and villagers as we go back in time—that is, they are not alive to be counted at the time of the survey. If old villagers are less likely to migrate, this will result in an upward bias in the estimated share of villagers in the United States (and thus a downward bias in the estimated migration trend), and this bias will be larger the farther back in time one goes. The key question relevant to our analysis is whether this bias alters the estimated effect of policy changes on migration. We explored this possibility by estimating the model separately for younger age cohorts of villagers (i.e., those who were sixteen–thirty-five years old in 1980 and thus less at risk of being affected by mortality over the study period). There were no significant changes to our econometric findings. Our findings on the effects of policy reforms on migration appear to be robust to the ways in which we construct our synthetic cohorts.

8.7 Conclusions

The impacts of NAFTA, IRCA and increased U.S. border enforcement are ambiguous a priori. Each policy change potentially has both positive and negative influences on migration. In the past, data limitations have made it difficult to test for impacts of policy shocks on Mexico-to-U.S. migration dynamics. The Mexico National Rural Household Survey provides retrospective migration histories from a nationally random sample of rural Mexicans. This makes it possible to isolate migration trends and control for place-of-origin characteristics while measuring the impacts of policy shocks on the share of rural Mexicans working in the United States.

Several general findings emerge from our analysis. First, international labor migration from rural Mexico has followed an upward trend from 1980 to 2002 but is driven overwhelmingly by past migration, reflecting the central role of migration networks. Second, policy variables significantly influence migration, but not as much as macroeconomic variables. The IRCA and NAFTA had some impact on curtailing migration; however, increased border enforcement appears to have had the opposite effect. No policies are able to counteract the effects of a changing macroeconomic environment. Third, the influences of both policy and macroeconomic variables are small compared with network effects embodied in past migration.

A unique contribution of this analysis is the insight it offers into the dynamics underlying female and male migration. Policy shocks and macroeconomic variables have differential effects on female and male migration, quantitatively (in the case of NAFTA and IRCA) and, in some cases, qualitatively (in the case of Mexico and U.S. GDP growth). The role of Mexico GDP growth in loosening liquidity constraints on migration appears to be more important for females than males, while the impact of U.S. income growth is greater for males.

Although own-gender migration networks are significant and large, cross-gender network effects are small. Past research has suggested that female migrants follow males, for example, for purposes of family reunification. However, we find that past labor migration by male villagers has a very small though significant effect on female labor migration. That is, *controlling for community effects and long-run migration dynamics,* labor migration networks are gender-specific. Future economic research is warranted on gender asymmetries in networks and their influence on migration propensities.

References

Borjas, G. 2002. *The impact of welfare reform on immigrant welfare use.* Center for Immigration Studies Report. http://www.cis.org/articles/2002/borjas.htm.

Boucher, S., A. Smith, and J. E. Taylor. 2006. Impacts of policy reforms on the supply of Mexican labor to U.S. farms: New evidence from Mexico. *Review of Agricultural Economics,* forthcoming.

Green, R., P. L. Martin, and J. E. Taylor. 2003. Welfare reform in agricultural California. *Journal of Agricultural and Resource Economics* 28 (1): 169–83.

Grieco, E., and B. Ray. 2004. *Mexican immigrants in the U.S. labor force.* Washington, DC: The Migration Policy Institute. http://www.migrationinformation.org/USFocus/display.cfm?10=206.

Judson, R. A., and A. L. Owen. 1999. Estimating dynamic panel data models: A guide for macroeconomists. *Econometric Letters* 65:9–15.

Levy, S., and S. van Wijnbergen. 1992. Mexican agriculture in the free trade agreement: Transition problems in economic reform. OECD Technical Paper no. 63. Paris: Organization for Economic Cooperation and Development.

Lucas, R. E. B., and O. Stark. 1985. Motivations to remit: Evidence from Botswana. *Journal of Political Economy* 93:901–18.

Martin, P. L. 2003. Promise unfulfilled: Unions, immigration, and farm workers. Ithaca, NY: Cornell University Press.

Martin, P. L., M. Fix, and J. E. Taylor. 2006. *The new rural poverty.* Washington, DC: The Urban Institute Press.

Massey, D. S. 1988. Economic development and international migration in comparative perspective. *Population and Development Review* 14:383–413.

Massey, D. S., and K. E. Espinosa. 1997. What's driving Mexico-U.S. migration? A theoretical, empirical and policy analysis. *American Journal of Sociology* 102: 939–99.

Mincer, J. 1974. *Schooling, experience, and earnings.* New York: Columbia University Press.

Munshi, K. 2003. Networks in the modern economy: Mexican migrants in the U.S. labor market. *Quarterly Journal of Economics* 18:549–99.

Public Policy Institute of California. 2002. *Has increased border enforcement reduced unauthorized immigration?* Research Brief no. 61. San Francisco: Public Policy Institute of California.

Robinson, S., M. E. Burfisher, R. Hinojosa-Ojeda, and K. E. Thierfelder. 1991. Agricultural policies and migration in a U.S.-Mexico free trade area: A computable general equilibrium analysis. University of California at Berkeley, Department of Agricultural and Resource Economics, Working Paper no. 617.

Schiff, M. 1996. Trade policy and international migration: Substitutes or complements? In *Development strategy, employment and migration: Insights from models,* ed. J. E. Taylor, 22–41. Paris: Organization for Economic Cooperation and Development.

Smith, J. P., and D. Thomas. 2003. Remembrances of things past: Test-retest reliability of retrospective migration histories. *Journal of the Royal Statistical Society* 166:23–49.

Taylor, J. E. 1987. Undocumented Mexico-U.S. migration and the returns to households in rural Mexico. *American Journal of Agricultural Economics* 69:626–38.

Torok, S. J., and W. Huffman. 1986. U.S.-Mexican trade in winter vegetables and illegal immigration. *American Journal of Agricultural Economics* 68:246–60.

U.S. Commission on Immigration Reform. 1997. *Binational Study: Migration between Mexico and the United States.* Washington, DC: U.S. Commission on Immigration Reform.

U.S. Department of Labor. 1991. Findings from the National Agricultural Workers Survey (NAWS) 1990: A demographic and employment profile of perishable crop farm workers. Office of the Assistant Secretary for Policy, Office of Program Economics, Research Report no. 8. Washington, DC: U.S. Department of Labor.

———. 2000. *Findings from the National Agricultural Workers Survey (NAWS)*

1997–1998: A demographic and employment profile of United States farmworkers. Office of the Assistant Secretary for Policy, Office of Program Economics, Research Report no. 8. Washington, DC: U.S. Department of Labor.

Yúnez-Naude, A. 2003. The dismantling of CONASUPO, a Mexican state trader in agriculture. *The World Economy* 26 (1): 97–122.

Yúnez Naude, A., and F. B. Paredes. 2004. Agricultural trade and NAFTA: The case of Mexico. In *The first decade of NAFTA: The future of free trade in North America,* ed. K. C. Kennedy, 117–44. New York: Transnational Publishers.

9

Emigration, Labor Supply, and Earnings in Mexico

Gordon H. Hanson

9.1   Introduction

Over the last several decades, migration to the United States has profoundly affected the Mexican economy. The most obvious change has been to Mexico's labor supply. Between 1970 and 2000, the share of the Mexican population (individuals born in Mexico) residing in the United States increased from 1.7 percent to 8.6 percent (see figure 9.1).[1] Emigration rates have been rising steadily over time and are highest for young adults. Between 1990 and 2000, 10.0 percent of males and 7.7 percent of females born in Mexico between 1965 and 1974 migrated to the United States, raising the share of this age cohort living in the United States to 17.5 percent for males and 12.6 percent for females (see table 9.1).

Not surprisingly, the outmigration of labor appears to have put upward pressure on wages in Mexico. Mishra (2004) estimates that in Mexico over the period 1970–2000, the elasticity of wages with respect to the outflow of migrant labor was 0.4 and that emigration raised average wages in the country by 8.0 percent. Upward pressure on wages has been strongest for young adults with above-average education levels (those with nine to fifteen years of schooling), who in the 1990s were the individuals most likely

Gordon H. Hanson is professor of economics at the University of California at San Diego, and research associate of the National Bureau of Economic Research.

I thank David Autor, George Borjas, Jose Ernesto Lopez Cordoba, Chris Woodruff, and participants in the NBER conference on Mexican Immigration for helpful comments. Jeffrey Lin provided excellent research assistance.

1. In this calculation, the numerator is the population of individuals born in Mexico, as enumerated in the U.S. population census, and the denominator is the sum of this figure and the population of individuals born in Mexico, as enumerated in the Mexican population census. This calculation ignores the small number of individuals born in Mexico who have migrated to third countries.

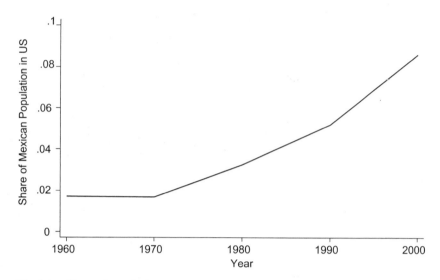

Fig. 9.1   Share of population born in Mexico residing in the United States

to migrate to the United States (Chiquiar and Hanson 2005). Increased labor flows between Mexico and the United States appear to be one factor
contributing to labor-market integration between the two countries. For
the 1990s, Robertson (2000) finds that a shock that raises U.S. wages by 10
percent raises wages in Mexico by 1.8 percent to 2.5 percent.

Were the only effect of emigration to raise wages for migrants and for
nonmigrating workers who substitute for migrant labor, the labor outflow
would yield static welfare losses in Mexico. However, an additional consequence of Mexican emigration has been an increase in the return flow of remittances. In 2003, remittances from Mexican immigrants in the United
States equaled 2.0 percent of Mexican GDP (Inter-American Development Bank [IADB] 2004). These appear sufficient to more than offset the
loss in GDP due to emigration.[2]

An important aspect of migrant behavior in Mexico is that the propensity to emigrate varies greatly across regions of the country. Due partly to
historical accident, central and western Mexico have long had the country's highest labor flows abroad. In figure 9.2, which shows the fraction of
households that sent migrants to the United States over 1995–2000 by
Mexican state, emigration rates are relatively low in states along the U.S.
border, sharply higher in states 600–1200 kilometers from the United
States and lowest in distant southern states. Regional variation in migration behavior suggests that the labor-market consequences of migrant out-

---

2. Based on Mishra's (2004) estimates, the emigration loss in Mexico for 2000 would be 0.45
percent of GDP (0.5 times change in wages due to emigration of 8.0 percent times loss in labor supply due to emigration of 16.0 percent times labor share of income of 0.70). In that year,
remittances were 1.1 percent of Mexican GDP.

Table 9.1   Share of U.S. immigrants from Mexico in the population of Mexico

| Age cohort | | Percent residing in United States | | | | | |
| Age in 1990 | Age in 2000 | Males | | | Females | | |
		1990	2000	Change	1990	2000	Change
	16–25		11.99			7.68	
16–25	26–35	7.57	17.53	9.96	4.89	12.62	7.73
26–35	36–45	10.87	15.49	4.62	7.69	11.90	4.21
36–45	46–55	9.18	12.21	3.03	7.47	10.44	2.97
46–55	56–65	7.00	8.64	1.64	6.44	8.36	1.92
56–65		5.70			5.84		

Source: Chiquiar and Hanson (2005).
Notes: This table shows Mexican immigrants in the United States as a percentage of the population of individuals born in Mexico (equal to the sum of the Mexican-born population residing in Mexico and the Mexican-born population residing in the United States) by age and sex categories. The sample is individuals sixteen–sixty-five years old (in the United States, excluding those in group quarters; in Mexico, excluding those not born in the country). Residents of Mexico in 1990 are the 1 percent microsample of the *XII Censo General de Población y Vivienda, 1990,* and in 2000 are a 10 percent random sample of the 10 percent microsample of the *XIII Censo General de Población y Vivienda, 2000.* Mexican immigrants are from the 1990 and 2000 5 percent U.S. Public Use Microsample.

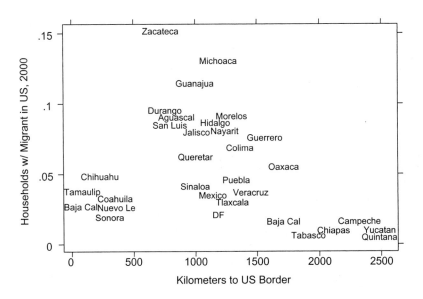

Fig. 9.2   Rate of migration to the United States: 1995–2000 by Mexican state

flows may be concentrated in specific areas. If this is true, estimates of the impact of emigration at the national level may understate its impact on the most affected regions. While the importance of specific sending regions in Mexican migration to the United States has long been recognized (Cardoso 1980), there is relatively little empirical work that assesses the regional economic effects of emigration in Mexico (Durand, Massey, and Zenteno 2001).

In this paper I examine the regional impacts of emigration on labor supply and labor market earnings in Mexico. I compare changes in labor market outcomes across individuals between 1990 and 2000 in two groups of states, states that had high emigration rates in the 1950s and states that had low emigration rates in the 1950s. There are two key identifying assumptions in my analysis. One is that labor is sufficiently immobile across Mexican regions for region-specific labor supply shocks to affect regional earnings differentials. Robertson (2000), Chiquiar (2005), and Hanson (2004) provide evidence of region-specific labor market shocks having affected Mexico's regional wage structure, which is consistent with some degree of regional labor immobility. The second identifying assumption is that current opportunities to migrate to the United States depend on regional historical migration patterns. One reason this may be the case is that migration networks are regionally organized and historically dependent. Munshi (2003) and Orrenius and Zavodny (2005) are recent contributions to a large literature that finds that in Mexico access to family or community networks helps migrants enter and succeed in the United States.[3]

In the estimation, I use migration rates in the 1950s as a reduced-form determinant of current migration opportunities. Because high emigration in the past could have altered regions in a manner that affects current labor market conditions, a reduced-form approach is more appropriate than using past migration behavior as an instrument for current migration. To control for internal migration, I use the 1950s emigration rate in an individual's *birth state,* rather than his or her current state of residence. Historical migration rates in an individual's birth state are thus meant to capture current access to migration networks, and so current opportunities to emigrate, in the Mexican regional labor market in which an individual is located. The persistence in regional differences in migration behavior (figure 9.3) is roughly consistent with my identifying assumptions.

The challenges to identifying the regional consequences of emigration in Mexico are analogous to those in identifying the regional consequences of immigration in the United States. Many studies have found that across U.S. cities and states immigrant inflows are only weakly negatively correlated with wage changes for U.S. native workers, suggesting that immigration has had little impact on the U.S. wage structure (see LaLonde and Topel 1997; Smith and Edmonston 1997; Borjas 1999; Card 2001). Borjas, Freeman, and Katz (1997) argue that cross-area wage regressions of this type identify the wage impact of immigration only under restrictive assump-

---

3. An implicit third identifying assumption is that emigration incentives for Mexicans were stronger in the 1990s than in previous decades, which in combination with the second assumption would imply that any negative labor supply shock associated with emigration would be larger in states with a longer history of U.S. migration. Data presented in section 9.3 are consistent with this assumption.

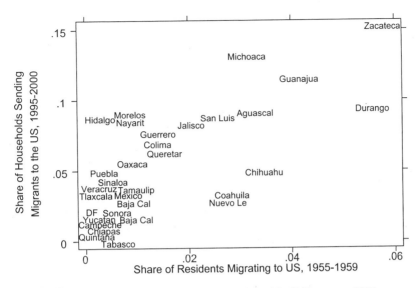

Fig. 9.3 State rates of migration to the United States in 1990s versus 1950s

tions. The tendency for immigrants to settle in regions with high wage growth makes estimates of the immigration wage impact based on cross-area regressions susceptible to upward bias. The standard practice of using the preceding decade's regional immigrant stock to instrument for current regional immigrant inflows may not be valid if regional labor market shocks persist over time. Borjas (2003) examines age and education cohorts at the national level and finds larger wage effects from immigration. He estimates that over 1980–2000 the elasticity of U.S. native wages with respect to immigrant inflows was 0.3–0.4 and that immigration contributed to a decrease in U.S. average wages of 3 percent.

Similar to the cross-area regression approach, I distinguish between Mexican states based on historical migration behavior. However, distinct from this approach I am able to use much longer lags on regional migration rates and to measure historical migration rates in an individual's birth state. These features help address the concerns that (a) regional labor market shocks may persist for more than a decade, and (b) an individual's current state of residence may be affected by current regional migration rates. The assumptions underlying my approach are thus perhaps less restrictive than those underlying the standard cross-area approach in literature on U.S. immigration.

An obvious challenge for the estimation is that there may be other, unobserved differences between high and low migration states that may affect current labor market outcomes. By examining regional differences in changes in outcomes, rather than regional differences in outcome levels, I am able to control for time-invariant–region-specific characteristics. Still, there may have been other shocks in the 1990s that had differential effects on regions with high versus low opportunities to migrate to the United States. Candidate shocks include the North American Free Trade Agreement (NAFTA), privatization and deregulation of industry, reform of Mexico's land-tenure system, and the 1994–1995 peso crisis.[4] The potential for these shocks to contaminate the analysis is an important concern, which I address in discussing qualifications to my results.

In the next section, I document further how migration behavior varies across regions of Mexico and discuss the criterion I use for selecting which Mexican states to include in my sample. In section 9.3, I describe how changes in labor supply vary across high- and low-migration states in Mexico and compare mean earnings and the distribution of earnings in high- and low-migration states. In section 9.4, I use standard parametric techniques and nonparametric techniques developed by DiNardo, Fortin, and Lemieux (1996) and Leibbrandt, Levinsohn, and McCrary (2004) to examine how earnings have changed over time in high- and low-migration states. By wage of conclusion in section 9.5, I discuss limitations of the estimation strategy and ideas for extending the analysis.

9.2   Regional Patterns of Emigration in Mexico

9.2.1   Data Sources

Data for the analysis come from two Mexican sources. In 1990, I use the 1 percent microsample of the *XII Censo General de Población y Vivienda, 1990,* and in 2000 I use a 10 percent random sample of the 10 percent microsample of the *XIII Censo General de Población y Vivienda, 2000.* Unfortunately, the 1990 Census contains no information about household emigration behavior. The 2000 Census includes two questions related to emigration: (a) whether anyone from the household migrated to the United States (or another foreign country) in the last five years (and the number, age, and gender of these individuals), and (b) whether anyone in the household received income in the previous month in the form of remittances from migrants located abroad (and the quantity received). These questions have obvious shortcomings. They provide no indication of the education of migrants, return or round-trip migration, migration before 1995, annual receipts of remittances, or transfers from migrants in kind rather than in cash. Still, the 2000 Census is useful in that it is the only nationally representative sample available for Mexico that contains information about migration to the United States.

---

4. See Chiquiar (2003) on recent policy changes in Mexico. For work on the labor market implications of globalization in Mexico, see Cragg and Epelbaum (1996), Feenstra and Hanson (1997), Revenga (1997), Hanson and Harrison (1999), Robertson (2000, 2004), Feliciano (2001), Fairris (2003), Ariola and Juhn (2003), Chiquiar (2005), and Hanson (2004).

For data on historical migration patterns, I use estimates of state emigration rates from Woodruff and Zenteno (2001). They calculate the fraction of each Mexican state's population that migrated to the United States over 1955–1959 by combining data on Mexican state populations with data on annual U.S. immigration of temporary legal workers from each Mexican state under the U.S. Bracero Program. The Bracero Program, which lasted from 1942 to 1965, allowed U.S. employers to import workers from Mexico (and the Caribbean) to fulfill short-term labor contracts. Most *braceros* worked in agriculture (Calavita 1992). Woodruff and Zenteno (2001) also provide data on state emigration rates in 1924, which I use in some empirical exercises.

For the analysis of earnings, I focus on men as their labor force participation rates are relatively stable over time, rising modestly from 73 percent in 1990 to 74 percent in 2000 (and are quite similar in high- and low-migration states). Labor force participation rates for women are low and variable over time, rising from 21 percent in 1990 to 32 percent in 2000. For women, this creates issues of sample selection associated with who supplies labor outside the home that complicates examining changes in the distribution of earnings.

9.2.2 Regional Patterns in Mexican Migration to the United States

Large scale migration from Mexico to the United States began in the early twentieth century. The construction of railroads in the late nineteenth century linked interior Mexico to the U.S.-Mexico border, which gave U.S. employers improved access to Mexican labor (Cardoso 1980). In the early 1900s, growers in Texas began to recruit farm laborers in Mexico. At the time, the population on the Texas-Mexico border was small and dispersed. To find workers, recruiters followed the main rail line into Mexico, which ran southwesterly through relatively densely populated states in the west-central region of the country. Early migrants came primarily from nine states in this region (Durand, Massey, and Zenteno 2001).[5] The recruitment efforts of U.S. employers intensified in the 1920s after the U.S. Congress imposed stringent quotas on U.S. legal immigration, which sharply reduced immigration of low-skilled labor from southern and eastern Europe. Recruitment intensified further in the 1940s, after Congress passed legislation allowing large-scale temporary legal immigration from Mexico under the Bracero Program (Calavita 1992). From the 1920s to the 1960s, the nine west-central states accounted for 44.0 percent to 56.1 percent of Mexican migration to the United States, but only 27.1 percent to 31.5 percent of Mexico's total population (Durand, Massey, and Zenteno 2001).

---

5. These nine states are Aguascalientes, Colima, Durango, Guanajuato, Jalisco, Michoacán, Nayarit, San Luis Potosí, and Zacatecas.

After working in the United States, many migrants return to Mexico where they often assist later generations in emigrating. Migrants remaining in the United States have created home-town associations that help members of their communities in Mexico make the transition to living north of the border (Cano 2004). In addition to home-town associations, there appear to be many informal networks through which current migrants help prospective migrants enter the United States, find housing in U.S. cities, and obtain jobs with U.S. employers. These networks are often embedded in relationships involving family, kin, or community of birth, which gives them a strong regional component. Of 218 home-town associations formed by Mexican immigrants enumerated in 2002 survey of such organizations in southern California, 86.6 percent were associated with one of the nine west-central states (Cano 2004). Networks appear to be important for migrant outcomes in the receiving country. Munshi (2003) finds that Mexican immigrants in the United States are more likely to be employed the larger is the U.S. population of residents from their home community in Mexico (where he instruments for the size of the home-community population using time series data on regional rainfall in Mexico). The importance of migrant networks for migration behavior and their strong regional character may help explain regional persistence in migration patterns.

Figure 9.3 provides graphical evidence of persistence in regional migration behavior. The states that had high migration rates in the 1950s, during the height of the Bracero Program, continue to be high-migration states. The correlation between state emigration rates in the 1995–2000 and the 1955–1959 periods is 0.73. The correlation between state migration rates in the 1995–2000 and 1924 periods is 0.48.

As figure 9.2 illustrates, high-migration states are not those closest to the United States. Nor does income appear to be the sole determinant of emigration. Table 9.2 reports regressions of state emigration rates in 1995–2000 on income and other state characteristics. In column (1), there is a negative correlation between state emigration rates and state per capita GDP, but the explanatory power of income is low. In column (2), adding distance to the United States (and distance squared) more than doubles the R-squared of the regression. The relation between emigration and proximity to the United States is nonlinear, with emigration initially rising with distance (reflecting low emigration in states on the U.S. border) and then declining with distance (reflecting high emigration for central states and low emigration for distant southern states). In column (3), adding the state emigration rate in 1924 as an independent variable raises the R^2 of the regression from 0.25 to 0.46. However, there appears to be little covariation between the 1995–2000 and 1924 emigration rates that is independent of the 1950s emigration rate. In column (4), once the 1955–1959 emigration rate is added, the R^2 rises further to 0.67, and the 1924 migration rate becomes statistically insignificant, reflecting the strong historical persistence

Table 9.2   **Emigration and characteristics of Mexican states**

	Migration to United States, 1995–2000			
	(1)	(2)	(3)	(4)
Constant	0.231	0.169	0.211	0.175
	(0.085)	(0.085)	(0.098)	(0.077)
Log per capita GDP in 1995	–0.025	–0.036	–0.03	–0.017
	(0.011)	(0.011)	(0.011)	(0.009)
Log distance to United States		0.070	0.006	–0.025
		(0.027)	(0.029)	(0.026)
Log distance to United States^2		–0.007	0.000	0.003
		(0.003)	(0.003)	(0.003)
Migration rate (1924)			32.813	4.295
			(10.210)	(10.210)
Migration rate (1955–59)				1.919
				(0.386)
Adjusted R^2	0.116	0.252	0.456	0.667
N	32	32	32	32

Notes: The sample is the thirty-one states of Mexico plus the Federal District. The dependent variable is the average share of households in a state that had sent a migrant to the United States in the 1995–2000 period. Standard errors are in parentheses.

in state emigration patterns. Columns (5)–(8) repeat the exercise using the fraction of households in 2000 receiving remittances from migrants abroad as the dependent variable, with similar results.

If states with relatively high emigration rates are also states that are more exposed to other aspects of globalization, then the empirical analysis might confound the effects of emigration with the effects of trade or capital flows. During the 1980s and 1990s, the Mexican government lowered barriers to international trade and foreign investment. Chiquiar (2005) and Hanson (2004) find that since 1985 Mexican states more engaged in international trade have enjoyed faster growth in average income and labor earnings. However, high emigration states do not appear to have benefited disproportionately from trade and investment reform. As expected, trade liberalization has affected states on the U.S.-Mexico border most strongly, and, as figure 9.2 shows, border states are not high emigration states. Most high-emigration states appear to have relatively low exposure to foreign trade and investment. This is seen in figures 9.4 and 9.5, which plot the fraction of the state population migrating to the United States over 1995–2000 against the share of foreign direct investment in state GDP and the share of imports in state GDP. Table 9.3 shows that across Mexico states in the 1990s, emigration rates are weakly negatively correlated with exposure to trade and foreign investment. It appears high exposure to emigration is not associated with high exposure to globalization. I discuss variation in state exposure to these and other shocks again in section 9.5.

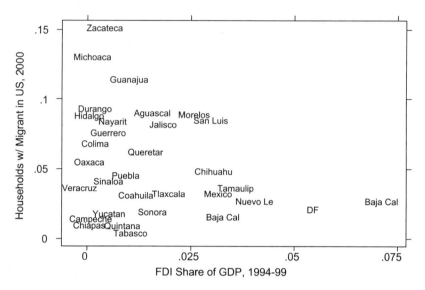

Fig. 9.4   State exposure to emigration and foreign direct investment

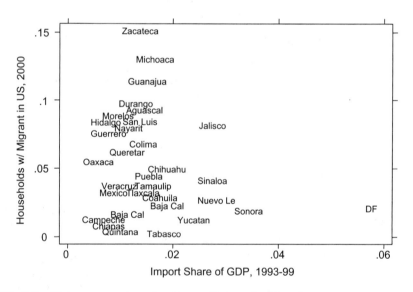

Fig. 9.5   State exposure to emigration and international trade

9.2.3   Sample Design

The goal of this paper is to examine the regional labor market consequences of emigration in Mexico. One approach would be to utilize data on
migration to the United States in Mexico's 2000 population census. Using
the 2000 data, I could compare labor market outcomes in households with

Table 9.3   **Correlation in measures of exposures to globalization across Mexican states**

	Maquiladora value added/ State GDP	Foreign direct investment/ State GDP	Imports/ State GDP	Share of state population migrating to United States, 1995–2000
Foreign direct investment/State GDP	0.391 (0.027)			
Imports/State GDP	−0.007 (0.968)	0.571 (0.001)		
Share of state population migrating to United States, 1995–2000	−0.128 (0.484)	−0.368 (0.038)	−0.253 (0.162)	
Share of state population migrating to United States, 1955–1959	0.188 (0.303)	−0.123 (0.502)	−0.133 (0.468)	0.725 (0.000)

Notes: The sample is the thirty-one states of Mexico plus the Federal District. Shares of state GDP (maquiladora value added, foreign direct investment, imports) are averages over the period 1993–1999. Correlations are weighted by state share of the national population (averaged over 1990 to 2000). *P*-values are in parentheses.

emigrants to outcomes in households without emigrants. Or, combining the household cross sections in 1990 and 2000, I could examine the covariation between the 1990–2000 change in household outcomes with the 1995–2000 state emigration rate. The obvious concern with either of these approaches is that household migration behavior is endogenous. The unobserved characteristics of households that affect their earnings and labor supply are also likely to affect whether households send migrants to the United States.

One way to address the endogeneity problem would be to use historical state emigration rates as an instrument for current opportunities to migrate abroad. The discussion in section 9.2.2 suggests that the 1950s emigration rate in an individual's birth state would be a good indicator of an individual's access to migration networks and so of an individual's relative opportunity to migrate to the United States. Using data from the 2000 Census, unreported probit regressions show that the likelihood a household either has sent a migrant to the United States in the last five years or has received remittances from abroad in the last month is strongly positively correlated with the 1955–1959 emigration rate in the household head's birth state.[6]

6. Additional controls in this regression are a cubic in age of the household head, dummies for the educational attainment of the household head, the sex of the household head, and dummy variables for the state of residence. Evaluated at mean values for the other regressors, individuals born in high-migration states are 24.3 percent more likely to have had someone in their household migrate to the United States in the last five years and 21.7 percent more likely to have received remittances from migrants located abroad in the last month (with both of these effects very precisely estimated).

However, historical state emigration rates are unlikely to be a valid instrument for current migration rates. Emigration opportunities in an individual's birth state may have affected an individual's accumulation of human capital, either by influencing the individual's early employment prospects (if local emigration rates affect local wage levels) or the quality of education the individual received as a youth (if remittances or local income levels affect the quality of local schools). Past emigration opportunities are thus likely to affect current labor market outcomes directly, through their impact on current emigration opportunities, and indirectly, through their impact on an individual's stock of human capital (which is observed imperfectly).

Given these concerns, I take a reduced-form approach by comparing changes in cross-section labor market outcomes, where I categorize individuals according to the historical emigration rate in their birth state. In so doing, I capture both the direct and indirect effects of historical emigration opportunities on current labor market outcomes. In presenting the empirical results, I will discuss whether the reduced-form effect of historical emigration rates on labor market outcomes is likely to under- or overstate the effect attributable solely to current emigration opportunities.

My empirical strategy is to compare labor market outcomes in regions that have been more or less exposed to opportunities to migrate to the United States. Table 9.4 describes the sample of high-migration and low-migration states.[7] I drop the six border states from the sample because these states have benefited disproportionately from trade and investment liberalization. Most border states had above average emigration rates in the 1950s, and including them in the sample could confound the effects of emigration with those of other aspects of globalization. To help isolate the effects of emigration, I limit high-migration states to those with emigration rates in the top three deciles of nonborder states and low-migration states to those with emigration rates in the bottom three deciles of nonborder states. In 2000, 10.4 percent of households in the seven high-migration states had sent a migrant to the United States in the previous five years, compared with only 2.1 percent of households in the seven low-migration states.

With the exception of the Federal District, in which part of Mexico City is located, all the low-migration states are in southern Mexico. Per capita income in the Federal District is over three times that in the southern low-

7. Figure 9.3 shows that while most states that had high emigration rates in the 1950s also had high emigration rates in the 1990s, there is some resorting between the groups. Some formerly high-migration states no longer are (e.g., the border states of Chihuahua, Nuevo Leon, and Sonora) and some formerly low-migration have become high-migration states (e.g., the central and western states of Hidalgo, Morelos, and Nayarit). Changes in state emigration rates over time suggest other factors, besides historical patterns, also affect migration behavior.

Table 9.4   **Ranking Mexican states by historical emigration rates**

| | Migration rate | | | |
Rank/State	1995–2000	1955–1959	Per capita GDP 1995	Population in 2000
High migration				
Aguascalientes	0.090	0.032	1,728	952
Durango	0.093	0.055	1,329	1,440
Guanajuato	0.114	0.041	1,062	4,604
Michoacán	0.130	0.031	901	3,921
San Luis Potosí	0.087	0.025	1,094	2,362
Zacatecas	0.151	0.059	878	1,348
Jalisco	0.082	0.020	1,479	6,272
Mean	0.104	0.033	1,197	2,986
Mean w/o Jalisco	0.114	0.038	1,077	2,438
Low migration				
Campeche	0.011	0.000	2,341	680
Chiapas	0.009	0.000	678	3,877
Quintana Roo	0.009	0.000	2,437	876
Tabasco	0.007	0.002	951	1,911
Veracruz	0.037	0.000	912	6,923
Yucatán	0.013	0.002	1,159	1,646
Federal District	0.021	0.001	3,823	8,544
Mean	0.021	0.001	2,006	3,494
Mean w/o Federal District	0.021	0.001	1,030	2,652
Other nonborder states (12)	0.049	0.007	1,096	2,925
Border states (6)	0.032	0.020	2,054	2,759

Notes: This table shows rates of migration to the United States, per capita GDP, and population for Mexican states. Means are weighted by the 2000 population of the subgroup. Population in the year 2000 is in thousands.

migration states. And, as figures 9.4 and 9.5 show, the Federal District has much higher exposure to international trade than the southern low-migration states. There is also heterogeneity among high-migration states. Jalisco, in which Guadalajara (the country's second largest city) is located, has high relatively high exposure to international trade. By way of checking the robustness of the results, I will perform the analysis with and without individuals born in the Federal District or Jalisco included in the sample.

9.3   Preliminary Analysis

9.3.1   Population Changes in High- and Low-Migration States

The most direct effect of emigration has been to reduce the relative population of young adults born in high-migration states. Figures 9.6 and 9.7

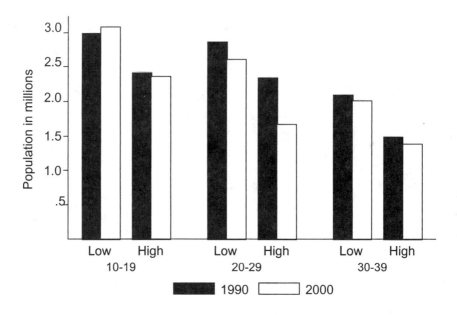

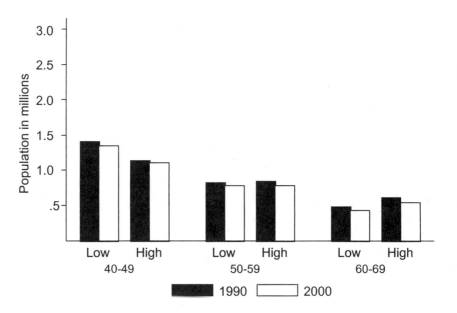

Fig. 9.6   Cohort sizes for men born in high- and low-migration states (based on age in 2000)

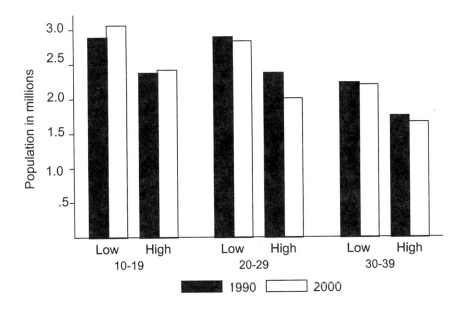

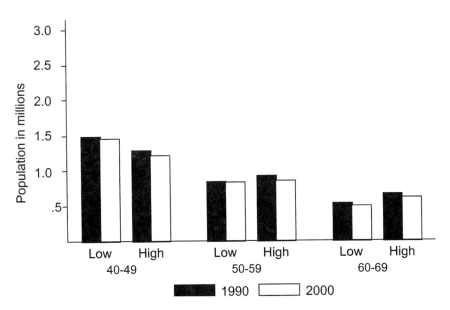

Fig. 9.7 Cohort sizes for women born in high- and low-migration states (based on age in 2000)

show cohort sizes based on age in 2000 for males and females born in high-migration or low-migration states. In the absence of measurement error, changes in population size are due to either net migration abroad or to death. Cohort sizes decline for all age-sex groups, except ten- to nineteen-year-olds.[8] Population declines are largest for twenty- to twenty-nine-year-old men (men born between 1971 and 1980) from high-migration states, whose number declines by 33.4 log points. In low-migration states, the number of twenty- to twenty-nine-year-old men drops by only 9.4 log points, such that the relative decline of the twenty- to twenty-nine-year-old male population in high-migration states over 1990–2000 is 24.0 log points. Overall, the population of twenty- to fifty-nine-year-old men declines by 9.8 log points in high-migration relative to low-migration states.[9]

Absolute and relative changes in female cohorts are smaller. The cohort of twenty- to twenty-nine-year-old women declines by 16.8 log points in high-migration states and 2.0 log points in low-migration states. Overall, the population of twenty- to fifty-nine-year-old women declines by 8.4 log points in high-migration relative to log-migration states.[10] Figure 9.8 shows that as a result of higher emigration rates for males, the share of men in the population of twenty- to twenty-nine-year-olds from high-migration states falls from 49 percent to 45 percent during the 1990s. In low-migration states the change is more modest, with a drop of 50 percent to 48 percent.

It appears men and women born in high-migration states in Mexico have become more likely to migrate abroad. One might also wonder whether they have become more likely to migrate internally. Table 9.5 reports probit regressions using data from 1990 and 2000 on whether individuals born in high-migration or low-migration states have changed their state of residence since birth. The regressors are (a) a cubic in age, dummy variables for

8. One explanation for the increases in cohort size for ten- to nineteen-year-olds is undercount of the population in the 1990 census (in which case figures 9.7 and 9.8 may understate reductions in cohort sizes over the decade). Conversations with INEGI (Mexico's statistical agency) suggest the precision of population estimates have improved with time. It is unlikely that regional differences in mortality could account for the differential regional population changes in figures 9.7 and 9.8. Migrants tend to be positively selected in terms of health, suggesting that mortality rates are likely to be higher among nonmigrants than migrants. If this pattern holds, then figures 9.7 and 9.8 would understate regional differences in population changes associated with migration as low-migration states would tend to have relatively high mortality rates. However, the fact that mortality rates among young adults are low suggests this is a minor issue.
9. One might imagine that internal migration in Mexico could have partly reversed the change in relative regional labor supplies due to emigration. The large exodus of individuals born in high-migration states might have given individuals from other states an incentive to move in. But data on population by state of residence (rather than state of birth) suggest that this is not the case. During the 1990s, high-migration states experienced the largest net decrease in resident population, followed by low-migration states. Border states had the largest net increase in resident population.
10. Dropping the Federal District and Jalisco, the relative population of twenty- to fifty-nine-year-olds in high-migration states declines by 9.4 log points for men and 7.3 log points for women.

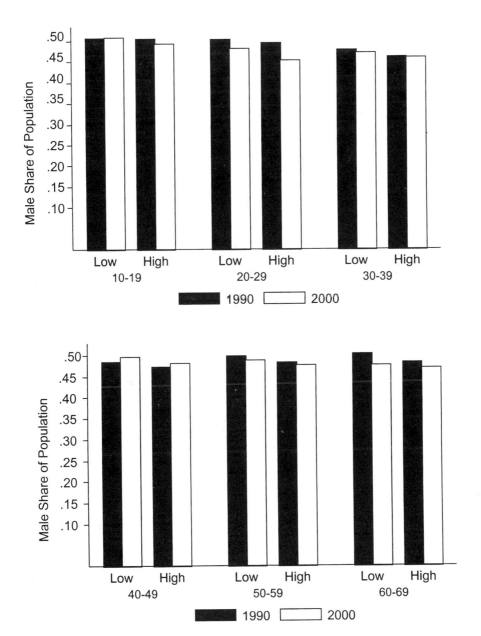

Fig. 9.8 Share of men in the population by age cohort in high- and low-migration states

Table 9.5   Probability of internal migration

	Moved since birth	
	Men	Women
A. All high-migration and low-migration states		
Year 2000 · high migration	0.034	0.041
	(0.014)	(0.130)
R	0.068	0.060
N	159,067	174,052
B. Excluding the Federal District and Jalisco		
Year 2000 · high migration	0.016	0.021
	(0.010)	(0.007)
R	0.077	0.066
N	107,310	116,864

Notes: This table reports results for probit regressions in which the dependent variable equals one if an individual resides in a different state than his or her birth state and zero otherwise. The sample is men and women in Mexico aged twenty–forty-nine in 1990 or thirty–fifty-nine in 2000 born in a high-migration or a low-migration Mexican state. The other regressors are: (a) a cubic in age, dummy variables for five categories of educational attainment (one–five years, six–eight years, nine–eleven years, twelve–fifteen years, or sixteen+ years), a dummy variable for marital status, dummy variables for presence of children in the household (ages zero–five, six–twelve, or thirteen–eighteen years), dummy variables for the state of birth, and a dummy variable for the year 2000; (b) interactions between the age, education, marital status, and children variables and the year 2000 dummy; and (c) interactions between the age, education, marital status, and children variables and a dummy variable for whether the individual was born in a high-migration state. The coefficients show the change in the probability of internal migration associated with an individual being from a high-migration state in 2000 versus that in 1990 (evaluated at mean values for other regressors). Standard errors (corrected for correlation in the errors within birth states) are in parentheses.

five categories of educational attainment (one–five years, six–eight years, nine–eleven years, twelve–fifteen years, sixteen+ years), a dummy variable for marital status, dummy variables for presence of children in the household (ages zero–five, six–twelve, thirteen–eighteen), dummy variables for the state of birth, and a dummy variable for 2000; (b) interactions between the age, education, marital status, and children variables and the year 2000 dummy; (c) interactions between the age, education, marital status, and children variables and a dummy variable for whether the individual was born in a high-migration state; and (d) the interaction between the year 2000 dummy and the dummy for whether an individual was born in a high-migration state. I report results only for this last variable, which captures the change in the likelihood of having migrated internally over 1990–2000 for individuals born in a high-migration state relative to those born in a low-migration state.

Between 1990 and 2000, men from high-migration states become 3.4 percent more likely to live in a state different than their birth state, relative to men from low-migration states. Excluding the Federal District and Jalisco, the estimate falls to 1.6 percent. Between 1990 and 2000, women from high-migration states become 4.1 percent more likely to live in a state different than their birth state, relative to women from low-migration states. Dropping the Federal District and Jalisco the estimate falls to 2.1 percent (and remains precisely estimated). It appears that during the 1990s, individuals from high-migration states were more likely to migrate either externally or internally.

9.3.2   Education and Earnings in High- and Low-Migration States

The educational profile of individuals by birth state varies between high- and low-migration states. Table 9.6 shows the distribution of schooling by age cohort in 2000 for the sample of Mexican states. For men, average schooling is higher in low-migration states. Among thirty- to thirty-nine-year-old men in 2000, 62.6 percent had completed nine or more years of schooling in low-migration states, versus 47.7 percent in high-migration states. For women, these figures are 57.5 percent and 42.7 percent, respectively. These differences, however, depend on including the Federal District among low-migration states, which has the most educated work force in the country. Once the Federal District and Jalisco are dropped from the sample, educational attainment is relatively similar in the two groups of states, with 46.9 percent of men and 40.1 percent of women in the thirty–thirty-nine age cohort having completed nine or more years of education in low-migration states and 45.9 percent of men and 40.6 percent of women in the thirty–thirty-nine age cohort doing so in high-migration states.

Despite comparable or higher education levels in low-migration states, wages appear to be higher in high-migration states. Table 9.7 shows average hourly wages by age and schooling cohort in 1990 and 2000.[11] For the full sample of states, wages are higher in high-migration states for most cohorts in 1990 and for all cohorts in 2000. In 1990, for men with six–eight years of education, which spans mean schooling levels in either year, average hourly wages are $0.06 to $0.44 higher in high-migration states, depending on the age cohort (based on age in 2000). In 2000, these wage differentials widen to $0.25 to $0.74. Wages in high-migration states increase relative to wages in low-migration states in fifteen of the eighteen age-schooling cohorts. Dropping the Federal District and Jalisco, wages remain higher in high-migration states in most cohorts for both years.

Figure 9.9, which shows kernel densities for log average hourly wages, gives another perspective on wages in high- and low-migration states. In

11. Average hourly wages are calculated as monthly labor income/(4.5 × hours worked last week). I need to assume individuals work all weeks of a month, which could bias wage estimates downward. To avoid measurement error associated with implausibly low wage values or with top coding of earnings, I restrict the sample to be individuals with hourly wages between $0.05 and $20 in Mexico (in 2000 U.S. dollars). This restriction is nearly identical to dropping the largest and smallest 0.5 percent of wage values.

Table 9.6   Schooling by age cohort in high-migration and low-migration states, 2000

Sex	State migration rate	2000 age cohort	Years of schooling					
			0	1–5	6–8	9–11	12–15	16+
Men	Low	30–39	0.042	0.131	0.201	0.262	0.200	0.164
	Low	40–49	0.064	0.192	0.241	0.174	0.145	0.184
	Low	50–59	0.119	0.289	0.240	0.124	0.097	0.132
	High	30–39	0.046	0.200	0.277	0.238	0.135	0.104
	High	40–49	0.084	0.283	0.290	0.142	0.084	0.118
	High	50–59	0.169	0.377	0.236	0.089	0.054	0.074
Excluding Federal District & Jalisco	Low	30–39	0.072	0.220	0.238	0.218	0.147	0.104
	Low	40–49	0.108	0.307	0.253	0.127	0.089	0.116
	Low	50–59	0.182	0.404	0.213	0.075	0.056	0.070
	High	30–39	0.052	0.215	0.274	0.233	0.129	0.097
	High	40–49	0.090	0.292	0.288	0.142	0.082	0.106
	High	50–59	0.174	0.386	0.235	0.089	0.050	0.065
Women	Low	30–39	0.064	0.155	0.205	0.237	0.210	0.128
	Low	40–49	0.105	0.227	0.255	0.162	0.156	0.095
	Low	50–59	0.197	0.278	0.238	0.125	0.113	0.050
	High	30–39	0.052	0.220	0.302	0.217	0.141	0.069
	High	40–49	0.103	0.350	0.292	0.122	0.083	0.050
	High	50–59	0.203	0.407	0.232	0.086	0.054	0.019
Excluding Federal District & Jalisco	Low	30–39	0.113	0.261	0.225	0.186	0.131	0.084
	Low	40–49	0.177	0.353	0.231	0.105	0.076	0.057
	Low	50–59	0.301	0.367	0.195	0.067	0.048	0.022
	High	30–39	0.060	0.236	0.298	0.205	0.135	0.066
	High	40–49	0.113	0.364	0.283	0.116	0.079	0.044
	High	50–59	0.218	0.414	0.216	0.083	0.052	0.017

Notes: This table shows the distribution of educational attainment by age cohort for individuals thirty–fifty-nine years old in 2000 born in high-migration or low-migration Mexican states (based on 1955–1959 emigration rates).

1990, wages have lower dispersion and a higher mean in high-migration states when compared to low-migration states. In 2000, these features are more pronounced. Relative to high-migration states, wages in low-migration states show an increase in relative dispersion and in relative mass in the lower tail. In figure 9.10, which shows wage densities excluding the Federal District and Jalisco, the relative rightward shift in the wage distribution for high-migration is more evident.[12]

Either in terms of average wages or wage densities, it appears that un-

12. In the United States, considerable research suggests that changes in minimum wages have affected wage distributions, particularly for women (e.g., DiNardo, Fortin, and Lemieux 1996). While Mexico does have a minimum wage (which varies by industry and region), it is widely regarded to matter only for very-low-wage workers. During the high inflation of the 1980s, the government allowed minimum wages to fall dramatically in real terms. By the mid to late 1990s, wages for workers in the middle of the wage distribution were typically quoted in two to three multiples of the minimum wage. See Woodruff (1999).

Table 9.7   Average hourly wages by age and schooling cohort, 1990 and 2000

Year	State migration rate	2000 age cohort	Years of schooling					
			0	1–5	6–8	9–11	12–15	16+
1990	Low	30–39	0.92	1.62	1.56	2.14	2.76	4.61
	Low	40–49	1.21	1.31	2.56	2.97	4.25	6.30
	Low	50–59	1.27	1.83	2.49	3.88	6.10	8.10
	High	30–39	1.41	1.77	1.76	2.77	2.80	5.00
	High	40–49	1.58	2.87	3.00	3.00	3.67	5.55
	High	50–59	1.53	1.93	2.55	3.80	4.76	7.13
2000	Low	30–39	0.61	1.06	1.19	1.50	2.59	5.11
	Low	40–49	0.54	0.70	1.31	1.84	3.25	6.19
	Low	50–59	0.60	0.85	1.57	1.89	3.56	6.97
	High	30–39	1.18	2.63	1.44	2.39	2.72	4.39
	High	40–49	1.21	1.22	2.05	2.02	3.51	5.12
	High	50–59	0.98	2.56	1.97	2.65	3.69	6.50
		Excluding the Federal District and Jalisco						
1990	Low	30–39	0.83	1.05	1.26	1.96	2.34	3.27
	Low	40–49	1.14	1.25	1.71	2.01	3.21	4.22
	Low	50–59	1.22	1.60	2.41	3.11	4.86	5.70
	High	30–39	1.31	1.74	1.68	1.75	2.80	4.36
	High	40–49	1.41	2.96	3.22	3.00	3.44	4.85
	High	50–59	1.49	1.64	2.43	3.96	4.47	6.71
2000	Low	30–39	0.56	1.05	1.06	1.23	2.28	3.79
	Low	40–49	0.51	0.63	1.11	1.70	2.64	5.54
	Low	50–59	0.56	0.79	1.29	1.75	3.20	5.88
	High	30–39	1.19	2.98	1.39	2.55	2.58	4.30
	High	40–49	1.10	1.11	2.19	1.86	3.13	4.96
	High	50–59	0.82	2.47	1.62	2.47	3.54	6.66

Notes: This table shows average hourly wages by age and schooling cohort for individuals aged twenty–forty-nine in 1990 or thirty–fifty-nine in 2000 born in a high-migration or a low-migration state. Wage levels are in 2000 U.S. dollars for men with average hourly earnings between $0.05 and $20. See footnote 10 on how wages are constructed.

conditional wages in high-migration states are higher than those in low-migration states and that this differential increases over the 1990s. This is seen clearly in figure 9.11, which shows the double difference in wage densities for high-migration and low-migration states (i.e., the 2000 difference in wage densities for high-migration and low-migration states, minus the 1990 difference in wage densities). Relative to low-migration states, high-migration states gain mass in the upper half of the wage distribution.

9.4   Decomposing Changes in Earnings

During the 1990s, the earnings gap appeared to increase between men born in high-migration states and men born in low-migration states. At face value, this change is difficult to interpret. It is possible that the large

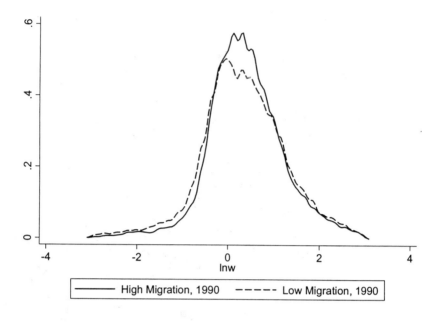

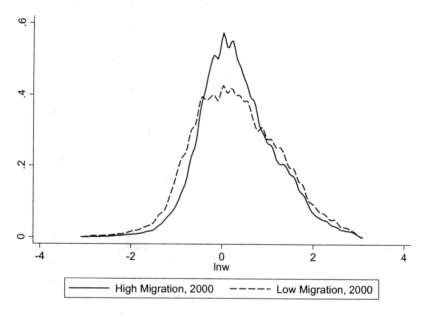

Fig. 9.9   **Kernel densities for average log hourly wages, 1990 and 2000**

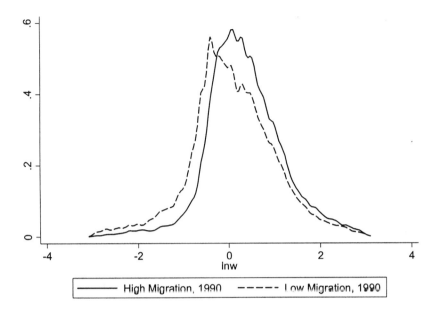

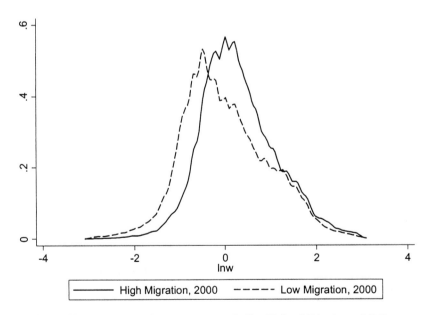

Fig. 9.10   Kernel densities for log wages, excluding Federal District and Jalisco

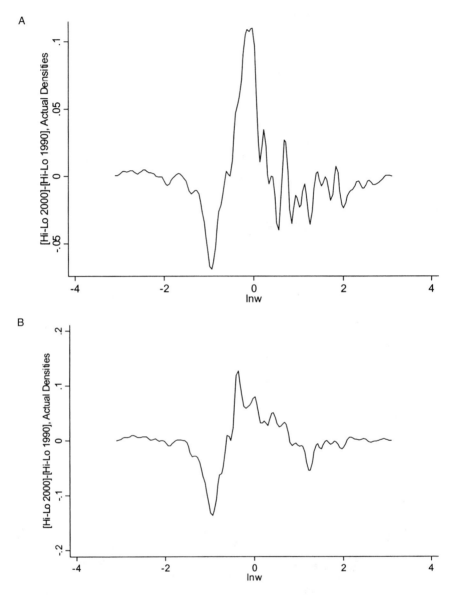

Fig. 9.11   1990 to 2000 change in wage densities for high-migration states relative to low-migration states: *A,* **Full sample;** *B,* **Excluding the Federal District and Jalisco**

exodus of individuals from high-migration states may have increased the wages of nonmigrating individuals from these states relative to wages for nonmigrating individuals from low-migration states. In this case, the national wage changes associated with emigration reported by Mishra (2004) would also be evident at the regional level.

However, other interpretations of the observed wage changes are plausible. Borjas (1987) suggests that in countries with high skill premia and high earnings inequality, such as Mexico, the less-skilled are likely to have the highest propensity to migrate to countries with low skill premia and low earnings inequality, such as the United States. In Mexico, if low-skill, low-wage individuals are more likely to migrate abroad (migrants are negatively selected in terms of skill), the apparent increase in wages in high-migration states may be due partly to shifts in labor force composition.

To describe wages changes in high-migration and low-migration states more thoroughly, I apply nonparametric techniques for constructing counterfactual wage densities developed by DiNardo, Fortin, and Lemieux (1996) and Leibbrandt, Levinsohn, and McCrary (2004). In the first exercise, I compare the 1990–2000 change in the distribution of earnings between high-migration and low-migration states, *holding the returns to observable characteristics (and the dispersion of residuals) constant.* By fixing the returns to characteristics but allowing the distribution of characteristics to vary over time and across regions, I isolate how regional differences in the composition of the labor force have changed. This will help reveal whether it is low-wage or high-wage individuals from high-migration states who are more likely to migrate abroad. In the second exercise, I compare the 1990–2000 change in the distribution of earnings between high-migration and low-migration states, *holding the distribution of individual characteristics constant.* By fixing the distribution of characteristics, but allowing the returns to characteristics to vary, I examine whether nonmigrating individuals in high-migration states have enjoyed wage gains relative to nonmigrating individuals in low-migration states.[13]

It is important to recognize that neither nonparametric exercise I perform amounts to a truly valid counterfactual. This is because emigration is likely to have changed both the distribution of worker characteristics *and* the returns to these characteristics. By looking at each change in isolation, the counterfactual differences in wage densities I construct represent only *partial* decompositions of the change in the wage distribution.[14] Neverthe-

---

13. DiNardo, Fortin, and Lemieux is not the only approach to nonparametrically decompose changes in wage distributions. See Machado and Mata (2005) and Autor, Katz, and Kearney (2004) for an alternative methodology.

14. A complete decomposition would separate wage changes into components due to changes in returns for given characteristics, changes in characteristics for given returns, and the interaction of changes in returns and changes in characteristics. The nonparametric analysis in effect ignores the third component.

less, the nonparametric analysis will be helpful for assessing the plausibility of the parametric results.

Following the nonparametric estimation, I consider a parametric regression of differential wage changes in high-migration and low-migration states on differential emigration opportunities (as summarized by historical emigration rates). The parametric approach will provide an estimate of the differential in wage growth between high-migration and low-migration states that is associated with emigration. There are several reasons why we might be reluctant to assign a causal interpretation to the parametric results, which I discuss in the concluding section.

Finally, the analysis doesn't address changes in the distribution of unobservables. If, holding observed characteristics constant, Mexican emigrants have low (high) unobserved ability relative to nonmigrants in Mexico, I would tend to understate the extent to which migrants are negatively (positively) selected in terms of skill.

9.4.1   Estimating Counterfactual Earnings Densities

Let $f(w \mid x, i, t)$ be the density of hourly labor earnings, w, conditional on a set of observed characteristics, x, in region i and time t. Define $h(x \mid i, t)$ as the density of observed characteristics among wage earners in region i and time t. For regions, $i = H$ indicates high-migration states, and $i = L$ indicates low-migration states; for time periods, $t = 00$ indicates the year 2000, and $t = 90$ indicates the year 1990. The observed density of labor earnings for individuals in region i at time t is

$$g(w \mid i, t) = \int f(w \mid x, i, t)h(x \mid i, t)dx.$$

Differences in $f(w \mid x, H, t)$ and $f(w \mid x, L, t)$ reflect differences in returns to observables in high- and low-migration states; differences in $h(x \mid H, t)$ and $h(x \mid L, t)$ reflect differences in the distribution of observables in high- and low-migration states. The empirical analysis examines how regional differences in these two sets of densities change over the 1990s.

In the first exercise, I compare the composition of the labor force across regions. I ask how the difference in earnings densities between high- and low-migration states changes over time, holding constant returns to observables such that only the distribution of observables varies across regions and years. The first decomposition I consider is how the wage density differs between high-migration and low-migration states in 1990 for a common set of returns to observable characteristics:

(1) $\int f(w \mid x, L, 90)h(x \mid H, 90)dx - \int f(w \mid x, L, 90)h(x \mid L, 90)dx$

The density difference in equation (1) evaluates the difference in the earnings distribution in high- and low-migration states in 1990, fixing the returns to observables to be that in low-migration states in 1990. This density difference characterizes the initial difference in the distribution of observables between high- and low-migration states. Applying DiNardo, Fortin, and Lemieux (1996), I rewrite (1) as

(2) $$\int(\theta^{L90\rightarrow H90} - 1)f(w\,|\,x, L, 90)h(x\,|\,L, 90)dx,$$

where

(3) $$\theta^{L90\rightarrow H90} = \frac{h(x\,|\,H, 90)}{h(x\,|\,L, 90)}.$$

Equation (2) is simply the observed marginal earnings density in low-migration states in 1990, adjusted by a weighting function. Given an estimate of the weighting function in (3), it would be straightforward to apply a kernel density estimator to equation (2). Following DiNardo, Fortin, and Lemieux, I estimate the weighting function in (3) by running a logit on the probability a Mexican male is from a low-migration state in 1990 for the sample of Mexican males from high-migration and low-migration states in 1990.

Consider the analogue to equation (2) for 2000. The 2000 difference in the earnings distribution in high- and low-migration states that is associated with differences in the distribution of observable characteristics can be written as

(4) $$\int f(w\,|\,x, L, 90)h(x\,|\,H, 00)dx - \int f(w\,|\,x, L, 90)h(x\,|\,L, 00)dx.$$

Using weighting functions analogous to (3), I rewrite equation (4) as

$$\int(\theta^{L90\rightarrow H00} - \theta^{L90\rightarrow L00})f(w\,|\,x, L, 90)h(x\,|\,L, 90)dx.$$

Putting (2) together with (5), we have the 1990 to 2000 change in the earnings distribution in high-migration versus low-migration states that is associated with changes in the distribution of observables:

(6) $$\left[\int f(w\,|\,x, L, 90)h(x\,|\,H, 00)dx - \int f(w\,|\,x, L, 90)h(x\,|\,L, 00)dx\right]$$
$$- \left[\int f(w\,|\,x, L, 90)h(x\,|\,H, 90)dx - \int f(w\,|\,x, L, 90)h(x\,|\,L, 90)dx\right]$$
$$= \int[(\theta^{L90\rightarrow H00} - \theta^{L90\rightarrow L00}) - (\theta^{L90\rightarrow H90} - 1)]f(w\,|\,x, L, 90)h(x\,|\,L, 90)dx.$$

Equation (6) shows the difference in the earnings distribution in high-migration versus low-migration states in 2000, relative to that in 1990, holding the returns to observables (and the dispersion of the residuals) constant. Because an individual's birth state is fixed, I can use (6) to evaluate changes in labor force composition in high-migration versus low-migration states, where I evaluate workers based on their place in the 1990 earnings distribution in low-migration states. To perform this exercise, I estimate a series of logit regressions to construct the weighting functions and then apply the weights to a kernel density estimator to obtain estimates for the densities described by (2), (5), and (6). The first two of these are for a *single difference* in densities and the third is for a *double difference* in densities.

The second exercise I perform is to examine how the returns to observable characteristics have changed in high- and low-migration states, holding the distribution of characteristics constant. For 1990, the difference in earnings densities we'd like to see is

(7) $\int f(w\,|\,x, H, 90)h(x\,|\,L, 90)dx - \int f(w\,|\,x, L, 90)h(x\,|\,L, 90)dx,$

which evaluates the difference in earnings distributions in high- and low-migration states in 1990, fixing the marginal density of observables to be that in low-migration states in 1990. Following the logic of DiNardo, Fortin, and Lemieux (1996), I rewrite equation (7) as

(8) $\int (\lambda^{L90\rightarrow H90} - 1)f(w\,|\,x, L, 90)h(x\,|\,L, 90)dx,$

where

(9) $$\lambda^{L90\rightarrow H90} = \frac{f(w\,|\,x, H, 90)}{f(w\,|\,x, L, 90)}.$$

The corresponding difference in densities for 2000 is

(10) $\int f(w\,|\,x, H, 00)h(x\,|\,L, 90)dx - \int f(w\,|\,x, L, 00)h(x\,|\,L, 90)dx,$

which evaluates the difference in earnings distribution between high- and low-migration states in 2000, again fixing the marginal density of observables to be that in low-migration states in 1990. Using the weights

(11) $\lambda^{L90\rightarrow H00} = \dfrac{f(w\,|\,x, H, 00)}{f(w\,|\,x, L, 90)}$ and $\lambda^{L90\rightarrow L00} = \dfrac{f(w\,|\,x, L, 00)}{f(w\,|\,x, L, 90)},$

I rewrite equation (10) as

(12) $\int (\lambda^{L90\rightarrow H00} - \lambda^{L90\rightarrow L00})f(w\,|\,x, L, 90)h(x\,|\,L, 90)dx.$

Putting equations (8) and (12) together,

(13) $\left(\int f(w\,|\,x, H, 00)h(x\,|\,L, 90)dx - \int f(w\,|\,x, L, 00)h(x\,|\,L, 90)dx \right.$

$\left. - \left(\int f(w\,|\,x, H, 90)h(x\,|\,L, 90)dx - \int f(w\,|\,x, L, 90)h(x\,|\,L, 90)dx \right) \right)$

$= \int [(\lambda^{L90\rightarrow H00} - \lambda^{L90\rightarrow L00}) - (\lambda^{L90\rightarrow H90} - 1)]$

$\cdot f(w\,|\,x, L, 90)h(x\,|\,L, 90)dx.$

Equation (13) shows the 1990 to 2000 change in earnings distribution in high-migration states relative to low-migration states, holding the distribution of observables constant. This is the component of the change in relative regional earnings densities associated with changes in relative regional returns to observable characteristics alone.

To estimate the weighting functions in (9) and (11), I use Leibbrandt, Levinsohn, and McCrary's (2004) extension of DiNardo, Fortin, and Lemieux (1996). As they show, applying Bayes' Axiom yields

$$(14) \quad \lambda^{L90 \to L00} = \frac{f(w \mid x, L, 00)}{f(w \mid x, L, 90)} = \frac{\Pr(t = 00, i = L \mid w, x)}{1 - \Pr(t = 00, i = L \mid w, x)}$$

$$\cdot \frac{1 - \Pr(t = 00, i = L \mid x)}{\Pr(t = 00, i = L \mid x)}$$

$$\lambda^{L90 \to H00} = \frac{f(w \mid x, H, 00)}{f(w \mid x, L, 90)} = \frac{\Pr(t = 00, i = H \mid w, x)}{1 - \Pr(t = 00, i = H \mid w, x)}$$

$$\cdot \frac{1 - \Pr(t = 00, i = H \mid x)}{\Pr(t = 00, i = H \mid x)}$$

$$\lambda^{L90 \to H90} = \frac{f(w \mid x, H, 90)}{f(w \mid x, L, 90)} = \frac{\Pr(t = 90, i = H \mid w, x)}{1 - \Pr(t = 90, i = H \mid w, x)}$$

$$\cdot \frac{1 - \Pr(t = 90, i = H \mid x)}{\Pr(t = 90, i = H \mid x)}.$$

Each weighting function in (14) is the product of odds ratios. In the first weight, the first ratio is the odds an individual is from a low-migration state in 2000 (based on a sample of individuals from low-migration states in 1990 and 2000), conditional on observables, x, and earnings, w; and the second ratio is the (inverse) odds an individual is from a low-migration state in 2000, conditional on just on x. To estimate the odds ratios, I estimate two logit models. In each case, the regressand is a $0-1$ variable on the outcome $i = L$ and $t = 00$ (based on a sample of $[i = L, t = 00]$ and $[i = L, t = 90]$). For the first logit, the regressors are x and w; for the second, the regressor is x alone. Other weights can be estimated analogously. After constructing the weights, I estimate (8), (12), and (13).

9.4.2 A Parametric Approach

To evaluate the association between emigration and earnings parametrically, I pool data on working-age men in 1990 and 2000 from high-migration and low-migration states and estimate the following difference-in-difference wage regression,

$$(15) \quad \ln w_{hst} = \alpha_s + \mathbf{X}_{hst}(\beta_1 + \beta_2 Y2000_{ht} + \beta_3 High_{hs})$$
$$+ \phi \cdot Y2000_{ht} \cdot High_{hs} + \varepsilon_{hst},$$

where w is average hourly earnings, $\mathbf{X}$ is a vector of observed characteristics, Y2000 is a dummy variable for the year 2000, and High is a dummy variable for whether an individual was born in a high-migration state. The regression includes controls for state-of-birth fixed effects and allows returns to observable characteristics to vary across regions and time. The coefficient, ϕ, captures the mean differential 1990 to 2000 change in earnings between high- and low-migration states.[15]

One important estimation issue is that shocks other than emigration may have had differential impacts on high- and low-migration states. I've already discussed the shock associated with NAFTA and other aspects of trade liberalization. Another shock was the peso crisis of 1995. After a bungled devaluation of the peso in 1994, Mexico chose to float its currency, which proceeded to plummet in value relative to the dollar. The ensuing increase in the peso value of dollar-denominated liabilities contributed to a banking collapse and a severe economic contraction. Low-migration states (excluding Mexico City) are modestly less industrialized than high-migration states and so may have been hurt less by the credit crunch. Also, low-migration states tend to have larger tourist industries, which may have benefited from the devaluation. Other shocks in the 1990s included a reform of Mexico's land tenure system in 1992, the privatization of state-owned enterprises, and industry deregulation. The existence of these shocks leaves the results subject to the caveat that factors other than emigration may have contributed to differential regional changes in earnings. I return to this issue in section 9.5.

9.4.3 Empirical Results

The sample for the analysis is the cohort of Mexican men aged twenty to forty-nine years in 1990 or thirty to fifty-nine years in 2000 who were born in one of the seven high-migration states or one of the seven low-migration states. By restricting the analysis to a single cohort, I limit possible contamination of the sample associated with more-educated younger workers entering the labor force and less-educated older workers exiting the labor force. The dependent variable is log average hourly labor earnings (see footnote 10).

Figure 9.12 shows kernel density estimates for the density differences in equations (2) and (5), which characterize the difference in earning distributions between high- and low-migration states holding constant the return to observable characteristics and residual dispersion. In 1990 and 2000, the density difference has negative mass above the mean and positive mass below the mean (where the mean over the entire sample of states is normalized to zero). This implies that in either year there are relatively few men from high-migration states with above-average earnings and relatively many men from high-migration states with below-average earnings. What-

---

15. Equation (15) is a standard difference-in-difference specification, which implies I estimate the mean differential in wage growth between high- and low-migration states. This approach ignores the possibility that the wage effect of being in a high-migration state may not be uniform throughout the wage distribution. A more elegant approach would be to estimate the regional differential in wage changes nonparametrically, as in the framework derived by Athey and Imbens (2003).

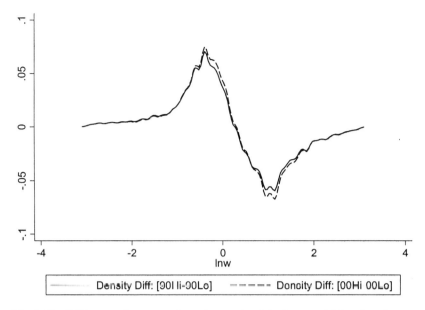

Fig. 9.12   Differences in counterfactual wage densities between high-migration and low-migration states (with returns to observable characteristics evaluated for low-migration states in 1990)

ever the source of this initial difference, it becomes modestly more pronounced during the 1990s. Between 1990 and 2000, the density difference loses mass above the mean and gains mass below the mean. Compared to low-migration states, it appears that men with above-average earnings from high-migration states disappear from the sample in larger numbers.

The change in the composition of the labor force is perhaps seen more clearly in figure 9.13, which shows the 1990 to 2000 change in the difference in earnings densities between high-migration and low-migration states (for constant returns to observables and constant residual dispersion). This (partial) double difference shows negative mass above the mean and positive mass below the mean, indicating that over time the relative scarcity of high-wage workers has increased in high-migration relative to low-migration states.

Comparing units on the vertical axes in figures 9.11 and 9.13, it is apparent that the counterfactual double difference in wage densities is small, but it is still informative about the nature of migrant selection on observables. Figure 9.7 shows that between 1990 and 2000 there was a relatively large loss in the population of working-age men born in high-migration states, which is consistent with individuals from high-migration states having a relatively high propensity to migrate abroad. What figures 9.12 and 9.13 suggest is that the men most likely to migrate abroad are those in the

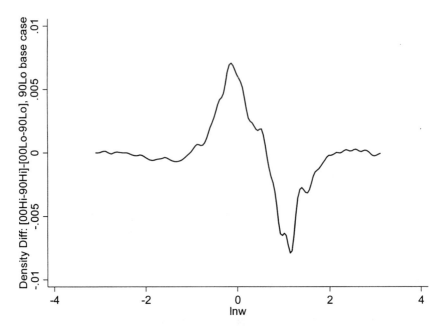

Fig. 9.13   Double difference in counterfactual wage densities (with returns to observable characteristics evaluated for low-migration states in 1990)

top half of the earnings distribution. This finding is inconsistent with negative selection of emigrants in terms of observable skills and suggests that emigrants exhibit intermediate or positive selection in terms of observable skills. Using data from Mexican and U.S. population censuses, Chiquiar and Hanson (2005) also find evidence against negative selection.[16]

One might also be concerned that including the relatively rich and globalized regions of the Federal District and Jalisco in the sample of birth states affects the results. In figure 9.14, I show the double difference in counterfactual wage densities reported in figure 9.13 (with returns to observables fixed at those for low-migration states in 1990) for a sample that excludes the two states. Comparing figures 9.13 and 9.14 shows that results are similar with or without these states in the sample. The results are also robust to dropping any one of the other states from the sample.

Over time, it appears that men born in high-migration states are emigrating from Mexico in relatively large numbers and that the emigrants include a disproportionately large number of individuals with relatively high earnings potential. In a simple labor supply–labor demand framework, a

16. Results are similar if I evaluate change in earnings densities between high-migration and low-migration states for returns to observables fixed at those for high- (rather than low-) migration states in 1990.

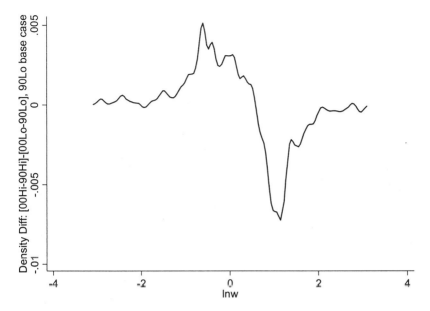

Fig. 9.14   Double difference in wage densities, excluding Federal District and Jalisco (with returns to observable characteristics evaluated for low-migration states in 1990)

decrease in the relative supply of more-skilled workers in high-migration states would put upward pressure on relative wages in these states (as long as labor was not perfectly mobile between regions of Mexico). Next, we examine how relative regional returns to observables have changed over time.

Figure 9.15 shows kernel density estimates for the density differences in (8) and (12), which characterize the difference in earning distributions between high- and low-migration states holding constant the distribution of observable characteristics. In 1990 and 2000, the density difference has positive mass above the mean and negative mass below the mean. In either year, returns to observables appear to be higher in high-migration states relative to low-migration states. Although one cannot identify from figure 9.15 the source of the initial difference in relative regional earnings, relatively high returns to observables in high-migration states is consistent with the relative scarcity of high-wage workers in high-migration states evident in figure 9.12.

Over time, the difference in returns to observables between high- and low-migration states appears to have become more pronounced. Figure 9.15 shows that from 1990 to 2000 the difference in wage densities between high-migration and low-migration states gains mass above the mean and loses mass below the mean. This is seen more clearly in figure 9.16, which shows the 1990 to 2000 change in the difference in earnings densities be-

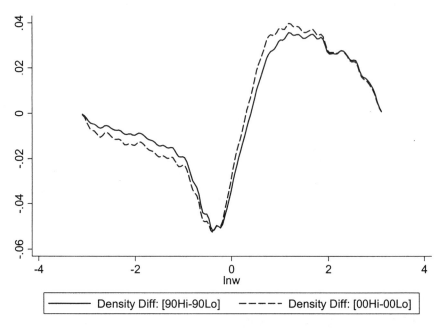

Fig. 9.15   **Differences in counterfactual wage densities between high-migration and low-migration states (with distribution of observable characteristics evaluated for low-migration states in 1990)**

tween high-migration and low-migration states, holding constant the distribution of observables. This double difference shows positive mass above the mean and negative mass below the mean, indicating that during the 1990s the wage premium for above-average wage earners increased for men born in high-migration states relative to men born in low-migration states. Though the partial double difference in wage densities is again small (compared to figure 9.11),[17] the increase in the relative wage for men born in high-migration states evident in figure 9.16 is consistent with the decrease in the relative supply of men born in high-migration states evident in figure 9.13. In unreported density estimates, I obtain similar results when I drop men born in the Federal District or Jalisco from the sample.

The nonparametric results suggest there has been an increase in relative wages for men born in high-migration states in Mexico. To evaluate the change in regional relative wages parametrically, table 9.8 shows estima-

17. Because both counterfactual double differences in densities are small, it appears that the interaction between changes in worker characteristics and changes in returns to characteristics accounts for a large portion of the total change in regional relative wages. However, the double differences in wage densities still appear to be informative about the direction of these changes. Relative regional wage changes appear to be larger where relative regional labor supply changes are larger.

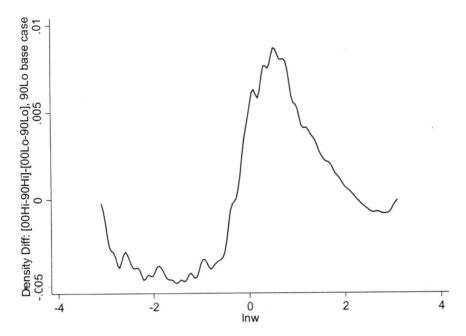

Fig. 9.16   Double difference in counterfactual wage densities (with distribution of observable characteristics evaluated for low-migration states in 1990)

tion results for equation (15). The dependent variable is log average hourly earnings. The regressors are dummy variables for educational attainment, a quadratic in age, a dummy variable for the year 2000 and its interaction with the age and education variables, a dummy variable for having been born in a high-migration state and its interaction with the age and education variables, dummy variables for birth state, and the interaction of the year 2000 and high-migration dummy variables. This last variable captures the differential change in wage growth in high-migration states relative to low-migration states. Standard errors are adjusted for correlation across observations associated with the same birth state.

Panel A of table 9.8 shows that during the 1990s the cohort of men born in high-migration states enjoyed labor earnings growth that was 6.3 log points higher than earnings growth for individuals born in low-migration states. These coefficients are precisely estimated. This is consistent with the nonparametric estimates and again suggests that men born in high-migration states enjoyed higher growth in labor earnings than men born in low-migration states. The second two columns of table 9.8 show results where the year2000-high-migration interaction is interacted with an indicator for an individual having nine to fifteen years of education (roughly, workers with above-mean schooling years but with less than a college edu-

Table 9.8   Regression results

	All workers (1)	Workers w/ 20–80 hour work week (2)	All workers (3)	Workers w/ 20–80 hour work week (4)
A. Full sample of workers				
Year 2000 · high migration	0.063	0.063	0.045	0.049
	(0.027)	(0.026)	(0.034)	(0.033)
Year 2000 · high migration · 9–15 years of education			0.057	0.043
			(0.030)	(0.030)
R	0.308	0.349	0.308	0.349
N	110,837	103,232	110,837	103,232
B. Excluding the Federal District and Jalisco				
Year 2000 · high migration	0.089	0.086	0.066	0.066
	(0.032)	(0.032)	(0.042)	(0.042)
Year 2000 · high migration · 9–15 years of education			0.084	0.065
			(0.046)	(0.048)
R	0.261	0.302	0.261	0.303
N	71,557	66,152	71,557	66,152

Notes: The dependent variable is log average hourly labor earnings. In columns (1) and (3), the sample is males born in a high-migration state or a low-migration state; in columns (2) and (4), the sample includes males who report working twenty–eighty hours a week. Other regressors (quadratic in age, dummies for year of education, and their interactions with year 2000 dummy and with high migration dummy; year 2000 dummy variable; state dummy variables) are now shown. Standard errors are in parentheses and are adjusted for correlation across observations within birth states. In panel A, the sample is working males in all high and low-migration states and time periods; in panel B, observations for the Federal District and Jalisco are dropped from the sample.

cation). This term allows relative earnings growth to be larger for more-educated workers. The education interaction term is positive, consistent with figure 9.12 (while the variable appears imprecisely estimated the two reported interaction terms are jointly highly statistically significant).[18]

Panel B of table 9.8 redoes the estimation, dropping observations for the Federal District and Jalisco. Estimated relative wage growth for high-migration states is higher for this sample, with men born in high-migration states enjoying labor earnings growth 8.6 to 8.9 log points higher than for men born in low-migration states. In the second two columns, the interaction between the year2000-high-migration interaction and the dummy variable for secondary education is again positive (and the two interaction terms are again jointly highly statistically significant).

Because emigration rates are highest for individuals in their twenties, one might expect that wage changes between high-migration and low-

18. Introducing interaction terms for more disaggregated schooling categories yields similar results.

migration states would have been largest for men who are more educated *and* young. In unreported results, I included additional interactions between the year 2000 dummy, secondary education, and age, but these proved to be imprecisely estimated in most regressions.

Based on the coefficient estimates, it is possible to construct an elasticity of the relative wage for high-migration and low-migration states with respect to the relative labor supply in high-migration and low-migration states. From figure 9.6, the supply of working-age men in high-migration states fell by 9.8 log points relative to the supply of working-age men in the same cohort in low-migration states. This implies a wage elasticity of 0.64. Excluding the Federal District and Jalisco, the wage elasticity is 0.91. Either elasticity is larger than the value of 0.4 that Mishra (2004) estimates using data on changes in wages and labor supply for age-schooling cohorts at the national level. Recall, however, that my estimates are reduced form. They include the direct effect of emigration on wages (through changes in the labor supply), and any indirect effect associated with differential labor demand growth in high-migration states that is associated with historical emigration patterns. Comparing my results to Mishra's suggests that the indirect effects of emigration on regional wages are positive.

9.5   Discussion

In this paper, I examine how emigration has affected regional labor supply and regional earnings in Mexico. Mexico has a long history of sending migrants to the United States. Since the early 1900s, emigration rates have varied widely across regions of the country, with individuals from west-central states having the highest propensity to migrate abroad. I exploit regional persistence in emigration behavior by focusing the analysis on individuals born in states with a history of either high migration or low migration to the United States, as measured by state emigration rates in the 1950s.

As in earlier decades, during the 1990s individuals born in Mexico's high-migration states appeared to have a relatively high propensity to migrate abroad. Between 1990 and 2000, the population of twenty- to fifty-nine-year-old men born in high-migration states declined by 10 log points relative to similarly aged men born in low-migration states. For women, the corresponding relative regional change in population was 8 log points. The relatively large exodus of individuals from high-migration states is concentrated among individuals with above-average earnings potential. This suggests that in terms of observable skills emigrants are positively selected. Controlling for observables, wages in high-migration states rose relative to low-migration states by 6–9 percent. This implies an elasticity of wages with respect to the labor supply of 0.7–0.8. This change reflects both the direct effects of emigration on the labor supply and any indirect effects of historical emigration patterns on current regional wage growth.

There are several possible interpretations of these results. One is that emigration raises wages in Mexico, with the effects being most pronounced in states that have well-developed networks for sending migrants to the United States. This interpretation is consistent with the findings in Munshi (2003), Hanson (2004), and Mishra (2004).

However, emigration was by no means the only shock to the Mexican economy during the 1990s. Other shocks may have also contributed to changes in regional relative wages. A large literature documents how NAFTA and other aspects of globalization appear to have increased regional wage differentials in Mexico. It is not clear how globalization interacts with emigration. States more exposed to globalization appear to have lower migration rates to the United States, suggesting that emigration and globalization may be complementary mechanisms for integrating Mexico into the North American labor market. Another important shock was the Mexican peso crisis in 1995. This may have hurt high-migration states more than low-migration states (as high-migration states have larger industrial bases and smaller tourist industries), suggesting my estimates may understate the true effect of emigration on regional wages.

Other policy changes, such as the privatization and deregulation of Mexican industry or the reform of Mexico's land-tenure system, may also have had differential regional impacts. Privatization and deregulation appeared to lower union wage premiums in these sectors (Fairris 2003). Since more heavily unionized industries are concentrated in Mexico's north and center and relatively absent in Mexico's south (Chiquiar 2003), we might expect a loss in union power to lower relative wages in Mexico's high-migration states, in which case my results would tend to understate the true effect of emigration. The reform of Mexico's land tenure system allowed the sale of agricultural land that had previously been held in cooperative ownership. We might expect this change to have raised relative incomes in southern Mexico, which specializes in agriculture. Because low-migration states are concentrated in southern Mexico, this is another reason my results may tend to understate the true effect of emigration.

A brief review of Mexico's other policy reforms during the 1990s does not suggest any obvious reason why they should account for the observed increase in relative earnings in high-migration states. Still, in an environment where multiple shocks have affected Mexico's labor market, it is important to be cautious about ascribing shifts in relative regional earnings to any specific event. In the end, we can only say that I find suggestive evidence that emigration has increased relative earnings in Mexican states that have stronger migration networks vis-à-vis the United States.

References

Ariola, Jim, and Chinhui Juhn. 2003. Wage inequality in post-reform Mexico. University of Houston. Mimeograph.

Athey, Susan, and Guido Imbens. 2003. Identification and inference in nonlinear difference-in-difference models. Stanford University. Mimeograph.

Autor, David, Lawrence Katz, and Melissa Kearney. 2004. Trends in U.S. wage inequality: Re-assessing the revisionists. Massachusetts Institute of Technology. Mimeograph.

Borjas, George J. 1987. Self-selection and the earnings of immigrants. *American Economic Review* 77:531–53.

———. 1999. The economic analysis of immigration. In *Handbook of labor economics,* ed. Orley C. Ashenfelter and David Card, 1697–1760. Amsterdam: North-Holland.

———. 2003. The labor demand curve is downward sloping: Reexamining the impact of immigration on the labor market. *Quarterly Journal of Economics* 118 (4): 1335–74.

Borjas, George J., Richard B. Freeman, and Lawrence F. Katz. 1997. How much do immigration and trade affect labor market outcomes? *Brookings Papers on Economic Activity,* Issue no. 1:1–90. Washington, DC: Brookings Institution.

Calavita, Kitty. 1992. *Inside the state. The Bracero Program, immigration, and the I.N.S.* New York: Routledge.

Cano, Gustavo. 2004. Organizing immigrant communities in American cities: Is this transnationalism, or what? Working Paper no. 103. San Diego: Center for Comparative Immigration Studies, University of California at San Diego.

Card, David. 2001. Immigrant inflows, native outflows, and the local labor market impacts of higher immigration. *Journal of Labor Economics* 19 (1): 22–64.

Cardoso, Lawrence. 1980. *Mexican emigration to the United States, 1897–1931.* Tucson: University of Arizona Press.

Chiquiar, Daniel. 2003. *Essays on the regional implications of globalization: The case of Mexico.* PhD diss., University of California at San Diego.

———. 2005. Why Mexico's regional income convergence broke down. *Journal of Development Economics* 77 (1): 257–75.

Chiquiar, Daniel, and Gordon Hanson. 2005. International migration, self-selection, and the distribution of wages: Evidence from Mexico and the United States. *Journal of Political Economy* 113 (2): 239–81.

Cragg, Michael I., and Mario Epelbaum. 1996. The premium for skills in LDCs: Evidence from Mexico. *Journal of Development Economics* 51 (1): 99–116.

DiNardo, John, M. Fortin, and Thomas Lemieux. 1996. Labor market institutions and the distribution of wages, 1973–1992: A semiparametric approach. *Econometrica* 64 (5): 1001–44.

Durand, Jorge, Douglas S. Massey, and Rene M. Zenteno. 2001. Mexican immigration in the United States. *Latin American Research Review* 36 (1): 107–27.

Fairris, David H. 2003. Unions and wage inequality in Mexico. *Industrial and Labor Relations Review* 56 (3): 481–97.

Feenstra, Robert C., and Gordon H. Hanson. 1997. Foreign direct investment and relative wages: Evidence from Mexico's maquiladoras. *Journal of International Economics* 42 (3–4): 371–94.

Feliciano, Zadia. 2001. Workers and trade liberalization: The impact of trade reforms in Mexico on wages and employment. *Industrial and Labor Relations Review* 55 (1): 95–115.

Hanson, Gordon. 2004. What has happened to wages in Mexico since NAFTA? In *FTAA and beyond: Prospects for integration in the Americas,* ed. Toni Estevade-ordal, Dani Rodrik, Alan Taylor, Andres Velasco, 505–38. Cambridge, MA: Harvard University Press.

Hanson, Gordon H., and Ann E. Harrison. 1999. Trade, technology, and wage in-equality in Mexico. *Industrial and Labor Relations Review* 52 (2): 271–88.

Inter-American Development Bank. 2004. *Sending money home: Remittances to Latin America and the Caribbean.* IADB Report. Washington, DC: IADB, May.

LaLonde, Robert, and Robert Topel. 1997. Economic impact of international migration and migrants. In *Handbook of population and family economics,* ed. Mark R. Rosenzweig and Oded Stark, 799–850. Amsterdam: Elsevier Science.

Leibbrandt, Murray, James Levinsohn, and Justin McCrary. 2004. Incomes in South Africa since the fall of apartheid. University of Michigan. Mimeograph.

Machado, Jose A. F., and Jose Mata. 2005. Counterfactual decomposition of changes in wage distributions using quantile regression. *Journal of Applied Econometrics* 20 (4): 445–65.

Mishra, Prachi. 2004. Emigration and wages in source countries: Evidence from Mexico. Columbia University. Mimeograph.

Munshi, Kaivan. 2003. Networks in the modern economy: Mexican migrants in the U.S. labor market. *Quarterly Journal of Economics* 118:549–97.

Orrenius, Pia M., and Madeline Zavodny. 2005. Self-selection among undocu-mented immigrants from Mexico. *Journal of Development Economics* 78 (1): 215–40.

Revenga, Anna L. 1997. Employment and wage effects of trade liberalization: The case of Mexican manufacturing. *Journal of Labor Economics* 15 (3): S20–S43.

Robertson, Raymond. 2000. Wage shocks and North American labor market inte-gration. *American Economic Review* 90 (4): 742–64.

———. 2004. Relative prices and wage inequality: Evidence from Mexico. *Journal of International Economics* 64 (2): 387–409.

Smith, James, and Barry Edmonston. 1997. *The new Americans: Economic, demo-graphic and fiscal effects of immigration.* Washington, DC: National Academy Press.

Woodruff, Christopher. 1999. Inflation stabilization and the vanishing size-wage effect. *Industrial and Labor Relations Review* 53 (1): 103–22.

Woodruff, Christopher, and Rene M. Zenteno. 2001. Remittances and microenter-prises in Mexico. University of California at San Diego. Mimeograph.

Contributors

Francine D. Blau
School of Industrial and Labor
  Relations
Cornell University
265 Ives Hall
Ithaca, NY 14853-3901

George J. Borjas
Kennedy School of Government
Harvard University
79 John F. Kennedy Street
Cambridge, MA 02138

David Card
Department of Economics
University of California, Berkeley
549 Evans Hall, 3880
Berkeley, CA 94720-3880

Brian Duncan
Department of Economics
University of Colorado at Denver
Campus Box 181
Denver, CO 80217-3364

Robert W. Fairlie
Department of Economics
University of California, Santa Cruz
Santa Cruz, CA 95064

Gordon H. Hanson
Graduate School of International
  Relations and Pacific Studies
University of California, San Diego
IR/PS, 9500 Gilman Drive
La Jolla, CA 92093-0519

Pablo Ibarraran
Inter-American Development Bank
Office B-0742
1300 New York Avenue
Washington, DC 20577

Lawrence M. Kahn
School of Industrial and Labor
  Relations
Cornell University
264 Ives Hall
Ithaca, NY 14853-3901

Lawrence F. Katz
Department of Economics
Harvard University
Cambridge, MA 02138

Edward P. Lazear
Graduate School of Business
Stanford University
518 Memorial Way
Stanford, CA 94305-5015

Ethan G. Lewis
Research Department
Federal Reserve Bank of Philadelphia
10 Independence Mall
Philadelphia, PA 19106

Darren Lubotsky
Department of Economics and
   Institute of Labor and Industrial
   Relations
University of Illinois at Urbana-
   Champaign
211 LIR Building
504 East Armory Avenue
Champaign, IL 61820

Susan M. Richter
Department of Agricultural and
   Resource Economics
University of California, Davis
2154 Social Sciences & Humanities
   Building
Davis, CA 95616

J. Edward Taylor
Department of Agricultural and
   Resource Economics
University of California, Davis
2107 Social Sciences & Humanities
   Building
Davis, CA 95616

Stephen J. Trejo
Department of Economics
University of Texas at Austin
1 University Station C3100
Austin, TX 78712-0301

Christopher Woodruff
Graduate School of International
   Relations and Pacific Studies
University of California, San Diego
IR/PS, 9500 Gilman Drive
La Jolla, CA 92093-0519

Antonio Yúnez-Naude
PRECESAM-CEE
El Colegio de México
Camino al Ajusco 20
México, D. F. 01000

Author Index

Subject Index